LOUIS LE VAU

LOUIS LE VAU

MAZARIN'S COLLÈGE, COLBERT'S REVENGE

HILARY BALLON

PRINCETON UNIVERSITY PRESS
PRINCETON, NEW JERSEY

Published by Princeton University Press
41 William Street
Princeton, New Jersey 08540

In the United Kingdom:
Princeton University Press
Chichester, West Sussex

Designed by Storehouse Co. / Charles Routhier and Joseph Jurewicz
Composed in Adobe Granjon by dix!, Syracuse, New York
Printed by Kwong Fat Offset Printing, Hong Kong

Publication of this book has been aided by grants from the
Graham Foundation and from the Millard Meiss Publication Fund
of the College Art Association of America

Printed and bound in Hong Kong
10 9 8 7 6 5 4 3 2 1 (cloth)
10 9 8 7 6 5 4 3 2 1 (paper)

Library of Congress Cataloging-in-Publication Data
Ballon, Hilary.
    Louis Le Vau : Mazarin's Collège, Colbert's revenge / Hilary
Ballon.
      p.   cm.
    Includes bibliographical references and index.
    ISBN 0-691-00186-3 (cloth : alk. paper)
    ISBN 0-691-04895-9 (pbk. : alk. paper)
    1. Collège des quatre-nations. 2. Architecture—France—Paris.
3. Architecture, Modern—17th–18th centuries—France—Paris.
4. Le Vau, Louis, 1612–1670—Criticism and interpretation. I. Title.
LF2395.P32B35   1999
727'.3'0944361—dc21
                                              99-25747
                                             CIP

For Orin

CONTENTS

ACKNOWLEDGMENTS

IT IS A PLEASURE TO ACKNOWLEDGE the friends and colleagues who helped improve this book in concrete ways. I am indebted to Philip Benedict, Joseph Bergin, Richard Brilliant, Richard Cleary, Joseph Connors, and Sarah McPhee, who read the manuscript in whole or in part; their insights, corrections, and suggestions were enormously valuable and made the writing of this book a learning process to the very end. For their help in unraveling historical puzzles, answering queries, reacting to my thoughts, and providing advice, my thanks go to James Ackerman, Nicholas Adams, Christy Anderson, Robert Berger, Giuseppe Dardanello, Elizabeth Easton, Pierre Force, Alice Jarrard, Susan Klaiber, Polly Maguire, Tod Marder, Claude Mignot, John Pinto, Orest Ranum, Victoria Sanger, John Beldon Scott, Peter Smith, Cathryn Steeves, Katherine Tachau, Patrice de Vogüé, and Carol Willis. The doctoral students whom I have been privileged to teach at Columbia University and my colleagues in the Department of Art History and Archaeology gave me the opportunity to present work in progress and enriched my work in significant ways. I do, indeed, feel fortunate to be part of this community of scholars.

Research for this book was undertaken mostly in the Archives Nationales, the Bibliothèque de l'Institut, and the Bibliothèque Nationale in Paris. I thank the many conservators and archivists in those institutions who facilitated my work. Writing began during a year at the Institute for Advanced Study in Princeton, where Irving Lavin created a tremendously stimulating environment.

It is my good fortune to work with Patricia Fidler, Curtis Scott, and Elizabeth Steiner at Princeton University Press; I am grateful for their attentiveness, efficiency, and editorial skill. A word of thanks as well to the Graham Foundation and the Millard Meiss Publication Fund of the College Art Association for the publication subventions they granted this book.

Finally, the contribution of my family, which was not at all concrete: it was impalpable, pervasive, and essential. I am incomparably blessed to be the mother of Sophie and Charles and to journey through life with Orin Kramer, my husband, to whom I dedicate this book.

LOUIS LE VAU

INTRODUCTION

GREAT BUILDINGS ARE exceptional by definition, but that does not entirely explain why praise for the Collège des Quatre Nations, now the Institut de France, always seems to fix on its singularity in Louis XIV's Paris. Constructed between 1662 and 1670 to designs by Louis Le Vau, the Collège borders the Left Bank of the Seine, gracefully extending its curved wings as if to embrace the royal palace on the opposite side of the river (FIG. 1). Today the two buildings are joined by a pedestrian bridge, built in the nineteenth century, which recalls an idea introduced by Le Vau and reinforces the message of his design. The Pont des Arts, makes the Collège veritably an annex of the Louvre; together they compose one of the world's great urban spectacles.

The most distinctive feature of the Collège, besides its orientation to the Louvre, is its kinship with contemporary buildings in Rome. The curved facade, domed temple front, and oval rotunda of the Collège are closer to the buildings of Gianlorenzo Bernini, Francesco Borromini, and Pietro da Cortona in seicento Rome than to the cold majesty of Louis XIV's Paris. Unlike the Louvre Colonnade, a building of reserve and intimidating grandeur that Le Vau himself helped to design only five years later (FIG. 2), the Collège is inviting, rich in contrasts, and eye-catching. Like a starlet in a clinging gown, the building captures your attention, draws you toward it, and shows you how it is put together. "One of the few [French] buildings to embody some of the principles of Roman Baroque architecture," Anthony Blunt explained in admiration, "[the Collège] presents a dramatically effective ensemble not to be paralleled in French architecture of the seventeenth century."[1] To put it simply, the Collège des Quatre Nations is a baroque building in a classical city.

To explain the anomalous appearance, some writers have suggested that its Italian patron, Cardinal Jules Mazarin, determined the building's style; after all, he was a devotee of Roman Baroque art and hailed from its heartland, the Barberini circle of Urban VIII in Rome. Mazarin was dead, however, when Le Vau designed the building; clearly he did not direct the project posthumously. True, Mazarin financed construction with a bequest in his will, but in all other respects, the Collège was a royal monument. It was designed by the king's architect, overseen by the chief minister, Jean-Baptiste Colbert, and situated opposite the Louvre at the king's explicit request. Mazarin's family played no part in the project,

FIG. 1. *Louis Le Vau, Collège des Quatre Nations (now the Institut de France), 1662–70*

FIG. 2. *Charles Le Brun, Louis Le Vau, and Claude Perrault, Colonnade of the Louvre, 1667*

whereas Louis XIV was actively involved and elevated Mazarin's Collège to the status of a royal foundation. The Collège des Quatre Nations was both a royalist—which is to say, categorically French—and an Italianate building, and that duality is a key both to Le Vau's design and to its critical fortune.

Given its undisputed status as a masterpiece, the Collège has drawn surprisingly sharp criticisms from the great critics (and guardians) of French architecture. Jacques-François Blondel, writing in the mid-eighteenth century, condemned the disunity between the domed centerpiece and the side wings; the variety of crowning elements, which include pediment, balustrade, and urns; and the juxtaposition of major and minor orders (Blondel thought the colossal order should extend across the entire facade). The massing, proportions, orders, and decoration of the Collège all came under fire because they violated Blondel's standard of uniformity, a standard satisfied by the Louvre Colonnade with its minimal projections, colossal order, crowning balustrade, and continuous, flat roof. Antoine Chrysosthôme Quatremère de Quincy summed up the problem a century later; even if the main facade of the Collège has "a monumental aspect that is not ordinarily encountered, . . . [the building] lacks the proportional finesse and purity of style that constitute a classical architecture."[2]

Quatremère was right; the Collège des Quatre Nations is not in the French classical style, and his criticisms serve as a useful reminder that the building's qualities cannot be properly seen through the prism of French classicism. With its emphasis on differentiation over uniformity, on articulation and juxtaposition over fusion, the Collège not only refers to contemporary developments in Baroque Rome. It also carries forward a French building tradition that extends from medieval fortresses (such as Vincennes) to the Renaissance châteaux of Philibert Delorme and Jacques Androuet Ducerceau the Elder, with their strongly projecting pavilions and towering frontispieces, and into the seventeenth century with the palaces of Salomon de Brosse (for instance, the Palais du Luxembourg, which stands a few blocks from Mazarin's Collège). Le Vau remained faithful to that traditional French compositional method and treatment of wall, mass, and roofs in his château designs of the 1650s and in the Collège des Quatre Nations. The Collège appears as an assemblage of discrete, separately roofed volumes—centerpiece, curved wings, and end pavilions—each individuated and dressed with a different order. But no sooner was the Collège designed than Colbert began promoting a rather different style inspired by ancient Rome, a classical style that would dominate French architecture for the next one hundred years.

The contrast between the Colonnade and the other wings around the Cour Carrée, the work of Pierre Lescot and Jacques Lemercier as well as Le Vau over the course of the preceding century, illustrates the change that occurred in French architecture during the 1660s (FIG. 3). In contrast to the tall pavilions, decorative dematerialization of wall surfaces, and variety of separate roofs of the older wings (features of the Collège as well), the Colon-

1. la grande Cour du Louure 2. les Thuilleries
3. la petite Ecurie 4. le Pont Royal
5. la Grenouillere
6. le Cours de la Reyne
7. Porte de la Conference

Veüe et perspectiue de la principale entrée du nouveau Louure à Paris

fait par Aueline *Auec priuilege du Roy*

FIG. 3. *Cour Carrée of the Louvre viewed from the east, before the reconstruction of the south range in 1668. Engraving by Pierre Aveline. Département des Estampes, Bibliothèque Nationale de France, Paris.*

nade stands as a flat-roofed monolithic block, its long stretch paced not by the play of receding and projecting volumes but by repetitive columnar bays. Pavilions—the quintessential building block of French architecture, which had previously been used to articulate the center and corners of a wing—are reduced at the Colonnade to shallow projections; its classical orders serve less as an ornamental motif responsive to the local building part (as at Mazarin's Collège) and more as an ordering system for the building as a whole.

Where did Le Vau stand in relation to the change in official style at Louis XIV's court and the reinvention of French architecture? That question, which remains unresolved, lies at the heart of the attribution debates surrounding Le Vau's late work. Between 1665 and 1670, the last five years of his life, Le Vau participated in designing three major buildings, each with an intricate history that complicates the issue of authorship: the Colonnade (1667) and south wing of the Louvre (1668–69), on which Le Vau collaborated with Charles Le Brun and Claude Perrault, and the Versailles Enveloppe (1668–73), which was completed after Le Vau's death. We will focus on these buildings at the end of the book; for now suffice it to say that the features of the Colonnade characterize the late work as a whole. The issue thus is how to explain Le Vau's evolution from Mazarin's Collège to the Enveloppe at Versailles, how to account for his dramatic change of style in the 1660s.

The standard response has been to deny any such change and to cleanse Le Vau's oeuvre of all classical designs by reattributing them to other architects. No one takes seriously the extreme position of Albert Laprade, who reattributed all of Le Vau's late works to his assistant François d'Orbay (d'Orbay's talents are addressed in Appendix B).[3] A consensus has gathered, however, around the view that Le Vau played only a minor role on the committee that produced the two facades of the Louvre and that Perrault was chiefly responsible for both designs. In other words, the one professional architect on the committee (Perrault was an amateur architect and Le Brun a painter) is marginalized—a problematic position particularly with regard to the south (or river) facade of the Louvre in as much as all the surviving drawings for that wing are from Le Vau's studio.

Those who acknowledge Le Vau's hand at the Louvre and Versailles face a different problem: making sense of an artistic change that they perceive as startling and unannounced. A leading scholar summed up the problem: the Versailles Enveloppe, he observed, "stands apart from Le Vau's oeuvre in a marked way, so that it is difficult to understand as an organic outgrowth of his evolving style. . . . The conclusion must be that Le Vau himself profoundly altered his style at the end of his career."[4] But the notion that Le Vau underwent a stylistic revolution founders on two points: first, features of the late work did, in fact, appear earlier at the château of Vincennes (1656–61), a building we will examine closely in Chapter 1; and second, Le Vau produced classical and baroque schemes for Versailles within a period of a few months, just as he designed classical and baroque buildings at virtually the same time in the mid-1650s—to wit, Vincennes and Vaux-le-Vicomte. In other words, baroque and classical were not stations on a linear path but rather expressive modes that Le Vau employed as a building project required. This is not to deny that his personal style changed over the course of his career, in particular in the 1660s. But the conception of baroque and classical as antithetical aesthetic systems—requiring an artist to bear allegiance to one or the other way of making art—misrepresents what was often a fluid movement between the two for many seventeenth-century artists (Bernini and Nicolas Poussin, for example).

The perspectives on Le Vau's late work outlined above—one insisting on consistency, the other on rupture—have yielded insights about particular buildings, but they neither satisfy all the facts nor clarify Le Vau's creative process. Mazarin's Collège can help us to rethink this problem because it stands at a turning point in Le Vau's career and in French architecture as a whole. Like most turning points, the Collège did not wholly belong to the past; it also contained seeds of the new aesthetic order that Colbert promoted. Illuminating that Janus-like turning point, in the context of the architecture and identity of Louis Le Vau, is our subject.

Most readers will be surprised to learn that Le Vau remains a relatively unstudied figure, despite his wide acclaim and an abundance of historical resources. Powerful, talented, and prolific, he was first architect in the court of Louis XIV and designed some of the most glamorous buildings of the age, many of which survive intact and continue to impress—the Hôtel Lambert, Vaux-le-Vicomte, Mazarin's Collège, and the Louvre. Yet whereas several books have been written about François Mansart, there is not a single monograph on Louis Le Vau. The imbalance does not reflect their relative importance in the seventeenth century as much as the historiographical constructs through which we view the field: Mansart is hallowed as the forefather of French classicism, while Le Vau is pushed to the margins of that cultural project.

This study brings Le Vau to the fore; it explores his approach to design, his relationship with Colbert and Bernini, and his roles from designer and building contractor to industrialist and entrepreneur. The book lacks the comprehensive coverage of a monograph; it focuses selectively on the 1650s and 1660s. But it is as much a revisionist portrait of Le Vau—who emerges in these pages as a man of great ambition, talent, and creativity—as a challenge to entrenched views about French classicism.

Chapter 1, "Mazarin's Bequest," concerns Cardinal Mazarin's motives in endowing the Collège and his vision of the institution. It also challenges the standard view of Cardinal Mazarin as an advocate of Baroque art and proposes a political interpretation of his patronage in France. Chapter 2, "Architecture and Imagery: The New Rome," tracks Le Vau's design process and reconstructs the pivotal role of Bernini. The argument about the building's message centers on its links to papal Rome, a city Le Vau never visited and knew only from prints and books. That learning process is the subject of the following chapter, "Le Vau's Library," which asks what role books played in his design process and takes a comparative look at other architects' libraries. Shifting from art to industry, Chapter 4, "Charges of Embezzlement," reopens a lawsuit brought against Le Vau for diverting building funds for the Collège to a cannon foundry, which, amazingly, became Le Vau's obsession in the last four years of his life. In unraveling the charges of embezzlement, we find Le Vau assuming different identities as a building contractor and industrialist, roles that underscore an architect's wide-ranging opportunities before the rise of academic culture and the professional regime it imposed. Occupying a place in the background, Colbert is omnipresent in the book. The conclusion looks squarely at his relationship with Le Vau, their collaboration at the Louvre and Versailles, and the invention of French classicism in the 1660s.

Ultimately Le Vau failed to meet Colbert's expectations—at the cannon foundry, at Mazarin's Collège, and at the Louvre—with respect to productivity, financial matters, and architectural design. Colbert's revenge took several forms. Sometimes he treated the first architect as an outcast at court. He also supported a punitive lawsuit. But most damaging for Le Vau's critical fortune and standing in history, Colbert rejected Le Vau's approach to architecture (and with it the whole tradition of French Renaissance design) and reoriented French building culture in the name of imperial grandeur and academic rigor.

CHAPTER I

MAZARIN'S BEQUEST

CARDINAL MAZARIN WAS ILL. Unable to join the ceremonial entry of Louis XIV into Paris on a late August day in 1660, he watched from the balcony of the Hôtel de Beauvais beside the Queen Mother and Queen Henrietta-Maria of England. Triumphal arches, obelisks, and other festive markers embellished the processional route from Vincennes to the Louvre. The parade celebrated two recent events: the long-awaited signing of a peace treaty between the superpowers of the age, France and Spain, and Louis XIV's marriage to the daughter of the Spanish king, Maria Theresa.[1] These events, which had altered the European balance of power, were the crowning achievements of Mazarin's diplomatic career: Mazarin had negotiated the treaty with Spain, the Peace of the Pyrenees, and arranged the marriage alliance of the Bourbon and Hapsburg dynasties. The royal entry was a time-honored ritual to honor the king; in 1660 it was also a tribute to Cardinal Mazarin.

For a brief moment in his tumultuous career, Mazarin enjoyed a hero's reception. Supporters put forward his name for the papacy. Even the Paris Parlement, which had forced Mazarin into exile a decade earlier, offered tributes "in consideration of the great and signal services . . . [he] has rendered the State."[2] Broadsheets, pamphlets, and prints, the early modern forms of mass publicity that had demonized him only a decade earlier, now championed Mazarin as architect of the peace and guardian of the French crown. The mood is captured in an engraving by Gabriel Le Brun that shows France and Spain embracing under the auspices of Cardinal Mazarin. His name and emblems identify him as patron of the Temple of Peace while unruly Spaniards on the right indicate who was to blame for the years of strife (FIG. 4).[3]

Although ephemeral, the entry was the most important tribute to Mazarin because of his costarring role in a ritual act of kingship. The triumphal arch at the entrance to Paris, the Porte Saint An-

FIG. 4. *Gabriel Le Brun,* Allegory of Peace between Spain and France, *1659. Engraving, Département des Estampes, Bibliothèque Nationale de France, Paris*

toine, detailed Mazarin's accomplishments; and an allegorical painting at the Marché Neuf, on the Cité, portrayed him as Mercury, messenger of the gods, in the act of bringing together the royal couple (who were depicted as Hercules and Minerva).[4] "As these two great events [the peace treaty and marriage] were realized under the wise direction of Cardinal Mazarin, there should be no surprise," the official handbook explained, ". . . that he appears as one of the principal figures in the painting, as the god of Eloquence, who interprets divine wishes and mediates truces and alliances."[5]

The celebrations came to a close two weeks later when Mazarin hosted a dinner party in honor of the king and his new queen. The reception at the Palais Mazarin gave the royal family and scores of dignitaries from courts across Europe an opportunity to admire their host's sumptuous palace and the unsurpassed library and art collection it contained.[6] The summer of 1660 was the climax of a remarkable career. Six months later Mazarin was dead. His timing was perfect; once an outcast, he managed to die a hero. Without that precondition, Mazarin's Collège would not have been built.

THE PHOENIX

Truth can be more surprising than fiction; Mazarin's swift ascent to power and sharp reversals of fortune, along with his change of national identity, constitute proof. Before the age of thirty, Mazarin had become a prominent diplomat at the papal court of Urban VIII.[7] Born into a Roman family of minor papal officials in 1602 and raised near the Trevi fountain, Giulio Mazarini received a proper Jesuit education at the Collegio Romano before entering the service of the constable Filippo Colonna, a distinguished member of the Roman elite, as a companion to his son. The young men spent two years in Spain, from 1622 to 1624, returning to Rome when Urban VIII was elected pope. The Colonna family was related by marriage to the pope—the constable's daughter Anna was married to the pope's secular nephew, Taddeo Barberini—and through them, Mazarin entered the Barberini circle, where he soon became a rising star. He joined the papal army in 1625 and then moved into diplomatic service, where his political skills and aptitude for pleasing powerful patrons served him well. Mazarin's job was to broker a truce between France and Spain. In a last-ditch effort to prevent renewed fighting in 1630, Mazarin reportedly rode onto the battlefield at Casale, brandishing new peace proposals, and forced the two armies to disengage.

After the legendary success at Casale, Mazarin attempted to negotiate, on behalf of the pope, a permanent peace between the superpowers. During his first missions to Paris in 1631 and 1632, the young papal diplomat greatly impressed the French prime minister, Cardinal Richelieu. Richelieu's favorable attitude inclined Urban VIII to appoint Mazarin as nuncio in Paris in 1635, but as Mazarin's fortune rose with Richelieu, it fell with the pope.[8] Suspecting that his agent had become partisan to the French cause, Urban VIII recalled Mazarin to Rome in 1636, then banished him to Avignon—a provincial assignment that the frustrated diplomat resented enormously. Eventually Cardinal Antonio Barberini, the pope's nephew, ended Mazarin's exile and installed him as *maestro di casa* in the Palazzo Barberini, but Mazarin's ascent in the Curia was blocked.

Paris became the promised land. In 1639 Louis XIII nominated Mazarin to the cardinalate—an appointment denied by the pope who argued that a papal subject could not fill a French seat in the College of Cardinals. By the time the pope relented and granted him the cardinalate in December 1641, Giulio Mazarini had become a naturalized French citizen (in April 1639), joined the government of Louis XIII as Richelieu's protégé, and moved to Paris (in January 1640). But the deaths of Richelieu and Louis XIII in the space of a few months in 1641 and 1642 plunged the French court into turmoil and left Mazarin to maneuver without the aid of his mentor. That Mazarin emerged from this crisis as the key adviser to the queen regent, Anne of Austria, and de facto first minister of France testifies to his exceptional adroitness and strategic skills.

Mazarin's spectacular rise in the early 1640s was matched with peculiar symmetry by an equally rapid fall at the end of the decade. In October 1648 the European states signed the Peace of Westphalia, which Mazarin had helped to negotiate. French publicists hailed it as a victory for France and a loss for Spain and the Catholic Church, but in reality French gains were limited, and the Treaty of Westphalia was a stalemate.[9] Spain, which did not want a treaty with France, reached an exclusive agreement with the republic of Holland. France was able to deal with the problem of succession to the Holy Roman Empire, but the continuing Franco-Spanish conflict was not resolved.

Mazarin's diplomatic problems were eclipsed by the outbreak of the Fronde. Whatever the underlying causes of the rebellion, a subject that historians continue to dispute, Cardinal Mazarin became the principal target. For four years, between 1648 and 1652, Mazarin was the most hated public figure in France, excoriated in a barrage of broadsheets and pamphlets—the *mazarinades*—charging him with every imaginable sort of crime, from blocking a European peace settlement and stealing royal funds to violating French customs and undermining the morals of the queen regent, his presumed lover. The Palais Mazarin was ransacked; his property was confiscated and sold by order of the Parlement. He was expelled from France and lived in exile for the better part of 1651 and 1652 before engineering a remarkable comeback. The irrepressible cardinal returned triumphantly to Paris in February 1653, reestablished his leadership at court, and launched a new phase of unbridled aggrandizement.[10]

The Peace of the Pyrenees completed Mazarin's metamorphosis from demon to hero. Spain was admittedly in a weaker position at the outset; still, Mazarin conducted the negotiations with indisputable skill. The treaty signed by the cardinal and his Spanish counterpart, Don Luis de Haro, on 7 November 1659 brought an end to some thirty years of war between the two great rivals, and the terms of settlement established France as the supreme European power, as several Spanish territories—roughly speaking, the provinces of Artois and Roussillon—passed into French hands.[11]

The arduous negotiations, which lasted three years, left Mazarin in a state of severe exhaustion with chronic insomnia, shortness of breath, and a variety of other medical problems. Eulogists would soon claim that Mazarin had sacrificed his life for the peace treaty. "The malady, so long and so cruel, was a result of the happy peace that he obtained for us by so much work. . . ," Louis XIV's confessor told the College of Cardinals in Rome. "[He] died in bringing forth . . . peace."[12]

Cardinal Mazarin was resting in his third-floor apartment in the Louvre, not far from the king's chamber, on the night of 6 February 1661, when a fire broke out in the royal palace. "I met him as he was leaving his room, supported under the arms by his captain of the guards and his chamberlain," Louis de Brienne reported. "He was very pale and de-jected, and death seemed painted in his eyes, either the fear of being burned in his bed hav-ing put him in this state, or he regarded the sudden outbreak of this great conflagration as a sign from God that his end was fast approaching."[13] The cardinal was brought temporarily to the Palais Mazarin, where he took leave of his artworks and jewels, then was moved to the royal château of Vincennes at the eastern edge of the city.[14]

Louis XIV and the Queen Mother Anne of Austria left Saint Germain-en-Laye to be at his side. They visited him re-peatedly, four to six times a day; the king sometimes came more often.[15] By all accounts, their affection for Mazarin was genuine. When Louis XIV lost his father at the age of five, Mazarin had become godfather to the king and assumed re-sponsibility for the youngster's education and political forma-tion (FIG. 5). Anne of Austria may have been in love with Mazarin. They were not secretly married, as was rumored at the time, but their relationship was intimate, judging from their correspondence, which was written in a secret code and filled with private terms of affection.[16]

The doctors who gathered at the cardinal's bedside— among them the king's personal physician, surgeon, and apothecary—could not agree on the nature of His Emi-nence's illness.[17] Some said Mazarin would recover, but no treatment eased his difficulty in breathing or revitalized his wasted body. His Theatine confessor, Angelo Bissaro, thought the doctors were dispensing false hope; he advised Mazarin to prepare a will. "This idea pleased him," Father Angelo reported, and on 3 March 1661, the cardinal began to dictate its terms.[18]

FIG. 5. *Mazarin as godfather and educator of the young Louis XIV. Reproduced from Marin Le Roy Gomberville,* La Doctrine des moeurs . . . *(Paris, 1646)*

THE FORTUNE

At the time of his death, Cardinal Mazarin was the richest man in France—the king, of course, excluded. According to Daniel Dessert's conservative tally, Mazarin was worth 39 million *livres* in 1661, an amount far surpassing the largest fortunes in seventeenth-century France.[19] The estate of Cardinal Richelieu, the second richest man, was worth 22.4 million *livres;* that of Prince Henri II de Condé, 14.6 million *livres;* and the fortunes of great nobles generally ranged from 1 to 3 million *livres.*[20] In fact, Mazarin's fortune had no equal throughout the history of the Old Regime, which is all the more astonishing because he amassed most of his riches in only nine years—between 1653, when he returned to France after the Fronde, and his death in 1661.

The formation of Mazarin's fortune falls into two phases, demarcated by the Fronde. Although there are no hard numbers for Mazarin's pre-Fronde holdings, we know that he accumulated substantial wealth during his first decade in France.[21] That Mazarin could personally lend large sums to the crown during the state bankruptcy of 1648 contributed to the widespread belief that he had "pillaged and carried away all the finances of the king and reduced His Majesty to extreme indigence," as one *mazarinade* put it.[22] Later Mazarin spent large sums to finance his return to power, but the extent to which the Fronde eroded his resources remains unclear. What is certain is that Mazarin rebuilt his estate with extraordinary rapacity after 1653 and entirely reconstituted the fortune in the next nine years; except for the Palais Mazarin, all of Mazarin's assets in 1661 were acquired after 1652.[23]

In the will, Mazarin attributed his wealth to the generosity of the king, yet only a small fraction of it came from outright royal gifts.[24] Mazarin traded on his rank and made money off the state in countless ways. He skimmed tax revenues and other royal funds he administered, set high interest rates on personal loans to the crown, and took payoffs from bankers, petitioners, and office seekers. For instance, during the 1640s Mazarin received annual payments of nearly a million *livres* from bankers seeking business with the crown.[25]

To be sure, Mazarin did not invent these corrupt practices. He followed the example of his predecessor, Cardinal Richelieu, who had profited enormously from his position as first minister to Louis XIII. Like other ministers and financiers of the seventeenth century, Richelieu and Mazarin exploited structural weaknesses in the French fiscal system—a system that blurred the boundaries between public and private resources, permitting royal officers to set exorbitant interest rates on money they loaned the crown. But Mazarin had far exceeded even Richelieu's rapacity and with good reason has been called "the most successful predator of the entire ancien régime."[26]

The enormity of his fortune presented Mazarin with a strategic problem when it came to disposing of his estate. In the normal course of events, there would be an inventory after death to assess the value of Mazarin's assets and to catalogue his personal papers. But this information was incriminating; it would expose the magnitude of Mazarin's wealth and quite possibly shake confidence in the crown's fiscal integrity, which its supposed guardian, the first minister of France, had manifestly violated. From the king's viewpoint, a simple solution might be to punish Mazarin posthumously by reclaiming his ill-gotten fortune. This scenario offered the French people a convenient scapegoat, and it obscured difficult structural problems that would be much harder to address. Mazarin legitimately feared that once he was gone, the crown would seize his estate, leave destitute the dynasty he had hoped to endow, if not to sire, and ruin the cardinal's name in history. He had to find a way of keeping his riches from the crown and of distributing the estate while concealing its disturbing size.

Mazarin responded boldly to the challenge and on 3 March 1661, he offered his entire estate to the king. One source tells us that Colbert had suggested the donation, convinced that the king's affection for Mazarin would lead to a prompt refusal.[27] As it happened, the cardinal's riches must have tempted the king, who witheld a response for three long days while Mazarin lay dying. After the king declined the gift, in effect agreeing to honor the cardinal's will, Mazarin made final revisions to the document and died two days later, before sunrise on 9 March at the age of fifty-nine.[28]

The bulk of the cardinal's estate passed to his primary heir, the duke of Mazarin, Armand-Charles de la Porte de La Meilleraye, who had agreed to bear the title and arms of his benefactor when he married Mazarin's niece Hortense Mancini a week before the cardinal's death.[29] There were important bequests to the royal family and to other relatives, smaller gifts to associates and servants, and some charitable donations.

The will included a ban against any sort of inventory. Mazarin asked the king to entrust all his papers to Colbert without undertaking "any inventory, description, register, or report" pertaining to his property and papers.[30] Against Mazarin's explicit wishes, the king called for an inventory of the estate, but he entrusted the job to Colbert, Mazarin's crafty secretary, who had a vested interest in whitewashing the investigation. Colbert had managed the cardinal's fortune, which implicated him in Mazarin's financial strategems and excesses. Unsavory news would have tainted Colbert. Thus, with his own career on the line, Colbert prepared an incomplete inventory that, nonetheless, satisfied probate standards.[31]

Having defused one bombshell that endangered his career, Colbert then masterminded another—one that propelled him to even greater heights. One day after Mazarin's death, Louis XIV announced the start of his personal rule, and five months later, in September 1661, ordered the arrest of Nicolas Fouquet. This action was intended to demonstrate the crown's determination to take charge of fiscal matters and reform abuses; it also made a scapegoat of Colbert's chief rival.[32]

Mazarin's death in March 1661 had removed the last obstacle to outright political warfare between his two ambitious assistants: the charming, gregarious Fouquet, who was in charge of raising money for the crown, and Colbert, Mazarin's wily, personal lieutenant.

Colbert outflanked his rival, engineered Fouquet's downfall, and consolidated his position at court, going on to serve as Louis XIV's chief minister for the next twenty-two years while Fouquet was condemned to spend the rest of his unhappy life in prison.

The events of 1661 involved two of the greatest monuments of seventeenth-century French architecture: the château of Vaux-le-Vicomte and the Collège des Quatre Nations, both designed by Louis Le Vau. It is often said that Louis XIV ordered Fouquet's arrest because the regal splendor of Vaux-le-Vicomte was a fatal violation of court decorum. In fact, the château was incidental to Fouquet's demise. The king had resolved to arrest Fouquet well before he laid eyes on the château, but Vaux was a useful distraction. So was the Collège des Quatre Nations; it shifted attention away from Mazarin's ill-gotten fortune.

TERMS OF THE BEQUEST

Since service to the state had made Mazarin a rich man, it behooved him to reciprocate the king's largesse. Cardinal Richelieu had set a fine example: he gave the king his magnificent Parisian palace, the Palais Cardinal (thereafter called the Palais Royal), as well as silver plate, jewels, and half a million *livres* in cash.[33] Cardinal Mazarin made an even greater show of generosity, befitting his far greater wealth. Besides paintings, tapestries, and the pick of his furniture, he gave the royal family a treasury of jewels: thirty-one emeralds and eighteen diamonds, which Mazarin renamed "dix-huit mazarins." The diamonds alone were valued at two million *livres* and included the largest stones in Europe, the sixty-carat Grand Sancy and the thirty-carat Miroir du Portugal.[34] These donations, however, did not satisfy Mazarin's desire for a public monument; for this, he created the Collège des Quatre Nations.

Mazarin set forth the terms of the bequest in a lengthy codicil to the will, which he signed on 6 March, after learning that the king had refused his donation.[35] The Collège was not a last-minute show of gratitude for the king's magnanimous renunciation. Mazarin had obviously given considerable forethought to the project and had specific ideas about the purpose and administration of the Collège. The terms of the bequest articulate the cardinal's conception of the foundation and help us gauge the ways in which Le Vau subsequently reconceived the project.

THE COLLEGE The name Mazarin selected for the foundation does not fully capture the scope of his ambitious program, which comprised a riding academy and public library in addition to the college that was the centerpiece. (In colleges of the seventeenth century, boys from about the age of fourteen studied for three or four years to obtain a bachelor's degree; girls were excluded.) The distinguishing feature of Mazarin's college was its clientele: sixty boys from territories France had annexed during the minority of Louis XIV— which is to say, the period when Mazarin was in charge of foreign affairs. Insofar as he negotiated the two peace treaties that authorized the annexations (the Treaty of Westphalia in 1648 and the Treaty of the Pyrenees in 1659), the Collège des Quatre Nations implicitly honored Mazarin's own achievements. Twenty students were to come from Flanders, Artois, Hainault, and Luxembourg; fifteen from Alsace and other former German lands; ten from Roussillon, Conflans, and Sardinia; and the remaining fifteen from Pignerol and the Papal State. France did not control any papal lands, but Mazarin, "out of affection for the place of his birth, wanted to include Italians from the ecclesiastical state, to increase their obligation to serve France with zeal."[36]

The mission of the college was to transform foreigners into Frenchmen by teaching them "how advantageous it is to be the subject of so great a king." When they returned home, the young men would induce others "to obtain the same teaching and the same feeling" of national identity so that over the long term, "all of the provinces would become French by their own inclination as much as they now are by the domination of His Majesty."[37] In short, the Collège des Quatre Nations was conceived as an instrument of national assimilation.

Mazarin's dual nationality—he was Roman by formation, French by political allegiance—may well have made him sensitive to conflicting cultural and political ties in the borderlands. As a result of territorial annexations, Flemish, German, and Catalan-speaking communities came under French rule. How could these foreigners be converted into Frenchmen? Mazarin recognized the role of education—that is to say, of cultural assimilation—in the process of political absorption; his college was probably the first and certainly the most prominent initiative in the capital to promote the goals of acculturation. But the Collège was also related to more modest local programs in the borderlands themselves. Historians have recently traced the efforts of the crown to promote French language and culture in the Catalan-speaking province of Roussillon, at the Spanish border, which included the establishment (in August 1661) of a Jesuit Collège in Perpignan for "the youth to learn according to the practice in France." Here assimilationist measures did not succeed, and Catalan remained the dominant language;[38] nevertheless, the linkage between the well-endowed college in the capital and such efforts at the periphery indicates a growing awareness of the role of culture, language, and education in nation building—an issue that Mazarin's Collège served to crystallize.

Although the name of the Collège alludes to the territorial expansion of the French state, France had actually conquered not four nations but rather discrete parts of ten different provinces.[39] The peace treaties spell out which valleys, counties, and seigneuries France obtained; in Flanders, for instance, it was the villages of Gravelines, Bourbourg, and Saint-Vennat.[40] It makes good rhetorical sense to describe this patchwork of small places as if they were whole provinces; why not then use the more accurate and more aggrandizing number ten in the title of the Collège?

As an educated European would have known, the "four nations" recalled the golden age of the University of Paris, the thirteenth and fourteenth centuries, when it was the European center of advanced learning. The guild of instructors who constituted the University were divided into four governing units, or nations; called French, Norman, Picard, and English, they were, in fact, heterogeneous groups where foreigners mixed with Frenchmen.[41] At a time when most of the instructors and their students—masters and scholars, in the parlance of the day—came from outside the Ile-de-France, the nations embodied the international character of the University. The Collège des Quatre Nations evokes this cosmopolitan model but with a crucial difference: the foreigners it welcomed were subjects of France. Mazarin's Collège was an imperial, not an international, institution.

Mazarin's Collège should be seen also in relation to the long-term encroachment of the crown in the realm of higher education, a trend that accelerated under the Bourbon kings, beginning with Henri IV's royal reform of the University in 1594.[42] Its nations, once a stronghold of self-governance, had become vestigial structures by 1617, when the crown banned them from meeting. The nations were replaced by the college system, which reached its height in the seventeenth century. In the medieval period colleges had functioned as boardinghouses where poorer university students lived at the expense of a pious benefactor. By the sixteenth century they had assumed a pedagogical role and become the setting for a new humanistic program of Latin studies.[43] Although some historians deny a correlation between the rise of the Parisian college and the long-term growth of state power, it is telling to compare Mazarin's Collège with its Renaissance prototype, the Collège de France, which François I founded in 1532.[44] Both royal institutions, the colleges each reflected a different understanding of the relationship between education and the state.

The Collège de France, wholly independent of the University of Paris, was set up in opposition to it as a showcase of royal patronage. By contrast, Mazarin envisioned his school as a full member of the University community and entrusted supervision of his foundation to the rectors of the Sorbonne, the prestigious, hard-line college of theology.[45] The alliance with the Sorbonne was a strategic move to overcome potential opposition from the University, which jealously guarded its shrinking authority. (Royal interference was not the only factor; more important, the University encountered in the seventeenth century the rise of an independent system of Jesuit schools.)[46] Thus, unlike the Collège de France, which operated on the fringes of the higher education system, serving a princely ideal of erudition and humanist learning, the Collège des Quatre Nations was fully integrated in a framework within which it promoted a new pedagogical mission: education in the service of elite formation, acculturation, and nation building.

THE ACADEMY The second component of Mazarin's foundation was a riding academy for fifteen graduates of the college to pursue a program in horsemanship, dance, arms, and mathematics. The curriculum stems from the twin spheres of aristocratic life—the court and the battlefield—which suggests that the academy was intended to draw students of the highest social rank. A relatively recent innovation in noble education, the academy had emerged in the sixteenth century as an alternative to the college where the Latin, humanist curriculum offered young aristocrats no relevant career training. Riding academies of the sort Mazarin envisioned proliferated in the court societies of early modern Europe; by one count there were seven equestrian academies in the faubourg Saint-Germain alone during the seventeenth century.[47] What distinguished Mazarin's academy was its linkage with a humanist college. Normally these institutions were unrelated, their curricula as different as the social classes they served; academies were for the old-line nobility, colleges for the officer class that ran the government bureaucracy. Mazarin sent a different message to the nobility: training in the equestrian and martial arts was not sufficient; humanist education was a prerequisite to enter his elite academy.[48]

Mazarin's initiative reflects a century-long effort to reform noble education in France.[49] Beginning in the 1580s, critics worried that the kind of training noblemen received limited their role in government; what help were horsemanship, fencing, and ballet in preparing to serve the state? One of the key reformers in this domain was Cardinal Richelieu, who opened two academies for young noblemen—one in Paris in 1636, the other in Richelieu in 1640. His academies offered an innovative program, combining standard aristocratic subjects (riding, military exercises, and mathematics) with humanist subjects that were deemed appropriate for a diplomatic career (letters, geography, and history). Significantly, instruction was in French, not in Latin as at the University.[50] Richelieu's academies closed soon after his death in 1642, but Mazarin, though less innovative than his role model, fashioned his academy along generally similar lines.[51] Both ministers recognized the role of education, and more specifically of a modern pedagogical program, in forming the political mentality and aptitude of the nobility.[52]

THE LIBRARY The third part of Mazarin's foundation was a public library, the Bibliothèque Mazarine, which entailed the reinstallation of his personal library in a new institutional setting. The entire contents of the library in the Palais Mazarin were transferred to the Collège: tables, chairs, and bookshelves, as well as the manuscripts and books—nearly 38,000 items in all—which made it the largest library in Paris.[53] Its holdings also outnumbered those of the other public libraries (as opposed to libraries that did not admit unaffiliated readers) in seventeenth-century Europe: the Ambrosiana in Milan (founded in 1608), the Bodleian in Oxford (founded in 1612), and the Biblioteca of Angelo Rocca in Rome (founded in 1629).

Although historians have heralded the Bibliothèque Mazarine as the first public library in France, its admissions policy was no different from that of the library in the Palais Mazarin: open twice a week to men of letters with the librarian's permission. Why, then, did Mazarin bother to move his palace library if only to preserve its policies and appearance in a new locale? By relocating the library, Mazarin succeeded in redefining its status.

From a private collection housed in the cardinal's palace, it became a public resource to which other educational institutions were attached. Once considered a sign of Mazarin's excessive wealth and rapacious collecting habits, the library in its new institutional framework became a cultural treasure of France, as it is regarded to this day—a perceptual shift that obviously enhanced Mazarin's standing in history.[54]

MONEY Mazarin provided generously for the foundation. He donated two million *livres,* roughly equal to his annual income at the time, and a stash of municipal bonds, which earned about 15,000 *livres* per year in interest.[55] Should additional funds be needed, the king could assign the revenue from the abbey of Saint Michel-en-l'Herme, one of the cardinal's many benefices, to the Collège. No other charitable or religious institution did nearly as well by the cardinal: he gave 600,000 *livres* to the pope for a crusade against the Turks; 300,000 *livres* to the Theatines for a new church; 60,000 to the Hôpital Général; 30,000 to the Hôtel Dieu, and 12,000 *livres* to the Hôpital des Incurables.[56] Of course, most of Mazarin's wealth remained in the hands of his family; the bequest to the Collège was only 5 percent of his fortune. In absolute terms, however, the gift of two million *livres* was enormous; the Place des Vosges had been built with half that amount.

The size of the bequest inevitably called attention to Mazarin's enormous wealth, the very issue that the Collège was meant to defuse. In crafting the language of the will, the challenge was to account for the unprecedented fortune without tainting either Mazarin's integrity or the financial structure of France. What appears as routine praise of the king's magnanimity, in fact, accomplishes this delicate task; the rhetoric converts Mazarin's greed into generosity and translates the recent past into a tale of private munificence:

> Knowing from experience that it was absolutely necessary to have secure capital in reserve to provide for the instability of events and urgent and unexpected emergencies, mainly during a very difficult war and against powerful enemies; and His Eminence [Cardinal Mazarin], knowing that the finances of the king were hardly in a state to give prompt assistance, guarded his savings to rescue the king, if he was in need, and to support and defend the grandeur of the kingdom, in case of necessity.[57]

The king was hard pressed to refute Mazarin's account, and by virtue of a posthumous gift, the cardinal was able to reshape his image for posterity. Yet Mazarin's money did not guarantee the future of his foundation. The critical factor was Louis XIV's decision to recognize the Collège des Quatre Nations as a royal institution.[58] If he chose to do so, it was in large part because Mazarin had structured the Collège as such. It is hard to imagine the crown granting its imprimatur to the personal monument of any subject, but Mazarin had devised a program that merged his self-serving dynastic aims with a tribute to the king.

There is no mistaking the self-aggrandizing purpose of Mazarin's bequest. The library would house his remarkable collection of books and manuscripts; installing the collection in a building open to the public was a civic deed but also a means of keeping his collection intact. The Collège would commemorate his two great diplomatic achievements as royal minister: the Peace of Westphalia and the Peace of the Pyrenees. The college chapel would also house his tomb. Understandably the foundation was usually called the Collège Mazarini in seventeenth-century documents: after all, Mazarin conceived it as a personal memorial. But the key to the project was the association of Mazarin's monument with a royalist program, representing the culmination of a strategy that was twenty years in the making. His identification with the crown was, in fact, the hallmark of his patronage in France.

MAZARIN'S PATRONAGE

Giulio Mazarini never learned to write properly in French. We do not know how well he spoke the language, but his handwritten letters are riddled with French spelling errors and with Italian words. Historians also have said that Mazarin never adjusted to the French cultural milieu, and that his taste in art was oriented to Rome. In the judgment of Madeleine Laurain-Portemer, whose influential studies of Mazarin have shaped the prevailing view of his cultural concerns, the cardinal, throughout his years in Paris, remained faithful to the Roman models he had absorbed at the Barberini court. Undoubtedly the Barberini family taught Mazarin two influential lessons: the political importance of patronage and the superiority of the Roman Baroque. But it cannot be claimed, as does Laurain-Portemer, that Mazarin launched "a Baroque offensive" during his first trip to Paris in 1634 and sustained it in "militant" fashion through the 1640s and 1650s. In this scenario Mazarin emerges as a vanguard figure whose preference for Baroque art was at odds with the conservative, even backward taste in Paris.[59]

As a generation of recent art-historical research has shown, Baroque art came to France well before Mazarin arrived in 1640. The process was set in motion by French artists such as Simon Vouet, who had been to Rome in the 1620s and 1630s. Moreover, Cardinal Richelieu, with the aid of Sublet de Noyers, Paul Fréart de Chantelou, and his brother Fréart de Chambray, had launched a program in the 1630s to recruit Italian artists and to promote classical culture in France. Mazarin played a small part in this enterprise: he helped Richelieu obtain paintings by Andrea Sacchi and Cortona, artists usually placed at opposite ends of the stylistic spectrum, and on several occasions Mazarin lobbied the Barberini cardinals, on Richelieu's behalf, to permit artists to work in France. But Mazarin did not initiate Richelieu's cultural program, nor was he attached to one style of art.[60]

No less troubling is the picture of Mazarin as a trend-setting patron. The cardinal was an insatiable collector, but as a patron he was only moderately active, even low key. Blinded perhaps by his collecting habits, most historians have emphasized Mazarin's generic ardor for the arts, without distinguishing between the distinct roles of patron and collector.[61] The intention of this subchapter is twofold: to demarcate the boundaries of Mazarin's architectural patronage, apart from his collecting, and to relate his patronage to the Cardinal's economic and political predicament in France. Compared with men of similar or even lower rank, Mazarin built very little, but the building projects he sponsored reflect a carefully considered strategy. They reveal how he enlisted art for political ends.

Recent historical studies stress Mazarin's contribution to the formation of the French state. The notion of Mazarin on a Baroque offensive, laboring mightily for an aesthetic cause, is at odds with the political pragmatism several modern historians have described.[62] The thrust of the argument presented here is to bring Cardinal Mazarin's cultural politics into realignment with his *raison d'état* and to demonstrate that what Mazarin brought from papal Rome were lessons not of style but of statehood.

To begin, we should acknowledge the strongest evidence for Mazarin's so-called Baroque offensive—namely, his well-documented efforts to recruit Roman artists for Parisian projects. Mazarin asked Cortona to decorate his *hôtel,* Bernini to design his tomb, and Carlo Rainaldi to plan what was to become the Collège. There were other invitations of this sort, amply documented by Laurain-Portemer, and they leave no doubt that Mazarin thought first of Roman artists when his imagination turned to matters of art and decoration.[63] Rebuffed by the famous artists, Mazarin's agents managed to recruit other, lesser-known Italians to decorate the cardinal's Parisian *hôtel* in the 1640s. The interiors may demonstrate a Roman bias, but it is inaccurate to characterize the Hôtel Mazarin as a Baroque haven in a hostile land because this view overestimates the Baroque exuberance of the *hôtel* and also underestimates French interest in the Roman scene.

Consider the upper gallery, often cited as a flagrant importation from Baroque Rome (FIG. 6). Giovanni Francesco Romanelli, a student of Pietro da Cortona, completed the ceiling during an extended stay in Paris, from June 1646 through September 1647.[64] Stucco frames divide the vault into variously shaped compartments in a fine application of the Roman practice of *quadro riportati,* but by 1646, Romanelli's scheme was in line with advanced art in Paris; five years earlier Poussin had proposed a comparable solution for the Grande Galerie of the Louvre.[65] In fact, there is a greater affinity to Roman Baroque art in Poussin's project—with its bold stucco figures, combination of media, and movement of figures from pictorial to real space—than in Romanelli's ceiling, which is more classical in terms of style, composition, and handling of figures.

If Romanelli's ceiling reflects Mazarin's Roman taste, it demonstrates just as forcefully his sensitivity to the French milieu. Romanelli had initially proposed scenes from Roman history, but Mazarin rejected the idea and changed the subject to Ovid's *Metamorphoses,* which he considered more in keeping with French taste.[66] It is clear that Mazarin chose the Ovidian decorative program with French values in mind; perhaps they also led him to select Romanelli, a classicizing Roman painter. The point is that Mazarin's instinct, honed by years of diplomatic service, was to accommodate, not to agitate. In art as in politics, the cardinal was a pragmatist. Passionate feelings about style, even if Mazarin had them, cannot account for the nature of his commissions.

FIG. 6. *Giovanni Francesco Romanelli, ceiling of the Galerie Mazarine (detail), 1646. Fresco. Palais Mazarin, Paris*

Mazarin's patronage was a strategic response to his predicament in France, where he had to reckon with two exceptional circumstances. First, he was both cardinal and first minister, a doubly exalted rank that only Richelieu had held before him. Second, he was an Italian at the helm of a foreign state, and his status as an outsider made him an inviting target, as the events of the Fronde were to confirm. Mazarin encompassed a demanding range of roles: prime minister and cardinal, Frenchman and Italian, man of church and state, savior and demon. In considering his patronage, the critical issue is how he used the arts to negotiate these difficult conditions.

Mazarin was an astonishingly acquisitive collector. He bought virtually all categories of movable property in unprecedented profusion; at the time of his death, he owned no less than 550 paintings, but the silver, crystal, furnishings, and jewels—more liquid forms of property—were even more valuable.[67] What accounts for the cardinal's relentless collecting? A quest for princely magnificence and the pleasures of connoisseurship are the standard answers, yet his experience during the Fronde, the bitter knowledge that power was short-lived, suggests other pyschological and strategic factors. Of his rapacious collecting habits, a psychologist might say Mazarin sought to stave off death, but a financial adviser would see that the cardinal found a way to take his fortune with him—should he need to liquidate it or take it out of France. Certainly the Fronde taught Mazarin the value of liquid assets, inasmuch as he was able to buy the compliance of adversaries and finance his return to power with his own hard cash.

Mazarin immediately translated the lessons he learned from this upheaval into an investment program of staggering success. In less than a decade, as we have seen, he amassed the largest private fortune in the history of the Old Regime, and the distribution of his assets was also unique. Instead of buying land and developing a seigneurial base in the countryside as was the practice of the French aristocracy, Cardinal Mazarin's wealth was concentrated in cash and treasury bills: more than 19 million *livres* was in cash and debt instruments; the cash alone (8.7 million *livres*) exceeded the bullion deposits at the bank of Amsterdam. Mazarin kept large stashes of cash in his residences—1.46 million *livres* at Vincennes and 766,000 *livres* in his Louvre apartment—and also at locations near the border, for convenient access if he were again forced into exile.[68] Both Cardinals Richelieu and Mazarin amassed what has been called a ministerial fortune because it was based on the financial opportunities arising from the privileges granted a minister of state.[69] But whereas Cardinal Richelieu concentrated his wealth in landholdings, Mazarin invested a relatively small portion of his fortune in land—less than 15 percent.[70] His landholdings included the duchies of Mayenne and Nivernais, which he went to some trouble to obtain; he was not entirely uninterested in seigneurial estates, but it is telling that Mazarin never built a private château in France.

This was a striking departure from the customs of the French court, where the norm was for noblemen to own one country seat and for high-profile ministers to own several, usually one of which was built anew and at great expense. Consider the other chief ministers of the seventeenth century: the duc de Sully, Henri IV's right-hand man, rebuilt the château of Rosny; Cardinal Richelieu owned several châteaux—Rueil, Limours, Bois-le-Vicomte, Champigny, and Richelieu, a lavish construction built along with the adjacent new town; Colbert bought the barony of Seignelay (in Burgundy) in 1657 and immediately dispatched Le Vau to renovate the château. To take another slice of court society, all the finance ministers with whom Mazarin worked earned a place in the history of French architecture by virtue of the country houses they had built: Jacques Bordier commissioned Le Raincy from Louis Le Vau; Michel Particelli had Le Muet rebuild Tanlay; Mansart built Maisons for René de Longueil; and Fouquet—to his regret, no doubt—had Le Vau build Vaux-le-Vicomte.

Of course, the seigneurial properties Mazarin acquired had manor houses, but he chose to ignore them; he undertook no renovations and rarely paid a visit to these houses. When Mazarin's purchase of the duchy of Nivernais in 1658 started rumors of his impending sale of the duchy of Mayenne, Colbert dispatched Louis Le Vau to make drawings of the town and its château, but as Colbert explained in a letter to the cardinal, Le Vau's mis-

sion was only a subterfuge "in order to dissipate the rumors circulating that Your Eminence wanted to sell the duchy."[71] Mazarin's interest in his seigneurial houses did not go
much beyond this ruse.

Cardinal Mazarin did not misunderstand the representational value of châteaux in
court society, but rather than build a château of his own, he chose to move into one of the
king's. In 1652, after the Fronde had ended, Mazarin obtained the mostly honorific title of
governor of Vincennes. The idea reportedly came from Colbert, who thought the royal
fortress at the eastern edge of Paris would make a secure treasury for Mazarin's cash;
imagine the dungeon, if you will, as a vault.[72] Mazarin moved into the governor's apartment, adjoining the Sainte Chapelle—the location a convenient reminder of his religious
rank. Next he refashioned Vincennes as the joint residence of the cardinal and the crown.

RECASTING VINCENNES

Mazarin's first task was to resurrect Vincennes as a royal retreat. From Paris, the crown
had traditionally looked to the south and west for recreation: to Fontainebleau, Saint-
Germain-en-Laye, and more recently Versailles. Vincennes lay to the east and was considered a defensive site: in recent times the dungeon was used as a royal prison, and shortly
after Henri IV's assassination, a new wing was built for Louis XIII as a security measure.
Although the château was dilapidated, as Silvestre's engraving illustrates, the chapel, dungeon, and towers remained forceful signs of royal power (FIG. 7).

Mazarin's mission was to reestablish the royal presence at Vincennes. If only to un-

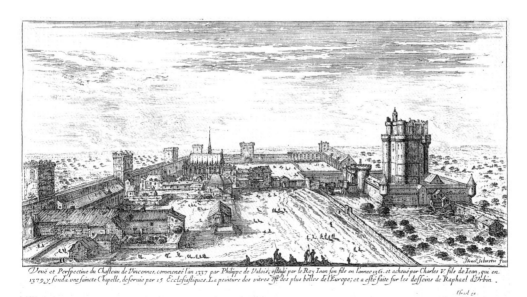

FIG. 7. *Château of Vincennes, ca. 1650, prior to Mazarin's renovations. Etching by Israel Silvestre. Département des Estampes,
Bibliothèque Nationale de France, Paris. The wing built by Louis XIII stands behind the dungeon, at right.*

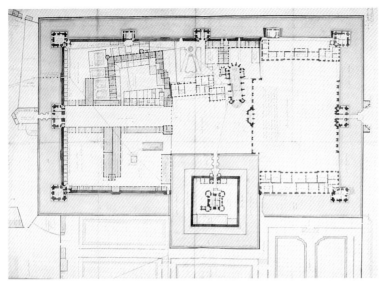

FIG. 8. *François d'Orbay, ground plan of the château of Vincennes, 1692. Pen, ink, and wash on paper. Archives Nationales, Paris (F21 3574/4). The Court of Honor, at right (south), comprises the King's Pavilion (below), the Queen's Pavilion (above), and the triumphal arch (right).*

derscore the royal nature of the enterprise, the project to renovate and enlarge Vincennes was probably destined for the royal architect; nonetheless, Colbert presented Mazarin with the names of three possible architects: François Mansart and Pierre Le Muet in addition to Le Vau. Mazarin instructed his secretary to choose, and Colbert, in turn, selected Le Vau. His assignment was to equip the old fortress with modern quarters and recreational facilities for the royal family, including new stables, a menagerie of exotic animals, and embellishments in the garden and the park, where the game stock was replenished. During the six years he worked on Vincennes, from 1654 to 1660, the scope of his interventions in the château gradually increased and moved to the north, from the court of honor to the service courtyards at the other end of the precinct. Even more striking is the growing importance of Cardinal Mazarin in the architectural program.

At an early stage, in 1654, a decision was made to double the width of the Louis XIII wing (visible in FIG. 7 beyond the dungeon) in order to provide apartments for Louis XIV and the Queen Mother; the enlarged wing was called the Pavillon du Roi, or King's Pavilion (though not a pavilion, properly speaking). Cardinal Mazarin remained outside the royal courtyard, in quarters adjacent to the Sainte Chapelle. In 1658, more secure in his power and close to a peace treaty with Spain, Mazarin decided to move his own lodgings to the court of honor and had Le Vau build another wing, only one room deep, opposite the King's Pavilion, with an apartment at each end—one for himself, another for Monsieur, the king's brother (see FIG. 8). Within a year, Louis XIV was engaged, and the living arrangements had to be altered to accommodate the new queen. The Queen Mother surrendered her apartment in the King's Pavilion and was reassigned to the wing under construction, thereafter called the Queen's Pavilion. To make room, either Monsieur or Mazarin had to go; Monsieur was displaced. The symmetry of the final layout—the king and queen in one wing, Mazarin and Anne of Austria in the other—explicitly installed the cardinal in the royal family and undoubtedly convinced some court watchers that Anne and Mazarin were lovers, as rumor had it.

Mazarin's presence at Vincennes became more emphatic also in the evolving designs for the triumphal arch that formed the entrance to the park on the south side of the court

FIG. 9. *Louis Le Vau, first project for the triumphal arch, château of Vincennes (detail of fig. 13)*

of honor (FIGS. 9–10). Whereas the ornament in Le Vau's first design refers only to the crown, the executed scheme incorporates multiple references to Cardinal Mazarin: in the frieze his signature fasces alternate with royal fleur-de-lis, and in the side bays his coat of arms appears above the niches, crowned by a cardinal's hat (the first scheme shows the royal crown in that location). In effect, Mazarin dominates the side bays of the triumphal arch, while the king controls the center, which features the royal escutcheon and medallion portraits of king and queen. The triumph evoked by the arch belongs jointly to the cardinal and the crown; in tandem they confer prosperity and peace, the qualities personified by the statues in the side niches who hold a cornucopia, on the left, and a palm frond, on the right.

By the time Mazarin died, his makeover of Vincennes was essentially completed, although he was unable to move into his new apartment. His patronage had brought the château back to life and insinuated the cardinal in the crown's domain. Visible from Le Vau's courtyard were the dungeon and royal chapel, buildings that embodied the secular and religious dimensions of royal power as did the presence of the king and his cardinal-minister (FIG. 11). During the late 1650s Vincennes was the hub of Mazarin's entourage. Fouquet established his primary residence nearby, the house of Saint-Mandé—famous as the

FIG. 10. *Louis Le Vau, triumphal arch, château of Vincennes, 1658. Engraving by Jean Marot. Département des Estampes, Bibliothèque Nationale de France, Paris*

seat of Fouquet's artistic activities—and the large number of period prints testifies to Vincennes's reemergence as an important royal site. The royal family and Mazarin gathered at Vincennes for several days before their entry into Paris in 1660. They gathered there again a few months later when Mazarin was brought to Vincennes to die, the deathbed vigil led by Louis XIV and his mother. The triumphal arch was not completed until after Mazarin's death; consequently, some of his devices were replaced by those of the king. In the side bays

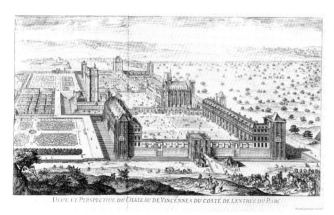

FIG. 11. *Château of Vincennes, ca. 1690. Etching by Pierre Brissart. Département des Estampes, Bibliothèque Nationale de France, Paris. The courtyard by Le Vau appears in the foreground.*

the face of Apollo supplanted the cardinal's coat of arms, but Mazarin's emblems remained intact in the frieze, a lasting homage to his renewal of Vincennes.[73]

In view of the issues raised in the introduction about classical and baroque in Le Vau's oeuvre, we must pause to assess the style of Vincennes before returning to the strategic goals of Mazarin's patronage. Le Vau's design has two distinctive features: it reformulates the standard château plan in order to leave open the park front, and it brilliantly adapts the medieval walls and bastions for entirely new purposes. In a preliminary project, Le Vau had converted the Louis XIII block into the side wing of a quadrangular plan; the arrangement centered on a new wing built against the perimetric wall (FIG. 12). The scheme satisfied the conventions of château planning by producing an enclosed courtyard, but it blocked visual and physical access to the park and shrank the new construction to an inappropriately intimate scale. Le Vau realized that the standard courtyard plan would not work—not if he wanted to create a space of grandeur, prolong the road from Paris through the grounds of Vincennes, and reveal views of the park.

The next design illustrates Le Vau's breakthrough idea: he reconceived the Queen's Pavilion as a freestanding wing on its current, lateral site; he perforated the curtain wall with an arcade, providing views of the countryside; and he brilliantly transformed the gate into a triumphal arch. Jean Marot's elevation and partial plan may give the impression of a thin screen,

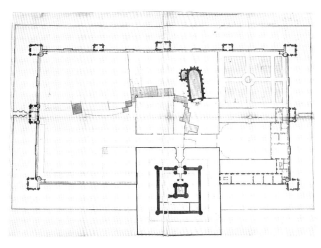

FIG. 12. *Louis Le Vau, first project to renovate the château of Vincennes, 1654. Pen, ink, and wash on paper. Bibliothèque Historique de la Ville de Paris (Réserve Plans E1500, no. 5)*

as with the arcade on the opposite side of the courtyard. In reality, however, the arcade and niches were carved from the thickness of the defensive wall (FIG. 13) and the triumphal arch from the immense southern gate; Le Vau's elevations of the side and exterior facade better convey the mass of masonry he had to remodel (FIG. 14). Here is a remarkably creative reuse of the medieval fabric, which was not just demilitarized but was adapted to a classical vocabulary and fitted with new functions. The arcade supported a balustraded promenade that permitted the king and queen to pass from their apartments on the second floor, stroll atop the medieval wall, and enjoy elevated views over the splendid park. The triumphal arch served also to demarcate an important ceremonial and urban route from the capital to Vincennes. Le Vau, in other words, translated the ephemeral triumphal arches seen on parade routes into a permanent marker of royal space.

Le Vau's use of the triumphal arch bears comparison with the temple front he applied to Vaux-le-Vicomte (FIG. 15). How, he asks in these two châteaux, can I adapt the forms of Roman classicism to the building types of France? The thought process is equivalent, al-

FIG. 13. *Louis Le Vau, first project for the triumphal arch and south arcade, château of Vincennes, ca. 1656–57. Pen, ink, wash, and graphite on paper. Bibliothèque Historique de la Ville de Paris (Réserve Plans E1500, no. 34)*

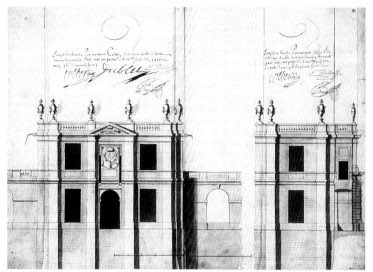

FIG. 14. *Louis Le Vau, south gate (exterior and side elevations and section), château of Vincennes, 28 May 1658. Pen, ink, and wash on paper. Bibliothèque Historique de la Ville de Paris (Réserve Plans E1500, no. 35)*

though the buildings produce different effects. Where Vaux's assemblage of differentiated units, comparable with his approach at Mazarin's Collège, adheres to the French tradition of composition and massing, Vincennes strikes a different note, comparable with the Versailles Enveloppe and Le Vau's other late designs, all royal buildings. At Vincennes the two wings appear as simple, rectangular blocks with a long, low roofline (FIG. 16). The facade is nearly flat, the four bays at each end of the facade barely project, and Le Vau reinforced the volumetric simplicity of the blocks by eliminating pediments originally sketched at each end.

The two châteaux, Vaux and Vincennes, deploy similar motifs from Le Vau's repertoire: scored masonry, colossal pilasters, flaming urns. But Vincennes is grander, more tectonic, and more severe than Vaux-le-Vicomte, where the decorative superabundance and play of robust volumes seem keyed to the rustic setting and the nonroyal standing of the patron, Fouquet. Fittingly, the classical aspect of Vincennes is keyed to its military pedigree, royal patron, and function as a center of court. What has been called the classical style of Vincennes should be understood as an attempt to tailor the expressive effects of architecture to its aulic role. Le Vau's differentiation of Vaux and Vincennes, two contemporary buildings, exemplifies what we mean by the modes in architecture.

For those who see Mazarin as a Baroque partisan, the classicism of Vincennes, its sobriety and rigor, has seemed odd. Two distinguished architectural historians (Alain Erlande-Brandenburg and Bertrand Jestaz) were puzzled in a recent book on Vincennes. The buildings "are nothing less than shocking," they averred, "when you consider the program launched by Mazarin, this great amateur of art, this Italian who ordinarily appears as the champion of Roman baroque in France."[74] But such an observation overlooks the fact that Vincennes perfectly championed Cardinal Mazarin's cause, which he defined in political, not artistic terms. The cardinal's aim was to ally himself with the crown in order to convey the unity of church and state.

THE ITALIAN LESSON

The copresence of Mazarin and the king at Vincennes, with its luminous palatine chapel, embodied the sacrosanct nature of the monarchy and its special relationship with the

FIG. 15. *Louis Le Vau, court elevation of the château of Vaux-le-Vicomte, 1656. Reproduced from Rodolphe Pfnor,* Le Château de Vaux-le-Vicomte *(Paris, 1888)*

FIG. 16. *Louis Le Vau, Queen's Pavilion and triumphal arch, château of Vincennes, 1658*

church. To insist on this political message is not to deny Mazarin other motives for rebuilding Vincennes. The cardinal obtained a country house at the crown's expense without freezing his own assets in real estate, while the enclosure of the château gave him a measure of personal security and an ideal stage for his self-aggrandizing iconography. But these self-interested motives coexist with the monarchical theme of the unity of church and state, a theme that runs through Cardinal Mazarin's other projects and accounts for the special character of his patronage.

Consider Mazarin's other building projects. First, he patronized the Theatines in Paris and left money for a new church, which was designed after the cardinal's death by the great Modenese priest-architect Guarino Guarini. Because the Theatines and their architect were Italian, the church is usually associated with Mazarin's "Baroque offensive," even though it was a posthumous project. No doubt Mazarin's support for the Theatines owed something to their Italian roots, but no less important was the order's strong connection with Anne of Austria to whom their church, Sainte Anne-la-Royale, was dedicated. It was the duty of a cardinal to foster piety, the duty of a minister to promote the ruler. Mazarin did more than meet these twin obligations in patronizing Sainte Anne-la-Royale. He also reinforced his personal identification with the crown.[75]

Second, Cardinal Mazarin created the finest private library in France, fulfilling the traditional responsibility of a cardinal to encourage learning and maintain a public studium. The library was housed in the Palais Mazarin, whose lavish furnishings have obscured its architectural deficiencies. Compared with the Palazzo Bentivoglio, the cardinal's official residence in Rome, the *hôtel* in Paris was something of a hodgepodge, formed by breaking through several neighboring townhouses, which made the structure large but decidedly unmonumental. The Palais Mazarin was an ongoing construction site for nearly twenty years; yet another enlargement was in the planning stages at the time of Mazarin's death.[76] Given his extensive resources, it may seem odd that he kept tinkering with the Hôtel Tubeuf instead of building a new and more perfect palace; after all, lesser men of finance were commissioning fine *hôtels* and driving a building boom in Paris. But Mazarin's conservative decision was sensible. First, the meliorist approach let the cardinal peg his renovations to the changing tide of his political fortunes. Second, it conformed to the model of Cardinal Richelieu, who made piecemeal enlargements to an extant structure in lieu of building a palace from scratch. And perhaps Mazarin did not mind the hodgepodge building because he did not live there. The Palais Mazarin was used only for receptions; Mazarin actually resided in a third-floor apartment of the Louvre. No other minister lived in the Louvre, but as at Vincennes, Mazarin did so in order to underscore his unusual bond with Louis XIV—the inseparability of cardinal and king, of church and state.

The one and only ex-novo building Mazarin commissioned was the Collège des Quatre Nations. As a posthumous commission, its design and site evolved beyond Mazarin's reach, but the basic program was his own. Library, college, chapel, and tomb—these were the sorts of projects cardinals typically sponsored; in fact, Mazarin virtually copied Cardinal Richelieu. The rebuilding of the college and church of the Sorbonne carried out by Richelieu set a magnificent standard of patronage that, in effect, authorized Mazarin's foundation. In addition, Richelieu had established two academies for noblemen, instructed his heirs to open his library to scholars, and destined his tomb for the collegiate church—all elements of Mazarin's Collège.[77] But the similarities should not obscure a telling difference between the programs of the two cardinals: Richelieu's college was devoted to theology, whereas the Collège des Quatre Nations served the state by making Frenchmen out of foreigners. In other words, within the traditional sphere of a cardinal's influence, Mazarin promoted the secular interests of a statesman.

The selective fashion in which Mazarin emulated his predecessor holds the key to the Italian's distinctive contribution. Richelieu, a prolific builder, met the two sets of demands implied by his twin office. As cardinal, he built a college, chapel, and tomb; as secular minister, he built two châteaux and a town. Mazarin, by contrast, built little; notably he never built a château of his own and eschewed the trappings of seigneurial power. But he redefined the image of cardinal-minister so as to fuse the religious and secular terms into one.

Mazarin took that step because he conceived the joint role of cardinal and first minister of France in terms of the cardinal-nephew at the Curia, the second-in-command whose hybrid powers, both political and spiritual, devolved from the pope. Historians regard the papacy as the prototype after which the monarchical states modeled their attempt to fuse secular and religious authority in the seventeenth century. The case of Mazarin translates this large-scale phenomenon into human terms. In the 1650s, at a time when the French crown was reeling from the crisis of the Fronde, Cardinal Mazarin reiterated an essential principle of the French state—unity of church and state—in his own activities as a patron. Once stability returned and Mazarin died, the Sun King appropriated the cardinal's message; after all, unity of church and state was the rightful claim of kingship.[78]

Mazarin's intrusion on royal ground may explain, at least in part, why he had no titular successor; after the cardinal's death in 1661, the king announced that he, rather than a new appointee, would assume Mazarin's duties. Mazarin's programmatic fusion of church and state explains also why his idea for a college did not suffer the fate of most posthumous projects. Instead of losing support and shrinking in scale, it materialized as a magnificent royal monument. Why? Because the Collège represented a powerful monarchical idea—the unity of church and state. That was Cardinal Mazarin's Italian lesson.

CHAPTER 2

ARCHITECTURE AND IMAGERY: THE NEW ROME

MAZARIN'S MANDATE WOULD have been fulfilled by an ordinary building on the edge of town, where land was plentiful and relatively inexpensive. Instead, Louis Le Vau designed a monument of unmatched splendor in the heart of Paris, opposite the Louvre. Handed the assignment to design a private foundation, Le Vau set an altogether different goal—to make a royal monument. His strategy went beyond embellishing the king's neighborhood; his intention was to fuse the Collège to the Louvre and make it part of an extended palace complex.

Insofar as the extensive literature on Mazarin's Collège deals with architecture—writers have been far more interested in the institutional history of the prestigious academies that meet under the dome—one point is made clear: more than any other building in Paris, the Collège has strong formal affinities with contemporary buildings in Rome.[1] The scenographic facade and curved walls, the portico and oval rotunda—these elements among others justify comparisons with the masterpieces of Roman Baroque architecture—Sant'Agnese, Santa Maria della Pace, and Sant'Andrea al Quirinale in Rome. But the Roman connections of the Collège go deeper than these surface similarities. Le Vau's borrowings were full of meaning and served to express basic values of Louis XIV's monarchy.

This chapter takes a close look at his design and asks what messages the Collège conveyed and what image it projected of the French state. While the forms of the building derive their expressive power from Roman models and archetypes, both ancient and modern, the overall message of Le Vau's monument is decidedly royalist. At the Collège des Quatre Nations, Rome was reborn on the banks of the Seine.

EARLY PROJECTS, 1656–60

Cardinal Mazarin took the first steps to build his *grand dessein*—library, college, church, and tomb—in 1656. At that time, Mazarin had made up his mind about one thing only: he wanted Gianlorenzo Bernini to design the tomb. In December 1656 he instructed his agent in Rome, Elpidio Benedetti, to obtain designs. Benedetti asked Mazarin for basic information: "a bit of a description of the site and the number of those who will be bound for the

Collège and for service in the church and library."[2] The cardinal was not helpful: "I cannot give the cavalier Bernini any information about the site, which is still uncertain, but he can make the design with every liberty because it will be up to me to choose."[3] This degree of freedom had no appeal to Bernini, who had the genius of seeing the artistic possibilities in site-specific constraints, as when he transfigured obtrusive portals into metaphors of death at the tombs of Urban VIII and Alexander VII. "[Bernini] told me that he does not know how to approach that which Your Eminence desires," Benedetti reported in May, "if he does not have the precise measurements of the place where [the tomb] will go, nor does he want to content himself with the complete liberty that is being offered him, or with your wish that the place be subordinated to the idea. The most important element should not yield to the secondary, and he does not have time to build castles in the air."[4] Knowing of his penchant for bargains, the cardinal's agent ended with some gossip about Bernini's high prices to mitigate the disappointment.

In November 1657, Benedetti sent Mazarin four drawings of tombs by a man he praised as "the most singular artist in Rome and of a talent that even Bernini might envy."[5] Three of the four drawings have been discovered recently in the archives of Turin; two illustrate a freestanding tomb, and the third depicts a wall monument. These projects are discussed in Appendix A; for now suffice it to say that Mazarin commissioned neither project.

As for the college, church, and library, Benedetti persuaded only one Italian architect to produce a design. Carlo Rainaldi, who would soon be associated with projects of the Mazarin family in Rome, reportedly sent sketches to Paris, but they do not survive, and we have no clues about Rainaldi's intentions.[6] The Italian negotiations had reached a standstill in June 1657, when Jean-Baptiste Colbert consulted with Mazarin on what to do.

> For the grand building project that Your Eminence has indicated he wants to proceed with, I very humbly request him to give me his orders: should I await a response from Monsieur E. Benedetti to learn if the architect from Rome [presumably Rainaldi] is coming to oversee the designs he made, or should I have some architect in our city work on it. In my opinion it is possible to use Le Vau, Mansart, or Le Muet. Your Eminence will please inform me which of the three he wants me to employ.[7]

Doubtful that Rainaldi would come to Paris, Mazarin answered: "It's fine to press Benedetti to send us the architect, but in the meantime, you must have one of the three in Paris work on the project, explaining my intention to him, with some gifts for Le Vau if you employ someone else, but I entrust this to you."[8] Mazarin, ever the diplomat, did not want to offend the king's first architect, hence the suggestion of a consolation prize.

As the letter makes clear, Mazarin did not choose the architect; that decision, so important in our eyes, he left to his secretary. "I have Monsieur Le Vau working on the *grand dessein* of Your Eminence," Colbert announced late in June, 1657. "Good," Mazarin responded, "because we can't expect anything from Rome, but perhaps it would be good to give some payment to the one who [according to Benedetti] made a beautiful design" (a reference either to Rainaldi or to the anonymous author of the tomb designs).[9]

That Mazarin delegated this key decision to his chief of staff deserves emphasis because it highlights the pragmatic, nonpartisan aspect of the cardinal's patronage. If he had strong artistic preferences, surely he would have cared who was the architect of his most ambitious commission. What is more, the artistic differences between Pierre Le Muet, François Mansart, and Le Vau could not have escaped Mazarin, since all three had worked for him before. The case at hand typifies his pattern of patronage: he initially requested a Roman artist and, failing that, relied on the best judgment of his advisers. The cardinal was not in the least preoccupied with style.

Le Vau's first design for Mazarin's foundation, produced in July 1657, does not survive, but we can reconstruct three key features. First, Le Vau situated the cardinal's buildings across the river from the Louvre, on the Porte de Nesle site and extending all the way to the Porte Dauphine. Second, the design included a large square similar to the Place des Vosges, then known as the Place Royale, a fact Le Vau disclosed in a later recollection.[10] Third, the project combined the cardinal's personal monument with service buildings for the Louvre, something we learn from a brief comment on the subject. "I'd like to know what the land would cost in building that square," Mazarin asked Colbert rhetorically, "and besides that, I tell you I don't at all approve what has been done with the barracks for the king's guard. On my word, if the project were to be executed as it is shown here, it would hardly be realized during my lifetime."[11]

Mazarin was right. Simply buying the land would have been a costly and time-consuming process, as he well knew from the crown's troubles in clearing the area between the Louvre and the Tuileries. Le Vau's project was too ambitous, but at its core was the brilliant idea of linking Mazarin's Collège to the Louvre, a possibility that the Porte de Nesle site afforded. Le Vau also made the interesting programmatic suggestion of moving the king's guard across the river, presumably to use the large square as a royal parade ground. This idea made an impression on Colbert, who resurrected it eight years later. In a memo to Bernini written during the planning of the Louvre in 1664, Colbert suggested building "a large square, square in shape, on the other side of the river [from the Louvre] laid out to lodge the gendarmes, light cavalry, musketeers, and even part of the regiment of guards, which could be used for important festivals and public celebrations, and in the middle of which could be erected a statue to the glory of the king."[12] Colbert's model was the Place Royale—which, by this time, had a royal equestrian monument in the center—and the proposal for a similar square on the Left Bank to house the king's guard revived Le Vau's lost project of 1657.

Le Vau's second design, from 1660, is recorded in a large drawing of the Louvre and Tuileries, which pointedly includes the general layout of Mazarin's monument on an other-

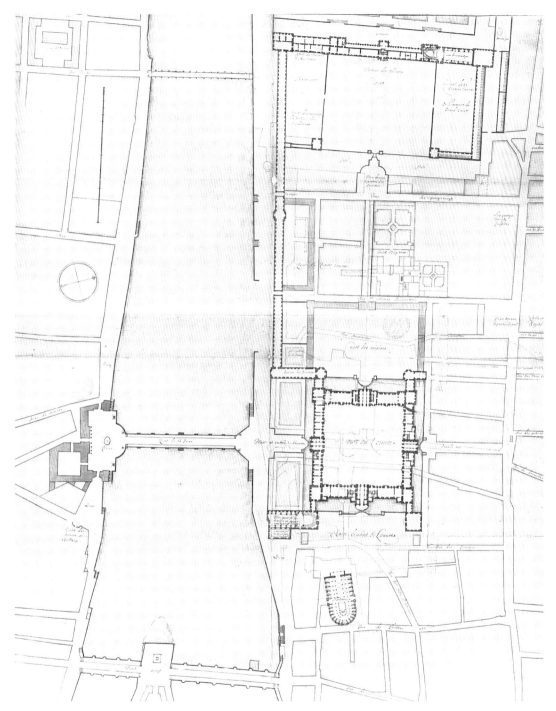

FIG. 17. *Louis Le Vau, plan of the Louvre and the Collège des Quatre Nations, 1660. Pen, ink, and wash on paper. Département des Arts Graphiques, Musée du Louvre, Paris (Recueil du Louvre I f21)*

wise blank Left Bank (FIG. 17). While the drawing focuses on the royal palace, it clearly establishes the Collège as an offshoot of the Louvre. The two buildings are connected by a bridge named the Pont de la Paix (Bridge of Peace) in honor of the peace treaty signed with Spain in November 1659. (Given this marker, it seems more likely that the drawing dates from 1660 than 1659, the more commonly given date.) The statues on the bridge and at each embankment would have celebrated the themes of victory and peace, and they confirm the ceremonial character of a roadway mostly disconnected from other streets. To generate some bridge traffic, Le Vau reopened the river entrance of the Louvre, previously closed off by a wall and private garden, and opened outlets to local streets on the Left Bank; unlike the Pont Neuf (at the bottom of FIG. 17), however, which was a key link in the network of city roads, the main purpose of the Pont de la Paix was to create a processional route between two monuments.[13] Le Vau's project taps an archetypal idea of the bridge as a sacred transit across water. The most likely way he encountered this tradition was in his library—specifically, in the modern reconstructions by Etienne Dupérac and Filippo de Rossi of Nero's bridge, the Pons Triumphans, and of the bridge that went to Hadrian's mausoleum, the Pons Aelieus (FIG. 18).[14] Like these ancient bridges, Le Vau's Pont de la Paix celebrates a triumphal journey in a landscape of royal power.

The bridge leads to an enclosed square in front of the Collège which entirely screens out the Left Bank neighborhood (FIG. 19). With Mazarin's buildings extending across the full width of the quay, the space reads not as a public square but as a private courtyard and pendant to the comparably shaped plaza beside the Louvre. Only three narrow passageways admit traffic, including one in the center of Mazarin's monument. It is unlikely that these passageways entailed complete breaks in the buildings; as with the entrances to the Collège quadrangle, they were probably only street-level openings, maintaining the effect of a continuous facade without entirely closing off traffic. Such *guichets* were a familiar feature in Paris; there were two in the Grande Galerie (see FIG. 17) and others at the Hôtel de Ville and Place des Vosges, to mention a few local examples of perforated facades.

FIG. 18. *Ponte Trionfale, Rome. Reproduced from Filippo de' Rossi,* Ritratto di Roma antica *(Rome, 1654), 186*

In response to Mazarin's criticisms, Le Vau radically scaled back the construction on the Left Bank. Gone are the buildings that service the Louvre; only Mazarin's buildings remain. Instead of a square as large as the Place des Vosges, a space comparable in size to the Cour Carrée, there is a modest courtyard with one corner of the buildings chipped away by an existing street; in deference to extant buildings behind the west wing, Le Vau devised an asymmetrical plan. Presumably the library was destined for the isolated west wing, while the Collège buildings surrounded the quadrangle, a traditional

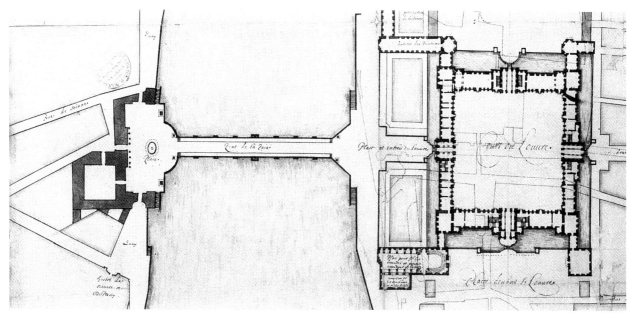

FIG. 19. *Louis Le Vau, plan of the Louvre, the Collège des Quatre Nations, and the Pont de la Paix, 1660 (detail of fig. 17)*

layout comparable with that at the Sorbonne (FIG. 20).[15] If the chapel is behind the facade, in the corner of the quadrangle, as seems likely, then the columnar centerpiece masks entrances to buildings with entirely different plans and purposes—a library and church—another bit of camouflage, like the *guichets,* and rival of any Baroque illusion.

The eight colossal columns in the middle gave monumentality to a facade intended to be seen from across the river. Lacking a corresponding elevation, the design is ambiguous, but the likelihood that the central opening is a typical French *guichet* suggests that Le Vau envisioned either a temple front (octastyle, as at the Pantheon) or a colonnade. Either way, Le Vau's scheme echoed the colossal order he had used on the central pavilion of the river wing of the Louvre.

THE SITE

Less than two weeks after Mazarin's death, his executors gathered to discuss the Collège des Quatre Nations. Colbert, who had assembled the group, took charge of the project; his close ties to Mazarin, administrative skills, and growing power at court, made him the natural leader. The executors included some of Louis XIV's top officers. Besides Colbert, there was Guillaume de Lamoignon, first president of the Parlement; Nicolas Fouquet, superintendant of finances; and Michel Le Tellier, secretary of state. The group included two representatives of the family's interests as well: Mazarin's primary heir, the duc de Mazarin; and Zongo Ondedei, the bishop of Fréjus, an old friend who had followed Mazarin to France. After setting the initial course of the project, the executors

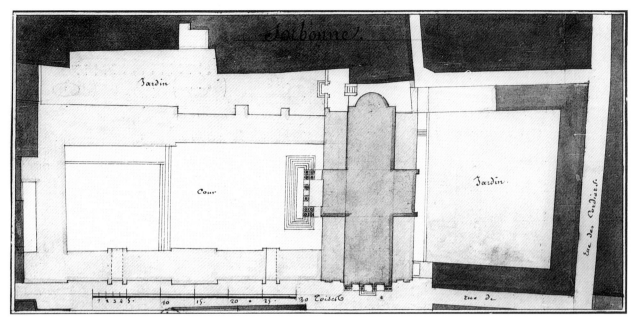

FIG. 20. *A. L. T. Vaudoyer, site plan of the college of the Sorbonne, 1817. Pen, ink, and wash on paper. Département des Estampes, Bibliothèque Nationale de France, Paris*

turned over the real work of creating the Collège to an administrative committee hand-picked by Colbert.

The project director was Jean de Gomont, a former agent of Mazarin's and a diligent administrator. He worked hard to appease the demanding rectors of the Sorbonne and to involve the tightfisted duke. He brokered conflicts between Le Vau, who preferred to have a free hand, and the controller, who was punctilious to a fault. Gomont consulted Colbert on every decision and in the early years held weekly meetings with Le Vau, which Colbert often attended. Gomont also had an eye on history and kept detailed minutes of committee meetings "so that posterity will be aware of the effort that led to the realization of this great design."[16] Besides tracking the nuts and bolts of the building project, Gomont's minutes capture Colbert's shifting ideas about the Collège, and they give us a better sense of Le Vau's personality than any other seventeenth-century source. Thanks to Gomont, we can enter the tangle of politics and personal rivalries, vision, and opportunism that gave rise to Mazarin's Collège.[17]

The first task was to choose a site, since the cardinal had not specified one in his will.[18] Surprisingly, Le Vau's previous designs for the Porte de Nesle site did not foreclose the matter. In fact, Colbert was wedded to a different location and suggested buying 35,000 square *toises* of land, roughly seven times the area of the Place des Vosges, farther upriver, opposite the Tuileries, where the faubourg Saint Germain was still sparsely settled. Such a large property was not needed for the Collège alone; Colbert wanted to merge it with another institution already located there—the convent of the Theatines, which Mazarin had also endowed.[19]

The Theatines were an Italian Counter Reformation order and from their first days in Paris had benefited from Mazarin's support. In 1647 he had bought the priests a house on the Quai Malaquais (now the Quai Voltaire), where they fashioned a simple chapel, and in 1659, at the height of his power, Mazarin initiated construction of a monumental church for the Theatines, Sainte Anne-la-Royale. He bought the Theatines additional land, hired the Piedmontese engineer-architect Maurizio Valperga to design the church, and ultimately bequeathed the monks 300,000 *livres* to finance its construction.[20]

Colbert had initially suggested a merger of the Collège and the Theatine convent to Mazarin while he was drafting his testament. "A remarkable thing happened during the reading of the will," Mazarin's Theatine confessor, Father Angelo, reported. "Monsieur Colbert got it into his head to attach our convent to the Collège.... He wanted the church of the Collège to be ours, and the exclusive right to say mass to go to the priests who governed and taught in the Collège, priests who are from the University and hate the regulars." Naturally, the two Theatines at Mazarin's bedside denounced Colbert's scheme, which would have deprived the order of an independent church. "His Eminence immediately agreed with us," Father Angelo reported, "and condemned the project of Monsieur Colbert." Colbert persisted and altered the will to read: "if the Fathers approve, the church of the Collège will be their church." Mazarin reportedly exploded: "[T]he Fathers do not want it; they do not want it; remove it. They want their own church, and I want that as well."[21]

Colbert did not heed the cardinal's wishes. After Mazarin's death, he made arrangements to buy the land surrounding the Theatine convent with the intention of building a single church for the joint use of the convent and the Collège. Colbert saw an opportunity to streamline the two projects, simplify his supervisory role, and perhaps maintain greater royal control over the enterprise. (He put Gomont in charge of the Theatine project as well as the Collège.) Endeavoring to scale back Mazarin's posthumous building program, Colbert reminded the executors that a single church would cost less to build.[22] Unlike the Theatines, he was insensitive to the tension between the University and regular clergy and the conflicting needs of college, parish, and convent. His thinking was bureaucratic, preoccupied with administrative efficiency and economy, and blind to the grandeur of Le Vau's Porte de Nesle scheme.

Mazarin's executors had a different perspective: they gave priority to the academic success of the Collège.[23] Toward this end, the executors focused on the requirements for membership in the University and more specifically on the standards of the Sorbonne, in compliance with the wishes of Cardinal Mazarin, who put the rectors of the Sorbonne in charge of his Collège. The rectors reluctantly agreed to oversee the Collège on three conditions. First, they opposed Mazarin's wish to involve the Theatines in the Collège (the will stipulated that Theatines were to direct the Italian division of the college and staff the chapel). According to the rectors, the Theatines were disqualified from collegiate posts because they lacked university degrees. Left unspoken was the Sorbonne's hostility toward the ultramontane clerics and a misplaced anxiety about the erosion of the University's authority by the crown and by the Jesuits. Conveniently, the Theatines declined the posts at Mazarin's Collège for reasons of their own, although the Sorbonne's sense of institutional vulnerability did not disappear.[24]

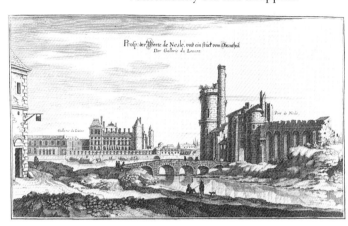

FIG. 21. *Porte de Nesle and the Louvre, ca. 1630. Engraving. Département des Estampes, Bibliothèque Nationale de France, Paris*

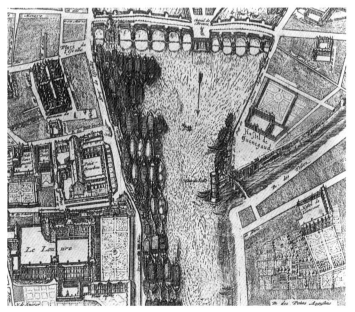

FIG. 22. *Jacques Gomboust, map detail of the Porte de Nesle and the Louvre, 1652. Engraving. Département des Estampes, Bibliothèque Nationale de France, Paris*

The leaders of the Sorbonne were also troubled by the riding academy, which they wanted to detach from the Collège and to locate outside the University quarter. Student discipline was a long-standing problem in a city rife with temptations, and the rectors regarded the academy, with its nonacademic program and aristocratic consituency, as a breeding ground for immoral behavior. But the issue of the riding academy took a back seat to the more immediate problem of a site for the Collège. The leaders of the Sorbonne required a location in the University quarter, a loosely defined area on the Left Bank that encompassed all of the existing colleges and centered, roughly speaking, on the Sorbonne. This pattern of settlement reinforced the urban presence and authority of the University, but it also gave a new college easy access to the target population of students. "To render the Collège illustrious, nothing is more important," Mazarin's executors noted, "than the attendance of external students and of officers and members of the University, because otherwise this would be a college of only sixty students, and in that case it would be hard to find capable professors willing to work there."[25] The executors rejected Colbert's site and agreed to focus on the University district.

It took Gomont's administrative committee another nine months to find a proper site, after deputizing Maurizio Valperga and a royal mason to evaluate five locations. The experts re-

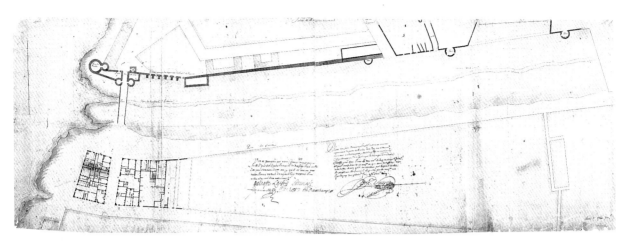

FIG. 23. *Louis Le Vau, site plan of the Tour de Nesle and environs, 23 June 1665. Pen, ink, and wash on paper. Archives Nationales, Paris (NIII Seine 710, no. 2)*

jected four of them, including the Porte de Nesle, and recommended taking over the Collège du Cardinal Lemoine, just inside the city wall at the Porte Saint Victor.[26] Beside the advantages of its site, the Collège du Cardinal Lemoine was one of the oldest and most prestigious colleges in Paris, and its pedigree might add some luster to a new upstart. The executors vetoed the suggestion for reasons worth mentioning only because they demonstrate complete disregard of architectural issues at this stage of the deliberations. The rationale was that it was poor public policy to eliminate one foundation to create another; the precedent set by the takeover would ultimately put Mazarin's Collège at risk; and the executors guessed that Cardinal Lemoine's name would stick in the public mind, overshadowing that of Mazarin.[27] No one mentioned, even in passing, the advantages a new building might offer.

Several other sites in the University were considered before Gomont's committee settled the matter at a meeting on Christmas Eve of 1661. With Valperga and Le Vau in attendance, the group made its decision in favor of the Collège du Cardinal Lemoine, this time focusing on vacant property it owned beside the city wall. The site required a new feeder street, but that was not a problem; someone—probably Le Vau because he made the same point at a later meeting—suggested building student housing on the street to generate rental income. So it was that "after the discussion of all issues, nothing was found to be more appropriate, more beautiful, or more convenient than the rear of the Collège du Cardinal Lemoine." The committee approved the site and asked Le Vau to sketch the layout of the new buildings.[28]

A week later, on New Year's Eve, Gomont reported that negotiations to buy the property had reached an impasse. Cardinal Lemoine's directors would not sell the land to a rival college unless it was under their control—a condition unacceptable to Mazarin's executors. "Regarding this difficulty," the minutes of the building commission report, "Monsieur Le Vau said that he had thought of another site that might be as advantageous as that of the Collège du Cardinal Lemoine, both for the establishment of the college and for the decoration of the city, as well as to render the memory of the late Cardinal Mazarin more illustrious: namely, to build the college opposite the Louvre, near the Porte de Nesle, where a public square can be built to embellish the view from the Louvre" (FIGS. 21–22).[29]

Colbert reconsidered the suggestion from a new vantage point. After a period of in-fighting and uncertainty culminating in Fouquet's arrest in September 1661, he had emerged as the king's chief minister and likely superintendant of royal buildings. As a minister of state, Colbert could see the merit of Le Vau's idea and instructed him to prepare a new design for the Porte de Nesle site. Le Vau presented his scheme three weeks later, on 21 January 1662. It greatly pleased the king and that, no doubt, is what pleased Colbert.[30] (For further details on the drawings, see Appendix C.) Gomont reported that Louis XIV found the drawings very beautiful and was delighted to have a majestic object to view from his apartment in the Louvre. On 11 March 1662 the building commission endorsed Le Vau's design.

The executors' earlier rejection of the Porte de Nesle site, for reasons unstated, is not hard to fathom. Besides being located outside the University, extensive work was required just to prepare the site for construction. Demolishing the wall of Charles V and the old city gate was the least of the expenses. As Le Vau's site plan delineates, the area was traversed by an open sewer, which had to be channeled into an underground sewer (FIG. 23). There were indemnities to pay to property owners and, above all, a quay to build along the ragged shoreline.

But to Le Vau's eye, the site had one overriding advantage: its proximity to the Louvre. Academic matters and the niggling concerns of the Sorbonne paled beside the opportunity to eliminate a prominent eyesore in the cityscape and embellish the environs of the Louvre. In fact, the crown had already taken steps to improve the area, which figured into Le Vau's budgetary calculations, as we will see in Chapter 4. Since the start of their deliberations nine months earlier, the executors and administrators had emphasized the pedagogical requirements of the Collège, whereas Le Vau set an entirely different agenda. In moving the Collège only a few blocks from the University quarter to the banks of the Seine, Le Vau had taken a great conceptual and creative leap. He had recast a conventional collegiate program into a monumental urban design, and Colbert had the good sense to follow his architect's lead. In the years to come, Le Vau was always credited for this compelling idea.[31]

THE DESIGN OF 1662

The new design (FIG. 24) was bolder than the 1660 scheme: the rectilinear wings of the earlier scheme were fused together, the straight walls bent into two fluid curves, and the central axis closed by a domed church. Never before had a curved facade been seen in Paris, and the domed temple front was no less a rarity. The bridge was dropped from this design,

FIG. 24. *Collège des Quatre Nations viewed from the Seine, ca. 1670. Drawing by Israel Silvestre. Département des Arts Graphiques, Musée du Louvre, Paris*

undoubtedly to economize. The Pont des Arts, built in the nineteenth century and still standing today, highlights an important feature of Le Vau's executed scheme: the main facade of the Collège is aligned with the axis of the Cour Carrée (FIG. 25).

Because of its singular qualities in a French context, the conventional underpinnings of the design are not recognized immediately. Behind Le Vau's method of composing forms stands a long French tradition, going back to medieval châteaux forts, of differentiating individual building units rather than submerging them in an all-encompassing block. The Collège facade combines three distinct elements. In the center is a projecting block with portico, pediment, and dome, which denote its sacral function as a church. The curved side wings are more demure; they have a simple balustrade and low roof (the urns Silvestre depicted over the curved wings were never built and may reflect an intermediary design). Another feature of the curved wings is a

FIG. 25. *Collège des Quatre Nations (now the Institut de France) viewed from the Cour Carrée of the Louvre*

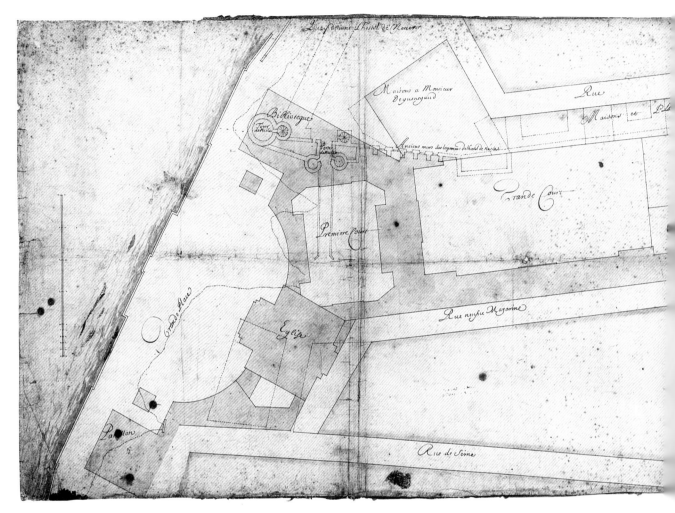

FIG. 26. *Louis Le Vau, site plan of the Collège des Quatre Nations, 23 June 1665. Pen, ink, and wash on paper. Archives Nationales, Paris (NIII Seine 710, no. 1). The dotted line indicates the original shoreline and extant properties on the site.*

two-story elevation with a double row of small pilasters, details that offended Jacques-François Blondel; he wanted to see a giant order applied across the entire facade to impart uniformity, but that was not Le Vau's aesthetic goal. Le Vau differentiated the building blocks to establish a compositional hierarchy, a goal well served by employing orders on a different scale. The end pavilions are like bookends; blocky and imposing with tall roofs and colossal pilasters, they anchor the composition and visually contain the dynamic forms in between.

While Le Vau was faithful to French tradition in composing the building, he managed to achieve an exceptional urban effect. The Collège does not border the street passively; it

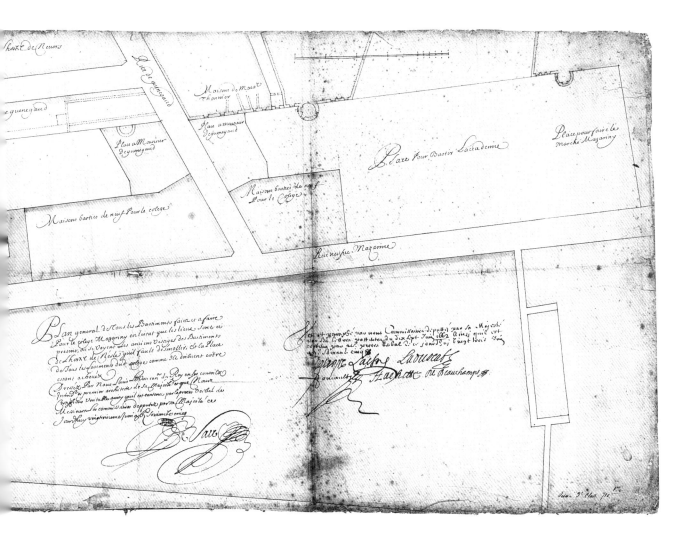

molds the space around it, like arms in an embrace, and captures our attention by its sceno-graphic placement in the cityscape. Writing in a guidebook of 1806, Jacques Guillaume Legrand and Charles Paul Landon considered this "picturesque and theatrical arrange-ment common enough in Italy but extremely rare in Paris, where most of the monuments are smothered and rarely arranged to form an agreeable sight."[32] But the controlling fact is unrecorded: the Collège can be seen properly only on axis from the Louvre. In other words, the king had the only good view.

The siting of the Collège stirred a controversy at the time of construction. The 1662 design may not be as brash as the earlier project, in which the Collège traversed the quay,

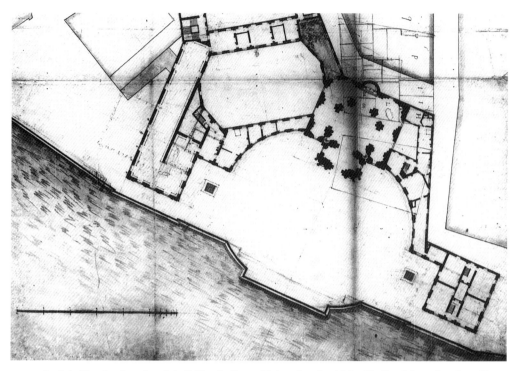

FIG. 27. *Louis Le Vau, first-floor plan of the Collège des Quatre Nations, here dated July 1662. Pen, ink, wash, and graphite on paper. Département des Estampes, Bibliothèque Nationale de France, Paris (Va 443). The drawing shows the original project for the Quai Mazarin with a straight quay drawn in pencil. The overdrawing on the library concerns a proposal to set the building farther back.*

but the forward placement of the pavilions—in line with the Tour de Nesle—meant that the quay had to be built out from the shoreline and molded around the buildings (FIG. 26). Predictably the municipal authorities protested Le Vau's scheme, which originally included a semicircular platform in the middle of the quay, extending another five *toises* into the Seine (FIG. 27). Historically the Hôtel de Ville protested all intrusions on the Seine, even if it meant taking on the crown, as in this case. The conflict erupted on 8 July 1662, as Le Vau was marking the site in the presence of representatives of the king and the city. After a stake was placed nine *toises* beyond the Tour de Nesle "to form a projection in the shape of a half-moon in front of the Collège," the *prévôt des marchands* protested that the protrusion in the river was a threat to navigation and the safety of the shore.[33]

Although the king had just approved the convex quay, the crown agreed to negotiate with the city. Experts for both parties recommended slicing off the semicircular projection; a drawing dated 10 July 1662, signed by the four experts, demonstrated that the revised design would not unduly narrow the Seine (FIG. 28).[34] Le Vau lost a platform for a statue—figure 27 shows a pedestal—but the basic contour of the quay, its orthogonal alignment with

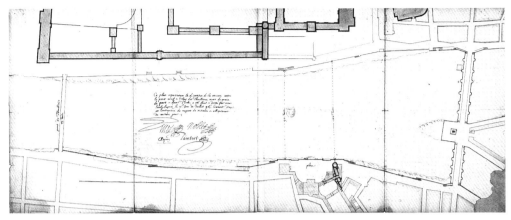

FIG. 28. *Louis Le Vau, plan showing the width of the Seine between the Collège des Quatre Nations and the Louvre, 10 July 1662. Pen, ink, and wash on paper. Archives Nationales, Paris (M176, no. 44)*

the Cour Carrée, and the implied connection between the Louvre and the Collège remained intact.

While the Hôtel de Ville may have been satisfied with this solution, the neighbors were not appeased. Gomont received "public complaints that the two pavilions [would] block the view from houses on the quay," and compel the road to bend around the buildings.[35] One irate citizen submitted a written complaint likening the quay to the meanderings of medieval streets and urged the king to imitate "the current pope [Alexander VII], who, in order to enlarge and straighten the roads leading to the Piazza San Pietro, demolished all parts of houses that project beyond the alignment."[36] On a site visit with Bernini, Paul Fréart de Chantelou complained that the Collège was "very badly planned and situated (on account of the alteration in the riverbed)."[37] We do not know what Bernini thought, but Christopher Wren echoed Chantelou's hostile view: "The Artist hath purposely set it ill-favouredly, that he might show his Wit in struggling with an inconvenient Situation."[38] Although Wren failed to recognize Le Vau's aim—perhaps Chantelou or another guide equally unsympathetic to Le Vau prejudiced his response to the site—the comment is interesting in light of Wren's effort to coordinate the street system of London with monumental buildings in his city plan of 1666, completed shortly after the Parisian sojourn.

Faced by public dissent, Gomont's group entertained a proposal to push the buildings back, farther inland. The move would have attenuated the link of the Collège to the Louvre, and the architect fought the suggestion tooth and nail. Besides pointing out the added land costs involved in this proposal, "Monsieur Le Vau has always said and still insists that [the view along the quay] will not be deformed when the buildings are finished. And to the contrary, the ornament will be more beautiful, especially the view from the Louvre, with the pavilions projecting beyond the alignment of the houses on the quay."[39]

FIG. 29. *View of the Seine east of the Pont Royal, ca. 1675. Etching by Lieven Cruyl. Département des Estampes, Bibliothèque Nationale de France, Paris*

Le Vau did not tell the whole truth; he surely knew that his buildings would obstruct views along the quay, as they do to this day (FIG. 29). On the other hand, the view from the Louvre is splendid. Privileging this viewpoint (the king's viewpoint) made clear that the Collège belonged not to the Left Bank but to the Louvre—no small feat, since a river runs between them.

As historic guardians of the quays, the municipal leaders could not have been insensitive to the disadvantages of Le Vau's design, yet they approved it unanimously. It was a political compromise, an imperfect but acceptable solution to a conflict between public commodity (a properly aligned quay) and royal privilege (a magnificent view). A century later Blondel condemned this solution; his judgment that the quay deserved priority indicates how much the notion of the public realm had expanded in the intervening period.[40] But Le Vau's design took shape in the fabled age of absolutism, and in that context the crown's willingness to bend deserves to be noted. Indeed, the proceedings over the Quai Mazarin illustrate the way that municipal and royal authorities negotiated over turf in Paris, the king rarely, if ever, getting his way without some degree of compromise.

If the buildings on the quay seek detachment, those to the rear blend with the surrounding urban fabric (FIG. 30; and see FIG. 26). Le Vau had begun the design process in 1657 with an ideal form in mind—a large square. He reversed that strategy in the 1662 design by working out from the site and confining his design to the area of the ruinous fortifications. Le Vau's plan brings to mind the image of a flower. A long stem is wedged in the Left Bank and constrained by its surroundings; the buildings on the stem are unremarkable, but they give rise to a beautiful blossom—the facade—which is oriented, if not toward the sun, then toward the Sun King's palace.

Responding brilliantly to a difficult site, Le Vau transformed wasteland into urban splendor. The east pavilion rose above the foundations of the Porte de Nesle, whereas the college courtyards filled the space between the city wall and the outer ditch of the fortifications. The preexisting street beside the ditch was changed in name alone, from the topographically descriptive rue des Fossez (Ditch Road) to the commemorative rue Mazarine. Circulation patterns were unchanged; rues Mazarine and de Seine were simply routed around the west pavilion, which was built mostly on infill. Le Vau appropriated private property only as needed for the facade; accordingly, a small block of houses was destroyed to make way for the right, or west, side of the Collège facade.

If the glamorous facade and the infill buildings to the rear show two sides of Le Vau's contextual urbanism, they come together in the pedestrian passageway that connects the back roads with the *place* along the Seine. The open arcade was originally located in the middle of the curved wing, symmetrical with the college entrance on the other side (see FIG. 30), but it was closed in 1700 and replaced by another passageway, which still survives, in the bay between the curved wing and the end pavilion. Perhaps because a person literally walks through the facade, the passageway creates the startling and dramatic sensation of entering a majestic stage—an effect as strong now as it was in the seventeenth century, when an English traveler observed that "the front [of the Collège] is stately, made like a theater."[41] Theatrical metaphors, which are often used to describe Baroque architecture, seem especially apt here because the entire right half of the facade functions as a screen. Le Vau's strategy here is no different from Pietro da Cortona's at Santa Maria della Pace (1656), where the facade also incorporates asymmetrical openings to the back streets of Rome.

THE ACADEMY AND RENTAL HOUSES Le Vau located the academy along the rue Mazarine at the south end of the site (at the top of FIG. 30). Consisting of two courtyards enclosed by stables and a riding area to the rear, the academy is as far removed from the college as the site permitted, but not far enough to satisfy the Sorbonne rectors. Gomont sided with the Sorbonne for economic reasons. Counting on a handsome profit from selling the desirable rue Mazarine property, he said the academy was cramped and would be better off on a larger and cheaper site on the outskirts of town. But Colbert disagreed, maintaining that foreigners would be more impressed by one large complex. Persuaded by Le Vau's royalist perspective, he now cared more about the appearance of central Paris than the pragmatic concerns that dogged Gomont.[42] In 1668 the building committee endorsed Colbert's position, but with no money to spare, the academy drifted down the list of priorities and was ultimately abandoned.[43]

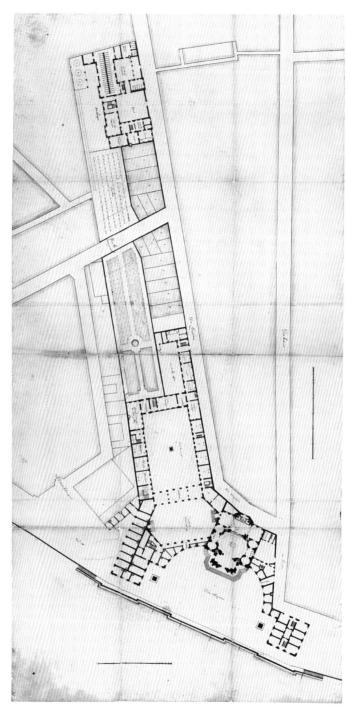

FIG. 30. *Louis Le Vau, ground plan of the Collège des Quatre Nations, 13 August 1662. Pen, ink, and wash on paper. Archives Nationales, Paris (M176, no. 52)*

Money—or rather, the shortage of it—led to another change in Mazarin's program (we will return to the financial pressures in Chapter 4). Although the cardinal had said nothing about rental housing, the commissioners made it a top priority. It was Le Vau's idea to build rental houses between the college and academy in order to supplement Mazarin's bequest, and a total of sixteen houses were built on the rue Mazarine and on the new cross street, the rue Guénégaud. Begun in August 1662, before anything else, they were ready to rent a year and a half later (FIG. 31).[44] Despite their simple elevations, the uniformity of the street front would have made for a dignified approach to the academy.

THE COLLEGE The college buildings were laid out around three courtyards (see FIG. 30): a small octagonal courtyard with symmetrical entrances to the chapel and library; a much larger courtyard where the classrooms and dormitories were located; and a service courtyard to the rear. Before making final plans for the college, Le Vau and Gomont consulted numerous experts and carefully inspected the Sorbonne. They measured classrooms and courtyards and examined the arrangement of beds and the installation of lamps.[45] Under pressure to economize, Le Vau incorporated several cutbacks in drawings he submitted in May 1664. Among them were two wings eliminated in the large courtyard—the long one adjacent to the city wall and the short one closing off the service courtyard—and replaced with screen walls (FIGS. 32–33). The Sorbonne doctors remained impressed by the size of the courtyard, "agreeing that there were not any other courtyards in the University that were as long, as wide, or in such good air."[46]

No space better demonstrates Le Vau's planning ingenuity than the first courtyard. The rear courtyards followed the oblique alignment of the rue Mazarine and the old city

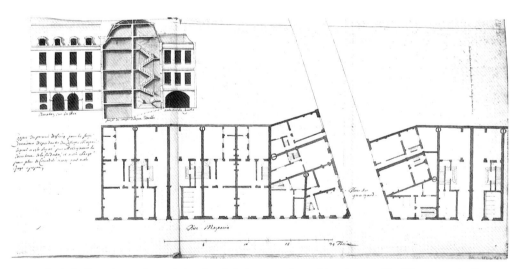

FIG. 31. *Louis Le Vau, plan, section, and elevation of the houses on the rue Mazarine, ca. 1665. Département des Estampes, Bibliothèque Nationale de France, Paris (Va 263d)*

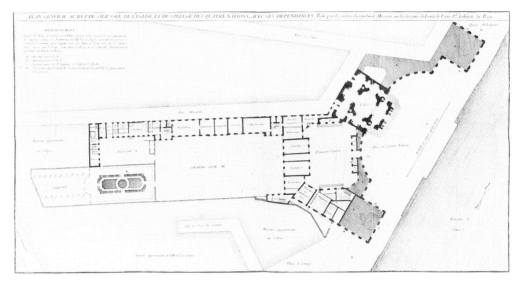

FIG. 32. *Ground plan of the Collège des Quatre Nations as built. Reproduced from Jacques-François Blondel,* Architecture françoise *(Paris, 1752–56), book 3, no. 1, pl. 1*

FIG. 33. *Second courtyard of the Collège des Quatre Nations. Etching. Département des Estampes, Bibliothèque Nationale de France, Paris*

wall, whereas the main facade was aligned with the orthogonal grid of the Louvre. These two geometries collided in the first courtyard, yet by molding the surrounding wings into irregular shapes, Le Vau created a symmetrical space. In the first scheme of August 1662, Le Vau applied porticos awkwardly to the short ends of a hexagonal space (see FIG. 30), whereas in the elegant final solution, much larger porticos dominate the sides of a rectangular space with canted corners (FIGS. 34–35).

THE LIBRARY On entering the courtyard from the street, the portico on the left (or east side) led to the Bibliothèque Mazarine, which Le Vau installed on the *premier étage*—the second floor, in American terms (FIG. 36). Mazarin's esteemed librarian, Gabriel Naudé, advised locating books above ground level to protect them from humidity, rain, and other ill effects of nature. Naudé also recommended a tranquil setting, away from the street, but Le Vau disregarded this advice by situating the Bibliothèque Mazarine on the bustling quay.[47] Evidently he felt that the stunning river views were worth more than a reader's solitude (FIG. 37).

The interior design of the library was essentially predetermined, since Cardinal Mazarin had bequeathed the furnishings from his palace library— the bookshelves, Corinthian columns, and woodwork—in addition to the books and manuscripts themselves. Having modeled the library in the Palais Mazarin after the one in the Palazzo Barberini,

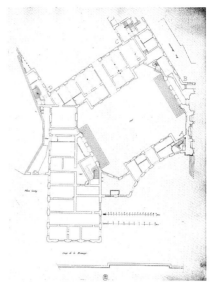

FIG. 34. *Ground plan of the first courtyard of the Collège des Quatre Nations. Anonymous 18th-century drawing. Département des Estampes, Bibliothèque Nationale de France, Paris (Va 261)*

FIG. 35. *Entrance of the chapel, first courtyard of the Collège des Quatre Nations (now the Institut de France), 1662–70*

Mazarin had obtained the plans in 1640 and spent enormous sums on furnishings of comparable splendor. The shelving from the palace was adjusted to fit the new building, which was smaller than the original setting but had more than twice as many windows. Palace furnishings survive virtually intact in the Bibliothèque Mazarine, with one exception: Le Vau's original vault was replaced by a flat ceiling in 1739 to create more shelf space.[48] Understandably most writers have focused on the handsome decor of the Bibliothèque Mazarine, but Le Vau's ingenious plan deserves our attention as well.

Although he had to work with an oddly shaped space, Le Vau carved out a regular L-

FIG. 36. *Entrance of the Bibliothèque Mazarine, first courtyard of the Collège des Quatre Nations (now the Institut de France)*

shaped plan (FIG. 38). It occupied the pavilion and a per-pendicular wing extending to the back of the octagonal courtyard, and the left-over spaces contained a triangular stairwell and other service functions. In accordance with the cardinal's wishes, the library received the public twice a week, after its delayed opening in 1691.[49] In the first design Le Vau accentuated the public nature of the institution by placing an entrance on the Place Mazarine (see FIG. 30), which he subsequently removed. The min-utes record two advantages of the new arrangement, pre-sumably as Le Vau explained them to his colleagues: the courtyard entrance permitted closer supervision of visi-tors who would have to pass through a monitored portal, as they do today, and enhanced the drama of entering the library by depositing the visitor at the far end.[50] It is a tribute to Le Vau's agile planning that we move from *place* to *cour,* up stairs, through smaller rooms, and finally into the spacious library with little sense of the ir-

FIG. 37. *Interior of the Bibliothèque Mazarine*

regularities Le Vau had to overcome. Wren saw the Bibliothèque Mazarine under construction in 1665 and 1666, and the lessons he learned about planning, local symmetries, and the magnificence a library might achieve informed his design for the library at Trinity College, Cambridge, where he would soon set a new standard for collegiate libraries.[51]

THE PAVILLON DES ARTS AND CURVED WINGS With the college and riding academy at the rear of the site and the library on an upper floor, Mazarin's requirements had been met without claiming much of the facade. The curved wings and end pavilions were mostly empty, and for these spaces Le Vau invented a program of his own. He conceived the west pavilion as the seat of four academies relating to the arts. The subjects are noted on the plan (see FIG. 38): architecture, mathematics, painting and sculpture, and engineering and fortifications. The pavilion contains four first-floor meeting rooms, one for each academy, and an apartment for the general director.[52]

Le Vau's proposal for a superacademy devoted to the arts probably reflects ideas float-

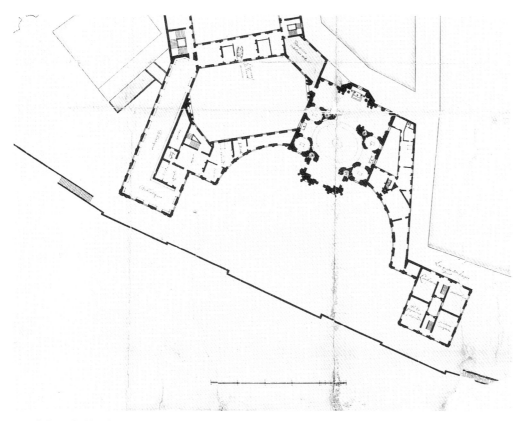

FIG. 38. *Louis Le Vau, first-floor plan of the Collège des Quatre Nations (detail), 13 August 1662. Pen, ink, and wash on paper. Archives Nationales, Paris (NIII Seine 710, no. 4). The caption on the west pavilion reads "Les quatre academyes pour l'architecture / mathématiques / peinture et sculpture / pour les ingenieurs fortifications."*

ing in Colbert's circle in the early 1660s. Before establishing individual academies, Colbert was planning a single *grande académie* with sections in belles lettres, history, philosophy, and mathematics.[53] Conspicuously missing from this list are the arts and related disciplines, precisely what Le Vau incorporated into his pavilion, perhaps to redress Colbert's omission. The Académie Royale de Peinture et de Sculpture existed at the time (according to Le Vau, "very badly lodged" in the Grande Galerie of the Louvre), but the other three were new. These subjects—architecture, mathematics, engineering, and fortifications— were eventually accommodated in the last of the academies established by Colbert, the Académie Royale d'Architecture, opened in 1671. No academic group ever convened in the pavilion, and college personnel took over the upper floors. It was a sensible use of a relatively small space, but it is hard to understand why Colbert waited nine years before acting on Le Vau's proposal to create an architectural academy and gave priority to virtually every other research field.[54]

The ground-level arcade of the facade provides another key to Le Vau's thinking. Unlike the open arches in the Cour Carrée and in Bernini's first two Louvre designs, the arches at the Collège were partially closed (see FIG. 1). The arrangement signifies a commercial arcade—ground-floor shops with mezzanine-level rooms above, as at the Place Dauphine. Elsewhere in Paris, shops flanking a church were customarily recessed and rendered visually inconspicuous behind a blank facade, as at the church of Saint Paul-Saint Louis on the rue Saint Antoine. Le Vau did just the reverse; he ennobled the shops with the orders and reinforced the connection with moldings that tie the storefronts visually to the church. The combination of church and shops in a monumental facade may stretch the standards of architectural decorum, but Le Vau had a local model: the Grande Galerie of the Louvre, where a select group of artists and artisans had ground-floor workshops.[55]

Inspired by royal example, Le Vau restricted the twenty-seven shops at the Collège to artisans from the prestige trades, which explains why Le Vau's name, the Pavillon des Arts, stuck after all. Over the next century (the shops were closed in 1804), tenants included jewelers and clockmakers, tapestry workers and cabinetmakers, booksellers and binders, and other skilled craftsmen who could afford higher rents.[56] Le Vau justified the shops on economic grounds but turned practical necessity into a coherent and compelling program. He envisioned the Collège as a center of artistic and intellectual activity, boasting the finest library in Paris, four royal academies, shops of accomplished craftsmen, and a prestigious college associated with the political and military ascendancy of Louis XIV's France. Le Vau explained his idea in a memo of 1662: "The buildings, with the library on one side and the four academies of the arts on the other, produce the beauty of the square, a public embellishment, and a beautiful view from the Louvre, while . . . artisans and merchants will bring convenience to the college and beauty to the Place Mazarine because it will always be filled with masters of the arts."[57] Le Vau recognized the importance of the luxury crafts to Colbert; as one historian of the minister explained: "[T]he relationship of the arts and technical progress seemed clear and important in Colbert's brand of mercantilist philosophy with its emphasis on luxury production."[58] The fine goods sold at the Collège would be living proof of Colbert's success in rebuilding the luxury trades in France.

The programmatic diversity of the Collège sheds light on the contentious issue of its formal pedigree. Usually the Collège is linked with two Roman churches of the mid-1650s, Santa Maria della Pace and Sant'Agnese (FIG. 39).[59] The *parti* is roughly similar, but the comparison serves to underscore the French features of the Collège. Le Vau did not express the curved wings as segments of a wall malleable enough to bend and curve without breaking, as in the Roman churches; his sweeping hemicycles are nearly self-sufficient forms with their own internal rules of articulation, and they terminate in typical French pavilions. Imagine the Collège without its curves, an effect achieved in one unartful period print (FIG. 40), and it is clear how closely its composition relates to standard French design.

Appropriately, the Collège has been related to the few châteaux with curved elements: Salomon de Brosse's Coulommiers (1613), Mansart's designs for Berny (1623) and Blois (1635–38), and Le Vau's own Vaux-le-Vicomte.[60] But we should not lose sight of what sets the Collège apart. At Blois a curved quadrant arcade is set before the wall and operates as a decorative riff (FIG. 41). At Vaux the curved wall remains a minor transitional element confined to the ground story (see FIG. 15). By contrast, at the Collège the curve ceases to be a minor contrapuntal note and becomes a fully plastic element in its own right.

In taking this formal step, Le Vau may well have been influenced by Antoine Lepautre's ideal château of 1652 (even if Le Vau did not own the book in which Lepautre

FIG. 39. *Francesco Borromini, façade of Sant'Agnese, Piazza Navona, Rome, 1653–55, completed by other architects in 1666*

FIG. 40. *"Collège Mazarin" (the Collège des Quatre Nations). Anonymous 17th-century engraving. Département des Estampes, Bibliothèque Nationale de France, Paris*

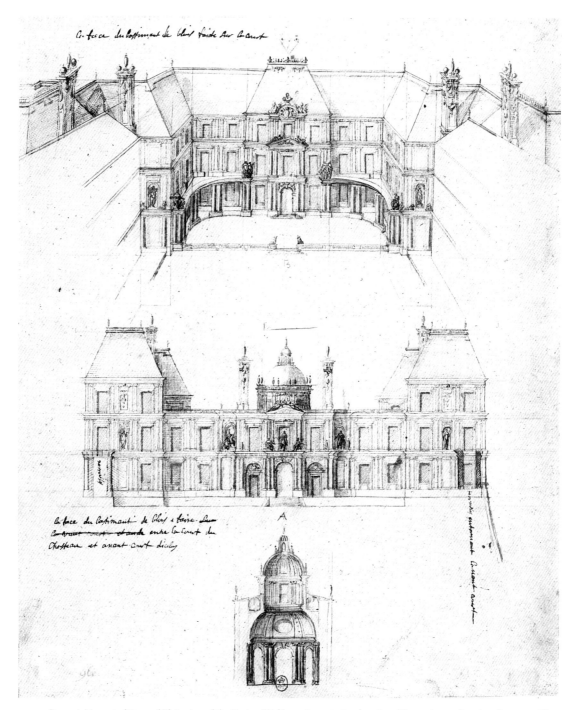

FIG. 41. *François Mansart, château of Blois, view of the Gaston d'Orléans wing, exterior elevation of front wing, and section of entry pavilion, ca. 1638. Pen, ink, and wash on paper. Département des Estampes, Bibliothèque Nationale de France, Paris (Va 407)*

FIG. 42. *Antoine Lepautre, project for a château. Reproduced from Lepautre,* Desseins de plusieurs palais *(Paris, 1652)*

published the château design);[61] the quadrant curves and colossal order are the most obvious signs of Le Vau's interest in Lepautre's scheme (FIG. 42). Once again, the differences between the Collège and château are revealing: Lepautre used flat roofs, Le Vau preferred tall French ones; Lepautre emphasized the overall unity of his building block with a continuous crowning balustrade, whereas Le Vau sharply individuated the building parts. Lepautre seemed to be after a consistent Roman effect, whereas Le Vau appeared to underscore the mixed heritage of his architectural language, as if he sought a declaratively Franco-Roman union. Is this not the message of juxtaposing a Roman temple front with steep French roofs?

Another factor must be added to this mix, since neither Roman churches nor French châteaux provided guidance with regard to a distinctive feature of the Collège: its combination of different functions in a monumental facade. For this Le Vau turned to Andrea Palladio. Specialists in French architecture have consistently maintained that Palladio, the most influential architect of all time, had virtually no influence in early modern France, but Le Vau disproves the thesis.[62] Throughout his career the Frenchman drew inspiration from Palladio's *Four Books on Architecture,* which he owned (in Italian, not in Fréart de Chambray's French translation). Le Vau's frequent use of the giant order and his juxtaposition of large and small orders goes back to Palladio. The temple front he used in domes-

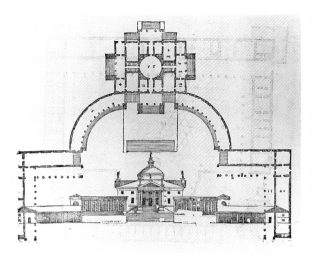

FIG. 43. *Andrea Palladio, plan and elevation of the Villa Trissino at Meledo. Reproduced from Palladio,* Les Quatres Livres de l'architecture, *trans. Fréart de Chambray (Paris, 1650), 129*

tic buildings derives from Palladio's villas, while his varishaped rooms echo those in the Italian master's palaces and reconstructions of ancient baths.

In the case at hand, Le Vau turned to Palladio's villas to solve the problem of combining different activities in a unified facade with a clear architectural hierarchy (FIG. 43). In particular, the unexecuted Villa Trissino at Meledo and the Villa Badoer at Fratta Polesine exhibit features that relate to the Collège des Quatre Nations: a dominant central volume raised on a stepped platform, preceded by a temple front, and attached to curved side wings, which accommodate lesser functions.[63]

THE CHURCH AS MAUSOLEUM

In the chapel Le Vau confronted what was arguably the quintessential design problem of the Baroque age: creating a space that fused two apparently opposite qualities, centrality and directionality. The issue arose from a liturgical need to place the high altar against a wall, contrary to the indications of a centralized space. It was a problem that the Renaissance had invented and that the seventeenth century set out to solve. The great architects of Le Vau's time had made a mark with centralized churches: Mansart at the Visitation (1632–34), Cortona at Santissimi Martina e Luca (1635–50), Rainaldi and Francesco Borromini at Sant'Agnese (begun 1652), Bernini at Sant'Andrea al Quirinale (1658–70). The Collège chapel was Le Vau's bid to join this enchanted circle, to try his hand at designing a space that was at once directionally focused yet centralized.

The church gave Le Vau trouble. The commission, which came late in his career, was his first chance to build a monumental dome, and the drawings betray an uncertain response to the challenge. Le Vau produced four schemes for the dome and three for the facade. Only the earliest set of drawings is dated, and although scholars agree on their sequence, there has been no attempt to understand the architect's thought process or to date the drawings, let alone relate them to other buildings and events. Yet it seems evident that some sort of creative disturbance agitated Le Vau and caused him to redesign the church over and over again. We will begin with the plan that he resolved early on; move to the dome, where Le Vau's problems centered; then step outside to look at the facade.

The chapel was an essential part of college life. Students gathered there for morning mass, vespers, and sometimes Sunday sermons, devoting as much as thirty to forty-five minutes a day to prayer.[64] Normally the public at large had no cause to use a collegiate chapel, but since Mazarin wanted his tomb erected in the Collège church (he gave his heart to the Theatines and his body to the Collège), Le Vau had to accommodate outside visitors.

FIG. 44. *Collège des Quatre Nations (now the Institut de France), 1662–70*

The dual program implied separate entrances and segregated spaces to minimize contact between the two constituencies. Yet the striking feature of Le Vau's design is the extent to which he subordinated collegiate considerations to the public role of the church.

Le Vau's most important design decision was to make the church the centerpiece of his composition. As best we can tell from the schematic plan of 1660, he had originally concealed the church behind the facade (see FIG. 19), whereas the design of 1662 recast it as a public monument in a salient relationship with the Louvre. Besides being legible from across the river, the large-scale forms of the church facade—temple-front and dome—were overtly classical elements rarely seen in Paris (FIG. 44). The one comparable portico discreetly faced the courtyard of the Sorbonne, and the city's skyline of Gothic spires contained only

FIG. 45. *Interior view of the dome, Collège des Quatre Nations (now the Institut de France)*

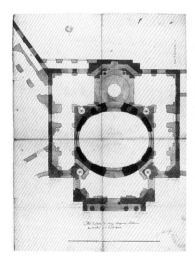

FIG. 46. *François d'Orbay, plan of the church at the level of the dome, Collège des Quatre Nations, ca. 1673. Pen, ink, wash, and graphite on paper. Archives Nationales, Paris (M176, no. 45)*

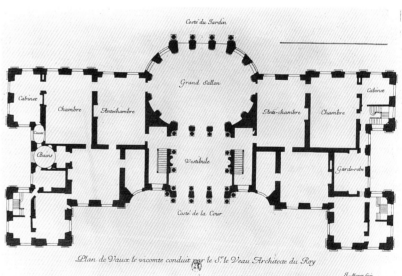

FIG. 47. *Louis Le Vau, ground plan of the château of Vaux-le-Vicomte, 1656. Engraving by Jean Marot. Département des Estampes, Bibliothèque Nationale de France, Paris*

three masonry domes—at Saint Paul, the Sorbonne, and Val-de-Grâce.[65] Obviously a college of sixty boys did not justify these conspicuous forms; they served to establish a relationship with the Louvre and to transform a collegiate chapel into an urban monument.

The double-shell dome epitomizes Le Vau's sense of spatial drama and his characteristic dexterity in freeing interior planning from exterior constraints. On the outside, the dome is nearly circular in plan and concentrates the composition on a perfectly stable and centralized form; inside, the dome is oval (FIGS. 45–46), a shape that attracted Le Vau, like other architects of his age, because of its tension between directional and centralizing forces.[66]

This oval is remarkable for its transverse orientation: its long axis is perpendicular to the main axis of the church. Church ovals, though relatively uncommon, were typically oriented the other way so that the long axis leads to the high altar. Le Vau, however, was intrigued by the transverse orientation, which he had exploited brilliantly at Vaux-le-Vicomte before reintroducing it at Mazarin's Collège and the east wing of the Louvre (FIG. 47).[67] As Vaux-le-Vicomte indicates, Le Vau's interest in the transverse oval predated Bernini's Sant'Andrea al Quirinale (1658–70), certainly the most famous and most successful tranverse-oval church (FIG. 48). In other words, the Collège chapel did not depend on Bernini's church; the two designs essentially emerged independently (which is not to say that Le Vau was unaware of Sant'Andrea). But if Bernini's church cannot be said to have caused or precipitated Le Vau's, their common interest in the transverse oval points to the more tangled subject of Le Vau's ongoing struggle with Bernini's influence—a matter to which we will soon turn.

Whereas Sant'Andrea involves an isolated oval, Le Vau embedded the volume in an interesting variant of a Greek-cross plan; the upper corners have been filled in to form an almost square block from which the entry vestibule projects (FIG. 49). The two types of congregants set up divergent axes of movement—a longitudinal one from the quay and a lateral one from the college courtyard—and the plan structures and

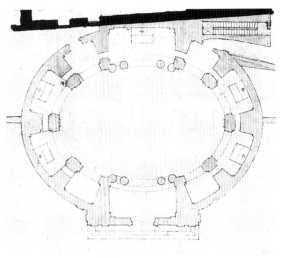

FIG. 48. *Gianlorenzo Bernini, ground plan of Sant'Andrea al Quirinale, Rome, 1658. Pen, ink, and wash on paper. Biblioteca Apostolica Vaticana*

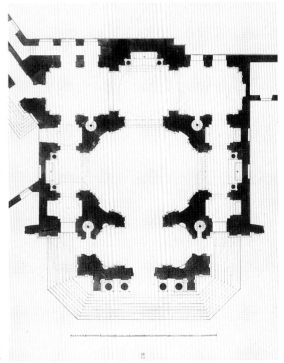

FIG. 49. *Louis Le Vau, final plan of the church, Collège des Quatre Nations. Pen, ink, and wash on paper. Département des Estampes, Bibliothèque Nationale de France, Paris (Va 261)*

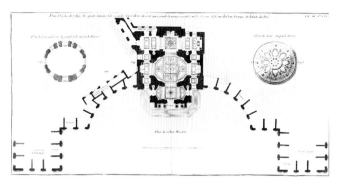

FIG. 50. *Ground plan of the church and shops, and plan of the dome as built, Collège des Quatre Nations. Reproduced from Jacques-François Blondel,* Architecture françoise *(Paris, 1752–56), book 3, no. 1, pl. 3*

accentuates this matrix of directional forces. A Parisian (as opposed to a student) moved from the entry vestibule to the high altar along a path, demarcated by the paving pattern, that internalized the urban axis of the Louvre and Collège (FIG. 50).[68] In the first scheme Le Vau used giant free-standing columns to accentuate the processional sequence toward the high altar, reserving the minor order for the cross axis (FIG. 51). In the second project he replaced the columns on the main axis with minor pilasters to render the four cross arms uniform; then he reasserted the directional focus by opening a dome in front of the high altar and filling that area with light (FIGS. 52–53). The long axis is countered by lateral pressures, which induce a reading of the plan as three horizontal bands (see FIG. 49). The private college entrance, at the upper left corner of the plan, sets this

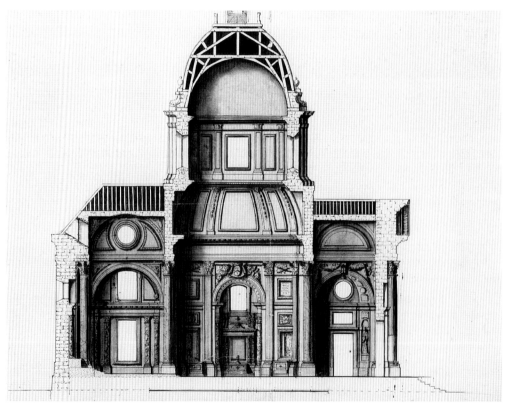

FIG. 51. *Louis Le Vau, longitudinal section of the church facing west, Collège des Quatre Nations, first scheme, 13 August 1662. Pen, ink, and wash on paper. Archives Nationales, Paris (M176, no. 9). The entrance is at right.*

FIG. 52. *Louis Le Vau, longitudinal section of the church facing east, Collège des Quatre Nations, second scheme, here dated 1664–65. Pen, ink, and wash on paper. Archives Nationales, Paris (M176, no. 32) The entrance is at left.*

FIG. 53. *Louis Le Vau, section of the church through the lantern and dome in front of the high altar, Collège des Quatre Nations, third scheme, here dated 1664–65. Pen, ink, and wash on paper. Département des Arts Graphiques, Musée du Louvre, Paris (Inv. 30249)*

lateral force in motion, and the theme is boldly restated both in the porch and in the transverse oval leading to side chapels, originally intended as burial chambers for members of the Mazarin family (FIG. 54).

Le Vau's plan may be understood as a response to two local models: Mansart's early masterpiece, the monastic church of the Visitation (FIG. 55), and Maurizio Valperga's plan for the Theatine church of Sainte Anne-la-Royale, under construction on a site neighboring the Collège and also financed by Mazarin (FIG. 56). (Soon after the foundations were built, the Theatines abandoned Valperga's scheme, and Guarino Guarini, himself a Theatine monk, redesigned the church.) Though confronting the same design problems as Mansart at the Visitation—segregating two congregations within a centralized space—Le Vau pointedly rejected its key features: the perfectly stable form of a

FIG. 54. *Interior of the Institut de France (formerly the church of the Collège des Quatre Nations), side chapel, facing east*

circular rotunda, chapels opening up the diagonal axes, and the lateral location of the nuns' choir, which afforded only blocked views of the main altar. Inverting the spatial hierarchy of the Visitation, Le Vau elevated its secondary oval dome into the primary space of the Collège, emphasized the transverse axis, and thereby established a more complex web of spatial forces. (That said, unlike Mansart and other Baroque architects, Le Vau never pursued diagonal planning.) In the end, despite substantial revisions, the Collège remains closer to Valperga's awkward Greek-cross plan for the Theatines, which Le Vau compressed, improved, and reinterpreted in a more Baroque key. On one level, the affiliation between the Collège and the Theatine project signals Mazarin's patronage of both buildings; on another, it underscores Le Vau's desire to engage the new architecture of Rome, which Valperga's scheme derivatively represented, and to rethink Mansart in Baroque terms.[69]

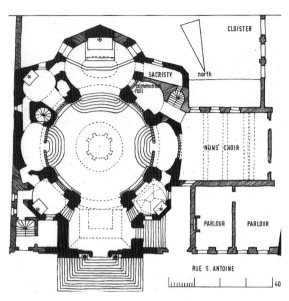

FIG. 55. *François Mansart, plan of the Visitation Sainte-Marie, 1632–34. Drawing by Peter Smith*

But the directional elements of Le Vau's design should not be overstated; the rotunda is experienced primarily as a centralized space, and a range of details reinforce its spatial autonomy. For instance, the rotunda sits on its own platform (see FIG. 49), and the crossing arches obey the geometry of the oval, not the side arms; in a marvelous display of French stereotomy, the arches curve in three dimensions.[70] In fact, Le Vau's rotunda seems to cramp the plan and compress the surrounding spaces, which are not adequate to serve the various practical requirements of a collegiate chapel. Le Vau gave short shrift to the students, who were the primary users of the chapel, and confined them to the top corners of the plan; the inscription in the upper left quadrant of figure 57 reads "lieu pour les escoliers" (area for the students). Much to the annoyance of the Sorbonne rectors, the sacristy was relegated to the far side of the college courtyard, at the end of a narrow corridor.[71] And although Le Vau pressed to have ordinary services in the church, to bring the liturgical program in line with the public character of the building, his scheme did not readily accommodate those basic liturgical needs; there was very little space in front of the high altar,

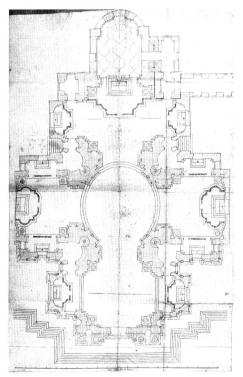

FIG. 56. *Maurizio Valperga, plan of Sainte Anne-la-Royale, Paris, 1660–61. Biblioteca Nazionale di Torino*

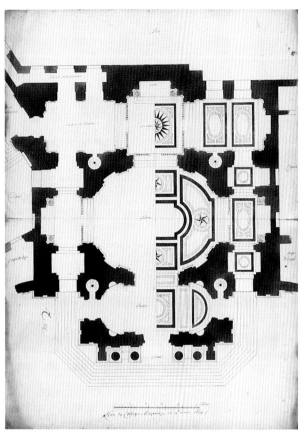

FIG. 57. *François d'Orbay, ground plan of the church and partial paving plan, Collège des Quatre Nations, 15 March 1684. Pen, ink, and wash on paper. Département des Arts Graphiques, Musée du Louvre, Paris (Inv. 30299)*

and within the oval, where congregants had more room, views of the altar were restricted.[72]

What was the purpose of this imposing rotunda? Le Vau conceived it as a mausoleum, and the earliest plans locate Mazarin's tomb beneath the dome (FIG. 58; and see FIG. 46, where the tomb is lightly sketched). Le Vau's idea made good architectural sense, but it was politically fool-hardy. Beyond the fact that the Italian-born minister and former antihero of the Fronde remained a controversial figure, it was inappropriate to build him a monumental mausoleum in central Paris when the kings of France had none. The Valois mausoleum had never been completed, its ruinous condition beside Saint Denis a sad reminder of the crown's failure to commemorate the royal line. Le Vau's mausoleum for Mazarin forced Colbert to confront this issue; he responded by commissioning designs for a Bourbon mausoleum at Saint Denis from Mansart, sometime between 1662 and 1665, and from Bernini during his trip to France in 1665. The Collège des Quatre Nations was the impetus for these projects.

Le Vau's startling idea comes into sharper focus by comparing his church with the one Jacques Lemercier built at the Sorbonne for Cardinal Richelieu in 1635, precisely because the building programs were identical: both were founded by a cardinal-minister to serve a college and shelter the founder's tomb. Save for its monumentality and splendor, Le Vau rejected the Sorbonne as a model in virtually every respect. First, the Sorbonne had a long nave (FIG. 59); Le Vau chose a compact centralized scheme— it begs the question to say the site dictated the plan since Le Vau was well aware of the constraints when he located the church. Second, Lemercier gave equal importance to the collegiate and public aspects of the Sorbonne, so that two monumental entrances initiate divergent but equally coherent readings of the interior space. As the students pass through a portico in the courtyard, they perceive a centralized church with two side arms extending from the great dome, while the public passes from the street through a modern Gesù-type facade into a long nave. No such balance obtains in the facades or layout of Le Vau's sanctuary, which was emphatic in favoring the public nature of his church.[73] Last, whereas Richelieu's tomb was placed in the choir, Le Vau planned to enshrine his patron's tomb beneath the central dome, instead of in a less conspicuous side chapel.[74]

As Mazarin faded into history, the importance of building a mausoleum in his honor

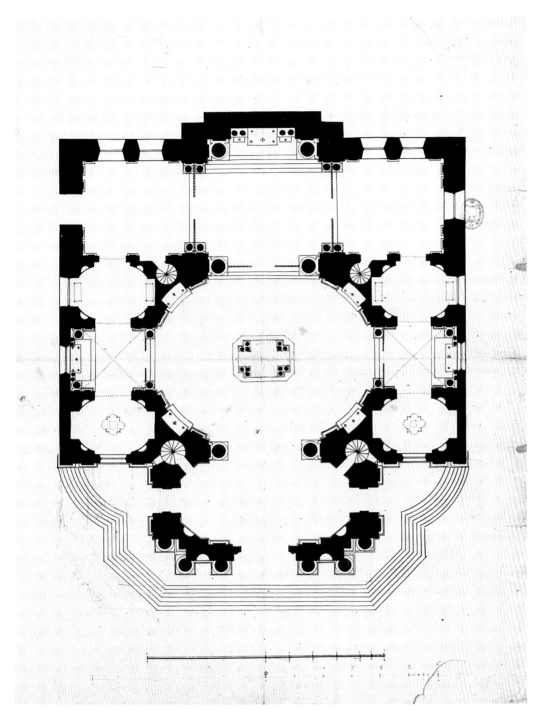

FIG. 58. *Louis Le Vau, ground plan of the church, Collège des Quatre Nations, first scheme, 13 August 1662. Pen, ink, and graphite on paper. Archives Nationales, Paris (M176, no. 37)*

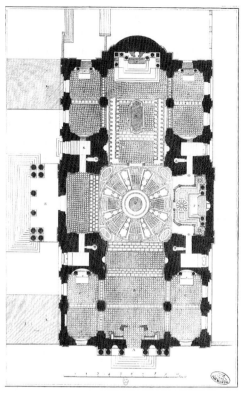

FIG. 59. *Jacques Lemercier, ground plan of the church of the Sorbonne, 1635. Engraving by Lucotte. Département des Estampes, Bibliothèque Nationale de France, Paris*

faded as well. That shift is registered in debates over the next twenty years about the proper place for Mazarin's tomb. The first complaints about the location under the dome came from Gomont in 1667, and it is interesting that Colbert went on record in favor of the central tomb; presumably he still expected to build a Bourbon mausoleum at the time.[75] When the issue was reopened in the mid-1670s, the key players had changed. Colbert's energies were absorbed elsewhere, Le Vau and Gomont were dead, and their successors had different views and different styles of working. Le Vau was succeeded by his chief assistant, François d'Orbay, who—despite efforts by Albert Laprade to portray him as a commanding figure responsible for much of Le Vau's work—emerges in the minutes of the building commission as a deferential and cautious man, producing designs as required but without any vision or a driving will.[76] On the contrary, the new chief administrator, Joseph Foucault, had strong opinions, among them that the Collège des Quatre Nations required a collegiate chapel, not a mausoleum for the founder. He acknowledged that the architecture was made to house a centrally placed tomb and that "no other space seems suitable" for it. Nonetheless, he stressed overriding functional problems: a central tomb blocked views of the high altar, obstructed the main axis, took up too much space, and conflicted with the needs of the college.[77]

Foucault consulted the Académie Royale d'Architecture, which gathered in the church in 1675 to consider the merits of three alternative locations for the tomb: beneath the dome, in the right side altar, and opposite the college entrance. The academicians submitted their views in March 1676, the majority opposing a central tomb because, as François Le Vau put it, "this church is not a mausoleum, like the Valois chapel." (Exposing the very premise of his brother's design and the underlying reason for its failure, François was giving vent to rivalrous feelings that evidently outlasted Louis's lifetime.) The academicians failed to reach a consensus: four backed Louis Le Vau's proposal for a tomb beneath the dome, among them Charles Perrault (whose views presumably reflected those of Colbert); three backed the right side chapel; and four, including the Académie's director,

François Blondel, supported Foucault's view that the tomb belonged opposite the college entrance.[78]

No action was taken at this time, but the discussions set the stage for the eventual abandonment of Le Vau's idea. In 1689 the Marquis de Louvois, who succeeded Colbert as minister-executor in charge of the foundation, commissioned a wall tomb opposite the college entrance. It is worth noting that Jules Hardouin-Mansart, who designed the tomb, had gone on record in 1676 against that location. He considered the spot too distant from the main entrance of the church, but in retrospect the location makes perfect sense (FIG. 60).[79] It relates to Mazarin's role as patron of the Collège, creates a visual focus for the collegiate axis, and gives a purpose to an otherwise useless corner. Indeed, so convincing is the actual placement that historians have overlooked Le Vau's intentions and lost sight of an important chapter in the history of failed attempts to build a royal mausoleum.

The absence of Mazarin's tomb beneath the dome meant that nothing impeded the primary affiliation of the Collège des Quatre Nations with the crown. Part of a network of royal buildings, the Collège finally expanded the crown's presence in Paris beyond the Louvre, a site that it still did not control—witness all the buildings between the Cour Carrée and the Tuileries—and onto the Left Bank. The next stage in the crown's territorial expansion was the Hôpital and Dôme of the Invalides, also on the Left Bank (FIG. 61). Planned as a mausoleum for the Bourbon kings, the Dôme would have met the challenge raised thirty years earlier by Le Vau's mausoleum for Mazarin. Moreover, Robert de Cotte's project for a plaza in front of the Dôme made significant reference to the Collège: as signs of royal power, the buildings dramatically extended the crown's claim on Paris.

THE STRUGGLE WITH BERNINI

In designing the elevation of the church, Le Vau had his eye on Rome, and more specifically, on Saint Peter's. There are references to that monument in several features of the first design—the temple front, dome, possibly the narthex, and statuary (FIGS. 62–63).[80] Le Vau's chief assistant, d'Orbay, had recently (sometime in 1661) returned from Rome with his own detailed renderings of Saint Peter's; he later presented them at a meeting of the Académie Royale d'Architecture. The facade of the Collège church was Le Vau's response to that immensely fruitful stimulus, and in the second design for the facade, he included more direct quo-

FIG. 60. *Mazarin's tomb viewed from the courtyard entrance of the church, Collège des Quatre Nations (now the Institut de France)*

FIG. 61. *Robert de Cotte, project for a royal square in front of the church of the Invalides, ca. 1717. Etching. Département des Estampes, Bibliothèque Nationale de France, Paris*

tations (FIG. 64): the tall attic and thirteen statues, exactly as in the Roman model. But the second design is awkward: the drum is too short and the dome too narrow, the attic is too tall and the whole overly fussy. In the final scheme Le Vau achieved a more massive and imposing effect (FIG. 65). He stripped away distracting ornament, composed the statues in more effective seated pairs, enlarged the drum, removed its base, and resolved the proportions. Beginning with an assemblage of borrowed elements, Le Vau arrived at a coherent response to Saint Peter's, albeit on a much smaller scale.

If the facade schemes imply a linear thought process, the sectional drawings give the opposite impression and suggest a sharp mid-course change in direction. Le Vau's first scheme features a three-part structure: curved base, drum, and hemispherical cupola (FIG. 66). Unlike pendentives, which make the transition from a square crossing to a circular dome, the curved base—the notable feature of this design—is not essential to the structure; given the oval ground plan, the drum could have rested directly on the piers, as it eventually did. But the curved base enabled Le Vau to attain an elevated effect by adding to the overall height of the dome and by reducing the circumference of the drum. The curved base is a standard feature of Le Vau's secular domes—for instance, the one in the grand salon at Vaux-le-Vicomte, which indicates his point of departure; Le Vau took his secular formula for a *salon à l'italienne* and inserted a drum.

But he was unhappy with the massive effect of the first scheme. In the second design Le Vau replaced the hemispherical vault with a more steeply pitched, ribbed dome and opened it up to the lantern (FIG. 67).[81] Le Vau took his cues from Mansart, the French master of dome construction, who favored tall, multitiered domes, as in Val-de-Grâce and the unexecuted projects for the entry pavilion at Blois and the Bourbon mausoleum (FIG. 68; and see FIG. 41). (Le Vau's second design also brings to mind Guarini's four-part dome at Sainte Anne-la-Royale, but the similarity does not go beyond the soaring effect.) Whatever Le Vau thought about its interior qualities, the tall, stacked dome produced ill effects on the exterior, as we see in the corresponding elevation (see FIG. 64).

In the third design Le Vau reversed direction and simplified the dome dramatically, reducing it on the interior from four parts to two—a simple duo of drum and vault (FIG. 69; there is no corresponding elevation for the third interior project). The drum sits directly on the piers so that the oval dome covers the entire crossing; the form is heavy, stable, and de-

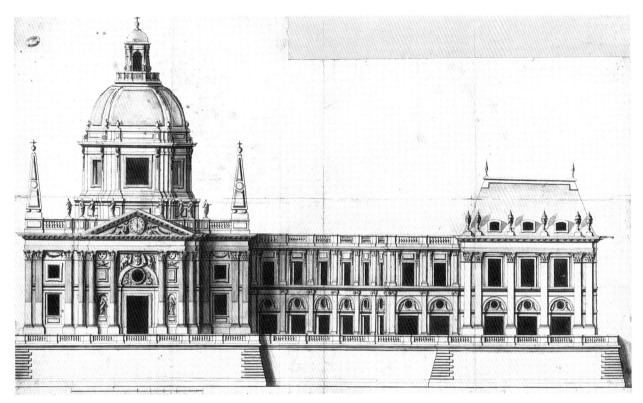

FIG. 62. *Louis Le Vau, elevation of the church and west half of the facade, Collège des Quatre Nations, first scheme, 13 August 1662. Pen, ink, and wash on paper. Archives Nationales, Paris (M176, no. 4)*

FIG. 63. *Carlo Maderno, facade of Saint Peter's, Rome, 1607–12*

FIG. 64. *Louis Le Vau, elevation of the church facade, Collège des Quatre Nations, second scheme, here dated 1664–65. Pen, ink, and wash on paper. Archives Nationales, Paris (M176, no. 24)*

FIG. 65. *François d'Orbay, elevation of the church facade as built, Collège des Quatre Nations, after 1673. Pen, ink, and wash on paper. Département des Estampes, Bibliothèque Nationale de France, Paris (Va 261)*

FIG. 66. *Louis Le Vau, transverse section of the church through the dome at left and the chancel at right, facing the main altar, Collège des Quatre Nations, first scheme, 13 August 1662. Pen, ink, and wash on paper. Archives Nationales, Paris (M176, no. 18)*

cidedly Roman. In the third scheme Le Vau eschewed Mansart as a model and coordinated the interior with the Roman orientation of the facade.[82] The fourth (and final) design refines this scheme by heightening the exterior shell, lengthening the drum slightly, and contrasting the windows on the diagonal and cross axes (FIGS. 70–71). As the corresponding elevation indicates (see FIG. 65), the exterior windows are all the same size, a pattern different from the interior and made possible by the double shell construction.

Two questions arise: What prompted Le Vau to reconceive his dome? And when did the changes occur? Answers begin to emerge from the construction history. The building of Mazarin's Collège began in the summer of 1662; after a year and a half, the site work was completed, and the two end pavilions reached roof level. Building of the church began in 1664; in June Gomont asked Le Vau to finish the foundations for Mazarin's tomb.[83] By the end of the year, the foundations were completed and work was continuing above ground when Le Vau brought construction to a halt in order to rethink his design for the dome and the roofline of the adjoining wings. Gomont pressed him in April 1665 to resolve his plans, and the architect promised to give the masons instructions within a day, but the spring building season came and went without the promised drawings.[84] To the dismay of Colbert, who urgently wanted the facade completed, some four hundred workers were diverted to less important structures at the rear of the site.[85] In July 1665 Le Vau reported that "there was still something to resolve, and that next week he would give the drawings to the contractors," but he broke that promise too.[86] Finally, in September 1665, Le Vau "gave his orders for the disposition of what remained to build, notably to begin the elevation of the church above the ground floor."[87] Thus, construction of the church resumed after a curious nine-month delay. Le Vau was, indeed, a busy man, but given the importance of the project and the weight of Colbert's wishes, he might have rearranged his schedule. It seems more likely that the problem was less an external than an internal resistance: Le Vau was gripped by a powerful force he could not immediately overcome.

FIG. 67. *Louis Le Vau, transverse section of the church facing the high altar, Collège des Quatre Nations, second scheme, here dated 1664–65. Pen, ink, and wash on paper. Archives Nationales, Paris (M176, no. 14)*

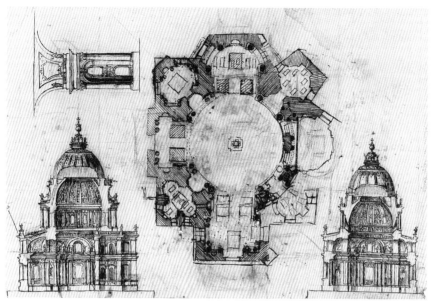

FIG. 68. *François Mansart, plan and sections of the Bourbon Mausoleum, ca.1663. Département des Estampes, Bibliothèque Nationale de France, Paris (Va 93)*

What accounts for Le Vau's hesitation as well as the sharp conceptual changes? The short answer is Bernini. The delay at the Collège coincided exactly with Bernini's Parisian sojourn: Bernini accepted the royal invitation to design the east wing of the Louvre in late 1664, left Rome in April 1665, reached Paris in June, and departed in October. Arguably, Bernini's presence precipitated a creative crisis; it caused Le Vau to halt construction, reconceive the dome, and produce antithetical schemes—first after Mansart (Scheme 2), then after Bernini (Schemes 3 and 4).

Le Vau had good reason to dislike the Italian interloper who had displaced him as architect of the Louvre, but the rivalry was even more complicated because of Le Vau's strong attraction to Bernini's architecture—a point that one modern critic recognized when he called Le Vau an "architetto berniniano suo malgrado" (a Berninian architect despite himself).[88] Le Vau regarded Bernini as both mirror image and model: one was architect of the pope, the other of the Sun King; they approached design with a similar appreciation for simple, geometric forms, strong volumes, and scenographic effects, which accounts for the kinship between the oval salon of Vaux-le-Vicomte and Sant'Andrea, and between Mazarin's Collège and Santa Maria dell'Assunzione at Ariccia (1662–64). Historians usually regard Bernini's first design for the east wing of the Louvre as a rebuke of Le Vau's foundation plan, yet it was also a kind of endorsement (FIGS. 72–73). The fact is that every other prospective architect of the Louvre, with the exception of one known as Candiani, significantly departed from Le Vau's foundation plan, whereas Bernini closely adhered to it; at least initially he embraced Le Vau's approach, with its protruding oval centerpiece, before recasting the design in Roman terms. Le Vau understood that message and tried to take the same Romanizing step in his designs for Mazarin's Collège.

It was not easy for Le Vau to admit his attraction to his arch rival, and he went in the opposite direction (toward Mansart) before returning to the Roman ideal that Bernini represented. To borrow one recent scholar's terminology: "[I]n an effort to hide this desperate admiration from others, and from himself," Le Vau was compelled to recast his hero as an

FIG. 69. *Louis Le Vau, transverse section of the church facing the high altar, Collège des Quatre Nations, third scheme, here dated 1664–65. Pen, ink, and wash on paper. Archives Nationales, Paris (M176, no. 26)*

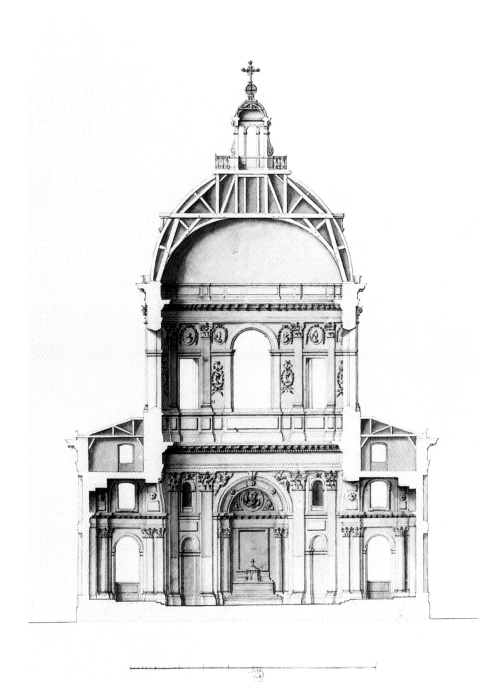

FIG. 70. *Louis Le Vau, transverse section of the church facing the high altar, Collège des Quatre Nations, final scheme, ca. 1666. Pen, ink, and wash on paper. Département des Estampes, Bibliothèque Nationale de France, Paris (Va 261)*

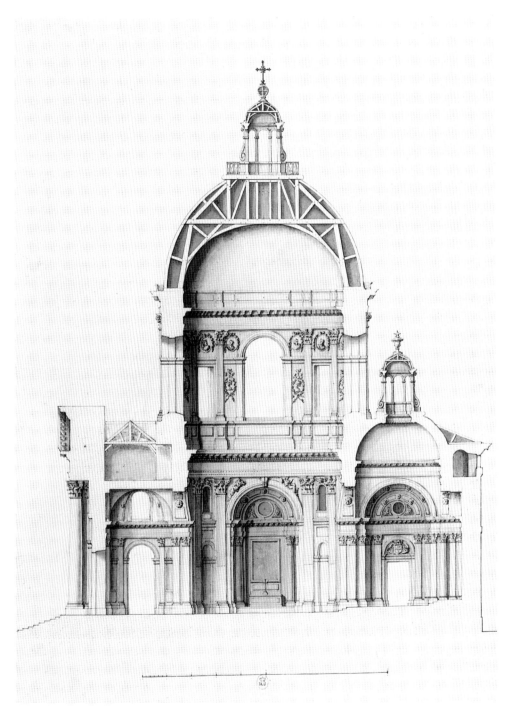

FIG. 71. *Louis Le Vau, longitudinal section of the church facing east, Collège des Quatre Nations, final scheme, ca. 1666. Pen, ink, and wash on paper. Département des Estampes, Bibliothèque Nationale de France, Paris (Va 261)*

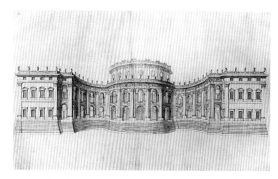

FIG. 72. *Gianlorenzo Bernini, first design for the east facade of the Louvre, exterior elevation, 1664. Départment des Arts Graphiques, Musée du Louvre, Paris (Recueil du Louvre I f4)*

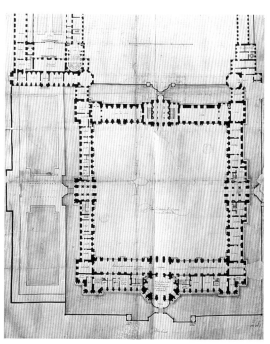

FIG. 73. *Louis Le Vau, ground plan of the Louvre, third scheme, ca. 1661. Pen, ink, and wash on paper. Départment des Arts Graphiques, Musée du Louvre, Paris (Recueil du Louvre I f12)*

enemy.[89] Le Vau was locked in a duel with Bernini, which events at the Louvre only intensified. Soon after laying eyes on the palace, Bernini announced his intention to alter the river facade, the very part Le Vau had just finished building. Bernini had already robbed him of the east wing; now his river facade was at risk. Le Vau was agitated, energized, definitely not resigned to losing the Louvre, and he continued to revise his designs for the palace in hopes of regaining the commission. When it became clear that Bernini would ignore the existing foundations, Le Vau followed suit and rethought his scheme from scratch. Likewise, as Bernini began to colonize the area west of the Cour Carrée with increasingly expansive plans, Le Vau would not be outdone and produced an equally ambitious design in July 1665 in which the Cour Carrée became the forecourt of a much larger courtyard with a semicircular wing to the west. We know about this project from Chantelou's description; no drawing of it survives, but Le Vau's preliminary thoughts appear on another plan, where he sketched the curved building and adjacent courtyards (FIGS. 74–75).[90] The faint pencil lines on this drawing are a dim reflection of his intense rivalry with the cavaliere—feelings that were ultimately productive for Le Vau.

His response to Bernini—a mixture of anger, rivalry, attraction, and envy—was so potent that Le Vau could not bring himself to visit Bernini during his five months in Paris, although a courtesy call by the king's architect was surely in order. On one occasion when the two men were at the very same country inn, Le Vau slipped out before dinner to avoid a chance encounter with Bernini.[91] By contrast, Guarini's presence in Paris was not charged in the same way, although his filigree dome would vie in the skyline beside Le Vau's. Guarini had arrived in Paris in the fall of 1662 to finish Sainte Anne-la-Royale and remained for four years. The difference is that Guarini had not displaced Le Vau on a royal project, and more important, Le Vau's formal preoccupations did not draw him to Guarini's skeletal vaulting and interlacing ribs as he was drawn to the Roman world of Bernini.

Nonetheless, during the nine-month period in 1665 when construction of the church was brought to a standstill, Le Vau overcame his resistance and succeeded in rethinking the dome in Roman terms. Le Vau could not face Bernini, yet his presence sparked a new phase of creativity, with consequences that would continue to reverberate during the last five years of Le Vau's life, from 1665 to 1670, in his final projects for the Louvre and Versailles.

THE DISPLACEMENT OF MAZARIN:
THE DECORATIVE PROGRAM

It was predictable that Mazarin's part in the decorative program would shrink over time and the crown's part grow larger. After all, Mazarin had entrusted the building to the crown, not his family, and had asked the king to make it a royal foundation, which the king did in patent letters of 1665.[92] The decision to place Mazarin's

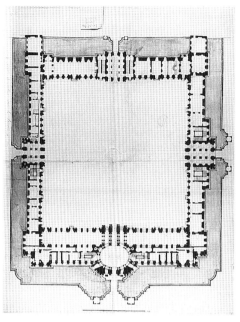

FIG. 74. *Louis Le Vau, ground plan (the foundation plan) of the Louvre, fourth scheme, ca. 1661. Pen, ink, and wash on paper. Départment des Arts Graphiques, Musée du Louvre, Paris (Recueil du Louvre I f5)*

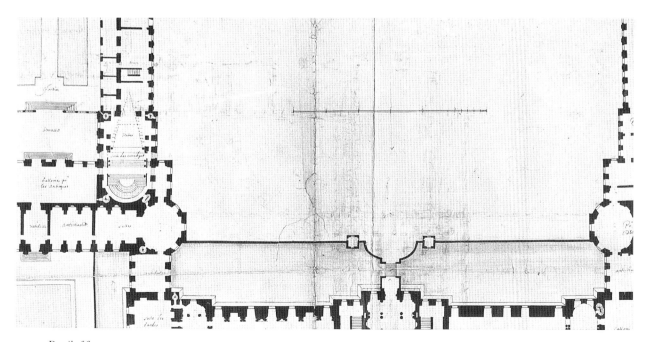

FIG. 75. *Detail of fig. 73*

tomb in a peripheral spot rather than the center of the church was only the culmination of an ongoing process of displacement. In the early designs Mazarin's portrait appears above the main door, and his heraldry—fasces and stars—appears in the side bays (see FIGS. 62 and 64); in the final design the portrait is gone and arms of the four nations decorate the entry wall (see FIG. 65). Likewise, within the church, the original intention was to decorate the rotunda with Mazarin's arms, but in the end they appear only above the college entrance and his tomb. Although his arms are placed prominently on the quay, it was built in 1663 and belongs to the earliest phase of the decoration (see FIG. 24). The other references to Mazarin—for instance, in the college courtyards and in the facade inscription—properly honor his role as benefactor of the Collège and do not constitute the central subject of the sculptural program.[93]

Mazarin's shrinking role in the ornamentation of the church naturally affected the main pediment, which shifted from a memorial to a royalist theme.[94] In the first two designs, essentially the same and dating from 1662–63, a large clock encircled by a wreath is framed by two figures with a trail of garlands (see FIGS. 62 and 64).[95] The design derives from a classical prototype—the *imago clipeata,* or winged image—where Victories support a medallion portrait of the deceased.[96] The most famous seventeenth-century variations on this theme are Bernini's tombs of Maria Raggi and Alessandro Valtrini, but the Collège pediment is an interesting attempt to depersonalize the idea since in lieu of a portrait is a clock. Rather than symbolizing the passage of time, the clock enacts it.[97]

In contrast to the sepulchral theme in the earlier projects, the executed design strikes a different note (FIG. 76). Gone are the garlands and *imago clipeata;* the clock is unadorned, and each flanking figure reclines on a globe. In the only commentary on this imagery, J. F. Blondel identified the woman at left, with a hammer and ready to strike the bell, as Vigilance. Since the hammer was used to symbolize the church's struggle with heretics, she might specifically connote vigilance against heresy. The presence of the church fathers, seated above on the attic, reinforces the role of the church.[98] The woman on the right side of the pediment holds a book and wears a winged helmet like Minerva's. Blondel identified her as Science; she can properly be construed more broadly as secular knowledge, encompassing the arts and crafts with which Minerva was associated. In the earlier drawings the figures looked outward; now they face one another to indicate that they are mates. The personifications represent complementary spheres of knowledge: the secular and sacred.[99]

It is worth asking if the pediment relates to the device Louis XIV adopted in 1663, *Nec Pluribus Impar* (not unequal to many).[100] Cryptic though it is, the device was understood to signify French supremacy over other realms, a theme that obviously pertains to the Collège des Quatre Nations, and it was commonly illustrated by two spheres, with the sun shining over the earth. Jean Warin cast this image in medals, and Le Vau used it in a project for the south wing of the Louvre (FIG. 77). If the clock is a symbol of the Sun King, who in his

FIG. 76. *Pediment of the Collège des Quatre Nations (detail of fig. 65)*

mythic guise as Apollo was master of Time, then its dominance over the two smaller globes might allude to the territorial conquests of France.

It is likely that Le Vau was not responsible for the final program of the pediment. D'Orbay drew the elevation of the executed project after Le Vau's death; we know this because the inscription in the entablature was composed by Charles Perrault in 1673.[101] As founding member of the Petite Académie and Colbert's chief iconographer, Perrault was the obvious figure to consult, not just for the inscription but also for the pediment whose original sepulchral theme no longer captured the mood in the 1670s, when the architectural decoration was completed. If not Perrault, then a like-minded thinker in Colbert's circle adjusted Le Vau's design to shift its symbolic focus from Mazarin to the king.

CROSS CONNECTIONS WITH THE LOUVRE: THE NEW ROME

Le Vau's work at Mazarin's Collège was closely connected to his designs for the Louvre. From the outset he had a unified vision of the two buildings, as his earliest drawing, the magnificent oversize sheet with the Pont de la Paix, discloses (see FIG. 17). The Collège is aligned with the Cour Carrée, and the two river-front plazas, joined by the bridge, form one continuous urban space.

As the designs evolved, Le Vau moved from rectilinear to rounded forms in both buildings. The curving facade and oval sanctuary of the Collège are echoed in the oval entry vestibule of the Louvre. Le Vau introduced the oval vestibule in his third project for

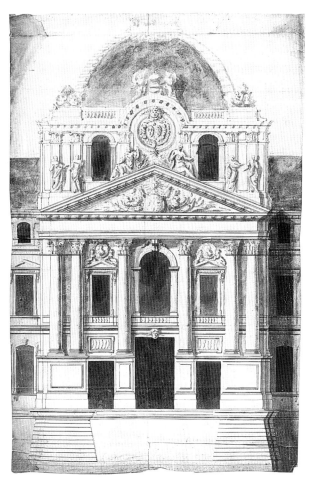

FIG. 77. *Louis Le Vau, project for the central pavilion of the south range of the Louvre (river façade), ca. 1660. Pen, ink, and wash on paper. Départment des Arts Graphiques, Musée du Louvre, Paris (Inv. 26076)*

the Louvre (see FIG. 73), and the fourth project (see FIG. 74) guided construction of the foundations, which were well advanced by March 1662. This chronology indicates, first, that the drawings for the fourth project as well as the third most likely date from 1661 (not 1662–63 as was once thought), and, second, that Le Vau designed the oval rotundas at the Collège and the Louvre at virtually the same time.[102]

The twin rotundas are the culmination of Le Vau's obsession with the oval form, which he had begun to explore twenty years earlier. He broached the idea at the château of Le Raincy by attaching semicircular lobes to a rectangular vestibule. At Vaux-le-Vicomte he perfected it in the grand salon, which was partially open to the elements and conceived as a gnomon, registering the movements of the sun.[103] For the east wing of the Louvre, Le Vau envisioned an unroofed vestibule, impractical in the rainy north, but the open oculus had the virtue of recalling the Roman Pantheon, an imperial space par excellence (FIG. 78). The twin ovals at the Collège and the Louvre are not simply the repetition of a motif Le Vau favored, like the flaming urns that appear on nearly every building he designed; they are part of an orchestrated exchange of motifs between the Louvre and the Collège for the purpose of enlarging the royal precinct to encompass the Collège des Quatre Nations and constituting its site on the Left Bank as royal space.

There is further evidence of this strategy in the church facade and the Quai Mazarin, both of which take their cues from the Louvre. The church facade has the same order (a colossal composite column), the same rhythm of bays, and the same type of openings and niches as the corresponding pavilion of the Louvre, which Le Vau designed in 1660 and 1661 (FIG. 79; and see FIG. 65). The wall of the Quai Mazarin is also a direct copy of the moat walls of the Louvre. The masonry contract for the quay specifically instructed the masons to copy the bosses, projections, and all other features of the foundation walls of the Louvre; and the inscription on the Quai Mazarin spelled out the connection.[104]

A second composite drawing Le Vau made of the Louvre and the Collège des Quatre Nations (FIG. 80), which dates from 1663–64, tells us nothing new about the Collège; in fact, the draftsman copied an out-of-date design (note the rectangular church narthex and the

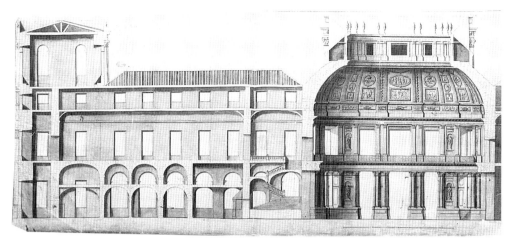

FIG. 78. *Louis Le Vau, project for the east wing of the Louvre, section, 1663–64. Pen, ink, and wash on paper. Archives Nationales, Paris (O1 1667, no. 77)*

hexagonal courtyard). But the drawing records Le Vau's changing thoughts about the Cour Carrée and forecourt. Apart from the key feature of this, his fifth design for the Louvre—namely the west wing, which has doubled in width and acquired an ovoid vestibule—we need to focus on the forecourt, where two curving colonnaded buildings mask the Gothic church of Saint Germain l'Auxerrois and irregular street openings. Designated "corps des gardes," the two buildings were intended to serve as barracks for the king's guard; and the square, previously a nondescript "place devant le Louvre," has become a "Place d'armes," or parade ground. This program reflects Le Vau's original idea to accommodate the soldiers in a square on the Left Bank. In moving that square across the river, albeit in a new form, Le Vau left a trace of the programmatic links he sought to establish between the palace and the Collège and therein attested to his integrated process of design.

The two themes we have been charting—connections of the Collège to the Louvre, on the one hand, and to Rome, on the other—come together in the Place Mazarine, the plaza in front of the Collège. Le Vau planned two large obelisks at opposite ends of the space, and their foundations were built at the same time as the quay (FIGS. 81–82; FIG. 82 also shows the footings for Mazarin's tomb in the crypt).[105] He then offered

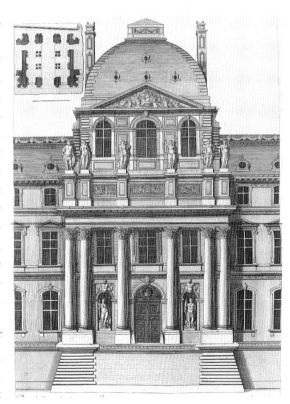

FIG. 79. *Louis Le Vau, plan and elevation of the central pavilion of the south wing of the Louvre (river facade), 1660–63 (destroyed). Engraving by Jean Marot. Avery Architectural and Fine Arts Library, Columbia University in the City of New York*

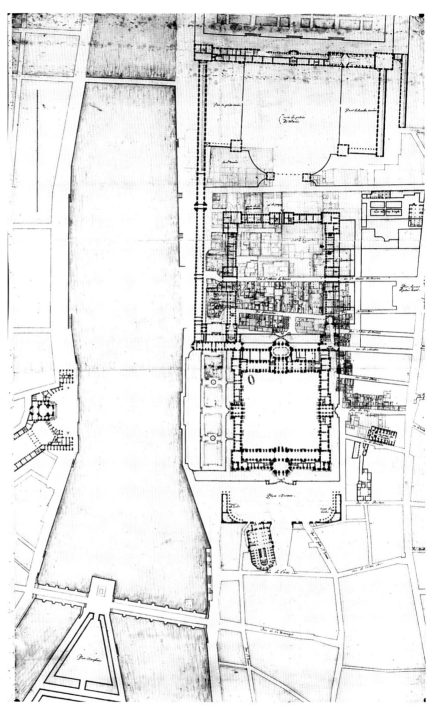

FIG. 80. *Louis Le Vau, plan of the Louvre, Tuileries, and Collège des Quatre Nations, ca. 1664. Pen, ink, and wash on paper. Archives Nationales, Paris (F21 3567/9)*

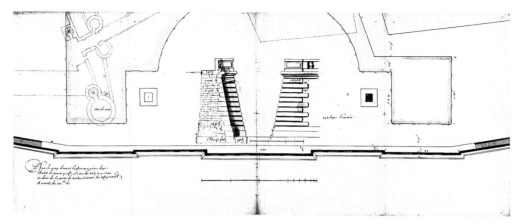

FIG. 81. *Louis Le Vau, partial elevation of the Quai Mazarin and plan of the Place Mazarine, 13 August 1662. Pen, ink, and wash on paper. Archives Nationales, Paris (M176, no. 43)*

the practical suggestion of making the obelisks into fountains and running water lines to nearby houses—an amenity that would make the rental houses more attractive. The Sorbonne, obstructive as ever, objected on account of the noise and mess fountains were bound to cause, but a more immediate problem was a shortage of funds. Although the city and Collège agreed in 1668 to split the cost of the fountains, the Collège was unable to pay its share, and the obelisks were never erected.[106]

There are no elevation drawings of the obelisks, only foundation plans, but their location and size are enough to shed light on their meaning. Obelisks were common symbols of death and resurrection; in the first elevation of the church (see FIG. 62), the finial-obelisks on the balustrade functioned in this way, symbolically analogous to the pair in front of the Mausoleum of Augustus (which pertains to Le Vau's conception of the chapel as a mausoleum as well as to the Augustan imagery surrounding Louis XIV; FIG. 83).[107] But the monumental obelisks in the square elaborate an imperial theme. Generic symbols of princely glory, their solar symbolism—the Egyptians created obelisks to honor their sun god—lent them particular relevance to the Sun King, which accounts for the proliferation of obelisks in Ludovican iconography (for instance, in the royal entry into Paris in 1660). The obelisks at the Place Mazarine likewise served to invoke the king's symbolic presence.

Proceeding a step further, we can situate the Place Mazarine

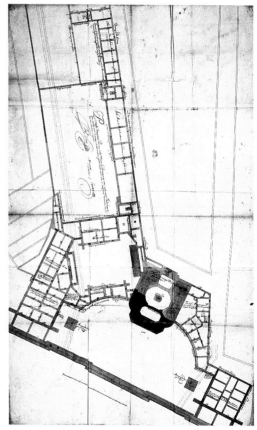

FIG. 82. *Louis Le Vau, foundation plan of the Collège des Quatre Nations, 28 November 1664. Pen, ink, and wash on paper. Archives Nationales, Paris (M176, no. 53)*

FIG. 83. *Mausoleum of Augustus. Reproduced from Giacomo Lauro,* Antiquae Urbis Splendor *(Rome, 1612), 77*

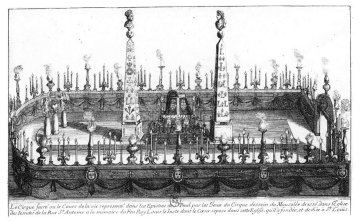

FIG. 84. *Funerary circus in memory of Louis XIII, Saint Paul, Paris, 1643. Etching. Département des Estampes, Bibliothèque Nationale de France, Paris*

in relation to a topical issue in seventeenth-century architecture—namely, the reinvention of the ancient circus as a modern urban form. Le Vau's obelisks were placed to fill a weak compositional link in the Collège facade, where the curved wings join the end pavilions, and to echo the fountains on the river front of the Louvre (see FIG. 80). But as end markers of an elongated space, they also recall the arrangement of obelisks along the *spina* of an ancient circus. The currency of this idea in Bourbon France is indicated by the "sacred circus" erected by Jesuits in Saint Paul when Louis XIII died in 1643 (FIG. 84). Unlike this ephemeral construction, the circus in ancient times was not a freestanding form; the Circus Maximus was built beside the Palatine palace, making it a prime setting of the imperial cult, and this pendant arrangement of palace-circus (or palace-hippodrome), as one historian explained, was "all but mandatory for the full expression of the late antique conception of the nature of the imperial palace and its master."[108]

Bernini gave new life to this archetype in his spectacular designs for the Piazza Navona and Piazza San Pietro, and it is precisely in that context that the Place Mazarine should be seen. The Piazza Navona, built by Innocent X (1644–55) on the site of Domitian's stadium, was the locus of Pamphili family power. At the pope's behest, his family palace and church were enlarged, and an obelisk was reerected in Bernini's Four Rivers Fountain to make the Piazza Navona an arena of Pamphili and papal influence (FIG. 85).[109] The piazza at Saint Peter's, built for Alexander VII (1655–67), also combined a papal palace and church (in this case official, not familial property), and the idea of the circus stands behind Bernini's brilliant square (FIG. 86). (It did not rise on the site of the ancient circus south of the church because in 1586 Sixtus V had moved the obelisk from its original location to embellish the front of Saint Peter's. This engineering feat evidently interested Le Vau, who owned a copy of Domenico Fontana's book on the transfer.) In forming an oval plaza around the Vatican obelisk, Bernini recalled the adjacent site of imperial power and Christian martyr-

FIG. 85. *Gianlorenzo Bernini, Piazza Navona, Rome, 1649–51*

FIG. 86. *Gianlorenzo Bernini, Piazza San Pietro, Rome, 1656–67*

dom, while giving it new meaning as a space of Catholic community. Situated in front of Saint Peter's and the papal palace, the piazza heralds a new era of Christian triumph.[110]

Like the two Roman squares, the Place Mazarine transformed the proximity of a palace and a church into a coherent statement about royal power. Le Vau's grand urban design expressed the king's sovereign power over religious as well as temporal matters. The duality of royal power, a basic principle of the French monarchy, was an implicit challenge to the authority of the pope, who claimed supreme spiritual power. In the language of architecture, Le Vau expressed this challenge by assimilating Bernini's papal squares and translating them into French terms.

The Collège des Quatre Nations looks in two directions—to the royal palace across the river and to papal Rome. In the execution of his design, Le Vau did much more than embellish Paris and give the king a pleasant view. He translated abstract ideas about kingship, state, and power into a compelling urban experience.

CHAPTER 3

LE VAU'S LIBRARY

WHAT SORT OF man was Louis Le Vau? A document of 1641 offers a clue. One of our earliest encounters with Le Vau in records from the period, the document was drawn up when he was twenty-nine years old and a promising architect, the rising star of the generation after François Mansart (Mansart being fourteen years older).[1] At the end of his sister's marriage contract, Le Vau signed his name in large, elegant, italic script (FIG. 87, second name in center column). The letters are beautifully shaped and fluidly rendered. The long, liquid strokes betray no trace of hesitation; their author was obviously adept with the pen. Le Vau's signature bespeaks a man of learning, self-assurance, and a sense of style. A splendid mark embellished with loops, curlicues, and a final flourish, it projects authority on the page. Indeed, its perfect design and execution establish the signature as a well-rehearsed, self-conscious, and fixed sign; thus it comes as no surprise to find that Le Vau's signature hardly changed over the course of his life (compare how he signed his name twenty years later on a drawing of the Collège; see FIG. 26). If we accept the premise that the signature is a form of self-authentication, then Le Vau fashioned an identity with this mark: his signature evokes education, civility, and authority, and sets him apart—first and foremost from his family.[2]

The same document was signed by Le Vau's father and his brother François, who was a decade younger (not a year, as is sometimes reported).[3] Neither of their signatures has the same presence as Le Vau's. The father has a tight scrawl; his hatched paraph lacks the cursivity of his son's and somewhat resembles the mark a mason carves in stone, as if the pen were a hardy chisel and not a featherweight plume (see FIG. 87, top of first column). But what

FIG. 87. *Signatures of Louis Le Vau, his father, and brother, 23 December 1641. Archives Nationales, Paris (Minutier central XXXVI 168, fol. 530)*

makes this document so revealing is not just the signatures, which are reproduced on other sheets; it is how the men spelled their common surname. Father and brother spelled it Le Veau (which means calf) whereas Louis Le Vau dropped the "e," thereby removing the bovine reference and differentiating himself from his namesake, father, and mentor—Louis Le Veau the elder. François eventually changed the spelling of his surname as well, but the father remained Le Veau with an "e" until the day he died. The name change and the signature announce Louis Le Vau's social ambition and cultivation; moreover, they expose a desire to distance himself from a father whom he also emulated.

Le Veau the elder was a master mason. He worked at Fontainebleau and in Paris, where his older son was born in 1612. Nothing is known about Le Vau's youth and training, but it is safe to say that he learned the fundamentals of masonry from his father. The role of teacher evidently suited the elder Le Veau, and in 1638, about the time Louis married, Le Veau reenacted that mentoring role with other young apprentices whom he contracted to train.[4] The son obligingly followed in his father's footsteps—becoming a mason and learning everything his father could teach him—but that did not suffice.

Early on Le Vau moved well beyond his father's range of talent, interests, and ambition, and redefined himself as a polished court architect. The architecture of Salomon de Brosse left a strong mark on Le Vau, but he was probably too young to have worked on the Palais du Luxembourg, which was completed in the early 1620s. It is more likely that the talented youth entered the entourage of Louis XIII's royal architect, Jacques Lemercier, who was at work on the Pavillon de l'Horloge and the west wing of the Cour Carrée in the 1630s, the period of Le Vau's formation. Experience at the Louvre and personal contact with Lemercier would help explain how Le Vau acquired the title of royal architect, *architecte ordinaire du roy,* by the age of twenty-seven. It seems likely also that Lemercier's persona influenced Le Vau. A cosmopolitan and learned man, who had spent an extended period of time in Rome and owned a vast library of architectural books and prints, Lemercier was the chief architect in France. Judging by the identity he created, Le Vau found Lemercier a more appealing professional model than his mason-father.

Yet Le Vau remained a loyal son and continued the family business of masonry contracting. He and his father lived together on the Quai des Celestins before moving to a house they built on the Ile Saint-Louis. In the 1640s Le Vau was the driving force in the development of the island and took on his father as a partner.[5] Left out of this father-son venture was François, who certainly could not match his brother's ability to patronize the family circle. Over time Louis Le Vau's stature helped to advance François's career, but François was destined to remain in the shadow of his more successful sibling, who doubled as his chief rival and sponsor. François's conflicting feelings of animosity and loyalty surfaced in his actions concerning the Louvre. In an implicit attack on his brother's plans, François Le Vau submitted his own scheme for the east wing, only to lead the defense of Louis's design for the enlarged river front of the Louvre a few years later.

Marriage ties are revealing also. Masons typically married within their tribe; for instance, the husband of Le Vau's sister Anne was a mason, Charles Thoison, himself the son of a mason.[6] Le Vau, however, went to a higher social rank and married Jeanne Laisné, the daughter of a well-established notary, Jacques Laisné.[7] The marriage, like the name change, was part of a strategy of social advancement and a fitting accoutrement for an architect at court.

That strategy was fulfilled in 1655. Le Vau was appointed first architect to the king, succeeding Lemercier, who had died the year before. At forty-three years of age, Le Vau became the most important architect in France; in rank, prestige, and power, he was in a class alone with the Cavaliere Bernini, architect of the pope. Yet even Le Vau's elevated standing at Louis XIV's court did not satisfy his manifold ambitions, quell his Oedipal struggle, or end his attachment to the family business of contracting and speculative building.[8]

THE STUDY A walk through the architect's house in 1670 provides other clues about his life and work.[9] Le Vau lived around the corner from the Louvre in the Hôtel de Longueville, a building that the crown had bought in 1657 and condemned for demolition; the intention was to clear the area east of the palace and build a proper entry square, but that project stalled, and the Hôtel de Longueville survived as an annex of the Louvre. Le Vau covered the walls of his house with paintings—nearly a hundred in all, including works by Jacques Fouquier, Paul Brill, and Jacopo Bassano. The most valuable painting was an architectural fantasy by Jean Lemaire, appraised at one hundred *livres.* In homage to his patrons, Le Vau hung portraits of the king and queen, Anne of Austria, Cardinal Mazarin, and Jean-Baptiste Colbert close to the entrance. There was no sign of fossils, medals, shells, and other precious bits of natural and antiquarian history that filled the curiosity cabinets of some of Le Vau's early patrons, like Louis Hesselin. The one curio was an astronomical clock; appraised at six hundred *livres,* it was the most valuable item in the house.

Le Vau's study was located in the front wing of the *hôtel,* overlooking the rue des Poullies (FIG. 88).[10] The street conveniently widened just outside the entrance of the *hôtel,* which received a constant stream of visitors on official business. In fact, the Hôtel de Longueville functioned as a royal office-building, the headquarters of the king's first architect. When a royal project was put out for bid, the building trades were convened in Le Vau's bureau to examine the drawings on display, and when questions arose during construction, as they inevitably did, administrators and contractors met under Le Vau's roof to consult drawings he stored. François d'Orbay and other draftsmen also did their work in the *hôtel,* perhaps in the well-lit vaulted side wing with the lovely view of Saint Germain l'Auxerrois.

Unlike the residential quarters at the back of the courtyard, Le Vau's study had only a few decorative touches: five paintings, including a large canvas of the muses and a smaller scene of a classical temple; several figurines in marble, bronze, and plaster; porcelain pots;

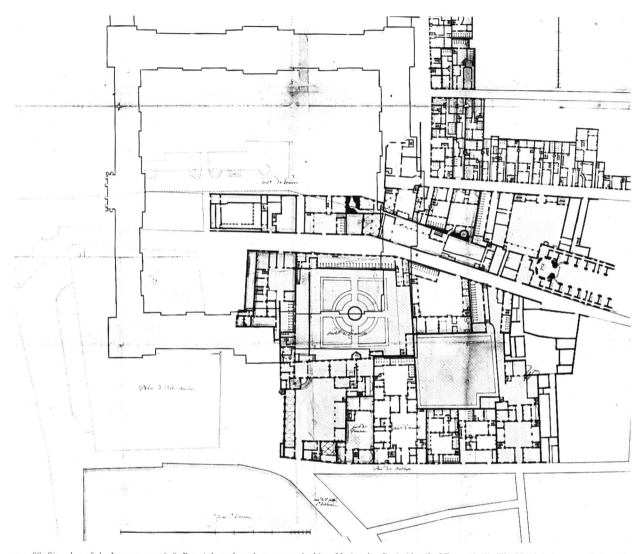

FIG. 88. *Site plan of the Louvre, ca. 1658. Pen, ink, and wash on paper. Archives Nationales, Paris (detail of F21 3567/8). The Hôtel de Longueville is at the corner of the rue des Poullies, at the bottom of the plan.*

and ten boxes of ivory pieces. For the most part, the room was equipped with the working tools of an architect: maps in rolls and boxes, measuring instruments, bundles of papers pertaining to Le Vau's real-estate investments and financial dealings, and boxes of drawings, contracts, and memoirs for each building he had designed. The furniture was functional: hanging shelves, some with compartments to sort out Le Vau's papers; five chairs, enough to receive several visitors; a locked trunk for important papers; two tables and a writing desk, where Le Vau could draft documents and drawings. (The dishes, plates, and sheets of tin kept in the study must have been samples manufactured by his factory, the subject of Chapter 4.) Most importantly, it was in this work space that Le Vau housed his impressive library. Although many collectors kept their books under lock and key in enclosed armoires, Le Vau stored his on open bookshelves for more convenient access. The wood shelves were covered with green serge and trimmed in silk, and they spanned an entire wall of the study.[11]

In examining the design of Mazarin's Collège, we encounter an architect well versed in the classical tradition, one with a profound interest in Rome, both ancient and modern. Le Vau knew reconstructions of the ancient city by Etienne Dupérac and Filippo de Rossi, studied Andrea Palladio, and kept tabs on Bernini's work and other recent building projects in Rome. The cultivated figure portrayed here bears no resemblance to the standing image of Le Vau as an intuitive, unschooled designer, a talented decorator with a careless grip on the orders. The revised picture of Le Vau raises the question of his education in the classical tradition, and our walking tour of his house points to the answer: Le Vau's library was his pathway.

In recent years scholars have redefined the activity of reading in the early modern period. Instead of dwelling on authorial intentions and recuperating meanings supposedly fixed in the text, historians have focused on the ways readers interact with books and discovered that variant reading practices produce different meanings.[12] This body of scholarship helps us understand the importance of Le Vau's library and the ways in which he used it—a subject we can broach thanks to a detailed inventory of his book collection (an edited list of titles can be found in Appendix D).

In trying to understand Le Vau's reading process, we face a critical limitation insofar as none of the books Le Vau actually owned has come to light. In the case of Inigo Jones, many of whose books have been located, scholars have been able to track his thought process on the basis of his marginalia.[13] Those annotations bear witness to what has been called a "transactional model of reading." As opposed to the Montaigne paradigm of a scholar closeted with a book in quiet contemplation, there emerges a goal-oriented reader who uses books on the job and discusses passages with fellow travelers in pursuit of answers to pressing questions.[14] Even without Le Vau's annotated copies, we can recognize him as this sort of directed reader. By temperament and formation, he was not prone to meditate in solitude; he was a man of action, a practitioner riding high on a building boom in the capital of Europe. Le Vau did not read for purposes of general education; he used his books, like his straight edge, to resolve design problems.

ARMCHAIR TRAVEL Le Vau's library is all the more important because it was the principal way he encountered the classical tradition—which is to say, he did not travel. The period of Le Vau's youth—the time for wandering about—remains murky, but to the best of our knowledge, he never set foot in Rome or traveled elsewhere in Italy. Although he was always on the move and crisscrossed the Ile-de-France from one royal château to the next, it appears that Le Vau left France on only one occasion. In the 1650s he traveled to Germany to learn the techniques of manufacturing iron, a matter taken up in the next chapter.

Odd as Le Vau's behavior seems from a modern perspective, it was not anomalous in his own time. Most French architects of Le Vau's generation and earlier—de Brosse, Pierre Le Muet, Mansart, Antoine Lepautre—men born between 1580 and 1620 who matured at a time of peace, prosperity, and architectural opportunity at home, did not go to Italy; French painters by contrast, flocked to Rome—Valentin, Nicholas Poussin, François Perrier and Simon Vouet, among the most famous. This difference is attributable to several factors. First, French architecture in the sixteenth century had effectively assimilated new Renaissance ideas, unlike French painting, which, relatively speaking, languished during the second half of the century. As a result, it was nearly impossible for an aspiring painter to develop in early-seventeenth-century France, so depleted were the country's resources in this domain, whereas the vitality of French architecture enabled a young practitioner to mature on native soil without the taint of provincialism, as had Mansart and Le Vau, the leading architects at mid-century. Second, the building boom in Paris put architects like Le Vau to work at a young age; Philibert Delorme went to Rome when he was unemployed and out of favor at court, but the abundance of work in the prosperous seventeenth century was a disincentive to leave. Finally, a great deal of information was available in printed books and prints, which produced a cosmopolitan culture at home. Owing to these various factors, it was the exception, not the rule, for French architects to visit the Eternal City between 1600 and 1670, and thus far only two exceptions have come to light: Lemercier and d'Orbay.

D'Orbay's trip is of particular interest because it was arranged by his employer, Le Vau, and testifies to Le Vau's intense interest in Rome. The trip took place in 1660, over the summer months and possibly continuing into the fall (its precise dates are unknown).[15] Whether Le Vau subsidized the trip is unclear; at the very least, he facilitated it and furnished his protégé with a letter of introduction from Cardinal Mazarin.[16] D'Orbay made contact with Mazarin's agent in Rome, Elpidio Benedetti, who presumably arranged for him to visit the workshops of Bernini and Carlo Rainaldi, both of whom were working on projects for Mazarin at the time. In the aftermath of the Peace of the Pyrenees, Mazarin decided to honor Louis XIV on his home ground by building a monumental staircase to the Trinità dei Monti. D'Orbay's trip coincided with the period of peak activity on this project: Benedetti was in the process of commissioning designs to send back to Paris. From the four drawings d'Orbay prepared for the Spanish steps (Appendix B) we sense his excitement at being in Rome and his sharp learning curve. No other drawings from d'Orbay's trip to Rome have yet come to our attention, but we know that he subsequently presented detailed renderings of Saint Peter's and other Roman buildings to the Académie Royale d'Architecture.[17] On this basis alone, it is safe to say that d'Orbay brought back a rich stock of images, providing Le Vau with an invaluable source of information about the architectural landscape of Rome, including works in progress in Bernini's studio.

Obviously d'Orbay was not the only source of visual information; Le Vau would have had access to drawings by other travelers and engravings by Israel Silvestre, de Rossi, Lieven Cruyl, and others in abundant supply on the print market. But what stands out in the inventory of Le Vau's house is his collection of books. Granted, ownership does not prove that Le Vau actually read his books, yet the size of his collection, which was extensive for a seventeenth-century architect, is enough to indicate that he considered books an essential resource.

SIZE Inventories after death do not necessarily reflect the size of a library at its peak. A dying person might give away or sell a share of his belongings; for instance, Mansart seems to have dismantled his library before he died. But the size and scope of Le Vau's library suggest that he kept it intact.

According to the inventory of his belongings, Le Vau owned about 308 books. The methodology involved in calculating this number, whether for Le Vau or any other individual, is not as straightforward as might be expected (the procedure is set forth in Appendix D). Besides the limitations imposed by documentary evidence (in particular, the frequent mention of unidentified packets) a problem arises from variations in the way historians tally a book list—some by title (as is done here for Le Vau), others by volume, but in most cases the method is left unexplained. In any event, the lack of descriptive information in the inventories makes it nearly impossible to apply either method consistently. The numbers cited below give the illusion of exactitude, but in truth they are only approximations.

Compared with the leading European book collections, Le Vau's library was small. A top library had a minimum of 4,000 books, according to Père Louis Jacob's book of 1644 on Europe's finest libraries. He identified ninety Paris libraries in this class, a figure confirmed by modern research. Interestingly, only twenty were owned by institutions, such as the abbey of Saint Victor or the crown; in 1661, the royal collection comprised nearly 17,000 volumes (which was small compared with Mazarin's 38,000 books). The other seventy libraries were owned by private individuals—collectors such as Cardinal Richelieu and Cardinal Mazarin—who made Paris the capital city of bibliophiles.[18] By contrast, well-to-do artisans and merchants typically owned no more than a half-dozen books.[19] But for our purposes, the more relevant comparison is with the libraries of other architects in the period preceding Le Vau's death.

Data about this narrow sector of the reading public is understandably limited. In a remarkable study of Paris libraries published in 1969, Henri-Jean Martin analyzed four hundred inventories from 1600 to 1670, of which only seven belong to artists and architects (the professions are not differentiated). Since then about two dozen inventories have come to light, providing a small but informative sample of architect-owned libraries.[20]

The largest library by far belonged to Lemercier, who owned slightly more than 3,000 volumes.[21] The size, scope, and quality of the collection (about a third of the books were in folio editions), unprecedented among early modern architects, reflects Lemercier's antiquarian interests and his experience in Rome. In addition, his position as first royal architect afforded advantages in developing the library: adequate financial resources, contacts with booksellers, priority in obtaining choice books, and relations with clients, courtiers, and publishers, who probably gave him some books as gifts.

After Lemercier, who was in a class of his own, the next largest architect-owned libraries belonged to Juan de Herrera (died 1597), the Spanish architect of Philip II, who had 400 books (including about a hundred Lullian works), and Francesco Borromini (died 1667), who owned at least 459 books.[22] Probably no other Italian architect owned a library comparable in size to Borromini's.

With about 308 titles, Le Vau's library comes just below this group. Because Mansart has been regarded as a more cerebral architect than Le Vau, it is interesting to note that his library was somewhat smaller than Le Vau's; thus far 166 books have been identified, although it is believed that at its peak, the library was larger (how much larger is impossible to know).[23] Pietro da Cortona (died 1669) owned about 222 volumes; the ducal architect in Piedmont, Amedeo di Castellamonte (died 1641), about 175; and Paolo Maruscelli (died 1649), who preceded Borromini as architect of the Filippini, about 123.[24]

Most architects and masons owned many fewer books. Of the seven such libraries Martin studied, five had fewer than 25 books; the other two had less than 100. De Brosse (died 1626) had only five books.[25] His cousin Jacques Androuet Ducerceau the Younger (died 1614) had many of his father's works, including 44 copies of *Les Plus Excellents Bastiments,* but that qualifies as inventory, not a library.[26] Perceval Noblet (died 1632), a high-ranking mason (and father of Michel Noblet, whom we will meet in the next chapter), owned 16 books, none of which was related to his profession.[27] Jean Thiriot (died 1647), the architect in charge of Richelieu's reconstruction at the Sorbonne, kept a bible and 7 architecture books in the cabinet beside his bedroom (including titles by Ducerceau, Le Muet, Giacomo da Vignola, and Alexandre Francine).[28] More typical of masons was Nicolas d'Yeray (died 1652), whose only brush with fame was at second hand—which is to say he sometimes worked with Thoison, Le Vau's brother-in-law; d'Yeray had a professional library of 21 books, plus a Lives of the Saints.[29] Michel Villedo (died 1685), one of the masons who built Vaux-le-Vicomte and the Louvre, kept 63 books in his study; his inventory does not mention a single title.[30]

Although some examples point to a correlation between library size and professional standing, this is not always the case. The papal architect Carlo Maderno (died 1629) owned only 24 books, while Augustin Guillain (died 1630), member of a dynasty of Parisian masons, had more books than Le Vau—484 titles, a large portion of which were religious handbooks and histories.[31]

Guillain's case is anomalous and points to one problem in comparing these numbers:

they tell us nothing about the composition of a library, the percentages relating to professional pursuits as opposed to, say, private devotional matters. Moreover, the book total does not measure how much the owner reads—reading need not be limited to the books on an architect's shelf. If Le Vau was like other readers of his time, he borrowed books from other collections—Cardinal Mazarin's, for instance. It is also true that the quantity of books does not measure the seriousness and dedication a reader brings to the reading process. No one in the early modern period was a more committed reader of architectural books than Inigo Jones (died 1652), yet the size of his library was not exceptionally large—it numbered about 200 volumes—and does not convey the intensity of Jones's reading practice.[32]

All the libraries surveyed above predate the establishment of the Académie Royale d'Architecture in 1671, one year after Le Vau's death. The Académie placed a higher priority than ever before on the role of books in architectural education; this changed the profession of architecture and the scale of architects' libraries. One such creature of the academic system, reflecting the ascendance of its book-oriented culture, was Jules Hardouin-Mansart, who owned 550 books when he died in 1708. Likewise, d'Orbay (died 1697), a founding member of the Académie Royale, owned close to 400 books. It is tempting to hypothesize that his trip to Rome awakened a curiosity that d'Orbay could satisfy only by acquiring books, but the concentration of contemporary French volumes points to the influence of the academy rather than that of Rome or even Le Vau.[33]

SUBJECTS Inventories were made to assess economic value; as a result, notaries routinely itemized and identified only books of value, bundling the inexpensive, small-format works in undifferentiated packets. Le Vau's inventory is typical; it names 137 volumes in folio, another 39 in quarto, and 6 in octavo, but the smaller books (most of the quartos and octavos) go unnamed. Although this procedure makes it impossible to identify inexpensive books, the ones with the widest circulation, it probably does not conceal the titles of most interest for our purposes—the art books, which were typically larger, illustrated, and more expensive.

The order of the inventory, which begins with folios then moves to quartos and octavos, indicates that the books were arranged on the shelves first by size and then, within each class, by subject. Not all titles fall in line, but the general organization is comparable with that of more extensive libraries: religion, modern history, literature, law, atlases, architecture and fortifications, mathematics and perspective, artists' lives, and collections of prints. Curiously, the Latin classics are scattered throughout. Number 19 in the inventory is blank; was this a slip of the pen, or does it imply the use of shelf marks?

The majority of books were in French. About 13 percent of those identified in the inventory (23 of 182) were in Italian; they are almost exclusively books on art and architecture. Close to the same number (22 books, about 12 percent of the titles) were in Latin, but they include several picture books with little or no Latin text, such as Gerardi Mercatoris's atlas and Antoine Lafrère's *Speculum*. No other languages were represented in Le Vau's library—no books in Greek, Dutch, German (one book was in French and German), Spanish, or English. Evidently Le Vau was not a scholarly reader; he had only 9 Latin classics (Plutarch, Pliny, Ovid, Livy, Tacitus, Seneca, Virgil, Lucian, and Horace), all of which were in French translation. He owned a dictionary (Ambrosius Calepinus) to help with unfamiliar Italian or Latin words; his degree of fluency in these tongues is unknown. (It bears repeating that this survey is based only on the 182 books whose titles are provided in the inventory.)

The paucity of the classics contrasts with the considerable number of books on modern history, all in French. There were histories of France by Jean de Serres, Etienne Pasquier, Bernard de Girard Du Hallien, Jean Du Tillet, Jacques de Bié, Claude Paradin, and Jean Loret; histories of England, Spain, the Netherlands, the popes, French cardinals, the order of the Knights of Malta, and the Council of Trent; several commemorative books on royal entries; and collections of French edicts and laws. What purpose did these books serve? Tracts on French geography and Parisian history might have been useful in the course of Le Vau's design work, yet except for one example by Claude Malingre, those titles are absent. The history books, although irrelevant to architecture, pertained to affairs of state, with which Le Vau had good reason to identify. After all, by the time of his death, he had assembled an impressive roster of titles, as listed in the inventory: "conseiller du roy en ses conseils, secrétaire de sa Majesté et de des finances, Intendant de ses bastiments, et son premier architecte."

One survey of urban reading practices between 1660 and 1780 finds that the aristocracy had an unusually strong interest in history, French history in particular. "The aristocracy shows a strong originality in this," Roger Chartier explained, "since works on history never accounted for more than 20 percent of book production." Inasmuch as an interest in history provided the aristocracy "with a base for their particular culture, rooting their aristocratic ambitions in the past and justifying them,"[34] Le Vau's library was decidedly aristocratic in character. The history books he owned attest to his association with the crown; his personal interaction with cardinals, kings, and ministers; and his sense of France's place in Europe. It is telling that many of the histories were available in small formats, yet Le Vau often possessed the more lavish folio versions. He may have received some of these books as gifts from distinguished clients—Nicolas Fouquet, Mazarin, Colbert, or even Louis XIV. Le Vau did not have an antiquarian or scholarly interest in history, but he did have a keen sense of his role as a servant of the crown. The shelf of folio books on modern history reflects that sense of responsibility and authority.

It is striking how little Le Vau's library reflected popular taste. The above-mentioned census of four hundred inventories, which included over 15,000 titles, shows, not surprisingly, that religion was the most prevalent subject. Le Vau's inventory names only 18 religious books (10 percent of the named books), although the unidentified quartos and octavos may well include missals, saints' lives, books of hours, and other common religious works that constituted the largest share of published books. (Since about half the books are not identified, we can be sure only of what was in Le Vau's library, not what was missing.) The library was not much richer in works of modern literature, poetry, and philosophy. Francesco Colonna and Lodovico Ariosto in French translation, Pierre de Ronsard, Honoré d'Urfé, Michel de Montaigne, René Descartes, and Madeleine de Scudéry found a place on Le Vau's shelf, alongside Louis de Lesclache, unheard of today but an author who greatly interested Le Vau, judging by the multiple copies of his books.

The main evidence that Le Vau developed his library as a professional tool comes from the preponderance of books on architecture and cognate subjects—fortifications, perspective, geography, and art theory. The area of greatest strength was modern architecture: of Le Vau's 20 books in this field, 14 were on French subjects (including books by Ducerceau, Le Muet, Alexandre Francine, Mathurin Jousse, and Jean Marot) and the other 6 on Italian subjects (including Lafrère, Peter Paul Rubens, Domenico Fontana, Girolamo Teti, and Pietro Ferrerio).

Next came architectural treatises—15 in all, including 5 editions of Vitruvius (whereas Mansart had 9). Le Vau was more interested in the writers of the sixteenth and seventeenth centuries—in particular, Sebastiano Serlio, 3 of whose treatises he owned, and Delorme, whose work he owned in duplicate. Le Vau also had books by Leone Battista Alberti, Palladio, Vincenzo Scamozzi, Hans Vredeman de Vries, Jacques Besson, Julien Mauclerc, and Ottavio Revesi Bruti. Surprisingly, Vignola is absent from this list.

Le Vau's interest in ancient Rome is manifest in the strong showing of related works in the library. In addition to 3 historical titles (by Scipion Dupleix, André Thevet, and Guillaume Du Choul), he had no less than 9 books on ancient Roman architecture, including the publications of Antonio Bosio, Giovanni Battista Montano, Scamozzi, Jean-Jacques Boissard, Antonio Labacco, Dupérac, and Lauro. Only 2 books on ancient Roman architecture have been traced to Mansart's library: titles by Lauro and Montano.

Unlike his brother, Louis Le Vau is not known to have been involved with military architecture. Nevertheless, the library was relatively strong in this area, with 8 books by specialists on fortifications and mathematics (among them Samuel Marolais, Simon Stevin, Matthias Dögen, Antoine de Ville, and Josèph Boillot). Surveying skills, which were the foundation of fortification planning, were, of course, broadly useful to an architect. These books may relate also to Le Vau's interest in artillery and metal casting (here Georg Agricola's *De re metallica* and Vannoccia Biringuccio's *De la pirotechnia* are noticeably absent). Close by on the shelves were 4 books on perspective by Ducerceau, Jean Dubreuil, Jacques Aleaume, and Père Jean-François Niceron (but not Abraham Bosse).

Maps were an important part of Le Vau's library. The inventory makes passing reference to maps in rolls and boxes, but only the bound volumes are detailed in the book list. Le Vau owned the atlases of François de Belleforest, Mercatoris, Georg Braun and Franz Hogenberg, Nicolas Tassin, and Claude Chastillon. By contrast, Le Vau had virtually no interest in small-scale, cultivated landscapes; only 2 titles related to gardening (one by Jacques Boyceau and a book on Roman fountains). The atlases were relatively costly, multivolume works; like the modern history books, they reflect both the high quality and cost of Le Vau's library and his sophisticated awareness of the broader European stage.

Having sketched the contents of the library, we might pause to note some surprising omissions. There were no books on masonry, meaning the art of stereotomy or techniques of the *toisé* (measuring stone)—a genre that is considered a particular strength of the French literature on architecture. The absence of books by Louis Savot and Girard Desargues in this category may be a function of Le Vau's expertise in masonry; he knew enough about the *toisé* and how to cut a vault. To a considerable extent the library was a research tool, a source of wanted information, but the books were also an attribute of his social standing. In this respect, the absence of masonry books may reflect Le Vau's desire to distance himself from his humble origins as a mason's son.

The question of Le Vau's self-image is raised also by the small number of books on painting. Four of his 5 books focus on artists' lives authored by Giorgio Vasari, Carlo Ridolfi, and Giovanni Baglione (two copies; the fifth book was by Giovanni Paolo Lomazzo). There is hardly a sign of interest in Baroque or Renaissance painting; only Teti's book on the Palazzo Barberini pertains, and no prints of contemporary painting are mentioned in the inventory. Architecture did not yet have its Vasari, but certainly Le Vau's narrow set of books could indicate historical self-consciousness, as if Vasari or Baglione helped Le Vau imagine himself projected into the annals of art history. At the same time, the artists' lives served as a repository of possible models of behavior and self-presentation. We have no concrete evidence of Le Vau's reactions to these books, but it is not unreasonable to suppose that Vasari and his followers helped Le Vau shape his public persona.

Perhaps more significant than the foregoing omissions, Le Vau owned neither of Fréart de Chambray's books: *Parallèle de l'architecture de l'antique et de la moderne* and his French translation of Palladio, both published in 1650, when Le Vau was certainly buying many other books. (If there was a slowdown in the growth of the library, it came in the 1660s; relatively few books date from the last decade of his life.) That Le Vau owned Palladio's treatise in Italian is not a satisfactory explanation; after all, he had multiple copies of Vitruvius, Serlio, and Delorme. The answer probably lies in the fact that Chambray had staked out an aesthetic position to which Le Vau was fundamentally opposed in practice. He could not have been sympathetic to Chambray's essentialist response to the orders and conservative attack on architectural invention. A theoretically oriented reader might be inclined to investigate a hostile position, but Le Vau's reading, it appears, was more oriented to action. Under those circumstances, he would not have been tempted to buy Chambray's books.

Chambray's absence begs a larger question: How did Le Vau study the classical orders? Besides the *Parallèle*, several obvious titles on the orders were missing from his library: Vignola's *Regola delli cinque ordini d'architettura* (Rome, 1563?), Jean Bullant's *Reigle*

FIG. 89. *Corinthian capitals by* (left) *François Mansart at the church of the Visitation and* (right) *Louis Le Vau at the Collège des Quatre Nations (now the Institut de France)*

généralle d'architecture des cinq manières de colonne (Ecouen, 1568), Le Muet's translations of Vignola's treatise (Paris, 1631) and of Palladio's Book 1 on the orders (Paris, 1645), and Bosse's *Traité des manières de dessiner les ordres de l'architecture antique* (Paris, 1664). Certainly Le Vau was not without written sources to consult—most of his treatises covered the topic—so given the importance of the orders in his designs, the absence of these specialized books in his library is remarkable.

For guidance on the orders, Le Vau relied less on graphic models than on the buildings of François Mansart. Mansart's Corinthian capitals (for example, those at the Val-de-Grâce, Blois, and Maisons) governed the order at the Collège and account for its distinctive features: the flatness of the acanthus leaves until the crowning curl; sharp delineation of the leaflets; and pronounced asymmetry between the elongated outer volutes (which extend to the corners of the abacus) and the shorter converging inner pair (FIG. 89). Likewise the unusual Ionic order Mansart used at the church of the Feuillants and at Maisons was the basis for the Ionic order at the Collège, where sprays of laurel drape the volutes and a leaf sprouts from the egg-and-dart molding (FIG. 90). But taking a cue from Philibert Delorme, who embellished the Ionic order at the Tuileries Palace in honor of his patron (the queen), Le Vau added the three stars from Mazarin's coat of arms in a comparable tribute. What was the need for picture books in the presence of Mansart's supremely thoughtful and resourceful essays on the orders? In essence this was Le Vau's attitude. It reflects a justified appreciation of Mansart's genius for architectural ornament, Le Vau's relative lack of originality in this sphere, and most important, a decorative approach to the orders.

Whereas Mansart rigorously respected the regulating system of design implied by the

FIG. 90. *Ionic capitals by* (left) *François Mansart at the château of Maisons and* (right) *Louis Le Vau at the Collège des Quatre Nations (now the Institut de France)*

orders, Le Vau disregarded the rules of proportion, placement, and tectonic expression, which the treatise writers explained at length. He basically regarded the orders as a repository of motifs and used them selectively to suit his decorative purposes. Consider, for instance, the way Le Vau panelized the second-story Corinthian pilaster by overlaying a strip of masonry, which floats above the pilaster footing (FIG. 91); as a result, the pilaster tends to read as an applied ornamental motif rather than as a tectonic element. Similarly, the attenuated form of the nearby window brackets undercuts their functional rationale as supporters for the entablature and converts them into weightless surface decor, in sharp contrast to the muscular window brackets at Maisons. Although Mansart sometimes sacrificed tectonic expression, he subscribed to the classical theory of the orders and deployed them as a regulating system to control the overall design of a building. By contrast, Le Vau eschewed classical doctrine and, consistent with French Renaissance tradition, used the orders to decorate wall surfaces as local circumstances required.[35]

As Le Vau's handling of the orders demonstrates, he did not read to discern the rules governing this heavily regulated aspect of classical architecture. He was indifferent to the authority of the ancients as codified in texts, and he repudiated correctness, the aesthetic standard championed by Chambray. When Inigo Jones compared the antiquities of Rome with Palladio's text in marginal annotations, he was implicitly comparing the authority of the building and that of the book. Never having been to Rome, Le Vau did not consult his books with that issue in mind. Text images did not trigger memories of corporeal forms seen earlier; they were entirely abstract ideas that he could adapt freely to different contexts—as he did, for instance, in going from Palladio's woodcut of the villa at Meledo to

Mazarin's Collège. Taking ideas from books selectively to suit his needs and formal impulses, Le Vau used his library as a laboratory of experimentation. He valued architecture over ideas, invention over authority, and in this regard was a decidedly anti-theoretical reader, less interested in the ideas of an author than in his own possibilities for action.

Le Vau's library constituted a professional tool that was geared primarily to his own needs as an architect. More specifically, the library enabled Le Vau to educate himself in precisely those areas where his traditional training as a mason had failed him; he learned about the culture of classicism from his books, and with that knowledge, his professional identity shifted from artisan to architect and courtier. Simply put, Le Vau became a humanist architect through his library.

The library was the most valuable possession in Le Vau's house at the time of his death. He had amassed a pile of debts, and creditors besieged the estate. The library, which had an assessed value of 785 *livres,* would have liquidated Le Vau's grocer's bill; nevertheless, it was not sold. Like the architect's drawings, the library was not regarded as a dispos-

FIG. 91. *Corinthian pilaster of the Collège des Quatre Nations (now the Institut de France)*

able asset. François Le Vau inherited the library, and his inventory after death contains a nearly identical list of books.[36] (As for the drawings, their fate is discussed in Appendix C.) That the library was transferred to François Le Vau, notwithstanding its economic value and the family's debts, indicates that the books had a status different from other forms of property. Instrumental in the making of a royal architect, they were personal—more like a cross between a diary and a straight edge, both self-projection and professional tool—and that close association with Le Vau converted the books from commodity to family treasure.

The Renaissance had opened a schism between the practice and theory of architecture. The great treatises of the sixteenth century articulated a new professional identity for the architect as a person of learning. Delorme, for instance, advised architects to study philosophy, mathematics, history, and music, but these subjects were not taught in stoneyards where architects, like Le Vau, traditionally learned their craft. In short, the emergent model of the architect as humanist was at odds with his artisanal formation. This conflict between theory and practice played out during the seventeenth century and produced a growing rift between the learned architect and the manually deft builder, a rift that the Académie Royale d'Architecture widened further. Under the academic regime, architects were formed in the classroom, not at the building site, and a new route to professional success was opened through teaching and writing, rather than designing and building. The profession of architecture was at last fully reconstituted as a liberal art.

Before then, what did architects do to resolve the conflict between theory and practice, between the normative standards of the treatises and the practical realities of construction? Le Vau's career corresponds with this period—the time between the publication of the humanist treatises of Delorme, Palladio, and others in the mid-sixteenth century and the establishment of the Académie Royale a century later—and his library enables us to understand how he responded to the broader cultural tension. In concrete terms, books helped prepare Le Vau to design the Collège des Quatre Nations.

CHAPTER 4

CHARGES OF EMBEZZLEMENT

AS PAUL FRÉART DE CHANTELOU tells it, Louis Le Vau was a scoundrel who made money improperly off the Collège. In conversation with Gianlorenzo Bernini one September day in 1665, he recounted a disturbing story. After buying one of Le Vau's earliest townhouses, the Hôtel Bautru (1634–37), Jean-Baptiste Colbert had learned unhappily that the foundations were flawed and had to be relaid.

> M. Colbert was having much difficulty in extricating himself from this mess for fear of letting it be known that he had made a mistake in his choice . . . ; if he acted suddenly, one thing would lead to another, and people would begin to criticize the Collège des Quatre Nations, which is very badly planned and situated (on account of the alteration in the riverbed) and shamefully executed. He would certainly make them pay heavily because he well knew that the whole thing had been done to enhance the value of the sites that Le Vau and his friends owned in the neighborhood.[1]

More or less taking Chantelou at his word, modern historians have alluded routinely to Le Vau's nameless improprieties at the Collège. We know enough about the intention of Le Vau's design to dismiss at once Chantelou's mercenary explanation of its site, but the possibility of Le Vau's financial interest in the Collège cannot be dismissed quite so quickly. A strange turn of events in the 1670s suggests that there might be a twisted truth in Chantelou's story.

Soon after Le Vau's death, officials of the Collège des Quatre Nations charged the royal architect with embezzling building funds and diverting them to a gun foundry. Le Vau's design had endowed the Collège with something of immeasurable value—monumental stature in Paris and a prominence that was forever linked to the Louvre. The Collège was an undisputed architectural success, but in lieu of feeling gratitude, the client felt cheated. Under the leadership of Colbert, their ex-officio head, the officers of the Collège sued their brilliant architect—or more precisely his estate, since he was dead. The beneficiary of the crime, according to the charges, was a gun manufactory that Le Vau had, in fact, operated with Colbert's unwavering support. Is it true that the royal architect stole Cardinal Mazarin's money to make munitions for the crown?

The literature on Le Vau has nothing to say about this remarkable lawsuit; the history of the case has essentially been forgotten and lies buried in legal petitions, briefs, and court orders from the 1670s and later. Yet the lawsuit opens a path into Le Vau's business affairs and clarifies the rumors that, thanks to Chantelou, have tarnished his reputation to this day. There is insufficient evidence to retry the case; too many financial records and other documents have been lost or were purposely destroyed when the events transpired in the 1660s. The best we can do by way of giving Le Vau a fair hearing is to lay out the charges and put the case in context. This means examining the cost overruns at the Collège, the difficulties of building for the crown, and Le Vau's work on the side as an industrialist. In re-opening a case closed three hundred years ago, we not only give a human face to Colbert's large-scale program to industrialize France. We also discover what being an architect meant to Le Vau and see, for the first time, the full orbit of his ambition and creativity.

THE PRICE OF GRANDEUR

One of the underlying assumptions of the plaintiffs in this case was that Le Vau's illegal actions caused the cost overruns at the Collège; therefore, we start by asking what it cost to construct the buildings.

Money was discussed at virtually every meeting of the building committee. Colbert, Jean de Gomont, and above all Le Vau paid close attention to costs, yet they skyrocketed and depleted Mazarin's bequest well before meeting his mandate. The cardinal had expected his donation to cover all expenses relating to the Collège—paying not just for construction but also for his tomb, furnishings, staff salaries, and operating expenditures, from horses for the academy to new books for the library.[2] But the two-million *livre* bequest did not even cover the cost of construction, and the budgetary problems were no last-minute surprise. Expenditures were discussed frequently, the design scaled back, and the budget tweaked precisely because the principals were worried from the outset about exceeding the bequest.

Le Vau made it clear that his design would consume the entire bequest. His budgets came in close to the mark, but as Gomont pointed out, everything but construction costs was left unfunded: taxes and indemnities, the cardinal's tomb, interior furnishings, decorations for the square in front of the Collège, staff salaries, and the equestrian academy.[3] Le Vau had a strategy for handling these expenditures—a combination of leveraging assets of the Collège and developing its real estate. Demonstrating his skill as a land developer, Le Vau advised the Collège to build rental properties: seventeen houses on the rue Mazarine and ground-floor shops on the main facade. Le Vau figured, not unreasonably, that the annual income derived from these properties, in addition to the other assets Mazarin had bequeathed to the Collège, would subsidize the cost of decorating and furnishing the buildings.[4]

It was also expected, at this early stage, that Mazarin's heirs would pay for the cardinal's tomb and other unbudgeted items. Gomont patiently courted the duc de Mazarin, Armand-Charles de La Porte—a peevish and demanding man who had married Mazarin's niece, Hortense Mancini, only two days before the cardinal's death. At that time he was named Mazarin's primary heir and agreed to surrender his family title, duc de La Meilleraye, for that of Mazarin. Alas, the cardinal pinned his dynastic hopes on a disastrous choice—certainly the feeling of Hortense Mancini, who left her husband in 1667. Even by modern standards, de La Porte was unusually litigious; according to the acerbic abbé de Choisy, he instigated some three hundred lawsuits—no doubt an inflated figure based on a grain of truth. In 1670 the duke vandalized the cardinal's antique nudes, and in later years he surrendered assets of Mazarin's estate that he considered ill-gotten. It would be kind to call the duke devout; more likely, he was mad, and before long Collège officials realized that he would make no financial contributions.[5]

Le Vau's costly project gave the building committee second thoughts about the Porte de Nesle site. The architect attempted to dispel their worries: "The foundation is the most beautiful and most advantageous there is in France, and the entire building will be seen from the Louvre," he reminded his colleagues.[6] Unpersuaded, the committee entertained the idea of buying the Luxembourg for 1.1 million *livres,* an option cheaper than building Le Vau's design. The duc de Mazarin supported the idea because he thought a royal palace—the Luxembourg had been built by Queen Maria de Medici—would add luster to Mazarin's legacy. Despite concerns about privatizing a royal foundation, Colbert instructed Le Vau to make a plan and raised the matter with the king, whose definitive views Colbert reported to the building committee: "The ornament that the structure of the Collège will bring the Louvre when it is built on the ditch by the Porte de Nesle has so strongly moved His Majesty that he much more approves this idea and he also wishes that it be executed as promptly as possible."[7] Louis XIV saw eye-to-eye with his architect on the benefits of the Porte de Nesle site, but Le Vau made the mistake of confusing the king's enthusiasm for his design with a willingness to provide financial aid.

Le Vau's expectation was not unreasonable. The king had designated the Collège des Quatres Nations a royal foundation, which in other cases meant that the crown paid staff salaries and absorbed operating costs, as at the Collège de France. Clearly, the king wanted to embellish the Louvre, which is why he insisted on building Mazarin's Collège at the Porte de Nesle site. From Le Vau's perspective, many expenses in improving the environs of the Louvre were incurred on the crown's behalf—higher expenses to meet the higher standards of royal construction. It followed that the king should defray those escalating costs. But the crown—which is to say, Colbert—did not reason in the same way.

He held that Mazarin's Collège was the primary beneficiary of these improvements;

hence, it should foot the bills—but Colbert's position was disingenuous, to say the least. In fact, Colbert engaged in cost shifting, which, in effect, imposed heavy taxes on the Collège because of its proximity to the Louvre. This strategy is clear in two particular areas where actual costs greatly exceeded Le Vau's budgeted expenditures.[8] First, a 37 percent increase in land costs was directly attibutable to the steep penalties the Collège suffered when Colbert voided a prior claim to the site. Colbert required the Collège to pay about 145,000 *livres* in damages to the city and a private syndicate that had lost the right to develop the fossé de Nesle.[9] Thanks to Colbert's high valuation (147 *livres* per square *toise* of land, 20 *livres* more than the developers had paid), the syndicate made a profit of 20 percent on land it had yet to improve, and the moat became some of the most expensive real estate in Paris. Naturally this induced other neighbors, including the powerful abbey of Saint Germain des Prés and the owner of the Hôtel de Nevers, to sue the Collège for damages and try to cash in on the higher land values.[10] True, the Collège would have driven up land values wherever it was located, but Colbert accelerated the process.

Even worse, he transferred the city's obligation to build a sewer and quay at the Porte de Nesle to Mazarin's foundation. To match the moat walls of the Louvre, Le Vau designed the Quai Mazarin with quoins, a fine balustrade, and the king's escutcheon. The going rate to build an ordinary quay was about 80 *livres* per cubic *toise* of masonry; the Quai Mazarin cost more than twice as much (140 livres per *toise*). The expense was incurred for the king; should he not pay for it?[11]

Le Vau made an analogous argument with regard to the sewer. The fossé de Nesle had functioned as an open sewer, channeling waste from Left Bank neighborhoods into the Seine. In accordance with the city's preexisting plan, Le Vau intended to enclose the sewer and bury it underground—a relatively inexpensive project that appeared on his first budget under the heading "Paving and Conduits, 20,000 *livres*."[12] But within months Colbert decided that one new pipe was not enough. An edict of September 1662 instructed the commissioners of Mazarin's Collège to solve all the sewage problems in the area in order to eliminate the malodors that disturbed His Majesty at the Louvre: "The stench that is often emitted in the heat of summer might cause a dangerous infection in the palace."[13] The Collège was compelled to build a more extensive underground sewer, regrade roads throughout the neighborhood, and repave several streets.[14] As a result, the cost of the quay and sewer cost 49 percent more than Le Vau had budgeted.

It was not that Colbert opposed infrastructural improvements in general; street widening, new quays, and sewers were the hallmark of his urbanism. But whatever fiduciary responsibility Colbert had as Mazarin's executor and trustee of the foundation was overtaken by his obligations as minister of state. Le Vau was deeply frustrated by Colbert's using the Collège to promote the royal agenda: had the Collège not been forced to pay for a magnificent quay and new sewer system, the Porte de Nesle site would have cost about the same as other properties in the University, and the pressure on Le Vau to make repeated cutbacks would have been lifted.[15] Le Vau believed the king would give him a more sympathetic hearing: "[I] will speak to the King," Le Vau warned Gomont, "about reimbursing the Collège for the cost of the quay, which is the most beautiful quay in the city, and which the king had built because it is opposite the Louvre, as well as the expenses for the sewer, which is a public work."[16] But his appeal, if executed, came to naught.

To summarize, it is crystal clear that Colbert and his lieutenant Gomont knew the high cost of Le Vau's building when they approved his design at the king's command. The deficit was not attributable to ineptitude or dishonesty on Le Vau's part; it resulted from the proximity of the Louvre, which converted Mazarin's Collège into a de facto royal building project, set a high standard of design, and raised the cost of construction. Half of Mazarin's bequest was consumed in buying the land, building the quay, and rerouting the sewer—costs driven not by difficult topography but by the crown's demands and Colbert's cost-shifting strategy with regard to the urban infrastructure. In effect, the decision to build the Collège opposite the Louvre cost a million *livres* before a single stone was in place; then the stones cost another million, roughly the total cost of building Vaux-le-Vicomte, a château of legendary splendor. Again, the high cost of construction has a clear explanation: the Collège was built to the same standards as the Louvre. It was built with the same stone—ashlar masonry of fine-grained, high-quality limestone from quarries around Paris.[17] It reproduced specific masonry features of the palace, as we saw in the Quai Mazarin; and it required the same high degree of skill and craft to build. Thanks to Le Vau's design, Mazarin's Collège enhanced the grandeur of the crown, but Colbert made the Collège pay the price of grandeur.

THE BUSINESS OF BUILDING

Under the circumstances, it was only normal for tensions to run high: expenses were mounting and money growing scarce, the founder's family was not forthcoming, and the crown was unexpectedly demanding. Le Vau was the pivotal figure, accountable for design, construction, and the budget. He was the middleman, caught not just between the interests of the king and the Collège, but also between an obtrusive bookkeeper and the building contractors. The charges of embezzlement hinge on Le Vau's role in the building process.

The process was set in motion in July 1662 with competitive bidding for the masonry contract. Of the contractors who inspected drawings on view at Le Vau's residence over a four-day period, few masons seemed to want the job. The complexity and scale of the project must have been a factor, but masons also considered the deadline for the finished building—1666, four years away—as unrealistic. They feared that construction at the Louvre would monopolize the supply of skilled workers and materials that the Collège required.[18] Six masons bid for the job, half of whom had personal connections to Le Vau: François d'Orbay was Le Vau's chief draftsman; Charles Thoison was Le Vau's brother-in-law; and

Simon Lambert's son worked in Le Vau's atelier.[19] Colbert awarded the contract, which was signed in August 1662, jointly to Lambert, the low bidder, and Thoison, whose projects at Vincennes, the Hôtel Tambonneau, and *hôtels* on the Ile Saint-Louis had all been designed by Le Vau.[20]

Colbert was preoccupied with graft on construction jobs; some degree of favor trading and paying kickbacks was probably endemic in the business. He pestered Bernini with his worries about this problem at the Louvre and even accused the late Sublet de Noyers, Louis XIII's superintendant of royal buildings, of skimming building funds.[21] Consequently, Colbert put various supervisory controls in place at the Collège; nevertheless, Le Vau managed to impose his free-wheeling style on the project. As controller general, Le Vau's job was to oversee construction. Once he approved the quality of finished work, the treasurer, Simon Mariage, was authorized to pay the contractors. They in turn appointed a paymaster, Etienne Blondet, whose job was to distribute the payroll.[22] Blondet was none other than Le Vau's personal agent; he lived in Le Vau's house, did his bidding on many matters, and often signed documents on Le Vau's behalf. In other words, the wages passed through Le Vau and at his command, as they had at Vaux-le-Vicomte, where Le Vau likewise paid the masonry contractors.

The royal architect was obviously a commanding figure; Gomont treated him with deference, and his polite requests to economize did not bother Le Vau as much as did the scrutiny of the punctilious assistant controller, one Meurset de La Tour, whose duty it was to measure and inspect finished work before the workers could be paid. Determined to ingratiate himself with Colbert, Meurset detailed each infraction he observed in long letters to his superior, casting a pall of suspicion and malfeasance over the building project. Meurset's criticisms often implicated Le Vau; for instance, he accused the architect of improperly allowing the masons and carpenters to use materials salvaged from the Tour de Nesle.[23] Le Vau defended his actions and tried to undermine Meurset's credibility, or at least Meurset suspected as much. "I well know that someone has misrepresented my conduct, in order to turn you against me," he wrote Colbert; "... the only cause was the exactitude and assiduousness with which I have executed the job you entrusted to me."[24] Le Vau was annoyed;[25] Meurset was a novice (he did not even know how to measure masonry), whereas he was the royal architect with more than twenty years of construction experience. Le Vau's bickering with the meddlesome controller also vented his deeper frustration with Colbert. The real problem facing the Collège was not bad construction, as Meurset suspected, but lack of money—a problem Colbert had in part created and might easily have solved.

Disbursements were not keeping up with the pace of construction. The contractors complained about the large sums they advanced to buy supplies and pay their masons. Likewise, the plumbers and carpenters complained that they had not been paid. Gomont disavowed responsibility; his oft-repeated message was that he had nothing to do with the finances of the Collège. In February 1667, as budgetary problems came to a head, the minutes record a particularly fervent denial: Gomont insisted that "he never wanted to become involved with personally issuing or directing others to issue payment orders, or to be informed of any payment, or even know who was paid, because that was not part of his profession, function. . . , interest or inclination."[26] Surely this was an odd position for the chief officer to take; the vehemence suggests something more than a simple cash-flow problem. Was Gomont trying to distance himself from a bigger concern?

An unsigned complaint written in the 1670s accused Le Vau not just of shoddy construction and inadequate oversight, but of reckless profiteering. The main charge was that Le Vau had taken half of the masons' pay and that the authorities had tolerated the arrangement in order to speed up construction. Everyone was complicit, but Le Vau was chiefly at fault: he let the contractors build as they pleased, was lax about inspections, and overlooked masonry of inferior quality.[27] Meurset de La Tour left a paper trail of similar recriminations—a screed he probably composed in another attempt to damage the architect, by then dead, who had held him in contempt.

As proof of Le Vau's deceitfulness and greed, the critic compared building costs for the Quai Mazarin and the adjoining Quai Malaquais: 105 versus 72 *livres* per cubic *toise* (in fact, the Quai Mazarin cost even more). The anonymous critic concluded that Le Vau had overcharged to build his design and pocketed profits of 94,000 livres.[28] This number is specious and the comparison unfair; we know why the Quai Mazarin cost more to build than an ordinary, undecorated quay, and as to the alleged inferiority of the masonry, the evidence is limited to Meurset's reports, which were nitpicky but failed to uncover a significant infraction. True, Le Vau's foundations at the Louvre were faulted by Bernini as well; he found misalignments, inadequate lime in the mortar, and holes between stones where rats were nesting. Colbert believed that the contractors, not Le Vau, were responsible for these problems.[29] In any event, Mazarin's Collège has stood the test of time, and modern restorers have found no unusual defects.

But what of the charge that Le Vau had a personal stake in the masonry contracts? With regard to the rental houses on the rue Mazarine, it is a fact that Le Vau purchased a 50 percent interest in the masonry contract, which means he built half the buildings, bore half the risk, and got half the money.[30] (Chantelou's belief, cited at the start of the chapter, that Le Vau owned property in the neighborhood of the Collège probably refers to the rue Mazarine houses.)[31] Why did the royal architect involve himself in construction of the sixteen houses on the rue Mazarine? Le Vau began his career as a mason-contractor and never lost a taste for that line of work; after all, contracting was a potentially lucrative activity, and Le Vau needed money. After 1654 he received an annual retainer of 6,000 *livres* as first architect plus individual design fees (he earned 1,000 *livres* for designing the Collège), but Le Vau lived beyond his means and had ambitions—in the 1640s to develop the

Ile Saint-Louis, in the 1660s to become an industrialist—which he could finance only by going into debt.[32]

Architects and masons made money, for the most part, in two ways—from construction and from real-estate development, activities that Le Vau pursued with great success on the Ile Saint-Louis. Beginning in 1638 he purchased several parcels of land on the island, most of which he developed (some lots were sold undeveloped). The documentation is patchy, but we know that in 1641 he undertook to build nine houses; he designed the structures either for clients, such as Jean-Baptiste Lambert, or on speculation; ordered building materials; hired subcontractors, including his father; then rented or sold the buildings, except for the house at 3 Quai d'Anjou (then Quai d'Alençon), where he lived for a brief time. Le Vau borrowed his working capital—1,000 *livres* from his brother-in-law Thoison, 24,000 from Lambert—and mortgaged one property against the next.[33] The situation was different with the rue Mazarine houses, which he obviously did not own. In addition to the money made from construction, Le Vau and the other contractors stood to earn an incentive fee; they guaranteed the Collège 60,000 *livres* in rental income for the first four years (1665–68), and they received a percentage of the rent above that threshold. The scandalmongers underestimated the risk this deal involved; the proof is that the rue Mazarine rents were only half of what the contractors guaranteed, and they lost money in their role as rental agents.[34]

If not improper, why did Le Vau conceal his stake in the rental houses, at least in documents where Blondet's name stands in for his own? The practice of using borrowed names, *prête-noms,* was common enough in seventeenth-century France and did not imply deception. In this case, Le Vau may have been concerned that commercial entanglements would harm the image and dignity of the royal architect. It was that worry that motivated a restriction against masonry contracting, which would soon become a condition of membership in the Académie Royale d'Architecture.[35] The imposition of the ban cut off architects from their most lucrative activity and forced a break between the business of building and the architectural profession—a difference that had not existed to the same extent during Le Vau's lifetime. While the culture of the Renaissance articulated a distinction between the mason and the architect, the process of construction kept the two, in actuality, rather closely linked. That common ground was wiped out by the Académie Royale and the academic culture it spawned. In this regard, Le Vau represents the end of an era in which he was able to play multiple roles—mason, contractor, designer, developer, and courtier—roles that were later deemed incompatible. The accusations of impropriety posthumously leveled against Le Vau signify the emergence of a value system that he had resisted.

The open question—and one that may answer the embezzlement charges—is whether Le Vau was, in fact, a co-contractor of the Collège. In 1672 Gomont, the chief administrator who heretofore had feigned ignorance of financial matters, discovered that 100,000 *livres* were unaccounted for.[36] In the normal course of construction, the treasurer (Mariage), upon giving money to the paymaster (Blondet), obtained receipts cosigned by

Le Vau, the contractors, and sometimes the workers; absent that, Mariage accepted a signed pledge from Le Vau to provide the proper paperwork in due course. The system broke down on thirteen occasions, between 1662 and 1666, when Mariage failed to obtain any paperwork from Le Vau. On 14 April 1666, reportedly after repeated requests, Mariage managed to secure a written promise from Le Vau to provide receipts from the contractors or else reimburse the treasurer the full amount in question (100,000 *livres*). Alas, the poor fellow got neither one, leaving him vulnerable to the charges of corruption and negligence raised in the 1670s.[37]

In justifying the undocumented payments to Le Vau, Mariage pointed out that the disputed sum was a fraction of the nearly 1.4 million *livres* that had uneventfully passed between the treasurer and the paymaster over the course of construction; that he had been instructed to obey Le Vau's orders and "would have failed in his duties . . . if he had not promptly furnished the funds needed to advance the work"; and finally—the key point—that the money reached its intended target because Le Vau was a copartner of the contractors. "There was every appearance and it is still presumed," Mariage explained, "that the late Le Vau had the same interest in work at the Collège [as he had at the rental houses], and that . . . agreements and secret declarations between [Le Vau and the contractors] that have not yet surfaced, . . . would show that in paying Le Vau, Mariage was paying the actual contractor and principal interested party."[38] According to Mariage, the routine practice was for Thoison, Lambert, and Le Vau to split the pay in three equal parts, but he supplied no proof, and none has surfaced since then.[39]

What if Mariage was right, as he likely is, given Le Vau's history as a developer on the Ile Saint-Louis in the 1640s and the rue Mazarine in the 1660s? Suppose that Le Vau was a co-contractor of the Collège des Quatre Nations, and suppose further that as a result, he loosened his control over Thoison and Lambert and did them favors. Maybe at the outset he helped them get the job and later let them take demolition materials (as the carpenters also did). As an experienced hand, Le Vau may have regarded that favor as an effective way to keep the building crews happy and work proceeding apace. At worst, Le Vau was a lax supervisor, but he did not violate conventional standards of the construction business; the public terms of his contract for the rue Mazarine houses make this point clear.

But if Mariage was wrong and Le Vau was not a co-contractor of the Collège, then he presumably had no right to money destined for the building crew. It was based on this premise that in the 1670s the Collège des Quatre Nations posthumously charged Louis Le Vau with embezzling 100,000 *livres:* "Le Vau wanted to make use of the Collège's money in his business; and to this end, concealing his plan, he entrapped Mariage into furnishing several sums, which together amounted to 100,000 *livres,* under the pretext of using the money to pay the contractors and workers."[40] To make sense of these charges, we need to leave Paris for the countryside around Nevers, where Le Vau set up a foundry.

THE ARCHITECT AS INDUSTRIALIST

In February 1665 the crown announced the creation of the Royal Manufactory for Tin, the Manufacture Royale de Fer Blanc.[41] Although the privilege was vested in an obscure metallurgist named Antoine Champion, the foundry was not, in fact, his creation.[42] It was Le Vau who planned the business, hired the work crew, constructed the manufacturing buildings, secured the start-up financing, and successfully lobbied for royal protection. So unexpected is this second career that, until recently, historians failed to recognize the industrialist and royal architect as one and the same Le Vau.[43]

Pursued in the context of Colbert's efforts to stimulate French protoindustrial activity, Le Vau's tinworks was, if not the first, among the earliest ventures Colbert sponsored under his Royal Council on Commerce. He formed the council in 1664 to coordinate an industrial campaign, and over the next decade new businesses opened across France, particularly in the area of textiles and metallurgy.[44] Colbert targeted the metallurgical industries, and especially gun foundries, because they were critical to national defense. Early modern warfare depended on cast cannon, yet France could not produce bombards on its own; for the constituent metals—iron, tin, and copper—the country relied on Sweden and Germany, leaders in early modern metallurgy. The primary goal was to make France self-sufficient in arms production, but from his unique vantage point—his ministerial portfolio covered finance, commerce, manufacturing, mining, and the navy—Colbert could anticipate commercial benefits from a developing metal industry.

Le Vau's foundry exemplified the bridge between civilian and military production that Colbert had in mind. The foundry had two missions. The first, which was spelled out in the 1665 edict, was to manufacture tableware and building parts in tin and tinplate. The second was to manufacture cannon and other ordnance for the French navy, which was undergoing a massive expansion under Colbert's leadership. Determined to make France a naval power, he sponsored initiatives ranging from new port construction—as at Rochefort, where, after 1670, François Le Vau was in charge of design—to the creation of a mining infrastructure, in which Louis Le Vau played an important part.

Le Vau obtained a significant aid package from the crown: 60,000 *livres* (half as a grant, half as an interest-free loan), tax exemptions (no tariffs would be levied on Le Vau's goods), a thirty-year monopoly on tinware (imitation or rival products would be confiscated), employee benefits (detailed below), the right to hang a shingle with the royal fleur-de-lis, and—most important—government commissions. These forms of state subsidy were not insignificant, but Le Vau required much more capital than the crown provided.[45] (The Gobelins workshop, by contrast, was fully funded by the crown.) Ultimately the success of Colbert's industrial campaign depended on private entrepreneurs, men willing to put their capital and careers at risk to forge a protoindustrial order in an economy that otherwise remained agrarian and rooted in seigneurial values. Le Vau was one of

those daring businessmen, "progenitors of industrial capitalism," in the words of one recent commentator.[46]

The timing of Le Vau's industrial initiative, which came on the heels of his fiasco at
the Louvre, raises the question whether the two events were related. Colbert halted construction of Le Vau's design for the east wing of the Louvre in February 1664, after a bit
more than the foundations had been built. At Colbert's invitation, French and Italian architects critiqued Le Vau's foundation design—obviously a humbling experience for the
royal architect—but the cruelest blow was Colbert's awarding the commission to Bernini.
Royal backing of Le Vau's foundry was in part compensatory for the loss of the Louvre,
and it promised to be mutually beneficial to Le Vau and Colbert. For Le Vau's part, the
business related to his lifelong engagement with commerce and craft, and in particular it
satisfied a long-standing interest in metallurgy.

Le Vau began to experiment with tin smelting in 1650, and like any serious metallurgist in the seventeenth century, he traveled to Germany to learn from masters of the craft.[47]
Ever since the publication in 1556 of Georg Agricola's treatise on German mining and
metallurgy, *De re metallica,* industrial spies trekked to the foundries of Bohemia and Saxony to capture their production secrets and to employ their master metalworkers. Le Vau's
trip may have been no different from that of Andrew Yarranton, an ironmaster from the
British Midlands, who went to Saxony in 1667, learned the local methods of tinplating, and
began production in Britain.[48] But it was notable because, to our knowledge, Le Vau made
no other foreign trips. He did not feel compelled to see the architecture of Rome, yet he
chose to go to Germany for the sake of a secondary pursuit. This choice reflects the relative
accessibility of information about European architecture through drawings, prints, and
books, but it also evokes Le Vau's restless and entrepreneurial character, his gambler's opti-
mism and indifference to risk.

In 1650 Le Vau set up furnaces and forges in the Norman village of Conches, just west
of Evreux, a historic center of French mining and metalworking because of its deposits of
iron ore. Despite commercial failure—the foundry closed after three years of operation—
Le Vau claimed a degree of technical success. He boasted that his tin matched that of Germany (an unlikely achievement) and, more plausibly, that it could be used on roofs and
elsewhere in construction in place of lead, a much heavier metal. This application serves to
explain how Le Vau went from developing houses on the Ile Saint-Louis to forging ridge
plates in Normandy. (The evidence of his experimental approach to construction reopens
the possibility that Le Vau had a hand in the system of iron reinforcements used at the
Colonnade.)[49] In taking on the more complex task of forging cannon, Le Vau entered a
realm familiar to military architects, who, if not knowledgeable about technical aspects of
metallurgy, were certainly well versed in fireworks, ballistics, artillery, fortifications, and
engineering—which is to say that Le Vau's foundry was not as far removed from the practice of architecture as may at first appear. The most famous illustration of this point is

Balthasar Neumann, who—in a reversal of Le Vau's trajectory—trained as a bell and artillery founder in the Franconia military and became a great architect.

In 1665, the second time around, Le Vau had a better idea of what the metal-casting business required in money, machines, and men. He planned an integrated operation that began with a supply of ore and charcoal timber and ended with cannon, anchors, and iron bars. To understand the capital investment this business required as well as the challenge facing Le Vau, consider what was involved in manufacturing a gun (FIG. 92).[50] Le Vau either mined the ore or purchased it from miners; the evidence is not clear on this point. Next the ore was roasted in blast furnaces with charcoal made on site from local timber. Le Vau's furnaces, if typical of the time, would have been square stone structures, divided into three or four hearths (large enough to cast cannon) and located by a watercourse, where a waterwheel drove the bellows needed to fan the fires. To ensure an adequate supply of power, Le Vau created a pond, the Etang de la Carrière, which drew upon the same hydraulics as André Le Nôtre's gardens at Vaux and Versailles. Herein we glimpse the hidden utility of the French formal garden—a phenomenon that helped to develop technology on which the country's industrial infrastructure was based. The next step was smelting: ore was heated beyond its melting point until it was altered chemically (by interacting with the charcoal) in ways that endowed the metal with new properties. Although the integrity of the cannon depended on the alloy, the chemistry of metals was then unknown. The metallurgy underlying gun founding was an art, and only an experienced smelter knew how to mix the alloys to achieve the proper density and purity that kept a cannon from exploding under pressure and determined the ballistics of a ball.[51]

Le Vau built his foundry in the village of Beaumont-la-Ferrière in the Nivernais, where Colbert had decided to concentrate industrial

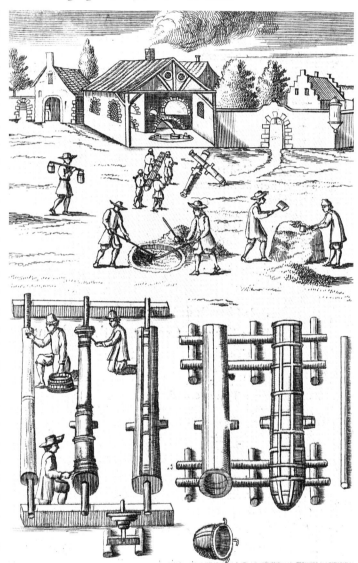

FIG. 92. *Forging cannon. Reproduced from Alain Manesson Mallet,* Les Travaux de Mars *(Paris, 1672)*

development. Soon other foundries opened in nearby towns, and the Nivernais became an immense arsenal.[52] Le Vau created a substantial operation, to judge from a list of assets in 1667: there were stockpiles of ore and charcoal, furnaces and at least seven forges, a battery mill where tinplate was hammered, warehouses, carriages to transport materials, and workers' housing dispersed in and around Beaumont.[53] Le Vau also bought and renovated the château of Beaumont, probably a modest manor house, and opened a refinery and slitting mill (to cut iron bars into rods and nails) on the grounds.

Le Vau's business got off to a good start, and he sent Colbert a characteristically optimistic report on 5 November 1665: "We know how to refine as well as in Germany.... We have all the proper material and the forges are as well arranged as one could hope for." Two forges were already in operation, three more were set to go on line by the end of the year. Le Vau was ready, as soon as Colbert gave the word, to begin manufacturing muskets, cannon, and shot. He had a sample musket to show and had reportedly hired a talented founder to mold and cast cannon. "The only thing we need are good hammer men who can move the work along more quickly than our Frenchmen."[54]

Besides a shortage of skilled labor, there was a dearth of working capital. Expenses were running high for the buildings, equipment, supplies, and transportation. An anonymous memorandum from late 1667 provides the following information about Le Vau's start-up and operating costs:

Budget for Le Vau's Foundry

Land	90,000
Buildings and Forge	50,000
Supplies	100,000
Other Expenses	110,000
Total Expenditures	350,000
Royal Subsidy	-30,000
Total Debt	320,000[55]

The math is straightforward, but it masks a murky financial structure. Only 60,000 *livres* have an identifiable source—the crown.[56] Who invested the remaining 290,000 *livres* in working capital, how much did each man pay, and in what order? That information was unavailable, Colbert's agent reported, which would pose a problem in raising additional funds. "The cost of the buildings, the upfront charges, and incidental expenses would be suspect to the most scrupulous investor," the adviser warned, "and since the order of payments [to creditors] was not drawn up with the proper paperwork, it would be almost impossible to induce large investments."[57] This picture of multiple creditors and casual bookkeeping is consistent with Le Vau's general modus operandi. The one certainty is that he borrowed money from several sources; the size of his personal investment remains unclear.

It is a sign of the importance Colbert attributed to Le Vau's foundry that he sent two leaders of his industrial campaign to shore up Beaumont: Abraham Besch and Samuel Dalliez de La Tour. Besch and his brother had come to France in 1666, at Colbert's behest, from their native Sweden, where they had acquired an expertise in smelting and manufacturing iron bar. Colbert put them in charge of the mines and gun foundries in Rouergue and Languedoc, before sending Abraham to Beaumont in September 1667, where he was favorably impressed and praised the lightweight cannon in letters to Colbert.[58] But Besch eventually disappointed Colbert; under his watch, the foundry continued to produce flawed products, and Colbert turned to Dalliez de La Tour to set things aright.

A Protestant financier, Dalliez began by operating foundries in the Dauphiné that rivaled Le Vau's.[59] "I am only thinking of how to serve M. Le Vau, who has the general privilege for the entire realm," Dalliez wrote Colbert disingenuously in August 1665, "and how for my part to contribute to the progress of a new industry so advantageous to the country and from which it is fair Le Vau should draw some utility, as he had the first idea."[60] Three years later Dalliez had become Le Vau's principal investor and the real head of Beaumont, although Le Vau retained operational control. With renewed confidence in the Beaumont foundry, Colbert awarded Le Vau a large government contract in March 1669 to deliver iron to the naval ports at Brest and Rochefort;[61] and at Le Vau's request and with Colbert's permission, Dalliez paid Le Vau in advance for two hundred cannon he was about to deliver to the navy.[62] Alas, the cannon failed inspection a few months later; some burst apart upon firing, and others had faults in the metal alloys.[63]

Colbert rebuked Le Vau. Beyond the poor performance of his cannon, Le Vau had neglected the foundry's original mission which was to make tin; and he showed no appreciation for the aid provided by Dalliez and Besch, whom Le Vau saw as menacing interlopers. "[I want] to make you realize the obligation you are under to make a success of the tin foundry," Colbert threatened Le Vau in October 1669.

> I was not obliged to find you partners, but in response to your request and in order to assist you, I gave you associates who sustained the entire loss so that all the changes you complain about have taken place to provide you with very considerable assistance, which, I repeat, I was not obliged to provide. In addition, I gave you a very advantageous license for your iron such that you had money from the king to buy the land in Beaumont and set up your establishment, and you received substantial aid from your associates and a good price for your iron. And, after all this, Your Majesty does not have tin.[64]

Le Vau had no choice but to revive tin manufacturing at Beaumont as Colbert instructed. "I have learned of the agreement you reached with Monsieur Le Vau for the tin foundry," Colbert wrote Dalliez in November 1669, "and it seems very likely that, having a significant interest in keeping it going, he will do his best to make it succeed."[65] And in an upbeat letter to Le Vau, Colbert commended his efforts and instructed him to concentrate on a naval contract for anchors.[66]

The foundries at Beaumont operated without notable problems over the next year. By February 1670 the anchors were ready for delivery to Nantes. Then Le Vau died in October 1670. Six days later Colbert sent Dalliez to Beaumont, instructing him to maintain order and to keep the foundry running.[67]

Dalliez's experience was not much different from Le Vau's. Colbert directed naval contracts to Beaumont, which was renamed the Compagnie du Nivernais, but the cannon and other arms consistently drew lukewarm reviews: the metal was weak, the alloy flawed, cannon kept failing trials.[68] These material problems reinforced the perception among the naval officer corps that cast-iron cannon *(canon de fer)* were inferior to guns of bronze *(canon de fonte)*.[69] The arsenals at Rochefort, Toulon, and Saintes, which specialized in bronze castings, took over the cannon market, and Beaumont was left making anchors and muskets until 1677, when the purchases, already greatly reduced, stopped altogether.[70]

Colbert's material achievements in stocking the arsenals of France were reinforced by scholars at the Royale Académie des Sciences, whom he encouraged to do related research. François Blondel and Nicolas de La Hire wrote treatises on ballistics; Christiaan Huygens studied the traction of gun carriages. Unlike the books by these learned men, Le Vau's gun foundry slipped away, entirely forgotten. Commercial, craft based, and industrial, it was the hidden side of the same Colbertian project—and the hidden side of Louis Le Vau.

THE VERDICTS

Le Vau was bankrupt when he died on 11 October 1670, at the age of fifty-eight. Although he owned several buildings and properties, they were all heavily mortgaged. To avoid liability for her husband's debts, Jeanne Laisné had to renounce the community-property act she had signed when they married thirty-one years before. On top of this, Madame Le Vau and her unmarried daughter, Hélène, were forced to leave their home; the Hôtel de Longueville, where the family had lived for nearly a decade, was owned by the crown, and their residential privilege expired upon the architect's death.

Creditors besieged the estate. Le Vau owed money left and right—to the heirs of Pierre Le Muet; the heirs of Charles Thoison; the carpenters who built the Collège, the brothers Pierre and Charles Sinson; his servant Etienne Blondet, to mention a few familiar names.[71] During the last year of his life, Le Vau hardly paid a household bill; the coachman, oat merchant, butchers, and doctors all had unpaid accounts. One grocer presented charges amounting to 750 *livres* for banquets and meals he provided Le Vau in 1667 and 1668; after more than sixty appeals, Le Vau had made a small down payment, leaving 520 *livres* unpaid. The long list of creditors confirms the financial strain of Le Vau's last years as well as his lifelong tendency to do business on credit and delay repayment. Indeed, many of the claims went back twenty-five years, to the period when Le Vau was developing the Ile Saint-Louis.

When the notaries entered the Hôtel de Longueville to inventory its contents, Le Vau's two married daughters, Jeanne and Louise, recounted an exchange with their father: "While he was sick, their father had described the sums of money he owed them, the continual expenditures he had had to make, and yet the girls had hardly any money to offer, and in the house, there was hardly anything at all; he had told them in these words, 'My daughters, take my silver plate and make use of it. I wish there were more, but you well know that I disposed of most of it some time ago.' "[72] How should we construe the story? Is it an accurate account of a dying father's moment of remorse, or was it invented by the daughters to justify their removal of the family silver?[73]

The ambiguity is symptomatic of the situation as a whole. The unpaid grocer remarked that Le Vau "was notorious as a man of intelligence and deceptive behavior."[74] Was Le Vau dishonest, shrewd, or merely careless in his business dealings? Did he steal from the masons at Mazarin's Collège or borrow recklessly to keep his foundry going? Litigants raised these questions in the French courts, which, after twenty years, provided answers of a legalistic kind.

Among Le Vau's numerous creditors, four were appointed as trustees to negotiate a bankruptcy agreement. The trustees had two responsibilities: the first was to sell Le Vau's assets and collect as much money as possible on behalf of the estate; the second was to validate the claims of Le Vau's creditors and arrange a payment schedule—that is, decide how much and in what order people were to be paid. This meant, in concrete terms, that the trustees were motivated to defend Le Vau's investment in Beaumont-la-Ferrière and to discount his debt to Mazarin's Collège.[75]

In one of their first actions, the trustees filed suit against the new regime at the Beaumont foundry: Dalliez de La Tour and the manager he installed at Beaumont in 1669, Paul Legoux.[76] According to the plaintiffs, Le Vau had invested 500,000 *livres* in the business, some of it his own money and some raised from family and investors. After six years of hard work, the brief explains, Le Vau died just as he was about to reap the fruit of his investment, leaving behind a business with assets of over 600,000 *livres*. Immediately after Le Vau's death, the brief continues, the defendants took over the foundry and proceeded to strip the business of its assets; in violation of testate laws, they prepared false inventories of the château of Beaumont and scattered manufacturing sites, destroyed records in the château, and doctored business accounts, all to deny Le Vau's ownership rights. Finally the architect's creditors identified his brother-in-law, the abbé Henri Laisné, whom Le Vau had put in charge of the foundry in 1667, as a co-conspirator and accused him of accepting a 200,000-*livre* bribe to ignore the illegal takeover of Beaumont.[77]

Dalliez and Legoux did not so much answer the charges as ridicule them. They wondered how they could stand accused of stealing from a man who was in debt to the tune of 300,000 *livres* and declared as much in a new financing agreement worked out between Dalliez and Le Vau in 1669. And how could the abbé Laisné be accused of criminal behavior when he was in fact "the protector and benefactor of the entire Le Vau family?"[78]

The truth must lie somewhere between these conflicting accounts. In the first place, the plaintiffs' valuation of Le Vau's assets at the foundry (500,000–600,000 *livres*) had to be way off the mark. We know that Le Vau did not own the foundry outright; thanks to Colbert's interventions, he had been propped up by outside investors—most significantly by Dalliez de La Tour, and Dalliez probably had sufficient proof of the monies he invested in Beaumont without having to make the point by rigging Le Vau's books. If money was, in fact, exchanged between Dalliez and the abbé, it may well have been a proper payment for administrative services the abbé rendered.

The uncontested fact is that Colbert had told Dalliez to keep the factory running and implicitly approved of his actions. It comes as a surprise, therefore, to learn that the court handed down verdicts in 1674 and 1675 against Colbert's allies, Dalliez and Legoux, but it was a pyrrhic victory for Le Vau's creditors.[79] Legal actions dragged on another dozen years, until 1687. Dalliez reimbursed the crown 30,000 *livres,* the amount of the original tax-free loan in 1665, and the estate received nothing.

While the Beaumont case was moving slowly through the courts, the estate trustees become embroiled in even more intricate legal maneuvers with the Collège des Quatre Nations. The bankruptcy agreement reached in September 1674 recognized a debt of 100,000 *livres* to Simon Mariage.[80] Convinced they had been cheated, since the missing money belonged to them, the Collège officials sued Mariage. Their case rested on two improbable claims: first, that in order to defraud the Collège of 100,000 *livres,* Mariage had conspired with Le Vau's trustees to forge the promissory note from Le Vau that acknowledged his receipt of the money; and second, that Le Vau was not in partnership with the masonry contractors. Two notaries had searched the Collège files and testified that they found no evidence of Le Vau's having done contracting work at either the rental houses or the Collège buildings.[81] Of course, the least likely place to find explicit evidence of Le Vau's double role was in the Collège's records. Be that as it may, the hard evidence of Le Vau's part in the rental houses undermines the credibility of the Collège's brief.[82]

The courts did not address directly the factuality of the three overarching charges that concern us here: whether Le Vau had a sweetheart deal with the contractors, whether he embezzled the masons' wages, and whether he diverted Collège funds to his foundry. Instead, the courts made a series of narrower rulings during the 1680s that in effect held both Mariage and Le Vau liable for 100,000 *livres* plus accumulated interest. Mariage was able to pay only 30,000 *livres;* and when he died in 1691, a broken man, the Collège seized what was left of his property.[83] Le Vau's impoverished estate paid what it could—about 17,000 *livres.*[84]

In view of the load of debt on Le Vau's estate and the negligible amount the Collège predictably extracted, we have to wonder why the Collège officials pressed forward with the lawsuit, taunting Le Vau's family with inflammatory criminal charges and dishonoring the first architect of the king. As the titular head of the Collège, Colbert must have approved this course of action. Perhaps he took Le Vau for a thief or sought revenge for Le Vau's failure to make a success of Beaumont. Whatever his motive, Colbert succeeded in exacting a powerful form of revenge: the charges of embezzlement besmirched Le Vau's name.

The judgments of the courts have the force of law, but they do not satisfy our yearning for a clear-cut ending to the detective story. The web of countercharges acts to discredit each and every brief. At best we can draw historically informed inferences, knowing that the truth about Le Vau is elusive, many sided, and probably conflictual.

Did Le Vau embezzle building funds? He had a comfortable and long-term working relationship with his brother-in-law Thoison, which must have included an exchange of favors—as when Le Vau, acting as construction supervisor, let him reuse salvaged stone. At Mazarin's Collège it is likely that the architect had a deal with the contractors, which may well have entitled him to a share of the building funds. Whatever the terms of the deal, which we will never know, it would have been mutually beneficial for the architect and his contractors—and probably a common, though undocumented practice. If some part of that 100,000 *livres* went to Le Vau by right—some but not all—does that mean he necessarily embezzled the rest?

Le Vau was financially overextended in the 1660s; once money went into his pocket, he might have used it to cover any number of bills that came due. Undeniably, the timing of Mariage's payments, which coincided with the first year of the foundry, makes them a likely target, given that Le Vau needed more working capital to run the foundry than the crown had provided. Nonetheless, why conclude that he stole money for his new business? It would be inconsistent with Le Vau's history of loans and mortgages to finance his ventures. To be sure, the bankruptcy agreement hammered out by the trustees of his estate does not mention any loans specifically for the Beaumont foundry, but Colbert's financiers would have assumed Le Vau's debt when they became co-owners. It is impossible to disprove the charges of embezzlement; at most, we can point to other plausible explanations of what transpired. Suppose, for instance, that Le Vau was entitled to the money, or that Thoison had approved an informal loan?

In seventeenth-century France the financial boundaries between the state and private financiers were rather blurred. Le Vau learned the methods of the financiers, and his personal finances exhibit an analogous erosion of boundaries between one investment and the next, one pocket and the other. His carelessness was symptomatic of his milieu, but in the end, Le Vau was probably not so much a dishonest man as a compulsive risk taker.

The charges of embezzlement should be set beside other accusations that the Collège officials made in court: that the president of the Chambre des Comptes, Nicolas Lambert, and the other trustees of Le Vau's estate forged a legal document; that Le Vau had no interest in the rental houses; that Mariage acted unreasonably when he gave money to the indisputable head of the building project. These charges were incredible, untrue, or simply unfair; nevertheless, they were effective legal strategies and moved a claim through court. The charges of embezzlement may have been no more than a plausible and effective legal argument, which interests us ultimately because it rested on a grain of truth. Le Vau borrowed freely, paid back slowly, leveraged and gambled as needed to feed his restless ambition. If his moral compass was basically intact, his fearless entrepreneurship and mercantile sensibility occasionally led him astray.

The fact is that being the highest-ranking architect at the court of Louis XIV did not satisfy Le Vau. He delighted in a range of roles that court society normally kept apart, and there is evidence that he honored the values of that world—as artist, courtier, and seigneur. For example, he bought (in 1644) the office of counselor and secretary to the king and (in 1657) the charge of intendant of buildings; he also lobbied hard to obtain one of Mazarin's lay benefices. During his five years in Beaumont (1665–70), Le Vau acted as the town's liege and protector; he paid for church bells and choir decorations, looked after the town fairs, the market, and communal woods.[85] But his commercial bent also led him down a path that aristocratic culture scorned. He developed Parisian real estate and operated foundries, and by no means as a casual pastime; even when work beckoned at Versailles, he was in Beaumont to tend to forges and cannon.

A self-made man, Le Vau went from the stone yards where his father trained him to Colbert's inner circle, but his ascent was different from the seventeenth-century norm. It was not fueled primarily by a desire for status or for wealth; his actions showed a disregard for both. He had a casual attitude toward money and, despite his entrepreneurial inclination, showed no talent for accumulating wealth; the man squandered nearly everything he made and was forced to live on credit. Le Vau was driven to multiply his generative powers in the tradition of the great artist-artificers—Filippo Brunelleschi, Leonardo da Vinci, Bernini, and Neumann to name a few early modern descendants of Daedalus. With opportunities, achievements, and failings that mirrored his times, Le Vau embodied that archetype in the context of seventeenth-century France.

CONCLUSION

MARIE DE SÉVIGNÉ called Jean-Baptiste Colbert (FIG. 93) "the North" (le Nord). To the witty doctor Guy Patin, he was "marble man." Although his savage treatment of Nicolas Fouquet more than justifies the sobriquets, they were probably earned on the basis of his ordinary conduct rather than one vile act. Colbert's relationship with Le Vau suggests the cool way he exercised power and achieved his goals. Colbert let Louis Le Vau die a thousand deaths by inviting international criticism of his Louvre foundation design and entrapped him in an impossible bind by shifting costs from the crown to the Collège. The Collège would have come in under budget if Colbert had paid the excess costs for infrastructural improvements required by the crown. Without question, these actions had strategic value; they advanced Colbert's goals—at Le Vau's expense. But the posthumous lawsuit had absolutely no utility, no hope of meaningful remuneration, and perhaps no just cause; the charges of embezzlement were guaranteed only to inflict damage on a dead man's reputation. Colbert had no loyalty for a long-time collaborator; instead he was bent on revenge. Le Vau had failed him—at his foundry in Beaumont and with his foundation plan at the Louvre, in speculative activities that did not meet Colbert's model of professional decorum, and on a larger scale, with his attachment to a historic French architectural tradition that Colbert rejected.

FIG. 93. *Robert Nanteuil, Jean-Baptiste Colbert, 1668. Etching and drypoint. Département des Estampes, Bibliothèque Nationale de France, Paris*

Colbert became a great cultural impresario, but he did not start out that way. His cultural policies and values took shape gradually during the 1660s; and although historians often project his mature views back to the start of his reign as Louis XIV's minister, Colbert's early years were more unsettled and experimental than is acknowledged. In contrast to the controlling historical image of Colbert as visionary patron, we will look for something else—a classicist still in the making.

Le Vau played an indispensable role in Colbert's cultural formation, beginning in the 1650s at Vincennes and continuing at Cardinal Mazarin's Collège, which Colbert selected him to design. The early history of the Collège affords a rare glimpse of the still-unformed Colbert, at heart an economizing accountant unable to appreciate the grandeur of Le Vau's idea. In 1661 Colbert wanted to merge Mazarin's two foundations—the Collège and Theatine convent—and build a single church that the two divergent institutions would share. By his calculation, erecting a grand structure opposite the Louvre was an inefficient use of Mazarin's resources—a sensible thought for a bookkeeper but foolish for a minister of state. Le Vau handed him an extraordinary opportunity to embellish Paris and enhance the crown, an opportunity it took Colbert a full year to comprehend.[1]

The Collège des Quatre Nations was a turning point in Colbert's education. It gave him a new perspective on the expressive power of classical forms, their transformative effect on perceptions of power and grandeur, and the importance of urban design—a field in which Colbert had had no prior experience. Although the standard art-historical emphasis on style has construed the baroque Collège as a negative model for the arch-classicist Colbert, just the opposite was true. The Collège helped him dream of Paris as a new Rome, but it was a dream that Colbert translated into far different terms.

Writing nearly thirty years after the events, Charles Perrault remembered that Colbert began devising monumental plans for Paris as early as 1662, not coincidentally the year of Mazarin's Collège. "He imagined that he would have to work not only on finishing the Louvre, a project begun so many times and always left incomplete," Perrault recalled, "but also on raising many monuments to the glory of the king, such as triumphal arches, obelisks, pyramids and mausoleums. Nothing was too grand or magnificent for him to propose."[2] Colbert's literary advisers reinforced this orientation. Jean Chapelain, a founding member of the Petite Académie, urged him to think about those "praiseworthy means of spreading and maintaining the glory of His Majesty, of which the ancients left us illustrious examples and which still summon respect in people's eyes, such as pyramids, columns, equestrian statues, colossi, triumphal arches, busts of marble and bronze, bas reliefs, all historic monuments."[3] Colbert heeded this advice and fixed his sights on commemorative monuments. Grandeur and magnificence were the oft-repeated watchwords of his building program, but what did these values mean in terms of a building style?[4] Obelisks and triumphal arches are straightforward set pieces, but how could he achieve architectural grandeur at the Louvre? The one thing Colbert knew in 1664 was that Le Vau's foundation plan did not provide the answer.

In the final scene of Paul Fréart de Chantelou's journal, Colbert explains his reasons for rejecting Bernini's Louvre design. The time is June 1668, and Colbert is clearly relieved that a resolution of the tortuous Louvre affair is at last at hand. The Petit Conseil—Le

Vau, Charles Le Brun, and Perrault—has taken charge, and the king has accepted their revised designs for the east and south wings of the Cour Carrée. Chantelou records the minister's parting words: "[Colbert] told me . . . [that] to house the king properly he was going to build out toward the river; he had been connected with buildings for so long that he was a good enough judge himself of what was needed; [and] he was very happy to have had the opportunity of telling me that he had not been influenced by others."[5]

With this unprompted defense of his independence and his judgment, Colbert unwittingly revealed the very fact that his words deny. Possessing a limited aptitude for architecture beyond his practical insights about programming, and having no real connoisseurship of design, Colbert relied extensively on advisers to bolster his unsteady judgment. He solicited the views of almost every important architect in France and Italy in 1664, when he sent Le Vau's foundation plan out for review. In addition to the Petite Académie, he consulted the Perrault brothers, mainstays of his inner circle, and Fréart de Chambray—men with whom Le Vau did not sympathize intellectually. The large number of designs Colbert commissioned, the changes of architect, the stop-and-go pace of construction—these are signs that Colbert was grappling with architectural problems he was still unable to resolve.

Granted, Colbert's well-known consultative methods are not necessarily a sign of insecurity; they arise in part from a corporate mentality that places more confidence in group work, like that of the Petit Conseil, than the solo flights of individual talents. It is wrong, however, to portray all of Colbert's outreach efforts as evidence of a directed vision, as if he knew exactly what he was searching for. Colbert's ideas about the Louvre took shape during this exploratory process, discovering by trial and error what path was appropriate to take. The Colonnade design in 1667 finally answered his uncertainty with a language of classical grandeur that Colbert comfortably embraced.

But the perception that Colbert broke with Le Vau in 1664 because the royal architect failed to satisfy his vision of the Louvre oversimplifies the dynamics of that decade. In fact, the two continued to collaborate productively throughout the 1660s, and Le Vau's work shifted in response to the changing cultural milieu. With no appreciable diminution of his workload after 1664, Le Vau remained in place as the king's first architect: he brought the Tuileries (1655–68) to completion, designed the Ménagerie at Versailles (1663–70), continued his oversight of other royal châteaux, worked on the east and south wings of the Louvre as a member of the Petit Conseil, designed the Versailles Enveloppe, and opened a gun foundry with Colbert's steadfast support. Moreover, he handled with deftness (as opposed to Gianlorenzo Bernini's disdain) all of Colbert's queries about programmatic and planning issues.[6] When Le Vau turned up in Colbert's company several times during Bernini's stay, Chantelou suspected that he had reemerged as one of Colbert's inside advisers.[7] But the strongest evidence of Le Vau's continuing importance to Colbert comes in the enlargement of the south wing of the Louvre in 1668.

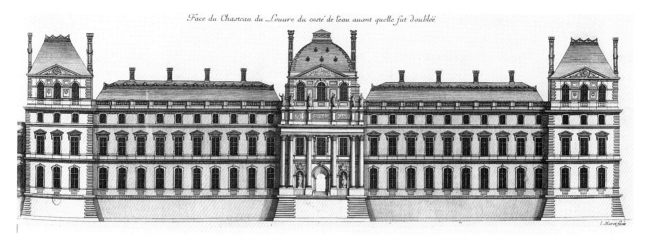

Face du Chasteau du Louure du costé de l'eau auant quelle fut Doublée

FIG. 94. *Louis Le Vau, river facade of the south wing of the Louvre, 1660–63 (destroyed). Engraving by Jean Marot. Département des Estampes, Bibliothèque Nationale de France, Paris*

The timing of Colbert's decision to rebuild the river wing seems curious at first. With the approval of the Colonnade in the previous year, Colbert was on the verge of realizing the century-old project of completing the Cour Carrée. Yet he unexpectedly decided to enlarge the scope of construction, notwithstanding two countervailing considerations: new construction would immure the river facade that Le Vau had completed in 1663, and the king was more interested in Versailles than in the Louvre. Colbert was greatly troubled by the latter development; in his view, Versailles merely served the king's private pleasures, whereas Paris was the measure of his glory.[8] That worry was what drove Colbert's building project: a splendid suite of rooms with a spectacularly improved view across the Seine was Colbert's last chance to contest the seductions of Versailles and lure the king back to work in Paris.[9]

We know that responsibility for the river extension fell to the Petit Conseil, but who among the trio bears chief responsibility for the design? Colbert's objectives in doubling the south wing essentially constituted a planning problem: provide the king with spacious rooms and knit them seamlessly to the old building. The task (which paralleled the intention of the Versailles Enveloppe) perfectly suited Le Vau, undisputed master of the art of planning. Even Bernini had admired the royal apartments Le Vau laid out at Vincennes, according to information Chantelou specifically relayed to Colbert and Louis XIV as proof that the hypercritical Italian admired a few things in France. "Bernini went into the king's rooms," Chantelou recounted, "and after looking at them passed into the queen's, remarking that it was a beautiful suite and the king was better accommodated there than in the Louvre."[10]

Despite two elevation drawings of the south facade by Le Vau's draftsman, François d'Orbay, historians have been reluctant to attribute to Le Vau a design that departs

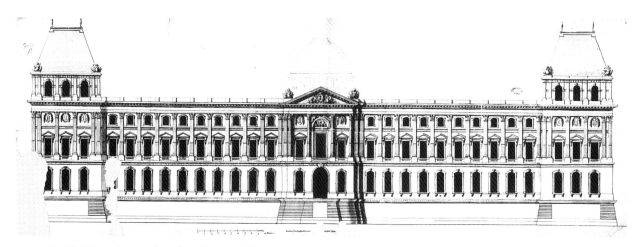

FIG. 95. *Louis Le Vau, project to enlarge the south wing of the Cour Carrée of the Louvre (river facade), 1668. Pen, ink, wash, and graphite on paper. Archives Nationales, Paris (O1 1667, no. 85)*

markedly from his first version. The character of the original facade, it is often forgotten, was set in the sixteenth century by Pierre Lescot (FIG. 94): Lescot designed the left (western) half of the range, and Le Vau matched it on the other side. His only original contribution was the central pavilion, where again he was constrained by the Pavillon de l'Horloge, Jacques Lemercier's western pavilion. Le Vau's domed pavilion has been criticized justifiably for its fussy decoration, but the main point of the design is his respectful revision of Lescot, which renders the tall end pavilions in a classical idiom and establishes a central focus on the long facade. Le Vau's approach, both here and at the Tuileries, where similar constraints applied, was to design in sympathy with the historic fabric and build on its symbolic associations.[11] This strategy of historical contextualism was cultivated at the French court—above all, at the Louvre, where preservation of the older buildings signified respect for the monarchy—a point lost on Bernini, who wanted to raze the old Louvre.

When Le Vau revisited the problem in 1668, the Colonnade had redefined the context—at the Louvre and in Colbert's mind. The only viable option was to echo the Colonnade design on the new adjoining wing. D'Orbay's elevation drawings show Le Vau's efforts to harmonize the two facades; the smooth ashlar base, swagged medallions, and colossal order of the second drawing show how far he had come (FIG. 95).[12] This drawing was subsequently revised to produce a still more unified and severe design in the executed facade (FIG. 96): instead of columns in the center, the building has only pilasters, and instead of tall pavilion roofs and a square dome, holdovers from the original building, the roofline is flat. Such revisions are the logical extension of the drawing, which captures an unresolved thought process. Indeed, the unfinished rendering of the dome stands for the transitional quality of this project, still in between the Renaissance pavilion system and the emergent model of a flat-roofed block.[13] Whether Le Vau was personally responsible for

FIG. 96. *Louis Le Vau, river facade of the Cour Carrée of the Louvre, 1668*

FIG. 97. *Louis Le Vau, garden facade of the Enveloppe, château of Versailles, begun 1668. Etching by Adam Pérelle. Département des Estampes, Bibliothèque Nationale de France, Paris*

the final revisions (as opposed to other members of the Petit Conseil or outside advisers) matters less than the revelation in the drawing of his thought in motion, harnessing his lifelong interest in the colossal order (from the Hôtel Lambert to Vincennes and the Hôtel de Lionne) to new architectural effects.

Two factors precipitated these changes: Colbert's equation of grandeur with imperial Roman forms and Le Vau's confrontation with Bernini in 1664 and 1665 which sparked his redesign of the Collège chapel. The latter encounter produced a rapprochement with Bernini's classical manner and enabled Le Vau to internalize aspects of Bernini's last Louvre design, the results of which we see most clearly in the Enveloppe at Versailles (begun in 1668), Le Vau's final building (FIG. 97). The Enveloppe eschews the segmented French pavilion system in favor of a uniform block, a uniformly articulated wall, and a flat roofline, where we find Le Vau's signature balustrade and urns set against the sky. Significantly, Le Vau did not evolve in a linear fashion; he offered classical and baroque schemes for Versailles within a period of a few months, as he had a decade earlier at Vincennes and Vaux-le-Vicomte. Le Vau was divided, an architect split in two, as he grappled with divergent approaches to the classical tradition. We cannot reckon with his oeuvre without granting him that duality and resourcefulness.

Emphasis is given here to Colbert's missteps and evolution, and to Le Vau's complexity and duality of styles, in order to break the static picture of French architecture and show that approaches to the classical tradition did, indeed, clash. Nevertheless, looking at the seventeenth century in general, a simple observation rings true: French architecture did not appear the same after Mazarin's Collège; Colbert set it on a visibly different path. His sponsorship of Roman classicism in Bourbon Paris produced a cultural rupture; and although Le Vau managed to cross the divide and make designs for the Louvre and Versailles in the new style, he nonetheless embodied the old, preacademic regime—from his roots as a mason, developer, and contractor to his affiliation with the tradition of French Renaissance design. Louis Le Vau and Mazarin's Collège may have helped Colbert define a new classical order, but it soon displaced them and left the architect's seminal contribution difficult to see—if only for the short term. After Colbert's death French architects eschewed the rigorous classicism he had promoted, and talents such as Jules Hardouin-Mansart and Robert de Cotte reclaimed the architecture of Louis Le Vau as touchstone and model. Ultimately Colbert and Le Vau represented opposite methods and solutions: whereas the minister championed a pure classicism imported from Rome and ideologically complete, the architect embraced a complex synthesis of building traditions that fused classical and baroque, French and Italian, past and present.

APPENDIX A

PROJECTS FOR MAZARIN'S TOMB

IN NOVEMBER 1657, after Bernini had declined to design Mazarin's tomb, Elpidio Benedetti sent the cardinal four tomb drawings from an unidentified designer. Benedetti boasted that the drawings "are by the most imaginative genius we have today and are of a quality even Bernini would envy," a claim that naturally brings to mind a talent like Borromini.[1] But that speculation can be dismissed now that three of the four drawings have been located in the Biblioteca Nazionale in Turin.[2]

FIG. 98. *Attributed to Elpidio Benedetti, project for a wall tomb for Jules Mazarin, ca. 1660. Pen, ink, and wash on paper. Biblioteca Nazionale di Torino (q. 165, dis. 154)*

One drawing headed "posato al muro" depicts a wall tomb (FIG. 98). Kneeling on a sarcophagus, the cardinal is flanked by winged figures of fame who herald his immortal feats. Just above him, Victory and Peace climb a stepped pyramid as they assemble Mazarin's coat of arms. One cherub tops it off with the cardinal's hat and ducal crown, while another cherub—holding an inscribed banderole under his arm—raises a cross and the funereal cloth of honor, which wraps around the curved niche.

Two other drawings depict the front and back of a freestanding tomb; "isolato" is written at the top of the frontal view (FIGS. 99–100).[3] Figures of Fame, Immortality, and Justice seem to raise the sarcophagus effortlessly, like the miraculous feat of the church fathers who lift Bernini's Cathedra Petri. In an explicit reference to Bernini's papal tombs, the artist included a seated skeleton who, while inscribing Mazarin's name in the book of death, is interrupted by Immortality, the right-hand figure with a serpent globe in hand and hourglass under foot; their exchange of glances reiterates the Berninian theme of truth triumphing over death, a fitting theme for the man demonized by the Fronde. The portrait medallion at the top of the tomb refers to the assumption of Mazarin's soul, while the historiated base narrates his deeds on earth in two scenes of peace-

FIG. 99. *Attributed to Elpidio Benedetti, project for a free-standing tomb for Jules Mazarin (front view), ca. 1660. Pen, ink, and wash on paper. Biblioteca Nazionale di Torino (q. I65, dis. I55)*

FIG. 100. *Attributed to Elpidio Benedetti, project for a free-standing tomb for Jules Mazarin (back view), ca. 1660. Pen, ink, and wash on paper. Biblioteca Nazionale di Torino (q. I65, dis. I56)*

keeping missions. (The parting of two armed camps on the plinth may refer to the battle of Casale.)

What can we say about the tomb designer? First, he was an amateur draftsman who had trouble conveying three-dimensional forms—the sarcophagus, for instance—and relating volumes in space, as suggested by the juxtaposition of the sarcophagus feet and maidens' arms. Second, the artist was well versed in the conventions of funerary architecture and inspired, in particular, by Bernini's tombs; the skeletal scribe, book of death, portrait medallion, and stepped pyramid with allegorical figures are among the motifs culled from Bernini's tombs for Urban VIII, Alexander VII, Maria Raggi, and Cardinal Pimentel. Third, the two designs, if not brilliant, are nonetheless skillful syntheses of current and long-established themes in funerary art; and there is even a touch of originality insofar as freestanding tombs were prohibited in Rome, and the artist had no direct local models for his second scheme.

Benedetti wanted to get Mazarin's attention; that would explain why he both exaggerated the skills of the artist and concealed his name. The anonymity makes sense only if the

FIG. 101. *Elpidio Benedetti, catafalque for Cardinal Mazarin, 1661. Etching by Domenico Barriere. Département des Estampes, Bibliothèque Nationale de France, Paris*

FIG. 102. *Elpidio Benedetti, catafalque for Anne of Austria, 1666. Reproduced from Benedetti,* Il mondo piangente *(Rome, 1666)*

artist were an amateur or relatively minor figure on the Roman scene, someone who obviously paled beside Bernini, whom the ambitious cardinal had wanted for his tomb. I believe the unidentified author of the tomb drawings is Elpidio Benedetti, and I base the attribution on three considerations: his other funerary designs; stylistic affinities between these sheets and a signed drawing by Benedetti; and Benedetti's handwriting.

To judge by his publications, Benedetti had a pronounced interest in funerary art. He published (in 1661) an illustrated account of Cardinal Mazarin's funeral in Rome and (in 1666) a similar pamphlet on the funeral of Anne of Austria with engravings of the funerary decorations that credit Benedetti as their "inventor."[4] For Mazarin's funeral, Benedetti dressed the facade of Santissimi Vincenzo e Anastasio with scenes of Mazarin's feats (the marriage of Louis XIV, which he brokered, and the truce at Casale) and with a winged skeleton, the fusion of Father Time and Death, which Bernini invented. Benedetti's catafalque for Mazarin elaborates the basic idea of the freestanding tomb of 1657 (FIG. 101); and there is further evidence of Benedetti's artistic evolution in the catafalque for Anne of Austria, where the sarcophagus and recurring skeletal figure of Father Time are set in an architectural frame—a work that probably involved an architect-collaborator, perhaps Gian Francesco Grimaldi, who assisted Benedetti on Mazarin's catafalque (FIG. 102). The catafalques have the same conceptual and artistic structures as the tomb projects for Mazarin, which reveal Benedetti's abilities at the start of his career in funerary decor.

The second piece of evidence is Benedetti's drawing of the Spanish Steps, dating from 1660. The circumstances of this submission parallel those of the tomb: after ruling out Bernini's participation, Benedetti sent Mazarin alternatives, including his own, which he recommended in the same boastful terms he used for the tomb drawings. In this case, however, Benedetti signed the 1660 drawing prominently, no longer fearful that his name would jeopardize the project (FIG. 103). Even if the underlying idea for the steps came from Bernini, as Tod Marder suggested, the drawing is in Benedetti's hand and bears a striking similarity to the tomb

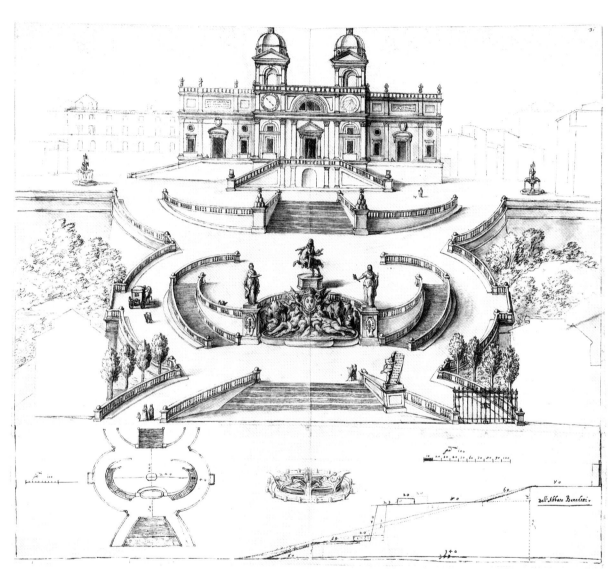

FIG. 103. *Elpidio Benedetti, project for steps on the Pincio, Rome, 1660. Pen and ink on paper. Biblioteca Apostolica Vaticana*

sheets.[5] Consider the use of wash, the draftsman's lack of mastery of scale and perspective, the representation of the stars on Mazarin's coat of arms, and the depiction of the standing female figures. In short, the drawings are awkward in comparable ways.

The third consideration is Benedetti's handwriting, admittedly a less reliable criterion because there is no way of proving that the same hand was responsible for the drawing and the text. Be that as it may, the long passage on figure 99, the freestanding tomb drawing, is identical to the inscription on figure 103, the Spanish Steps drawing, which is in Benedetti's hand.

The tomb drawings here attributed to Benedetti informed Maurizio Valperga's project for a catafalque for Mazarin (FIG. 104).[6] The catafalque combines a triangular base, a perforated domed structure with an obelisk on top, and an effigy of Mazarin beneath the dome—a skillful conflation of elements from Benedetti's tomb projects, the base coming from the freestanding project and the priant from the wall tomb. Valperga has, however, replaced Benedetti's oblong sarcophagus with a rounded form that more satisfactorily engages the rotating perspectives on the statue. The catafalque would have been designed shortly after Mazarin's death in March 1661; at that time Valperga may have consulted the unexecuted tomb projects, which would explain how the tomb drawings found their way into his

FIG. 104. *Maurizio Valperga, catafalque for Cardinal Mazarin, 1661. Pen, ink, and wash on paper. Biblioteca Nazionale di Torino (q. 165, dis. 150)*

album, now in Turin. The drawing was made in Paris; the watermark is French and the scale is in French feet. But the one misspelling betrays the Italian hand: the scale on the left reads "l'echelle dell'elevation."

Interestingly, there is no evidence that a catafalque for Mazarin was ever constructed in Paris. Despite the king's private outpouring of grief, the crown did not sponsor obsequies, and Valperga may have devised his scheme to stir interest at the highest levels in a tribute to the cardinal. Valperga had good reason to be loyal to Mazarin. The minister had lobbied for his release from a Neapolitan prison; when Valperga was set free in 1659,

Mazarin brought him back to Paris and employed him steadily on personal and royal projects at the French court.

Mazarin's corpse was moved from Vincennes to the Collège crypt in September 1684; after more than twenty years, the time had come to give him a proper tomb. Five years later the marquis de Louvois, who succeeded Colbert as minister-executor in charge of the foundation, commissioned a wall tomb that was installed in 1692 in the alcove opposite the student entrance to the church (FIG. 105). The sculptors Antoine Coysevox, Jean-Baptiste Tuby, and Etienne Le Hongre executed the design of Jules Hardouin Mansart who was faithful to the idea he had originally presented in 1676, when the Académie Royale d'Architecture convened in the church to discuss the tomb and its location.[7]

The tomb celebrates the cardinal's political leadership. Mazarin kneels beside a Victory, who holds a Roman fasces, the symbol of just rule in Mazarin's coat of arms. His pious gesture gains more spiritual force from the contrast of the white marble figures and the dark marbles and bronze around them. The three bronze allegorical figures at the base of the sarcophagus honor his worldly achievements as a statesman: on the left, Prudence holds the rudder of state that Mazarin had steered as royal minister; in the middle, Peace refers to the car-

FIG. 105. *Antoine Coysevox, Etienne Le Hongre, and Jean-Baptiste Tuby, tomb of Cardinal Mazarin, Collège des Quatre Nations, 1692*

dinal's diplomatic successes; and on the right, Fidelity holds the royal crown and arms to recall Mazarin's loyal service. Religion is consigned to the tympanum overhead, where Charity and Vigilance support the cardinal's escutcheon. The figure of Vigilance holds a Temple of Virtue, which may well be an allusion to the Collège des Quatre Nations.[8]

APPENDIX B

D'ORBAY'S DRAWINGS FOR THE SPANISH STEPS (1660)

SOON AFTER SIGNING the Peace of the Pyrenees, Cardinal Mazarin decided to erect a monument in honor of Louis XIV in Rome. In January 1660 he instructed Elpidio Benedetti to invite Gianlorenzo Bernini to design a monumental staircase at the foot of the French Minim church of Trinità dei Monti. Benedetti considered Bernini an inappropriate choice and supplied designs by François d'Orbay, Carlo Rainaldi, Giovanni Francesco Grimaldi, and himself. This chapter in the history of the Spanish Steps has been studied extensively; the objective here is to focus on the four drawings by d'Orbay, which record two different projects.[1]

Benedetti sent two drawings, a plan and corresponding elevation, to Paris in August 1660 (FIGS. 106–7). In a preliminary letter, Benedetti commended d'Orbay's project as "assai bello, nobile e magnifico," but the note he penned on the elevation was less enthusiastic: "This is the design of the young Frenchman Monsieur Orbais [sic], who was sent here by Monsieur Le Veau [sic] to work on the Trinità dei Monti. If he had rendered it

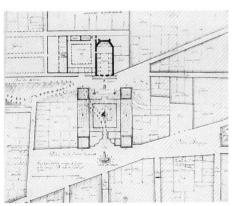

in perspective, it would have been more pleasing; this is evident also from the plan. The design is too extravagant and costly for a staircase."[2] Pairs of pavilions at the bottom and top of the stairs dominate the design and counterbalance the church. The staircase splits in front of a fountain, wraps around the perimeter of a square, and returns to the central axis in front of an equestrian statue of Louis XIV. The most striking aspect of the design is the uncompromising Frenchness of the architectural conception: the hierarchical arrangement of volumes, the vertical stress accentuated by the quoining, the mansard roofs, and the ornamental repertory—in particular, the wall busts omnipresent in Le Vau's oeuvre. These French characteristics suggest that d'Orbay prepared the design soon after arriving in Rome and before he absorbed anything from that city.

FIG. 106. *François d'Orbay, site plan of the Pincio with first scheme for steps, August 1660. Pen, ink, and wash on paper. Département des Estampes, Bibliothèque Nationale de France, Paris (Vb 132)*

In a letter to Mazarin of 16 August 1660, Benedetti advised him that d'Orbay's project was impractical and too expensive. Mazarin

FIG. 107. *François d'Orbay, elevation of the Trinità dei Monti and first project for steps on the Pincio, August 1660. Pen, ink, wash, and graphite on paper. Département des Estampes, Bibliothèque Nationale de France, Paris (Réserve B11)*

did not comment directly on the drawings, but he informed his agent that he preferred the design by Rainaldi.[3]

At a later point during his stay in Rome, d'Orbay prepared a revised design. Although the plan and elevation, which were published originally by Wolfgang Lotz, are neither signed nor mentioned by Benedetti, the drawings are unquestionably in d'Orbay's hand (FIGS. 108–9).[4] If the first project came on the heels of his arrival in Rome, the second one shows some signs of d'Orbay's encounter with Roman architecture. Having removed the pavilions and most of the sculptural ornament, d'Orbay built on tensions between solid walls and hollow niches, and between axial and diagonal forces. The staircase navigates around an octagon, a dynamic form that cuts the wall up into triangular wedges and undermines the stacked-up verticality of the first design, as do variations in the masonry. The levels alternate between surfaces of rocky stone—more fitting for a grotto—and smooth

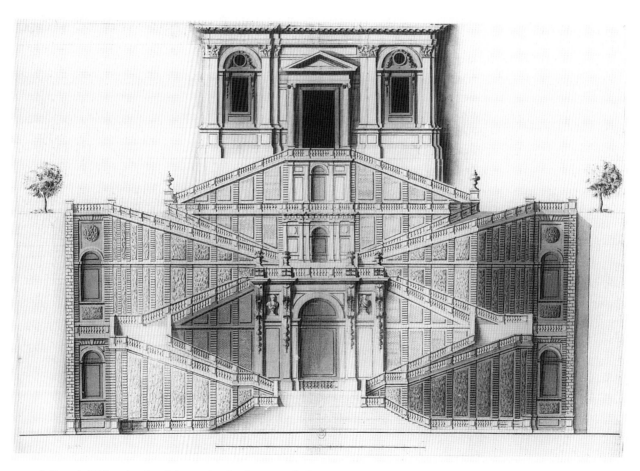

FIG. 108. *François d'Orbay, elevation of the second project for steps on the Pincio, 1660. Pen, ink, wash, and graphite on paper. Département des Estampes, Bibliothèque Nationale de France, Paris (Vb 132)*

panels of brick. As the wall rises, the overall effect is one of increasing simplicity; for instance, the decor of the niches on the central axis evolves from brackets and busts (at the base) to the Doric order and to un-adorned pilaster strips at the top. The forceful sim-plicity of that top niche, compared with any one in his first design, marks d'Orbay's evolution in Rome.

Noticeably, the second project no longer refers to Louis XIV; both the equestrian monument and the Bourbon arms are gone. On 1 November, Benedetti informed Mazarin that the idea of displaying a royal statue in a public space was raising hackles in Rome.[5] In addition to the evolution in d'Orbay's personal style, his second design reflects a programmatic change in the project. For these reasons, the two later drawings can be dated to the fall of 1660, October or November, when Mazarin's idea of the *scalinata* was beginning to unravel.

The two projects for the Spanish Steps are the only hard evidence we have of d'Orbay's response to Rome and his artistic formation. Despite the marked changes in the second design, d'Orbay remained more interested in the decorative effects of masonry than in the austere power of ancient Roman forms. The drawing still relates more to the terraces at Saint Germain-en-Laye than to those at Palestrina. D'Or-bay had grown considerably during his three or four months in Rome, but he fell far short of the classicist portrayed by his twentieth-century champion Albert Laprade. Laprade knew only the first design for the Spanish Steps, which he considered out of line with d'Orbay's true classicizing style. (Laprade considered

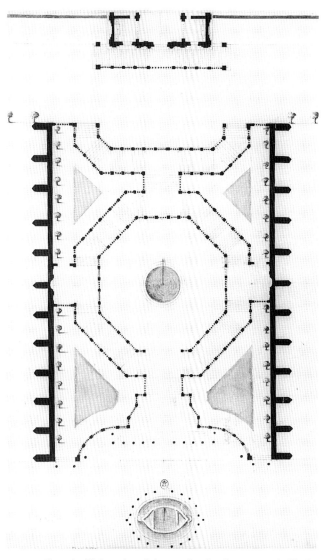

FIG. 109. *François d'Orbay, plan of the second project for steps on the Pincio, 1660. Pen, ink and wash on paper. Département des Estampes, Bibliothèque Na-tionale de France, Paris (Vb 132)*

the arch of triumph at Vincennes a work by d'Orbay, not Le Vau.) He also believed that d'Orbay played a key role in the making of French classicism over the next decade.[6] The second project for the Spanish steps dispels this image of François d'Orbay as an ardent classicist upon his return from Rome. At twenty-six he was a talented draftsman with much to learn about architectural design.

APPENDIX C

DRAWINGS OF MAZARIN'S COLLÈGE: A CHECKLIST

LE VAU STORED his architectural drawings—along with his books, building contracts, and financial papers—in his studio. The inventory after death indicates the number of items in a folder and the general topic; and although the date and signatories of some transactions are specified, no details about the drawings are provided other than the project name.

The drawings pertain to both private and royal commissions; there was no sharp separation between the two dimensions of Le Vau's career, at least in his lifetime, but the survival pattern of the drawings suggests that after Le Vau's death, the drawings for private and royal buildings were handled differently. A considerable number of drawings for royal buildings survive. After his death they probably remained in place at the Hôtel de Longueville, which subsequently became the official office of the Surintendance des Bâtiments, and in effect entered the royal archives. By contrast, relatively few drawings for private and municipal commissions (the *hôtels,* châteaux, and churches; the Châtelet; and the pump on the Pont Neuf) survive; neither Le Vau's family nor his clients were as successful in safeguarding the drawings.

The one exception was the Collège des Quatre Nations. The same historical self-consciousness that led Gomont to keep a journal of the building process served to protect Le Vau's drawings. As a result, we have more drawings of the Collège than of any other building by Le Vau. Alas, no working sketches survive—only finished presentation drawings, which were probably drafted by François d'Orbay. We know that Jules Hardouin-Mansart did not draw and relied on draftsmen in the royal building works. Whether this model applies to Le Vau remains unclear. Given his extensive responsibilities, Le Vau was surely too busy to assume the time-consuming task of preparing the finished drawings of the Collège, but that does not necessarily mean he did not draw at all. The drawings for the Collège are highly informative about Le Vau's thought process but not about his drawing style.

Le Vau presented five drawings at the decisive meeting on 21 January 1662, when Colbert approved his design for the Porte de Nesle site. According to the minutes, the drawings included a site plan, a ground plan of the foundation as a whole, a plan or elevation of the college, a plan or elevation of the church, and a plan or elevation of the library. I suspect that some of these were included among the nine drawings dated 13 August 1662, all of which were signed on the reverse by the duc Mazariny [*sic*]; Colbert; the masonry contractors Simon Lambert and Charles Thoison; two of the cardinal's executors, Guillaume de Lamoignon and Michel Le Tellier; and the notary François Le Fouyn. The drawings of August 1662, which were probably attached to the masonry contract, give a comprehensive picture of the starting point of the design process.

The following checklist organizes the drawings from the 1660s and 1670s by subject. Eleven drawings entered the collection of Robert de Cotte; de Cotte's inventory number is clearly visible in the corner of each. For further details on those drawings, see François Fossier, *Les dessins du fonds Robert de Cotte de la Bibliothèque Nationale de France: Architecture et décor* (Paris, 1997), 264–67.

THE SITE

1. Plan of the Seine between the Pont Neuf and the Louvre, 10 July 1662: AN M176, no. 44 (FIG. 28). Signed by the masonry experts who studied the width of the Seine and determined that the Quai Mazarin did not present a danger.

2. Site plan of the Tour de Nesle and environs, 23 June 1665: AN Cartes et Plans NIII Seine 710, no. 2 (FIG. 23). Duplicate: BN Est. Va443; Robert de Cotte 2581. Both plans are signed by Le Vau and representatives of the crown delegated to resolve problems arising from claims against the Collège for damages.

3. Site plan of the college and academy with preexisting buildings and shoreline shown in dotted lines, 23 June 1665: AN Cartes et Plans NIII Seine 710, no. 1 (FIG. 26). Signed by Le Vau and representatives of the crown delegated to resolve problems arising from claims against the Collège for damages.

4. Elevation of the Tour and Porte de Nesle, west facade, 23 June 1665: AN Cartes et Plans NIII Seine 710, no. 3. Signed by Le Vau and representatives of the crown deputized to resolve problems arising from claims against the Collège for damages.

5. Elevation of the Tour and Porte de Nesle, west facade: AN M176, no. 54. Signed by Le Vau and probably drawn in June 1665 at the same time as the preceding elevation. AN M176, no. 55, is a variant elevation.

6. Plan of property belonging to Henri de Guénégaud, 21 February 1665: AN M176, no. 35.

GENERAL PLANS

1. Site plan of the Collège with the Louvre and Pont de la Paix, 1660: Musée du Louvre, Département des Arts Graphiques, Recueil du Louvre I, fol. 21 (FIG. 17).

2. First-floor plan of the college and site plan of the academy: BN Est. Va443; Robert de Cotte 2582 (FIG. 27). The plan has two distinguishing features: preexisting buildings on the site are shown in outline, and the quay has a curved projection into the Seine, a detail that indicates the plan antedates 13 August 1662.

3. Ground plan of the college and academy with straight quay, 13 August 1662: AN M176, no. 52 (FIG. 30).

4. First-floor plan of the college and academy with a straight quay, 13 August 1662: AN Cartes et Plans NIII Seine 710, no. 4 (FIG. 38).

5. Foundation plan, 28 November 1664: AN M176, no. 53 (FIG. 82); duplicate: AN M176, no. 51. Signed on the recto by Le Vau, the controller Meurset de La Tour, the masonry contractors Thoison and Lambert, and a notary.

7. Ground plan of the Collège, Louvre, and Tuileries, c. 1665: AN F21 3567/9 (FIG. 80). The plan of the Collège was copied from an earlier plan and was out of date when this plan was drawn.

THE CHURCH

SCHEME I, AUGUST 1662

1. Elevation of the church facade, western concave wing, and pavilion, 13 August 1662: AN M176, no. 4 (FIG. 62).

2. Ground plan of the church, 13 August 1662: AN M176, no. 37 (FIG. 58). The plan reflects a slight modification in the shape of the porch, which is rectangular in the general plans (nos. 3–4 above) and here has canted corners.

3. Half foundation plan and half plan of the upper walls of the church, 13 August 1662: AN M176, no. 11. A duplicate plan is marked on the verso "fourny par Mons. Lambert": AN M176, no. 21. The plans were meant to provide guidance for the *toisé*.

4. Longitudinal section of the church, facing west, 13 August 1662: AN M176, no. 9 (FIG. 51).

5. Transverse section through the dome and chancel, 13 August 1662: AN M176, no. 18 (FIG. 66).

SCHEME II, HERE DATED 1664–65

1. Elevation of the church facade: AN M176, no. 24 (FIG. 64).

2. Longitudinal section, facing east: AN M176, no. 32 (FIG. 52).

3. Transverse section, facing the high altar: AN M176, no. 14 (FIG. 67).

SCHEME III, HERE DATED 1664–65

1. Longitudinal section, facing east: AN M176, no. 25.

2. Transverse section, facing the high altar: AN M176, no. 26 (FIG. 69).

3. Section through the lantern and dome, in front of the high altar: Musée du Louvre, Département des Arts Graphiques, Inv. 30249 (FIG. 53).

4. Half plan, east side with college entrance, September 1665: AN M176, no. 38.

EXECUTED DESIGN, 1665

1. Elevation of the church facade, after 1673: BN Est. Va261 fol. 10; Robert de Cotte 910 (FIG. 65). Claude Perrault devised the entablature inscription in 1673.

2. Elevation of the church facade: BN Est. Va261, fol. 11. An unfinished variant of the preceding elevation.

3. Ground plan of the church: BN Est. Va261, fol. 22; Robert de Cotte 907 (FIG. 49).

4. Plan of the church at the level of the dome, 1670s: AN M176, no. 45 (FIG. 46). Mazarin's tomb is sketched under the dome, and the sculptors of the facade statues are identified.

5. Ground plan of the church and partial paving plan, 15 March 1684: Musée du Louvre, Département des Arts Graphiques, Inv. 30299 (FIG. 57).

6. Ground plan with superimposed plan of the dome and vaults, c. 1680: BN Est. Va261, fol. 21; Robert de Cotte 906. Mazarin's tomb appears in its wall niche.

7. Longitudinal section, facing east, 1670s: BN Est. Va261c, fol. 4; Robert de Cotte 912 (FIG. 71).

8. Longitudinal section facing east, 15 March 1684: Musée du Louvre, Département des Arts Graphiques, Inv. 30294.

9. Transverse section, facing the high altar, 1670s: BN Est. Va261c, fol. 5; Robert de Cotte 911 (FIG. 70).

THE BIBLIOTHÈQUE MAZARINE

1. Elevation of the east facade of the Bibliothèque Mazarine, facing the Pont Neuf, 13 August 1662: AN M176, no. 42.

2. First-floor plan of the library and adjoining concave wing: AN M176, no. 36.

3. Ground plan of the western concave wing: AN M176, no. 46

4. Section and plan of the shops below the Bibliothèque Mazarine: AN M176, no. 39

COLLEGE BUILDINGS

1. Elevation of the wing between the two courtyards, south facade, c. 1663: AN M176, no. 31. The drawing predates the economizing decision not to build a wing on the east side of the rectangular courtyard.

2. Elevation of the rue Mazarine wing, west facade: AN M176, no. 30.

3. Elevation of the buildings along the rue Mazarine, east facades: Bibliothèque de l'Institut MS. 1039, no. 22.

4. Elevation of the entrance to the first courtyard from the Place Mazarine, AN M176, no. 22. Three flaps show alternative designs for the ornament and inscription above the portal.

5. Elevation of the grill between the two courtyards, 22 September 1673: BN Est. Va261b; Robert de Cotte 2584.

6. Ground plan of the wing between the first and second courtyard: AN M176, no. 47.

THE PLACE MAZARINE

1. Plan of executed scheme with dimensions: BN Est. Va261 fol. 19; Robert de Cotte 908.

2. Partial elevation of the Quai Mazarin and plan of the Place Mazarine, 13 August 1662: AN M176, no. 43 (FIG. 81).

3. Plan with a project for a pedestal and parapet, 1670s: BN Est. Va261; Robert de Cotte 909. According to Fossier (*Dessins du fonds*), the drawing relates to a project to erect an equestrian statue to Louis XIV.

HOUSES ON THE RUE MAZARINE

1. Plan, section, and elevation of the houses on the rue Mazarine. BN Est. Va263d; Robert de Cotte 2583 (FIG. 31).

LOUIS LE VAU'S LIBRARY: THE INVENTORY

EDITORIAL NOTES

After Le Vau's death, his heirs engaged two notaries to take an inventory of the contents of his house. For the library they turned to two booksellers qualified to appraise the books. The inventory of the library consists of a numbered list with abbreviated titles for some items, the format of the publications, and their appraised value in *livres tournois* (LT) and *sols* (s).

Each entry has been transcribed without modernizing the spelling or punctuation. It is followed by bibliographical information: author, title, and publication date. Rather than list the first edition of the book, I have identified the edition (or editions) matching the format of Le Vau's copy. In cases of such a match, the format and number of volumes are not repeated in the modern bibliographical data. But in many instances it is impossible to determine the particular edition Le Vau owned; there are multiple editions in the appropriate format, often with several different publishers. For that reason and for the sake of consistency, the names of publishers have been omitted. To shed light on his collecting preferences, however, I have tried to indicate whether the books Le Vau owned in folio editions were available also in smaller formats.

Ascertaining the author's name was the key to identifying Le Vau's books. In many cases the inventory does not supply the author's name, but even if it does the name can be truncated and misspelled, at least by modern bibliographical standards. I relied on a number of bibliographical reference works, short-title catalogues of French and Italian books in the British Library, and general catalogues of several libraries—above all, the Bibliothèque Nationale (Paris)—in the research process; these sources are cited in the bibliography.

Two sets of numbers appear below. The inventory number appears beside the transcribed short title. The assessors typically grouped several titles by the same author under a single inventory number; for instance, no. 91 covers four different books by Jacques Androuet Ducerceau. As a result, the final inventory number, 203, does not correspond to the total number of books in the library. In order to determine the actual size of Le Vau's collection, the number in square brackets provides a running tally of book titles, as opposed to volumes, thus the five-volume edition of *Astrée* counts as one book. The inventory identifies 182 separate titles.

The problem is that we do not know how many titles were included in the unidentified multivolume packets at the end of the inventory. I made the assumption that each unidentified packet (nos. 165–83 and 190–203) contained half as many titles as volumes. If the packet comprised one series, I reasoned, the booksellers would have mentioned the series title, as they did with packets 184–89. The small format of the packets, however, made it likely that any title had at least two volumes. If, on the one hand, every anonymous packet actually comprised one multivolume title, which seems unlikely, then I have overestimated the number of books in Le Vau's library by 95. On the other, if each packet comprised as many titles as volumes, then I have underestimated the total by a slightly larger figure. The inventory fails to specify the number of volumes in packets 182 and 203; I supplied estimates consistent with the size of the surrounding packets.

These uncertainties underscore the fact that the total of 308 books calculated here is only an approximate figure; depending on how the unidentified packets are counted, the number of titles might range from 212 to 486. This warning applies to other libraries as well. The scholars whose work I cited in chapter 3 inevitably used different methods of calculating library size, but their procedures and assumptions are rarely made explicit.

Very few inventories of architects' libraries have been published; none has been edited properly. It is hoped that the publication of this book list will facilitate research into other architects' libraries and aid future scholars in tracking down the particular books Le Vau owned, some of which are probably deposited in French libraries and may well be covered with his marginalia.

THE INVENTORY
Inventaire prissé et estimation des livres de la Bibliotheque de feu Mr Le Vau, conseiller du Roy, secretaire et premier architecte de ses bastimens.

LIVRES IN FOLIO

[1]   1. Biblia sacra gotique in folio 1 LT
      A Latin Bible.

[2]   2. Vilalpendus in Ezechielem en trois volumes in folio prisé dix livres 10 LT
      Prado, Jeronimo de, and Juan Bautista Villapando. Hieronimi Pradii et Joannis Baptistae Villapandi . . . In Ezechielem explicationes et apparatus urbis ac templi Hierosolymitani commentariis et imaginibus illustratus. *Rome, 1596–1604.*

[3]   3. Bible en francois in folio paris du puys 8 LT

The brothers Jacques and Pierre Dupuy edited, compiled, and translated numerous seventeenth-century publications, including perhaps this French Bible.

[4]   4. Sancti Augustini de civitate dei in folio 2 LT

Augustine, Saint. D. Aurelii Augustini, . . . de Civitate Dei libri XXII . . . cum commentariis novis et perpetuis R. P. Leonardi Coquaei . . . et Joa. Lud. Vivis. *Paris, 1613.*
Cited above is the only seventeenth-century Latin edition in folio of The City of God *published before Le Vau's death (he might have owned an earlier edition).*

[5]   5. St. Augustin de la Cite de Dieu in folio 2 LT

Augustine, Saint. De la Cité de Dieu, traduite par le sieur de Ceriziers, ... *Paris, 1655.*
Alternatively, Le Vau might have owned the 1585 French edition.

[6]   6. Summa Sancti Tomae en trois volumes folio 3 LT

A Latin edition of writings of Saint Thomas Aquinas, probably the Summa Theologiae.

[7]   7. Summa Becani in folio 2 LT 10 s

Becanus, Père Martinus. Summa theologiae scholasticae, authore R. P. Martino Becano. . . . *Paris, 1634; 2d ed., 1666.*

[8]   8. Laymani Teologiae in folio 3 LT

Laymann, Père Paul. R. P. Pauli Laymann, . . . Theologia moralis in quinque libros distributa. Editio tertia. . . . *Antwerp, 1634.*
Other folio editions were published in 1642, 1653, and 1664.

[9]   9. Praxia Reginaldi in folio 2 LT

Regnault, Père Valère. Praxis fori poenitentialis ad directionem confessarii in usum sacri sui muneris, auctore P. Valerio Reginaldo. . . . *Cologne, 1626.*

[10]   10. Lessiue de Justitia et Jure in folio 1 LT 10 s

Lessius, Leonardus [Père Leonard Leys]. De Justitia et jure caeterisque virtutibus cardinalibus libri quator. *Louvain, 1605.*

[11]   11. Chrisostomi Homilioe in folio 1 LT

Chrysostom, Saint John. Sancti Christosomi Homiliae et Commentarii in Psalm. David. . . . *Paris, 1614.*
The short title does not specify the subject of the homilies; I selected the volume that matches the format of Le Vau's copy.

[12]   12. Perez de Valentia in psalmoe in folio 1 LT

Perez de Valentia, Jacob. I. Parez de Valentia expositiones in Psalmos Davidicos. *Paris, 1521. The second edition has a variant title that is slightly closer to the short title of the inventory:* Jacobi Perez de Valentia . . . In psalmos davidicos lucubratissima expositio. . . . *Paris, 1533.*

[13]   13. Oeuvres de Coeffeteau in folio 1 LT 10 S

Coëffeteau, Nicolas. Oeuvres de R. P. en Dieu F. Nic. Coëffeteau, . . . contenant un nouveau Traicté des noms de l'Eucharistie, auquel est refuté tout ce que les Srs Du Plessis, Casaubon et M. Pierre Du Moulin, ministre de Charenton, ont escrit sur ce sujet contre la doctrine de l'Eglise, avec divers autres traictez ci-devant publiez par le mesme autheur. *Paris, 1622.*

[14]   14. Oeuvres de Sales in folio pouris 1 LT

François de Sales, Saint. Les Oeuvres de messire François de Sales. . . . *Toulouse, 1637.*

[15]   15. Une idem in folio 3 LT 10 S

Père Nicolas Talon brought out an enlarged edition, with a slightly revised title, Les Oeuvres de bienheureux François de Sales, *in Paris, 1641. Le Vau's second copy was probably this edition, which was reissued in 1647 and 1652.*

[16]   16. Histoire eclesiastique de Nicefore in folio 2 LT

Calliste, Nicéphore. L'Histoire ecclésiastique de Nicéphore, fils de Calliste Xantouplois, . . . traduicte nouvellement de latin en françois . . . de nouveau corrigée et mise en meilleur françois qu'auparavant, par deux docteurs en la faculté de théologie à Paris. *Paris, 1586.*

[17]   17. Histoire de Josephe in folio 2 LT 10 S

Josephus, Flavius. Histoire de Fl. Josèphe . . . escrite premièrement par l'auteur en langue grecque et nouvellement traduite en françois par François Bourgoing . . . *Lyons, 1562. The first French edition, cited above, was supplanted by a new translation by D. Gilb. Genebrard in 1578; it was republished numerous times in the seventeenth century.*

[18]   18. Histoire de lesglise par M. Godeau en deux volumes in folio 9 LT

Godeau, Antoine. Histoire de l'Eglise, par Mr. Antoine Godeau, . . . Nouvelle edition . . . augmentée. *Paris, 1653–78. Le Vau presumably owned the first two volumes of the five-volume edition cited here.*

19. [No entry]

[19]   20. Calepini dictionarium sixto linguae in folio 3 LT

Calepinus, Ambrosius. Ambrosii Calepini Dictionarium octolingue. *Paris, 1609. Originally published in 1514, the dictionary went through numerous editions; none, however, refers to only six languages, as in the inventory. Most editions cover eight languages, as in the first seventeenth-century edition cited above.*

[20]   21. Histoire de France par de Sere in folio 3 LT
Serres, Jean de. Inventaire général de l'histoire de France depuis Pharamond jusques à present . . . par Jean de Serres. *Paris, 1627.*

[21]   22. Histoire de France par du Hallien in folio 2 LT
Girard, Bernard de, seigneur Du Hallian. L'Histoire de France. . . . *Paris, 1576.*
A six-volume edition was published in octavo in 1585.

[22]   23. Les Memoires du Tillet in folio 1 LT
Du Tillet, Jean. Les Mémoires et recherches de Jean Du Tillet . . . contenans plusieurs choses mémorables pour l'intelligence de l'estat des affaires de France. *Rouen, 1578.*

24. La France metalique et le portrait des Roys de France en deux volumes in folio, manque une volume 7 LT
[23]   *Bié, Jacques de.* La France métallique, contenant les actions célèbres tant publiques que privées des rois et des reines remarquées en leurs médailles d'or, d'argent et de bronze. . . . *Paris, 1636.*
[24]   *Bié, Jacques de.* Les Vrais Portraits des rois de France, tirez de ce qui nous reste de leurs monumens, sceaux, médailles ou autres effigies. . . . *Paris, 1634; 2d ed., 1636.*

[subtotal:] 72 LT 10 S

[25]   25. Histoire des guerres civiles de France par Davilla en deux volumes in folio 8 LT
Davila, Enrico Caterino. Histoire des guerres civiles de France, contenant tout ce qui s'est passé de mémorable en France jusqu'à la paix de Vervins, depuis le règne de Francois II écrites en Italien par Davila, mises en français par Baudoin. *Paris, 1644; 2d ed., Paris, 1647.*

[26]   26. Le ceremonial francois par Godefroy en deux volumes in folio 10 LT
Godefroy, Théodore. Le Cérémonial françois. *Paris, 1649.*

[27]   27. Histoire des Cardinaux francois par Mr du Chesne en deux volumes in folio 12 LT
Du Chesne, François. Histoire de tous les cardinaux françois de naissance ou qui ont esté promeus au cardinalat par l'expresse recommandation de nos roys pour les grands services qu'ils ont rendus à leur Estat et à leur couronne. . . . *Paris, 1660.*

[28]   28. Histoire des Papes par M. du Chesne en deux volumes in folio 4 LT

Du Chesne, André. Histoire des Papes et souverains chefs de l'Eglise, depuis S. Pierre, premier pontife romain . . . augmentée en cette dernière édition jusques à présent 1645. *Paris, 1645.*

[29]   29. Recherche de la France par Pasquier folio 3 LT

Des Recherches de la France, *by Etienne Pasquier, comprised two books originally published in 1560 and 1567, respectively, and combined in a folio edition of 1621; a third book was added in 1633. Le Vau probably owned one of the seventeenth-century editions—1633, 1643, or 1665— which included further additions.*

30. Les Antiquitez et Anale de Paris en deux volumes in folio 6 LT

[30]   *Malingre, Claude.* Les Antiquitez de la ville de Paris, contenans la recherche nouvelle des fondations et establissemens des eglises . . . la chronologie des premiers présidens, advocats et procureurs généraux du Parlement, prévosts gardes de la prévosté . . . prévosts des marchands et eschevins de la diteville. . . . *Paris, 1640.*

[31]   *Malingre, Claude.* Les Annales générales de la ville de Paris, représentant tout ce que l'histoire a peu remarquer de ce qui s'est passé . . . en icelle. *Paris, 1640.*

[32]   31. La Pucelle de Mr. Chapelin in folio 2 LT 10 s

Chapelain, Jean. La Pucelle ou la France délivrée, poeme héroique. *Paris, 1656.*

[33]   32. Les oeuvres de Plutarque en quatre volume 10 LT

This is probably an edition of Plutarch's Les oeuvres morales *translated by Jacques Aymot.*

[34]   33. Les hommes illustres de André Teues en deux volume in folio 16 LT

Thevet, André. Pourtraits et vies des Hommes illustres Grecz, Latin, et Payens. . . . *Paris, 1584.*

[35]   34. Histoire de Malthe en deux volume in folio 8 LT

Baudouin, Jean. Historie de Malte avec les statuts et les ordonnances de l'ordre. *Paris, 1659*

[36]   35. Histoire dEspagne par Turques en deux volumes in folio 10 LT

Turquet de Mayerne, Louis. Histoire générale d'Espagne, comprise en XXX livres . . . jusqu'à la conquête du royaume de Portugal faicte par Philippe IIe. . . . *Paris, 1635*
The original edition of 1587 (one volume in folio) was followed in 1608 by a two-volume folio edition. Given the format of Le Vau's copy, he would have owned either the 1608 or the 1635 edition.

[37] 36. Histoire des pays-bas par Metteran fol. 5 LT

Meteren, Emanuel van. L'Histoire des Pays-Bas, d'Emanuel de Meteren, ou Recueil des guerres et choses mémorables advenues tant es dits pays qu'es pays voysins depuis l'an 1315 jusques à l'an 1612. . . . *Traduit de flamend en françois par IDL Haije [Jean de La Haye] . . . avec la vie de l'autheur. The Hague, 1618.*

[38] 37. Histoire d'Angleterre in folio 4 LT

Du Chesne, André. Histoire générale d'Angleterre, d'Ecosse et d'Irlande. . . . *Paris, 1614. Le Vau might have owned one of the later editions (Paris, 1634 and 1641), which were printed also in folio.*

[39] 38. Histoire des Turcs par Viginere en deux volumes in folio 6 LT

Chalcondyle [Laonicus]. L'Histoire générale des Turcs, contentant l'Histoire de Chalcondyle, traduite par Blaise de Vigenaire, avec les illustrations de mesme autheur et continuée jusques en . . . 1612 par Thomas Artus et . . . par le Sr de Mézeray jusques en . . . 1612. *Paris, 1662.*

[40] 39. Histoire Romaine par Dupleix 3 vols. 12 LT

Dupleix, Scipion. Histoire romaine depuis la fondation de Rome. *Paris, 1638–44.*

[41] 40. Le Monde par Davity en quatre volume 10 LT

Avity, Pierre d', seigneur de Montartin. Le Monde, ou la Description générale de ses quatre parties, avec tous ses empires, royaumes, estats et républiques . . . avec un discours universel comprenant les considérations générales du monde celeste et terrestre. . . . *Paris, 1643.*

[42] 41. Histoire de Pline en deux volume in folio 4 LT 10 s

Pliny the Elder. L'Histoire du monde de C. Pline Second . . . A quoy a esté adjousté un traité des prix et mesures antiques réduites à la facon des françois . . . Le tout mis en françois par Antoine Du Pinet. . . . *Lyons, 1566.*
The first French translation (Lyons, 1562) appeared in one volume. The two-volume format of Le Vau's copy corresponds with the edition of 1566 cited above or that of 1581. A new edition in 1615 reverted to the one-volume format.

[43] 42. Les Triomphe de Louis le Juste par Valdor in folio 7 LT

Valdor, Jean. Les Triomphes de Louis le Juste XIII du nom . . . contenans les plus grandes actions où Sa Majesté s'est trouvée en personne, representées en figures aenigmatiques exposés par un poème héroique de Charles Beys et accompagnées de vers françois sous chaque figure, composez par P. de Corneille. Avec les portraits des roys, princes et généraux d'armées qui ont assisté ou servy ce belliqueux Louis le Juste combattant, et leurs devises et expositions en formes d'éloges, par Henry Estienne. . . . Ensemble le plan des villes sièges et batailles. . . . Le tout traduit en latin par le R. P. Nicolai . . . ouvrage entrepris et finy par Jean Valdor. *Paris, 1649.*

[44]   43. La Cosmographie de Belleforest en trois volume in folio 8 LT
Belleforest, François de. La Cosmographie universelle de tout le monde. . . . *Paris, 1575.*
This two-volume format differs from Le Vau's copy.

[45]   44. Tite live par Blaise de Vigenere en deux volume in folio 5 LT
Livy. Les Décades . . . mises en langue françoise la 1re par Blaise de Vigenere. . . . *Paris, 1606.*
Le Vau owned either the first edition or the second edition in 1616 or 1617.

[subtotal:] 151 LT

[46]   45. La Mere des Histoire in folio 1 LT 10 S

[47]   46. La Mithologie des Dieux in folio 6 LT
Conti, Natale. Mythologie, ou Explication des fables contenant les généalogies des dieux . . . cy devant traduite par J. de Montlyard. Exactement revue en cette dernière édition et augmentée . . . par J. Baudouin. *Paris, 1627.*

[48]   47. Les Metamorphose dOvide par Renoüar 3 LT
Ovid. Les Métamorphoses d'Ovide, de nouveau traduittes en prose françois par Nicolas Renouard. *Paris, 1619, 1637, 1651.*
Numerous editions of Renouard's translation were published in the seventeenth century. Le Vau probably owned a folio edition of the book, which was originally published in octavo. The inventory does not specify the format, but the entry appears among other folio editions.

[49]   48. Les Lettres du Cardinal dOssat in folio 1 LT
Ossat, Cardinal Arnaud d'. Lettres de l'illustrissime . . . cardinal d'Ossat . . . au roy Henri le Grand et à M. de Villeroy depuis l'année 1594 jusques à l'année 1604. *Paris, 1624.*

[50]   49. Les Oeuvres de Corneille Tacite par Le Maistre in folio 1 LT
Tacitus. Les Oeuvres de C. Tacite. Traduction nouvelle augmentée des six derniers livres des Annales de supplémens et annotations . . . et ensemble des vies de Tite Vespasian, Nerva, Trajan, avec un bref traitté des monnoyes romaines. Le tout par Rodolphe le Maistre. *Paris, 1636.*
The first edition of 1627 was not in folio and did not include the treatise on coins.

[51]   50. Les Essays de Michel sr de Montagne 2 LT

      Montaigne, Michel de. Les Essais de Michel seigneur de Montagne, édition nouvelle trouvée
après le décéds de l'autheur, reveüe et augmentée par luy. . . . *Paris, 1595.*
*The essays were published originally in 1580; cited above is the first folio edition. Later folio
editions appeared in 1640, 1652, and 1657.*

[52]   51. Les Hyerogliphique de Pierius in folio 2 LT

      Bolzani, Giovanni Pierio Valeriano. Les Hiéroglyphiques de Jan Pierre Valerian,
vulgairement nommé Pierius, autrement Commentaires des lettres et figures sacrées des
Aegyptiens et autres nations, oeuvre réduicte en cinquante huict livres ausquels sont
adjoincts deux autres de Coelius Curio, touchant ce qui est signifié par les diverses effigies et
pourtraicts des dieux et des hommes, nouvellement donnez aux François par J. de
Montlyard. . . . *Lyons, 1615.*

[53]   52. Larmonie du Monde par George Venitien in folio 2 LT

      Giorgio, Francesco. L'armonie du monde divisée en trois cantiques. Oeuvre . . .
premièrement composé en latin par François Georges Venitien & depuis traduict & illustré
par Guy Le Fèvre de La Boderie . . . Plus l'heptaple de Jean Picus comte de la Mirande
translaté par Nicolas Le Fèvre de La Boderie. *Paris, 1578.*

[54]   53. Les oeuvres de Seneque par Chalues in folio 1 LT 10 s

      Seneca. Les Oeuvres de L. Annaeus Seneca, mises en françois par Mathieu de Chalvet &
augmentées. . . . *Paris, 1638.*
Earlier folio editions appeared in 1604, 1616, and 1624.

[55]   54. Les oeuvres de du Bartas in folio 1 LT 10 s

      Du Bartas, Guillaume de Saluste. Les Oeuvres de G. de Saluste, sr Du Bartas, reveües,
corrigées, augmentées de nouveaux commentaires, . . . Plus a esté adjousté la première et
seconde partie de la suitte, avecq l'argument général et amples sommaires au
commencement de chacun livre par S. G. S. *[Goulart]*. . . . *Paris, 1610–11.*
*Several earlier editions were published in smaller formats; the copy cited above is the first one in
folio.*

[56]   55. La Religion des Anciens Romains par Du Choul in folio 2 LT

      Du Choul, Guillaume. De la Religion des anciens Romains. *Lyons, 1556.*

[57]   56. Les figure de la Bible du Bé in folio 2 LT

      Cousin, Jean. Figures des histoires de la Saincte Bible. . . . *Paris, 1635.*

This volume, the third edition of Cousin's woodcut illustrations, was published by Guillaume Lebé II. An identical edition was published by Guillaume Lebé III in 1643 and reprinted in 1660.

[58]   57. Les Oeuvres de Ronsar en deux volumes 3 LT

Ronsard, Pierre de. Les Oeuvres de Pierre de Ronsard . . . reveues et augmentées et illustrées de commentaires et remarques [par M.-A. Muret et N. Richelet]. *Paris, 1623.*

Although there were many earlier editions of Ronsard, only the 1623 edition matched the format of Le Vau's copy.

[59]   58. Les oeuvres de Mr La Motte Le Vayer en deux volumes in folio 9 LT

De La Mothe Le Vayer, François. Oeuvres de François de La Mothe Le Vayer. *Paris, 1654.*

[60]   59. La Cronologie de la Peyre, grand papier 3 LT

Auxoles, Jacques d', sieur de Lapeyre. La Saincte Chronologie du monde. . . . *Paris, 1632.*

A pendant study by d'Auxoles, La Saincte Géographie *(Paris, 1629), was issued both in folio and on "grand papier." It appears that the same was true of* La Saincte Chronologie, *although the Bibliothèque Nationale catalogue mentions only the folio edition.*

[61]   60. Les Aliance genealogique de Paradin in fol 2 LT

Paradin, Claude. Alliances généalogiques des rois et princes de Gaule. *Lyons, 1561.*

[62]   61. Manuscript des Interest d'Espagne in fol 3 LT

[63]   62. La Musse historique de Loretts en deux volumes in folio 5 LT

Loret, Jean. La Muze historique, ou Recueil des lettres en vers contenant les nouvelles du temps, écrites à Son Altesse Mademoizelle de Longueville. *Paris, 1658–65.*

The Bibliothèque Nationale catalogue does not mention a folio edition in two volumes, the format of Le Vau's copy. The first folio edition, in one volume, appeared in 1658 and 1659.

[64]   63. Les Oeuvres d'Ambroise Paré in folio 3 LT

Paré, Ambroise. Les Oeuvres d'Ambroise Paré . . . divisées en 27 livres, avec les figures et portraicts, tant de l'anatomie que des instruments de chirurgie, et de plusieurs monstres, reveuz et augmentez par l'autheur pour la seconde édition. *Paris, 1579.*

Originally published in 1575, Paré's works went through many editions; I have cited the first folio edition above; however, Le Vau may well have owned a later, seventeenth-century edition—for example, the ninth edition of 1633 or the eleventh edition of 1652. (The Bibliothèque Nationale catalogue does not mention the tenth edition.)

[65] 64. Les Oeuvres de du Laurens in folio 3 LT

Du Laurens, André. Toutes les Oeuvres de Me André Du Laurens, sieur de Ferrières, . . . traduites de latin en françois par Mᶜ Théophile Gelée . . . reveues, corrigées et augmentées . . . par G. Sauvageon. . . . *Paris, 1639 and 1646.*

An earlier edition, prior to Sauvageon's revision, was published in Rouen in 1621.

[66] 65. Mathiole des plants in folio 1 LT

Mattioli, Pietro Andrea. Commentaires de M. Pierre André Matthiolus, . . . sur les six livres de Pedacius Dioscoride . . . de la matière médicinale, traduits de latin en françois par M. Antoine Du Pinet. . . . *Lyons, 1572.*

Originally published in Latin in 1554, the French translation was republished numerous times in the seventeenth century.

[67] 66. Le Coustumier general 1635 en deux volumes in folio 9 LT

Les Coustumes générales et particulières de France et des Gaules, corrigées et annotées de . . . décisions . . . & autres choses . . . par M. Charles du Moulin . . . augmentées . . . par Gabriel Michel. *Paris, 1635*

[68] 67. Le Code Henry Quatre 1615 in folio 3 LT

Le Code du très-chrestien et très-victorieux Roy de France . . . Henry IIII. Du droit civil iadis descrit, à nous délaissée . . . par . . . Justinian. . . . Dernière edition. *Rouen, 1615.*

The format differs from Le Vau's copy, which was in folio.

[69] 68. Les Office de France par Joly en deux volumes in folio 6 LT

Girard, Etienne, avocat au Parlement. Trois Livres des offices de France: le premier traitte des parlements . . . le second des chanceliers, gardes des sceaux . . . le troisiesme des baillifs, séneschaux . . . par Me E. Girard . . . avec plusieurs additions . . . qui contiennent l'histoire de l'origine et progrès des offices susdits . . . le tout vérifié . . . par Me Jacques Joly. *Paris, 1638, 1644, 1658.*

[70] 69. Les Ordonance de Neron in folio 3 LT

Girard, Etienne, and Pierre Néron. Les Edicts et ordonnances des très chrestiens roys François Ier, Henry II, François II, Charles IX, Henry III, Henry IV et Louys XIII, sur le faict de la justice et abréviation des procez, avec annotations, apostilles et conférences sous chacun article. . . . Nouvelle et dernière édition, corrigée et augmentée . . . par M. F. P. A. *Paris, 1656.*

Several earlier editions were available in smaller formats.

[71] 70. Atlas Mercator en deux volume in folio 12 LT

Mercatoris, Gerardi. Atlas, sive Cosmographicae meditationes de fabrica mundi et fabricati figura. . . . *Amsterdam, 1628.*

We do not know which of the many available editions Le Vau owned—whether his copy was in Latin, the language of the original publication in 1607, or in French translation: L'Atlas, ou Méditations cosmographiques de la fabrique du monde et figure d'ieceluy, commencé en latin par le très docte Gérard Mercator, parachevé par Jodocus Hondius, traduit en francois par le sieur de la P[opelinière] *(Amsterdam, 1609).*

The inventory mentions two volumes, but no such edition is recorded. It may be that Le Vau owned the most lavish edition, in three volumes (cited first above) and was missing one of the volumes in the series.

[72]   71. Roma sotteranea un volume in folio 6 LT

Bosio, Antonio. Roma sotterranea, opera postuma di Antonio Bosio. . . . *Rome, 1632.*
The format of Le Vau's copy indicates that he owned the original edition, which was followed in 1650 by a more modest version in quarto and a more extensive Latin edition in two volumes in folio.

[73]   72. Speculum Romanae magnificentiae folio 10 LT

Lafreri, Antonius [Antoine Lafrère]. Speculum romanae magnificentiae, omnia fere quaecunque in Urbe monumenta extant, partim juxta antiquam, partim juxta hodiernam formam acuratissime delineata reprasentans. *Rome, 1579.*

[74]   73. Entré du Cardinal Infant a Anvers 5 LT

Aedo y Gallart, Diego de. Le Voyage du prince Don Fernande infant d'Espagne cardinal, depuis le douzieme de l'an 1632 qu'il partit de Madrit pour Barcelone avec le roy Philippe IV, son frere, jusques au jour de son entrée en la vaille de Bruxelles le quatrieme du mois de novembre de l'an 1634. *Antwerp, 1635.*

[subtotal:] 111 LT 15 S

[75]   74. Les Oeuvres de Mr. Voet en un volume en folio 12 LT
This is probably an album of prints by Simon Vouet.

[76]   75. Deux volumes de diverse piece tant anciene que moderne in folio 30 LT

[77]   76. Le Teatre des citez en quatre volume 10 LT

Braun, Georg, Simon Van den Noevel, and Franz Hogenberg. Théâtre des cités du monde premier volume. . . . *Cologne, 1579.*
The first volume, published originally in Latin as Civitates orbis terrum *(Cologne, 1572), was followed by five more volumes with variant titles: vol. 2, c. 1575; vol. 3, 1583; vols. 4–5, n.d.; and vol. 6, 1618. It appears that Le Vau did not have a complete set of six volumes.*

[78] 77. La philosophie de Lesclache par Tables 4 LT

> *Lesclache, Louis de.* La Philosophie, expliquée en tables. . . . *Paris, 1651–56.*

[subtotal:] 161 LT 10s

[79] 78. Palazi di Genova in folio 10 LT

> *Rubens, Peter Paul.* Palazzi de Genova. *Antwerp, 1622.*

[80] 79. Il fontana de lobelisco Vaticana 6 LT

> *Fontana, Domenico.* Della Trasportatione dell'obelisco vaticano et delle fabriche di nostro signore papa Sisto V. fatte dal cavallier Domenico Fontana. *Rome, 1590.*

[81] 80. Les Machine de Besson et Vitruve 4 LT

> *Besson, Jacques.* Théâtre des instrumens mathématiques et mechaniques de Jacques Besson . . . avec l'interprétation des figures d'iceluy par François Béroald. *Lyons, 1578.*

[82] 81. Entré du Roy Louys XIIII^em a Paris 3 LT

> L'Entrée Triomphante de leurs Majestez Louis XIV. Roy de France, et Marie Therese d'Austriche son Espouse dans la ville de Paris, . . . au retour de la signature de la paix generalle, et de leur mariage. . . . *Paris, 1662.*

[83] 82. Traité du jardinage par Boissau 2 LT

> *Boyceau de La Baraudière, Jacques.* Traité du jardinage, selon les raisons de la nature et de l'art. . . . *Paris, 1638.*

[84] 83. Architetura di Serlio in folio 3 LT

> *Jean Martin had published French translations of books 1–2 (Paris, 1545), book 5 (Paris, 1545), and the* Extraordinario Libro *(Lyons, 1551), all with Italian and French titles, but whether Le Vau owned one of these translations or an Italian edition is impossible to say.*

[85] 84. Architetura di Vitruvio gaste 1 LT

> *This may be an edition by Guillaume Philander.*

[86] 85. Topographie francoise par Boiseau folio 4 LT

> *Chastillon, Claude.* Topographie françoise, ou Représentations de plusieurs villes, bourgs, plans, chasteaux, maisons de plaisance, ruines et vestiges d'antiquitez du royaume de France, dessignez par defunct Claude Chastillon et autres, et mis en lumière par Jean Boisseau. . . . *Paris, 1648.*

[87]   86. Architecture de Vitruve en francois in folio 1 LT 10 s

Martin, Jean. Architecture, ou Art de bien bastir de Marc Vitruve Pollion, . . . mis de latin en francoys par Jan Martin. . . . *Paris, 1547; 1572.*

Le Vau passed over the seventeenth-century editions (1618 and 1628), which were in quarto, for a folio edition.

[88]   87. Architettura di Scamosi in folio 10 LT

Scamozzi, Vincenzo. L'Idea della architettura universale di Vincenzo Scamozzi. *Venice, 1615.*

[89]   88. Maniere de bastir par Le Muet in folio 3 LT

Le Muet, Pierre. Manière de bien bastir pour touttes sortes de personnes. *Paris, 1623; 2d ed., Paris, 1647.*

[90]   89. Architettura di Paladio in folio 2 LT 10 s

Palladio, Andrea. I Quattro libri d'architettura di Andrea Palladio. . . . *Venice, 1581; 1642.*

[91]   90. Architecture de Vitruve par Maucler folio 2 LT

Mauclerc, Julien, sieur de Ligneron-Mauclerc. Traitté de l'architecture suivant Vitruve, où il est traitté des cinq ordres de colomnes . . . suivant la pratique des plus anciens architectes grecs et romains . . . mis en lumière par Pierre Daret, graveur. *Paris, 1648.*

The short title suggests that Le Vau owned this posthumously published edition rather than the original edition: Le Premier Livre d'Architecture de Julien Mauclerc, Gentilhomme Poitevin . . . Traictant tant l'ordre Tuscanique, Doricque, Ionique, Corinthe, que Composite *(La Rochelle, 1600).*

91. Quatre volume de Du Cerceau in folio 2 LT

Androuet Ducerceau's book on perspective appears later in the inventory (see no. 128); hence, the four volumes grouped together here probably consist of his printed books on architecture.

[92]   Livre d'architecture de Jacques Androuet Du Cerceau, contenant les plans et dessaings de cinquante bastimens tous différens, pour instruire ceux qui désirent bastir, soient de petit, moyen ou grand estat. . . . *Paris, 1559.*

[93]   Second Livre d'architecture par Jacques Androuet Du Cerceau, contenant plusieurs et diverses ordonnances de cheminées, lucarnes, portes, fonteines, puis et pavillons . . . avec les desseings de dix sepultures toutes différentes. *Paris, 1561.*

[94]   Livre d'architecture de Jacques Androuet Du Cerceau, auquel sont contenues diverses ordonnances de plants et élévations de bastiments pour seigneurs, gentilshommes et autres qui voudront bastir au champs. . . . *Paris, 1582; 1615.*

[95]   Le Premier [& Second] volume des plus excellents bastiments de France. . . . *Paris, 1576–79; 1607; 1648.*

[96] 92. Serlio et Vitruve in folio 5 LT

The short title may refer to Sebastiano Serlio's book 4 on the orders, the only one of his books that mentions Vitruvius in the title: Sebastiano Serlio, Regole generali di architetura sopra le cinque maniere degli edifici, cio e thoscano, dorico, ionico, corinthio et compositio, con gli essempi dell'antiquita, che, per la magior parte concordano con la dottrina di Vitruvio *(Venice, 1537).*

[97] 93. Un petit morceau de Serlio in folio 1 LT

This was Le Vau's third book by Serlio.

[98] 94. Architecture de Philiber de Lorme 1567 2 LT 10 s

Delorme, Philibert. Le Premier tome de l'architecture de Philibert de L'Orme conseiller et aumosnier ordinaire du Roy, & Abbé de S. Serge lez Angiers. *Paris, 1567.*

[99] 95. Un Idem. 1626 2 LT

Delorme, Philibert. L'Architecture de Philibert de L'Orme, conseiller, aumosnier ordinaire du Roy et abbé de Saint-Serge les Angiers. Oeuvre entière contenant onze livres, augmentée de deux; et autres Figures non encore veuës, tant pour desseins qu'ornemens de maison avec une belle invention pour bien bastir et à petits frais. . . . *Paris, 1626.*
This edition includes forty plates that were included in the first edition and were probably intended for the unexecuted second volume. On the various editions of Delorme's treatise, see Jean-Marie Pérouse de Montclos, "Les éditions des traités de Philibert de L'Orme au XVIIe siècle," in Les traités d'architecture de la Renaissance, *ed. Jean Guillaume (Paris, 1989).*

[100] 96. Architecture de Leon Baptiste Albert 2 LT

Alberti, Leone Battista. L'Architecture et art de bien bastir, du seigneur Léon Baptiste Albert, . . . divisée en dix livres, traduicts du latin en françois par deffunct Jean Martin. . . . *Paris, 1553.*

[101] 97. Architettura delle Milanesse in folio 3 LT

Montano, Giovanni Battista. Architettura con diversi ornamenti cavati dall'antico, da Gio. Battista Montano, Milanese . . . dati in luce da Calisto Ferrante. *Rome, 1636.*

[102] 98. Architecture et portique de Francine 2 LT 10 s

Francine, Alexandre [Alessandro Francini]. Livre d'architecture contenant plusieurs portiques de differentes inventions, sur les cinq ordres de colomnes. . . . *Paris, 1631; 2d ed., 1640.*

[103] 99. Architecture de Barber 1 LT 10 s

Barbaro, Daniele. I Dieci libri dell'Architettura di M. Vitruvio, tradutti et commentati da Monsignor Barbaro, eletto patriarca d'Aquileggia. *Venice, 1556.*

Barbaro's work was not translated into French; hence, the short title in the inventory does not necessarily indicate the language of the book. The short title cited above may have been prompted by the revised title of a later edition: L'Architettura di Vitruvio libri dieci, *tradotta e commentata da Monsig. Daniel Barbaro. Venice, 1641.*

[104] 100. Artifices de feu et Instrumans de guerre Aleman et francois in folio 3 LT
   Boillot, Josèph. Artifices de feu et divers instruments de guerre, das ist künstlich Feuerwerck und Kriegs Instrumenta . . . aus dem Französischen transferirt durch Joannem Brantzium junior. . . . *Strasbourg, 1603.*
   The original French edition (Chaumont, 1598) was in quarto.

[105] 101. Antiquita di Roma di Vincenzo Scamossi 4 LT
   Scamozzi, Vincenzo. Discorsi sopra l'antichità di Roma. *Venice, 1582.*

[106] 102. Antiquita di Roma Boosardi 2 volume 12 LT
   Boissard, Jean-Jacques. I. Pars Romanae urbis topographiae et antiquitatum . . . Jano Jacobo Boissardo autore . . . figurae . . . in aere incisae artificie Theodoro de Bry. . . . II. Pars antiquitatum romanarum, seu Topographia Romanae urbis. . . . *Frankfurt, 1597–1602.*
   The Bibliothèque Nationale has a copy bound in two volumes, as did Le Vau.

[107] 103. Architetura di Labacco in folio 2 LT
   Labacco, Antonio. Libro d'Antonio Labacco appartenente a l'architettura, nel qual si figurano alcune notabili antiquità di Roma. *Rome, 1557; Venice, 1576.*

[108] 104. Aedes barbarinae in folio 5 LT
   Teti, Girolamo. Aedes barberinae ad Quirinalem, a comite Hieronymo Tetio. . . . *Rome, 1642.*

105. Trois volumes d'entrée dont une de Louis XIII^em et deux de Marie de Medicis dans Amsterdam in folio 3 LT
[109]   *Le Vau might have owned any one of a number of commemorative publications documenting Louis XIII's entries into Bordeaux (1615), Chartres (1619), Niort (1621), Arles (1622), and Lyons (1622).*
[110]   *Van Baerle, Kasper.* Marie de Medicis entrant dans Amsterdam: ou histoire de la reception faicte à la reyne mère du roy très chrestien par les bourgmaistres et bourgeoisie de la ville d'Amsterdam. *Amsterdam, 1638.*
[111]   *The third volume was either the Latin edition of Van Baerle's text mentioned above, which focuses specifically on Amsterdam, or the following wider-ranging volume: Jean Puget de La Serre,* Histoire curieuse de tout ce qui s'est passé à l'entrée de la Reyne Mère (Marie de Medicis) du Roy tres-chrestien dans les villes des Pays Bas. *Antwerp, 1632.*

[**112**] 106. Arts liberaux 2 LT

> *This is possibly an album of etchings illustrating the liberal arts by Hieronymus Cock and Frans*
> *Floris, or perhaps other printmakers.*

> *[subtotal:]* 161 LT 10 S

[**113**] 107. Cartes de Tassin in folio 1 LT 10 S

> *Tassin, Nicolas.* Cartes générale[s] et particulières de toutes les costes de France, tant de la
> mer Océane que Mediterranée où sont remarquées toutes les iles, golphes, ports, havres,
> rades, bayes, bancs, escueils et rochers plus considérables avec les anchrages et profondeurs
> nécessaires. . . . *Paris, 1634.*

[**114**] 108. Teatrum florae in folio 1 LT 10 S

> Theatrum florae, in quo ex toto orbe selecti mirabiles . . . flores . . . proferuntur. *Paris, 1633*
> *[or 1623].*

[**115**] 109. Hortus palatinae in folio 2 LT

> *Caus, Salomon de.* Hortus palatinus a Friderico rege Boemiae, electore Palatino
> Heidelbergae exstructus, Salomone de Caus, architecto. *Frankfurt, 1620.*

[**116**] 110. Les Oeuvres de Samuel Marolois en deux volumes in folio 8 LT

> *Marolois, Samuel.* Opera mathematica, ou Oeuvres mathématiques traictans de la géometrie,
> perspective, architecture et fortification, par Samuel Marolois, de nouveau reveue,
> augmentée et corrigée par Albert Girard. . . . *Amsterdam, 1651.*
> *Earlier editions were in a smaller format, one volume either in folio (1616) or in quarto (1628).*

[**117**] 111. Les Memoire mathematique de Stevin 2 LT

> *Stevin, Simon.* Les Oeuvres mathématiques de Simon Stevin, . . . où sont insérées les
> Mémoires mathématiques, esquelles s'est exercé . . . Maurice de Nassau, prince d'Aurenge
> . . . Le tout reveu, corrigé et augmente par Albert Girard. . . . *Leiden, 1634.*

[**118**] 112. Les Fortifications dogen in folio 6 LT

> *Dögen, Matthias.* L'Architecture militaire moderne, ou Fortification, confirmée par diverses
> histoires tant anciennes que nouvelles et enrichie des figures des principales forteresses qui
> sont en l'Europe, par Matthias Dögen . . . mise en françois par Hélie Poirier. . . . *Amsterdam,*
> *1648.*

[**119**] 113. Les fortifications du Chevalier de Ville 4 LT 10 S

> *Ville, Antoine de.* Les Fortifications du chevalier Antoine de Ville, contenans la manière de

fortifier toute sorte de places . . . avec l'ataque et les moyens de prendre les places . . . plus la défense. . . . *Lyons, 1636.*

[120] 114. Variae Architecturae Vredemani in folio en long 2 LT
Vredeman De Vries, Hans. Varia architecturae formae, a Joanne Vredemanni Vriesio, magno artis hujus studiosorum commodo, inventae. *Antwerp, 1601.*
This quarto edition is not in the same format as Le Vau's copy.

[121] 115. Appiaria Mathematica 2 vols. in folio 8 LT
This is possibly an edition of writings by Petrus Apianus [Peter Benewitz] on cosmography, which was published originally in quarto as Cosmographicus liber Petri Apiani mathematici studiose collectus *(Landshut, 1524).*

[122] 116. La perspective du Pere Niceron in folio 2 LT
Niceron, Père Jean-François. La Perspective curieuse, ou Magie artificielle des effets merveilleux de l'optique par la vision directe, la catoptrique, par la réflexion des miroirs plats, cylindriques et conqiues, la dioptrique par la refraction des crystaux. *Paris, 1638.*

[123] 117. Archisesto del Signor Ottavio Revesi 1 LT
Revesi Bruti, Ottavio. Archisesto per formar con facilità li cinque ordini d'architettura. *Vicenza, 1627.*

[124] 118. Un volume du Cesar et Imperatrice folio 1 LT
This may be Jean-Baptiste Le Menestrier, Médales illustrées des anciens empereurs et impératrices de Rome. . . . *(Dijon, 1642), but it was published in quarto, not in folio.*

[125] 119. Albohazen haly de Judicis Astrorum 3 LT
Haly, Albohazen [Aboul Hasan Ali ibn Aboul Ridjal]. Liber de Judiciis astrorum Albohazen Hali filii Abenragel revisus per Bartolomeum de Alten. *Venice, 1485.*
It is more likely that Le Vau owned a later edition; other folio editions appeared in 1520, 1551, and 1571.

[126] 120. Cardani in Ptolomerum in folio 3 LT
Cardano, Girolamo. Hieronymi Cardani in Cl. Ptolemaei Pelusiensis IIII de astrorum judiciis, aut, ut vulgo vocant, quadripartitae constructionis libros commentaria . . . nunc primum in lucem aedita. . . . *Basel, 1554.*

[127] 121. Antichitta di Roma de Duperac en long 1 LT 10 s

Du Perac, Etienne. I vestigi dell'antichità di Roma raccolti et retratti in perspettiva . . . da Stefano Du Perac. *Rome, 1575.*
The format differs from Le Vau's copy.

[128] 122. Antiquae Urbis Splendor en long 3 LT 10 s
Lauro, Giacomo. Antiquae urbis splendor, hoc est praecipua ejusdem templa, amphitheatra, theatra, circi . . . aliaque sumptuosiora aedificia . . . opera et industria Jacobi Lauri. . . . *Rome, 1612–13.*

[129] 123. La Maisson de Lyancour par Silvestre 3 LT
This is probably a suite of twelve engravings by Israel Silvestre: Différentes veües du Chateau et des Jardins, Fontaines, Cascades, Canaux et parterres de Liencourt. Dessiné au naturel et gravé par Israel Silvestre, 1656. *Silvestre did a variant suite of ten engravings of the château in 1655 and a suite of eight engravings of the Hôtel de Liancourt in Paris, which are alternative possibilities.*

[130] 124. Richelieu palais en long 2 LT 10 s
Marot, Jean. Le Magnifique Chasteau de Richelieu, en général et en particulier, ou les plans, les élévations et profils généraux et particuliers dudit chasteau. . . . *N.p. [Paris], n.d. [c. 1660].*

[131] 125. Palazzi di Roma en long 2 LT
Ferrerio, Pietro. Palazzi di Roma de' più celebri architetti, disegnati da Pietro Ferrerio . . . Libro primo. Nuovi disegni dell'architetture e piante de' palazzi di Roma . . . disegnati et intagliati da Gio. Battista Falda, dati in luce da Gio. Giacomo de Rossi. *Rome, n.d. (1655).*

[132] 126. Vitruvio de l'archittetura in folio 1 LT
This is another edition of Vitruvius.

[133] 127. Piante di Tera Sancta in folio 2 LT
Amico, Père Bernardino. Trattato delle piante immagini de sacri edifizi di Terra Santa disegnate in Ierusalemme. . . . *Florence, 1620.*

[134] 128. Leçons de perspective par du cerceau 1 LT 10 s
Androuet Ducerceau, Jacques. Leçons de perspective positive. . . . *Paris, 1576.*

129. Le Teatre des charpentiers et serruriers 2 LT 10 s
[135] *Jousse, Mathurin.* Le Théâtre de l'art de charpentier, enrichi de diverses figures, avec l'interprétation d'icelles, faict et dressé par Mathurin Jousse. *La Flèche, 1627.*

[136]   *Jousse, Mathurin.* La Fidelle ouverture de l'art de serrurier, où l'on void les principaulx préceptes, desseings et figures touchant les expériences et opérations manuelles dudict art, ensemble un petit traicté de diverses trempes, le tout faict et composé par Mathurin Jousse. *La Flèche, 1627.*
The two books were presumably bound together in Le Vau's copy.

[137] 130. Divers cartouches in folio 1 LT 10 s

LIVRES IN QUARTO

[138] 131. Deux volumes des Ephemerides dorigan in quarto 4 LT
Unidentified works by Origan.

132. Deux volumes de Magini dont Ephemerides et Tabulae in quarto 3 LT

[139]   *Magini, Giovanni Antonio.* Ephemerides coelestium motuum J. Antonii Magini . . . ad annos XL ab anno Domini 1581 usque ad annum 1620. . . . *Venice, 1582.*

[140]   *Magini, Giovanni Antonio.* Tabulae secundorum mobilium coelestium . . . congruentes cum observationibus. . . . *Venice, 1585.*

[141] 133. Les Ephemerides de dures in quarto 1 LT
Duret, Noël. Novae motuum coelestium ephemerides Richelianae annorum 15, ab anno 1637 incipientes. *Paris, 1641.*

134. Cinq volumes dargolius dont Ephemerides en trois volumes. Tabulae et pandosium Sphericum in quarto 10 LT

[142]   *Argoli, Andrea.* Exactissimae coelestium motuum ephemerides, ad longitudinem Almae Urbis et Tychonis Brahe hypotheses ac deductas e coelo accurate observationes, ab anno 1641 ad annum 1700, auctore Andrea Argolo. *Passau, 1648.*
Earlier editions of Argoli's Ephemerides (1621 and 1638) were issued in one volume and do not match the enlarged, three-volume format of Le Vau's copy.

[143]   *Argoli, Andrea.* Tabulae primi mobilis Andreae Argoli . . . Tabulae positionum . . . a grad. altitud. poli 36 usque ad grad. 60. *Rome, 1610.*

[144]   *Argoli, Andrea.* Andreae Argoli, . . . Pandosion spaericum, in quo singula in elementaribus regionibus atque aetherea mathematice pertractantur. Editio secunda. . . . *Passau, 1653.*

[subtotal:] 84 LT

[145] 135. Les plans de Tassin in quarto 2 LT 10 s
Tassin, Nicolas. Les Plans et profils de toutes les principales villes et lieux considérables de France; ensemble les cartes générales de chacune province et les particulières de chaque gouvernement d'icelles, par le Sr Tassin. *Paris, 1634.*

The inventory mentions only one volume. In later editions the two volumes were published independently.

[146] 136. La Geographie de Bertiers in quarto 1 LT
Bertius, Pierre. La Géographie racourcie, de Pierre Bertius. *Amsterdam, 1618.*
The book was published simultaneously in Latin but in a folio edition. It is conceivable, despite the French short title in the inventory, that Le Vau owned the second Latin edition of 1628: Geographia vetus ex antiquis et melioris notae scriptoribus ruper collecta. . . . *(Paris, 1628).*

[147] 137. Vassari, Vitae di pittori en trois volumes quarto 5 LT
Vasari, Giorgio. Le Vite de' piu eccellenti pittori, scultori e architettori, scritte da M. Giorgio Vasari, . . . di nuovo del medesimo riviste et ampliate, con i ritratti loro et con l'aggiunta delle vite de' vivi e de' morti dall'anno 1550 insino al 1567. . . . *Florence, 1568.*
The format of Le Vau's copy indicates that he did not own the original, 1550 edition, which consisted of two volumes; another three-volume edition was published in Bologna in 1647.

[148] 138. Ridolfi miravoglio de l arte di pittori in 4° 2 LT
Ridolfi, Carlo. Le Maraviglie dell'arte overo le Vite degl' illustri pittori Veneti e dello stato . . . descritte dal cavalier Carlo Ridolfi. *Venice, 1648.*

[149] 139. Baglione Vitae di pittori in quarto 1 LT
Baglione, Giovanni. Le Vite de' pittori, scultori et architetti, dal pontificato di Gregorio XIII del 1572, in fino a' tempi di Papa Urbano Ottavo nel 1642, scritte da Gio. Baglione. *Rome, 1642.*

[150] 140. un autre 1 LT
Perhaps the second copy is the later edition of Baglione's Vite *published in 1649.*

[151] 141. P. Lomazzo. Della de la pittura in quarto 3 LT
Lomazzo, Giovanni Paolo. Trattato dell'arte de la pittura. . . . *Milan, 1584.*
The short title makes no sense. If not the Trattato, *it may refer to Lomazzo's,* Idea del tempio della pittura. *Milan, 1590.*

[152] 142. Le deux ou troisieme volume de la perspective pratique in quarto 2 LT 10 s
Du Breuil, Jean. La Perspective practique [Second et troisiesme parties de la Perspective practique] . . . par un Parisien religieux de la Compagnie de Jésus. *Paris, 1642–49.*

[153] 143. Porte et cheminé in quarto 1 LT 10 s
Marot, Jean. Recueil de diverses pieces modernes d'architecture, et nouvelles inventions de portes, cheminees, ornemans et autres. *Paris, n.d.*

[154] 144. La perspective Daleaume in quarto 1 LT 5 s

Aleaume, Jacques. La Perspective spéculative et pratique . . . de l'invention du feu sieur Aleaume, . . . mise au jour par Estienne Migon. *Paris, 1643.*

[155] 145. Un livre concernant la menuiserie 1 LT

This is possibly Jean Barbet's model book Livre d'Architecture et de cheminees *(Paris, 1633), illustrated with etchings by Abraham Bosse, or an album of prints relating to fine carpentry.*

[156] 146. Fontana di Roma in quarto 1 LT 10 s

This is possibly an album of early prints by Giovanni Battista Falda—a volume that would have been compiled many years before the publication of his series of thirty-one engravings of Roman fountains, Le Fontane di Roma *(Rome, c. 1675).*

[157] 147. Recüelle d'elevations par Marot in quarto 2 LT

Marot, Jean. Recueil des plans, profils et élévations des plusieurs palais, chasteaux, églises, sépultures, grotes et hostels bâtis dans Paris et aux environs . . . desseignez, mesurés et gravez par Jean Marot. *N.p., n.d.*

[158] 148. Antiquarum Urbis Romae in quarto 1 LT 10 s

Cavalleri, Giovanni Battista. Antiquarum statuarum vrbis Romae, quae in publicis privatisque locis visuntur, icones. . . . *Rome, 1621.*

[159] 149. Ruyne de Rome in quarto 1 LT

This is possibly Hieronymus Cock, Praecipua Romanae Antiquitatis Ruinarum Monimenta, Vivis Prospectibus, ad veri Imitationem Affabre Designata *(Antwerp, 1551).*

[160] 150. Les Songes de Poliphile in quarto 1 LT

Colonna, Francesco. Le Tableau des riches inventions couvertes du voile des feintes amoureuses qui sont représentées dans le Songe de Poliphile, desvoilées des ombres du songe et subtilement exposés par Béroalde. *Paris, 1600.*

All editions of Jean Martin's better-known translation of the Hypnerotomachia Poliphi—*from 1546, 1554, and 1561—were in folio, not the format of Le Vau's copy.*

[161] 151. Les Oeuvres de Monsieur Lesclache en sept volume in quarto 12 LT

[162] 152. Idem. Quatre volumes Tabl. 6 LT

It is unclear which works by Louis de Lesclache are encompassed in these two entries. Lesclache was evidently one of Le Vau's favorite authors; see also inventory no. 77.

[163] 153. Lucien de M. Dablencour en deux volumes 3 LT

    Lucian of Samosata. Lucien de la tradution de N[icolas] Perrot, Sr d'Ablancourt. *Paris, 1654.*

[164] 154. Quinto Curce de M. Vaugelas in quarto 2 LT

    Vaugelas, Claude Favre de (translated by Quinte-Curce). De la Vie et des actions d'Alexandre
    le Grand de la traduction de M. de Vaugelas, avec les supplémens de Jean Freinsihemius . . .
    traduits par Pierre Du Ryer. *Paris, 1653.*

[165–67] 155. Trois volumes separé de M. des Cartes 3 LT

    It is impossible to say which books by René Descartes Le Vau owned.

[168] 156. Les femmes ilustre en deux volumes 2 LT

    Scudéry, Madeleine de. Les Femmes illustres, ou les Harangues héroïques de Mr de Scudery,
    avec les veritables portraits de ces heroines, tirez des medailles antiques. *Paris, 1642.*
    This edition, unlike Le Vau's, is in one volume.

[169] 157. Les oeuvres de M. Charon in quarto 1 LT 10 s

    Charron, Pierre. Toutes les Oeuvres de Pierre Charron. . . . Dernière édition. *Paris, 1635.*

[170] 158. Leneide de Virgile par Perrin en deux vols. 2 LT

    Virgil. L'Enéide de Virgile, fidèlement traduite en vers et les remarques à chaque
    livre pour l'intelligence de l'histoire et de la fable. . . . 1re partie . . . par messire P. Perrin.
    Paris, 1658.
    Virgil. L'Enéide de Virgile fidèlement traduite en vers heroiques, avec le latin à costé. . . .
    2e partie . . . par messire P. Perrin. *Paris, 1658.*
    When first published in 1648, Perrin's translation did not bear his name.

[171] 159. La Teologie de P. Ive en quatre vols. 3 LT

    Yves de Paris, Père. La Théologie naturelle où les premières véritez de la foy sont éclaircies
    par raisons sensibles et morales, par le P. Ives de Paris. . . . *Paris. 1633*
    Yves de Paris, Père. La Théologie naturelle. Tome second. De l'Immortalité de l'âme, des
    anges et démons. . . . *Paris, 1635.*
    Yves de Paris, Père. La Théologie naturelle. Tome troisieme. Des Perfections de Dieu, de sa
    providence, de sa justoce. . . . *3e ed. Paris, 1640.*
    Yves de Paris, Père. La Théologie naturelle. Tome quartiesme. De la Religion. Que la
    religion chrestienne est la vraye. Des mystères de la religion chrestienne. . . . *3e ed. Paris.*
    1641.

[172] 160. La Morale du Pere Ive en quatre vols. 3 LT
　　　　Yves de Paris, Père. Les Morales chrestiennes. *Paris, n.d. (c. 1643).*

[173] 161. Les Emblesme dorace in quarto 3 LT
　　　　Horace. Q. Horatii Flacci Emblemata imaginibus in aes incisis cotisque illustrata, studio
　　　　Othonis Vaenii. . . . *Antwerp, 1607.*
　　　　The 1612 edition included translations in several languages including French; there was, however,
　　　　no French edition of Emblemata, *as the short title implies.*

[174] 162. Les Lettres de M. Costar en deux vols. 3 LT
　　　　Costar, Abbé Pierre. Lettres de Monsieur Costar. *Paris, 1658–59.*

[175] 163. Roland le furieux in quarto 1 LT 10 s
　　　　Ariosto, Lodovico. Le divin Arioste, ou Roland le Furieux, traduict nouvellement en françois
　　　　par F. de Rosset, ensemble la suitte de cette histoire continuée jusques à la mort du paladin
　　　　Roland conforme à l'intention de l'autheur. . . . *Paris, 1615.*

[176] 164. Histoire du Concile in quarto 1 LT 10 s
　　　　Sarpi, Paolo. Histoire du concile de Trente, traduite de l'italien de Pierre Soave Polan par
　　　　Jean Diodati. *Geneva, 1621; 2d ed., 1635.*

LES PAQUETS IN FOLIO
[180] 165. paquet de 8 volumes in folio *[4 titles?]* cotte ung 4 LT
[184] 166. paquet de 9 volumes in folio *[4 titles?]* cotte deux 3 LT 10 s
[186] 167. paquet de 5 volumes in folio *[2 titles?]* cotte trois 2 LT

　　　[subtotal:] 85 LT 5 s

LES PAQUETS IN QUARTO
[189] 168. paquet de 6 volumes in quarto *[3 titles?]* cotte quatre 3 LT
[192] 169. paquet de 7 volumes in quarto *[3 titles?]* cotte cinq 4 LT
[194] 170. paquet de 5 volumes in quarto *[2 titles?]* cotte six 4 LT
[197] 171. paquet de 7 volumes in quarto *[3 titles?]* cotte sept 2 LT 10 s
[200] 172. paquet de 6 volumes in quarto *[3 titles?]* cotte huit 4 LT
[202] 173. paquet de 5 volumes in quarto *[2 titles?]* cotte neuf 3 LT
[205] 174. paquet de 7 volumes in quarto *[3 titles?]* cotte dix 3 LT 10 s
[209] 175. paquet de 8 volumes in quarto *[4 titles?]* cotte onze 6 LT
[213] 176. paquet de 9 volumes in quarto *[4 titles?]* cotte douze 5 LT 10 s
[217] 177. paquet de 8 volumes in quarto *[4 titles?]* cotte treize 7 LT

[220] 178. paquet de 7 volumes in quarto *[3 titles?]* cotte quatorze 2 LT 10 s

[222] 179. paquet de 5 volumes in quarto *[2 titles?]* cotte quinze 3 LT

[225] 180. paquet de 7 volumes in quarto *[3 titles?]* cotte seize 3 LT 10 s

[228] 181. paquet de 7 volumes in quarto *[3 titles?]* cotte dixsept 3 LT 10 s

[230] 182. paquet de plusieurs volumes *[5 volumes, 2 titles?]* in quarto telle quelle cotte dixhuit 2 LT

[232] 183. paquet de cinq volumes *[2 titles?]* in quarto cotte *191 lt 10 s*

LES PAQUETS IN OCTAVAU

[233] 184. paquet de *6 volumes in octavau Almahyde cotte vint* 4 LT

> *Scudéry, Madeleine de.* Almahide, ou l'Esclave reine par Mr de Scudéry. *Paris, 1660–63.*
> *This edition, unlike Le Vau's, is eight volumes in octavo.*

[234] 185. paquet de *10 volumes de Cyrus cotte vint et un* 7 LT

> *Scudéry, Madeleine de.* Artamene, ou le Grand Cyrus. . . , *2d ed. Leiden and Paris, 1656.*

[235] 186. paquet de *10 volumes in octavo de Cassandre cotte vint et deux* 5 LT

> *La Calprenède, Gautier de Coste de.* Cassandre. *Paris, 1644–60.*

[236] 187. paquet de *8 volumes in octavau Cyrano et Scipion cotte vint et trois* 3 LT

> *This item probably refers to two different works of literature: Savinien Cyrano de Bergerac,* Les Oeuvres diverses de Mr. De Cyrano Bergerac *(Paris, 1654), and Pierre de'Ortigue de Vaumorière,* Le grand Scipion *(Paris 1658–62).*

[237] 188. paquet de *8 volumes de Cleopatre cotte vint et quatre* 4 LT

> *La Calprenède, Gautier de Coste de.* Cléopatre. *Paris, 1653–63.*
> *This edition, unlike Le Vau's, is twelve volumes in octavo.*

[238] 189. paquet de *5 volumes in octavo Astrée cotte vint cinq prise* 3 LT

> *Urfé, Honoré d'.* L'Astrée de messire Honoré d'Urfé . . . 3e édition, reveuë et corrigée. *Paris, 1633; 1647.*

> *[subtotal:]* 84 LT 10 s

[241] 190. paquet de huit volumes in octavo *[4 titles?]* cotte vint et six 3 LT 10 s

[244] 191. paquet de sept volumes in octavo *[3 titles?]* cotte vint et sept 5 LT

[247] 192. paquet de six volumes in octavo *[3 titles?]* cotte vint et huict 4 LT

[252] 193. paquet de dix volumes in octavo *[5 titles?]* cotte vint et neuf 4 LT

[259] 194. paquet de quinze volumes in octavo *[7 titles?]* cotte trente prise 3 LT

[265] 195. paquet de douze volumes in octavo *[6 titles?]* cotte trente et un prise 1 LT 10 s

[**269**] 196. paquet de huit volumes in octavo *[4 titles?]* cotte trente et deux 2 LT 10 s

[**276**] 197. paquet de sept volumes in octavo *[7 titles?]* cotte trente et trois prise 2 LT

[**280**] 198. paquet de huit volumes in octavo *[4 titles?]* cotte trente et quatre 2 LT 10 s

[**284**] 199. paquet de neuf volumes in octavo *[4 titles?]* cotte trente et cinq 1 LT 10 s

[**292**] 200. paquet de dix sept volumes in octavo *[8 titles?]* cotte trente et six prise 1 LT 5 s

[**297**] 201. paquet de dix volumes in octavo *[5 titles?]* cotte trente sept prise 1 LT

[**303**] 202. paquet de douze volumes octavo *[6 titles?]* cotte trente huit 1 LT 5 s

[**308**] 203. paquet de plusieurs volumes *[10 volumes, 5 titles?]* in douze cotte trente neuf 2 LT

　　　[subtotal:] 35 LT 10 s

Tous les livres mentionez à l'inventaire cy devans ce monte à la somme de sept cent quatre vint cinq [785] livres et dix solz sauf les der[nier] du calcul. Faict à Paris ce quatriesme decembre mil six cent soixante et dix en foy de quoy nous avons signé: Dumas; Jean de Latourette.

Nous avons receu la somme de quarante et quatre livres pour l'inventaire cy devant des mains de Monsieur Grand Huissier et ce des deniers provenant de la veuve de feu Mr. Le Vau pour nos vacations dont nous la quitons. Faict a Paris ce 16me fevrier mil six cent septente et un: Dumas; Jean de Latourette.

AN Minutier central LXXXV 198, 14 decembre 1670.

Citations from seventeenth-century French documents contained in the notes are faithful to the original spelling, which means that accents are used infrequently and inconsistently. Throughout the notes, the following abbreviations have been used:

AN   *Archives Nationales, Paris*
Boll. CISA *Bollettino del Centro Internazionale di Studi di Architettura Andrea Palladio*
BN   *Bibliothèque Nationale de France, Paris*
BSHP   *Bulletin de la Sociéte de l'Histoire de Paris et de l'Ile-de-France*
BSHAF   *Bulletin de la Société de l'Histoire de l'Art Français*
GBA   *Gazette des Beaux-Arts*
JSAH   *Journal of the Society of Architectural Historians*

INTRODUCTION

1. Anthony Blunt, *Art and Architecture in France, 1500–1700,* 4th rev. ed. (New York, 1986), 326. Jacques Guillaume Legrand and Charles Paul Landon made a similar comment in their guidebook *Description de Paris:* "[T]he happy effect of the combined mass of the dome and pavilions . . . present a picturesque and theatrical disposition which is common enough in Italy but extremely rare in Paris where most of the monuments are crowded and rarely disposed to form an agreeable point of view" ([Paris, 1806], 1:107). For other positive assessments of Le Vau as a Baroque architect, see Guglielmo De Angelis d'Ossat, "Louis Le Vau, architetto bernini-ano suo malgrado," in *Gian Lorenzo Bernini architetto e l'architetettura europea del Sei-Settecento,* ed. Gianfranco Spagnesi and Marcello Fagiolo (Rome, 1984), 2:511–24; Robert Berger, "Louis Le Vau's Château du Raincy," *Architettura* 6, no. 1 (1976):36–46; Berger's entry on Le Vau in *Macmillan Encyclopedia of Architects* (New York, 1982), 2:695–97; Dietrich Feldmann, "Das Hôtel de la Vrillière und die Raüme 'à l'italienne' bei Louis Le Vau," *Zeitschrift für Kunstgeschichte* 45, no. 4 (1982):395–422; and Feldmann, *Maison Lambert, Maison Hesselin und andere Bauten von Louis Le Vau auf der Ile Saint Louis in Paris* (Hamburg, 1976).

2. Jacques-François Blondel, *Architecture françoise, ou Recueil des plans, élévations, coupes et profils des églises, maisons royales, palais, hôtels et edifices . . .* (Paris,

1752–56), vol. 2, bk. 3, chap. 1. The comments on Le Vau in Antoine Joseph Dezallier d'Argenville, *Vie des fameux architectes* ([Paris, 1787], 380–81), derive from Blondel. Quatremère's comment reads in full: "Le plan exigea une très-grande intelligence, et . . . l'élévation présente, sur le quai en face du Louvre, un aspect monumental qu'il n'est pas très-ordinaire de rencontrer. . . . On est obligé de convenir qu'il règne dans les profils, dans les ornemens et dans l'exécution, quelque chose de lourd, et que le tout manque de cette finesse de proportion et de cette pureté de style qui constituent une architecture classique" (Antoine Chrysosthôme Quatremère de Quincy, *Dictionnaire historique d'architecture* [Paris, 1832], 2:648). For similar appraisals of the Collège, see Henry Lemonnier, *Le Collège Mazarin et le Palais de l'Institut (XVIIe–XIX siècle)* (Paris, 1921), 33; and Reginald Blomfield, *A History of French Architecture from the Death of Mazarin till the Death of Louis XV, 1661–1774* (1921; reprint, New York, 1973), 55–67. Blunt also criticized Le Vau's sloppy use of the orders and his decorative approach to design, in *Art and Architecture in France,* 222.

3. Albert Laprade, *François d'Orbay, architecte de Louis XIV* (Paris, 1960).

4. Robert Berger, *Versailles: The Château of Louis XIV* (University Park, Pa., 1985), 26–27.

CHAPTER I

1. The royal entry of of 1660 was the last one in Paris, and the tradition died out during the reign of Louis XIV. On the transformation of royal ceremonial under Louis XIV, see Ralph Giesey, "Models of Rulership in French Royal Ceremonial," in *Rites of Power: Symbolism, Ritual and Politics Since the Middle Ages,* ed. Sean Wilentz (Philadelphia, 1985), 41–64. For a full description of the 1660 royal entry, see the official publication: [Jean Tronçon], *L'entrée triomphante de leurs majestez Louis XIV roy de France et de Navarre et Marie Thérèse d'Austriche son espouse dans la ville de Paris . . .* (Paris, 1662). The entry has been studied in detail by Karl Möseneder, *Zeremoniell und monumentale Poesie: Die 'Entrée solennelle' Ludwigs XIV, 1660 in Paris* (Berlin, 1983), which includes a reprint of the 1662 program. On the political dimension of sixteenth-century royal entries, see Lawrence Bryant's several publications: "Politics, Ceremonies, and Embodiments of Majesty in Henry II's France," in *European Monarchy: Its Evolution and Practice from Roman Antiquity to Modern Times,* ed. Heinz Duchhardt et al. (Stuttgart, 1992), 127–54; *The King and the City in the Parisian Royal Entry Ceremony: Politics, Ritual and Art in the Renaissance* (Geneva, 1986); and "Parlementaire Political Theory in the Parisian Royal Entry Ceremony," *Sixteenth Century Journal* 7, no. 1 (April 1976):15–24.

2. "[C]onsiderant les grands et signalez services que Monsieur le Cardinal Mazariny luy avoit rendus et à son Estat en cette occasion" ([Jean Tronçon], *L'entreé triomphante,* "Retour du roy et son séjour à Vincennes," 3). According to Loménie de Brienne, Mazarin had made arrangements with Spain to permit his election to the papal throne upon the death of Alexander VII (Paul Bonnefon, ed., *Mémoires de Louis-Henri de Loménie, Comte de Brienne,* [Paris, 1916–19], 2:19–21).

3. Gabriel Le Brun's engraving illustrated a poem by Cavalier Ascanio Amalteo in honor of the cardinal, *Il Tempio della pace edificato dalla virtù dell'eminentissimo cardinale Mazarino* (Paris, 1660). Jean Loret reported (in *Muze historique,* 5 March 1661) that 30,000 people prayed for Mazarin's convalesence. Although the number is fictitious, the verse indicates the popular support Mazarin enjoyed following the peace treaty. For other tributes to Mazarin, see R. P. Du Bosc, *Lettre à Monseigneur le Cardinal duc Mazarini sur la paix générale: avec le panégyrique du Cardinal de Richelieu* (Paris, 1662); Nicolas Le Maistre, *Irenicus* (Paris, 1659); *Le triomphe de son eminence dans la conclusion de la paix* (Paris, 1660); and a verse attributed to Charles Perrault, *Ode sur la paix* (Paris, 1660). Unlike these panegyrics, a pamphlet by the sieur de Coquerel, *Le navire de la France arrivé heureusement au port de la paix sous la conduite de son éminence* (Paris, 1660), pays even-handed tribute to numerous ministers and ambassadors.

In a more elaborate allegory painted by Theodoor van Thulden for the court, *Allegory of the Alliance of Louis XIV and Philip IV of Spain* (Musée du Louvre Inv. 1905), Mazarin is equated with the column he touches to the left of the royal couple, a bulwark and support of the French crown. See Alain Roy, ed., *Theodoor van Thulden (1606–1669): Un peintre baroque du cercle de Rubens* (Zwolleand and 's Hertogenbosch, 1991), 229–31.

4. The inscription on the arch at the Porte Saint Antoine reads: PACI / VICT LUDOV XIV ARMIS / FEL ANN CON AVG M T NUPTI / ASSID IVL CARD MAZ CVR / PART FVND AET FIRMAT / P VRB AE Q SS ANN CD D CLX. Views of the towns where the peace treaty was signed decorated the city side of the arch.

5. "Commes des deux grandes actions [the peace and marriage] ont esté ménagées par la sage conduite de Monsieur le Cardinal Mazarin, il ne faut pas s'estonner qu'il intervienne à leur conclusion, et qu'il face l'une des principales parties dans ce Tableau, sous l'habit du Dieu de l'Eloquence, de l'interprete des volontez divines, de l'Entremetteur des Treves et des alliances, puis qu'il a fourny icy bas si heureusement toutes ses fonctions" ([Jean Tronçon], *L'entreé triomphante,* "Preparatifs dans la ville," 22).

6. The party on 9 September 1660 is described in

Loret, *Muze historique,* 11 September 1660, and in *Muse royale,* 9 September 1660; these sources are cited in Alfred Franklin, *Histoire de la Bibliothèque Mazarine et du Palais de l'Institut,* (Paris, 1860; rev. ed., 1901), 118–20.

7. Among the numerous biographies of Mazarin, two recent studies are commended: Pierre Goubert, *Mazarin* (Paris, 1990); and Geoffrey Treasure, *Mazarin: The Crisis of Absolutism in France* (London and New York, 1995). On Mazarin's early years in Rome, see Georges Dethan, *The Young Mazarin,* trans. Stanley Baron (London, 1977); the contents of that book are abridged in Dethan's comprehensive biography *Mazarin: Un homme de paix à l'âge baroque, 1602–1661* (Paris, 1981). A text by Mazarin's agent in Rome covers his life up to 1652: Elpidio Benedetti, *Raccolta di diverse memorie per scrivere la vita del Cardinale Giulio Mazarini* (Lyons, n.d.).

8. On Mazarin's relationship with Richelieu, see Dethan, *The Young Mazarin,* 89–101; Pierre Blet, "Richelieu et les débuts du Mazarin," *Revue d'histoire moderne et contemporaine* 6 (1959):241–68; and Guido Quazza, "Giulio Mazzarini mediatore fra Vittorio-Amedeo I e il Richelieu (1635–1636)," *Bolletino storio-biografico subalpino,* 1950:53–84.

9. France won control of Pignerol and parts of Alsace, and the treaty confirmed French control of the bishoprics of Metz, Toul, and Verdun. The Protestant princes won territorial control over the churches in their lands. For the text of the treaty, see the facsimile edition, Heinz Duchhardt and Franz-Josef Jakobi, eds., *Der Westfälische Frieden,* (Wiesbaden, 1996); and Henri Vast, *Les grands traités du règne de Louis XIV* (Paris, 1893–99), 1:1–64. For analysis of its terms, see Klaus Bussman and Heinz Schilling, eds., *1648: War and Peace in Europe* (Munich, 1999); Kenneth Setton, *Venice, Austria, and the Turks in the Seventeenth Century* (Philadelphia, 1991), 89–102; Fritz Dickmann, *Der Westfälische Frieden,* 2d ed. (Münster, 1965); Ludwig von Pastor, *The History of the Popes,* trans. Dom Ernst Graf (London, 1957), 30: 94–126; and Hermann Weber, "*Une Bonne Paix:* Richelieu's Foreign Policy and the Peace of Christendom," in *Richelieu and His Age,* ed. Joseph Bergin and Laurence Brockliss (Oxford, 1992), 45–69. Unlike the other authors mentioned above, Weber does not regard the treaty as a great victory for France because it failed to meet the two principal goals of Richelieu's foreign policy: universal peace and collective security. Spain and the Netherlands were not party to the treaty, and France remained at war with Spain. On Mazarin's personal contribution to the Treaty of Westphalia, see Pierre Goubert, *Mazarin* (Paris, 1990), 179 (describing the treaty as "pitiful"); and Richard Bonney, "Mazarin et la Fronde: La question de responsabilité," in *La Fronde en questions,* ed. Roger Duchêne et Pierre Ronzeaud (n.p., 1989), 331–33.

10. On the Fronde, see Orest Ranum, *The Fronde: A French Revolution, 1648–1652* (New York, 1993); Bonney, "Mazarin et la Fronde," in *La Fronde en questions,* ed. Duchêne and Ronzeaud, 329–38; Bonney, "Cardinal Mazarin and the Great Nobility during the Fronde," *English Historical Review* 96 (1981): 818–23; Roland Mousnier, "Mazarin et le problème constitutionnel en France pendant la Fronde," in Accademia Nazionale dei Lincei, *Il Cardinale Mazzarino in Francia,* Atti dei convegni Lincei 35 (Rome, 1977), 7–16; and Bonney, "The Secret Expenses of Richelieu and Mazarin, 1624–1661," *English Historical Review* 91 (1976):825–36. For an evaluation of the charges of financial impropriety, see Françoise Bayard, "Du rôle exact de Mazarin et des Italiens dans les finances françaises," in *La France et l'Italie au temps de Mazarin,* ed. Jean Serroy (Grenoble, 1986), 19–26. Several interesting studies of the *mazarinades* have been published recently by Christian Jouhaud: *Mazarinades: La Fronde des mots* (Paris, 1985); "Propagande et action au temps de la Fronde," in *Culture et idéologie dans la genèse de l'état moderne,* Ecole Française de Rome 82 (Rome, 1985), 337–53; and "Readability and Persuasion: Political Handbills," in *The Culture of Print: Power and the Uses of Print in Early Modern Europe,* ed. Roger Chartier (Cambridge, 1989), 235–60.

11. The treaty is published in Jean Dumont, *Corps universel diplomatique du droit des gens . . .* (Amsterdam, 1726–31), vol. 6, pt. 1, pp. 450–59 and vol. 6, pt. 2, pp. 264–83; and Vast, *Les grands traités,* vol. 1, 79–187. Among the key provisions are article 4, which concerns the renunciation of Maria Theresa's claim to the Spanish throne, and articles 35–38, which address the transfer of territory. The earliest history of the peace conference was written by Count Galeazzo Gualdo Priorato, *Histoire de la paix conclue*

sur la frontière de France et d'Espagne entre les deux couronnes, l'an M.DC.LIX. (Cologne, 1667). For evaluations of the Peace of the Pyrenees, see Goubert, *Mazarin,* 417–21; and von Pastor, *The History of the Popes,* 31:82–83, who concluded: "Mazarin had achieved the main purpose of his life: Germany and Spain were broken and France was the first power in Europe." The peace treaty granted Spain only one concession: Louis XIV pardoned the Grand Condé, Louis II Bourbon, the Spanish ally who had rebelled against the crown. Although his property was restored, the Grand Condé was compelled to live in retirement at the château of Chantilly.

12. "Cette maladie si longue et si cruelle n'est certainement autre chose qu'un fruit de cette heureuse pais qu'il nous a procurée par tant de travaux. . . . Le Cardinal Mazarin . . . meurt en enfantant non plus la guerre, mais la paix." Père Léon Macé (Léon des Carmes was his religious name), confessor to Louis XIII and Louis XIV, delivered the eulogy. This passage is cited by Raymond Darricau and Madeleine Laurain in "La mort du Cardinal Mazarin," *Annuaire-Bulletin de la Société de l'Histoire de France,* 1958–59: 68 n. 1; for the full text of the eulogy, see R. P. Léon, *L'éloge funèbre de l'éminentissime Cardinal Jules Mazarin* (Rome, 1661).

13. "Je courus à l'appartement du Cardinal. Je le rencontrai comme il sortoit de sa chambre, soutenu sous les bras par son capitaine des gardes et son maître de chambre. Il étoit fort pâle et fort abbatu, et la mort paroissoit peinte dans ses yeux, soit que la peur qu'il avoit eue d'être brûlé dans son lit l'eût mis en cet état, soit qu'il regardât l'accident inopiné de ce grand embrasement comme un avertissement que le Ciel lui donnoit de sa fin prochaine. Jamais je ne vis homme si embrassé ni si défait qu'il me le parut" (Bonnefon, ed., *Mémoires de Loménie de Brienne,* 2:27–28).

14. Loménie de Brienne was supposedly hiding behind a tapestry at the Palais Mazarin when he observed the Cardinal bidding farewell to his paintings; although he must have embellished the scene, it captures Mazarin's well-documented materialism. See Bonnefon, ed., *Mémoires de Loménie de Brienne,* 2:27–28, and 3:88–90.

15. Two sources provide eyewitness details of

Mazarin's death: Mazarin's Theatine confessor, Father Angelo Bissaro ("Relation précise des incidents qui se produisirent pendant la dernière maladie et la mort du Cardinal Mazarin survenue le [9] du mois de mars 1661") and the curate Claude Joly, who attended Mazarin at Vincennes ("Relation succinte de ce qui s'est passé à la mort de M. le Cardinal Mazarini premier ministre d'Estat"); both accounts are published in Darricau and Laurain, "La mort du Mazarin," 59–120. An excerpt from Joly's report had been published previously in *Lettres, instructions et mémoires de Colbert,* ed. Pierre Clément (Paris, 1861–70), 1:532–36. A less reliable but more widely circulated account of Mazarin's death was written by the abbé [François Timoléon] de Choisy: Jacques-Joseph Champollion-Figeac, ed., "Mémoires pour servir à l'histoire de Louis XIV," in *Nouvelle collection des mémoires pour servir à l'histoire de France,* ed. Joseph Fr. Michaud and Jean Joseph François Poujoulat, 3d ser., vol. 6 (Paris, 1850), 569–79.

16. On the relationship between Mazarin and Anne of Austria, see Claude Dulong, "Les signes cryptiques dans la correspondance d'Anne d'Autriche avec Mazarin, contribution à l'emblématique du XVIIe siècle," *Bibliothèque de l'Ecole des Chartes* 140 (1982):61–83; Ruth Kleinman, *Anne of Austria* (Columbus, Ohio, 1985), 226–32; Pierre Goubert, "Anne d'Autriche et Giulio Mazzarino, jusqu'où?," in *Correspondances, mélanges offerts à Roger Duchêne,* ed. Wolfgang Leiner and Pierre Ronzeaud (Tübingen, 1992), 155–58; and Jeffrey Merrick, "The Cardinal and the Queen: Sexual and Political Disorders in the Mazarinades," *French Historical Studies* 18 (Spring 1994):667–99.

17. On Mazarin's medical condition, see Darricau and Laurain, "La mort du Mazarin," 78, 92, 115 n. 4; and Dr. J. Sottas, "La maladie et la mort du Cardinal Mazarin," *Chronique médicale* (Poitiers, 1925).

18. "Je crois qu'elle ferait mieux si elle se mettait à couvert d'un désagrément imprévu en disposant de son bien par un testament car si le mal augmentait . . . le testament ne pourrait être que laborieux et Votre Eminence ne pourrait pas s'y appliquer comme maintenant. Cette proposition lui plus" (Darricau and Laurain, "La mort du Mazarin," 98).

19. The fundamental study of Mazarin's fortune is Daniel Dessert, "Pouvoir et finance au XVIIe siècle: La fortune du Cardinal Mazarin," *Revue d'histoire moderne et contemporaine* 23 (1976):161–81, which concentrates on the period after the Fronde (1652–61). The figure 39 million *livres* reflects only documented assets and may underestimate Mazarin's wealth if he had secret assets beyond French borders, as his contemporaries believed. Dessert found no firm evidence to substantiate the charge advanced by Fouquet in particular that Mazarin had transferred money abroad; he indicated, however, that the fortune might have reached 40 million *livres* (164 n. 17).

For an analysis of Mazarin's ecclesiastical benefices, which formed a substantial component of his wealth, see Joseph Bergin, "Cardinal Mazarin and His Benefices," *French History* 1, no. 1 (Mar. 1987):3–26.

20. The figures come from Dessert, "Pouvoir et finance," 165; and Sharon Kettering, *Patrons, Brokers, and Clients in Seventeenth-Century France* (New York, 1986), 180. For a comparison of the fortunes of Richelieu and Mazarin, see Joseph Bergin, *Cardinal Richelieu: Power and the Pursuit of Wealth* (New Haven and London, 1985), 140, 253.

21. Claude Dulong's work on Mazarin's pre-Fronde finances is invaluable, but her contempt for the cardinal leads to unsubstantiated inferences in *La fortune de Mazarin* (Paris, 1990). Dulong's related articles have a more neutral tone: "Mazarin et ses banquiers," in Accademia Nazionale dei Lincei, *Il Cardinale Mazzarino in Francia,* Atti dei convegni Lincei 35 (Rome, 1977):17–40; "Mazarin et les frères Cenami," *Bibliothèque de l'Ecole des Chartes* 144 (1986): 299–354; "Mazarin, ses banquiers et prête-nom," in *La Fronde en questions,* Actes du 18e colloque du Centre Méridional de Rencontres sur le XVIIe Siècle, Marseille-Cassis, 28–31 Jan. 1989 (n.p., 1989), 85–93; "Les comptes bleus du cardinal Mazarin," *Revue d'histoire moderne et contemporaine* 36 (1989): 537–58; and "Le processus d'enrichissement du cardinal Mazarin d'après l'inventaire de l'abbé Mondin," *Bibliothèque de l'Ecole des Chartes* 148 (1990):355–425.

22. "[P]illé et ravi toutes les finances du roy et réduit

Sa Majesté en une indigence extreme" (cited by Richard Bonney, *The King's Debts: Finance and Politics in France, 1589–1661* [Oxford, 1981], 213).

23. Dessert, "Pouvoir et finance," 170, 178.

24. "Ce n'est pas dans les bienfaits du roi qu'il faut trouver l'explication de sa fabuleuse fortune," Daniel Dessert explained, "mais bien plutôt dans cet affairisme qui se manifeste dans son intérêt pour les impôts engagés par la couronne" (Dessert, "Pouvoir et finance," 169).

25. Dulong, *La fortune de Mazarin,* 20–23; and Bonney, *The King's Debts,* 213.

26. Bergin, *Cardinal Richelieu,* 5. Although these financial practices were endemic at court, it should be noted that Henri IV's first minister, Sully, did not engage in them. In 1610, at the height of his power, most of Sully's income came from royal gifts and pensions. He never accumulated a massive fortune on the scale of his successors, and at the time of his death in 1641, Sully's holdings were estimated at 5 million *livres* (Isabelle Aristide, *La fortune de Sully* [Paris, (1989)], 92, 170, 409–12, 463).

27. In his memoirs the abbé de Choisy credited the idea of a donation to Colbert (*Nouvelle collection,* 569). Most historians regard it as a virtually foolproof strategy; Richard Bonney, for instance, argued (in *The King's Debts,* 260) that the public would have perceived the king's acceptance of the gift as a disavowal of Mazarin's recent diplomatic achievements. But this judgment reflects the wisdom of hindsight, not the uncertainties of the time.

28. "This business [of writing the will] took so long it went on until three days before his death," the confessor reported. On 6 March, Mazarin "ordered that his will be brought to him to read with the intention of signing it that night. The reading was long; he had many changes to make, and as he was very exacting about the terms, he criticized everything so that midnight arrived and the reading was not yet finished." ("Cela a été une affaire si longue qu'elle a duré jusques trois jours avant la mort. Elle ordonna qu'on lui apportât son testament à lire dans l'idée de le signer ce soir-là. L'histoire était longue; elle avait beaucoup de changements à faire et comme elle était très pointilleuse sur les termes, elle les critiquait tous de sorte que minuit arriva et que la lecture n'était pas finie" [Darricau and Laurain, "La mort du Mazarin," 100]).

29. The marriage contract was signed on 28 February 1661; the marriage took place on 1 March. A copy of the marriage contract is preserved with Mazarin's will in BN MS Mélanges de Colbert 74. The will was published by comte Gabriel-Jules de Cosnac, *Mazarin et Colbert* (Paris, 1892), 2:441–79. Cosnac did not, however, include the two codicils describing donations to the Theatines and the Collège des Quatre Nations; they are discussed below in "Terms of the Bequest." The king confirmed the will on 18 March.

30. Cosnac, *Mazarin et Colbert,* 2:464.

31. The order was dated 29 March 1661, and work on the inventory began the next day. For the inventory, see BN MS Mélanges de Colbert 75. The inventory provides an incomplete account of Mazarin's assets; many items were not appraised and private bequests were excluded.

32. On the political significance of Louis XIV's personal rule, see Daniel Dessert, *Louis XIV prend le pouvoir: Naissance d'un mythe?* (Brussels, 1989), and the analysis of Fouquet's trial in Dessert, *Fouquet* (Paris, 1987).

33. On Richelieu's will, see Bergin, *Cardinal Richelieu,* 257. In one interesting provision of the will, Richelieu asked the king to demolish the Hôtel de Sillery, which was part of the donation, and to build a proper square in front of the Palais Cardinal.

34. Mazarin purchased the Grand Sancy and the Miroir du Portugal from Henrietta-Maria, queen of England and sister of Louis XIII, in 1657 while she was living in exile in France. The eighteen *mazarins* remained among the crown jewels until 1792, when all but five disappeared; they were sold by the state in 1887. On Mazarin's diamonds, see Germain Bapst, *Histoire des joyaux de la couronne de France d'après des documents inédits* (Paris, 1889), bks. 3 and 6; Dulong, *La fortune de Mazarin,* 63–64; and Daniel Alcouffe,

"The Collection of Cardinal Mazarin's Gems," *Burlington Magazine* 116, no. 858 (Sept. 1974):514–26. For the passage in the will concerning Mazarin's gifts to the royal family, see Cosnac, *Mazarin et Colbert,* 2:446–47 and 474.

35. The foundation act was published by Alfred Franklin, *Recherches historiques sur le Collège des Quatre-Nations* (Paris, 1862), 141–60.

36. "Par l'affection qu'il a eûe au lieu de sa naissance, vouloit joindre les Italiens de l'Estat Ecclésiastique, pour les obliger de plus en plus à continuer leur zèle au service de la France" (Franklin, *Recherches historiques,* 145).

37. The full passage reads as follows: "Que comme toutes ces Provinces sont nouvellement venues ou retournées sous la puissance du Roy, il estoit à propos de les y conserver par les moyens les plus convenables. Qu'on pouvoit les affermir et les lier au service de Sa Majesté, en établissant dans la ville de Paris, qui est la Capitale du Royaume, et le sejour ordinaire des Rois Tres-Chrétiens, un College et une Académie, pour y nourrir, élever, et instruire gratuitement des Gentilshommes et des Enfans des principaux Bourgeois des Villes des Nations cy-dessus. Qu'on pouvoit aussi leur apprendre les veritables sentimens du Christianisme, la pureté de la Religion, la conduite des moeurs, et les regles de la discipline, n'y ayant point de lieu ou toutes ces choses soient avec tant d'avantages que dans ce Royaume. Que pendant ces instructions, ceux des Nations cy-dessus connoistront ce qui est necessaire à leur salut, aux sciences, et à la police, et combien il est avantageux d'estre soûmis à un si grand Roy. Que ceux qui auroient ainsi pris leur éducation en France, porteroient ce qu'ils y auroient appris au païs de leur naissance, quand ils y retourneroient, et que par leurs exemples ils y en pourroient attirer d'autres, pour venir recevoir successivement les mesmes instructions, et les pareils sentimens. Qu'enfin toutes ces Provinces deviendroient Françoises par leur propre inclination, aussi-bien qu'elles le sont maintenant par la domination de Sa Majesté" (Franklin, *Recherches historiques,* 144–45).

38. Peter Sahlins, *Boundaries: The Making of France and Spain in the Pyrenees* (Berkeley, 1989), 25; and

David Stewart, *Assimilation and Acculturation in Seventeenth-Century Europe: Roussillon and France, 1659–1715* (Westport, Conn., 1997). On the issue of cultural assimilation, see also M. M. Martin, *The Making of France: The Origins and Development of the Idea of National Unity* (London, 1951).

39. I am skeptical of Alfred Franklin's claim that Mazarin initially favored the more aggressive name Collège des Conquêtes (*Histoire de la Bibliothèque Mazarine et du Palais de l'Institut*, [Paris, 1860; rev. ed. 1901], 126). Franklin provided no supporting evidence, and I have found none. Collège des Quatre Nations is, in fact, a more evocative name for reasons indicated below.

40. The boundaries of the French annexations are described in articles 35–38 of the Treaty of the Pyrenees; see Vast, *Les grands traités,* 1:58–64, 109–11. On annexations and the idea of national boundaries, see Daniel Nordman, "Les limites d'état aux frontières nationales," in *Les lieux de mémoire,* ed. Pierre Nora, vol. 2, *La Nation* (Paris, 1986), 44.

41. The nations pertained only to the Faculty of Arts, the largest constituent group of the university comprising about two-thirds of the masters. The nations had a major role in university governance; they regulated the curriculum, administered exams, and elected the rector of the university. My thanks to Katherine Tachau for guiding me through the vast literature on the University of Paris. The following works were of most help in understanding the role of the four nations and relations between the crown and the university: Stephen Ferruolo, "*Parisinis-Paradisus:* The City, Its Schools and the Origins of the University of Paris," in *The University and the City from the Medieval Origins to the Present,* ed. Thomas Bender (New York, 1988), 22–43; Pearl Kibre, *The Nations in the Mediaeval Universities* (Cambridge, Mass., 1948), and *Scholarly Privileges in the Middle Ages* (Cambridge, Mass., 1962); Gordon Leff, *Paris and Oxford Universities in the Thirteenth and Fourteenth Centuries* (New York, 1968); and Hastings Rashdall, *The Universities of Europe in the Middle Ages,* 2d ed., ed. F. M. Powicke and A. B. Emden (Oxford, 1987), vol. 1.

42. On French universities in the seventeenth century, see the superb book by Laurence Brockliss,

French Higher Education in the Seventeenth and Eighteenth Centuries: A Cultural History (Oxford, 1987); Howell A. Lloyd, *The State and Education: University Reform in Early-Modern France* (Hull, 1987); and Jacques Verger, ed., *Histoire des universités en France* (Toulouse, 1986), 141–253. For a comparative perspective, see *A History of the University of Europe,* vol. 2, *Universities in Early Modern Europe (1500–1800),* ed. Hilde de Ridder-Symoens (Cambridge, 1996); Willem Frijhoff, "L'état et l'éducation (XVIe-XVIIe siècles): Une perspective globale," in *Culture et idéologie dans la genèse de l'état moderne,* Ecole Française de Rome 82 (Rome, 1985), 99–116; and Richard Kagan, *Students and Society in Early Modern Spain* (Baltimore, 1974).

43. On the college system, see Rainer Müller, "Student Education, Student Life," in *A History of the University of Europe,* vol. 2, *Universities in Early Modern Europe (1500–1800),* ed. Hilde de Ridder-Symoens (Cambridge, 1996), 333–39; Marie-Madeleine Compère, *Du Collège au lycée (1500–1850): Généalogie de l'enseignement secondaire français* (Paris, 1985); Jean de Viguerie, *Les institutions des enfants: L'education en France XVIe–XVIIIe siècle* (Paris, 1978); Roger Chartier et al., *L'education en France du XVIe au XVIIIe siècle* (Paris, 1976), chap. 5; and A. L. Gabriel, *The College System in the Fourteenth-Century Universities* (Baltimore, n.d.). On the decline of the nations, see Kibre, *The Nations in the Mediaeval Universities,* 115.

44. In *From Humanism to the Humanities: Education and the Liberal Arts in in Fifteenth- and Sixteenth-Century Europe* (London, 1986), Lisa Jardine and Anthony Grafton argued that educational reform in the humanities and the establishment of *studia humanitatis* in the early fifteenth century served the growing absolutist state. For a contrary view, see Paul Gehl, *A Moral Art: Grammar, Society, and Culture in Trecento Florence* (Ithaca, 1993). See also the sources on seventeenth-century French higher education cited in note 43.

45. The twelve most senior doctors of the Sorbonne were to select four colleagues as inspectors or overseers of the Collège des Quatre Nations. The headmaster and treasurer had to be graduates of the Sorbonne (Franklin, *Recherches historiques,* 149–50).

46. The key source on Jesuit schools remains François de Dainville, *La naissance de l'humanisme moderne: Les Jésuites et l'éducation de la société française* (Paris, 1940).

47. On riding academies, see Norbert Conrads, *Ritterakademien der frühen Neuzeit: Bildung als Standesprivileg im 16. und 17. Jahrhundert* (Göttingen, 1982). The most famous French riding academy was founded by Antoine Pluvinel, riding master at the court of Henri III and Henri IV, in 1594 near the royal stables in the faubourg Saint Honoré, where he instructed the dauphin and other members of the royal family. On Pluvinel's academy, see Alexandre de Pontaymery, *L'académie ou l'institution de la noblesse* (Paris, 1595); Antoine de Pluvinel, *Maneige royale* (Paris, 1625); and Pluvinel, *L'instruction du roy en l'exercise de monter à cheval* (Paris, 1625).

48. If, however, the Collège failed to provide a full class of fifteen students, openings could be filled by students from the so-called four nations who had not studied at the Collège (Franklin, *Recherches historiques,* 147, 154). Laurence Brockliss (*French Higher Education,* 450) believes Mazarin was out of step with government opinion in seeing a a traditional humanist education as suitable for a military man.

49. On aristocratic education and efforts to reform it in the sixteenth and seventeenth centuries, see Chartier et al., *L'education en France,* 168–85; J. R. Hale, "Military Academies in the Venetian Terraferma in the Early Seventeenth Century," in *Renaissance War Studies* (London, 1983), 285–307; J. H. Hexter, "The Education of the Aristocracy in the Renaissance," in *Reappraisals in History,* 2d ed. (Chicago, 1979), 45–70; and Mark Motley, *Becoming a French Aristocrat: The Education of the Court Nobility, 1580–1715* (Princeton, 1990), especially chap. 3.

One proposal notable for its ambitious scope came from François de La Noue (*Discours politiques et militaires* [Basel, 1587]), who, in the early 1580s, envisioned a national network of four royal academies where young nobles beginning at age fifteen would pursue a four-year course of study. Classes were divided into two fields: training for the body, which amounted to the standard arts of wars—equitation, use of arms, athletics—and training the mind, an innovative reform of humanistic studies tailored

to prepare young men for government service: reading the ancients in French so that time was not wasted in studying Latin, ancient and modern history, geography, fortifications, and vernacular languages. Not one of de La Noue's schools was ever founded.

50. At the academy in Paris, twenty young nobles were to study for two years before serving in the king's guard or navy for two more years. Cardinal Richelieu provided an annual subsidy of 22,000 *livres* to the academy in his new town; it reportedly attracted two hundred students its first year and double that number a year later. On Richelieu's views about education and his two academies, see Cardinal Richelieu, *Testament politique,* ed. Louis André (Paris, 1947), 204–6; *Lettres, instructions diplomatiques et papiers d'état du cardinal de Richelieu,* ed. D. L. M. Avenel (Paris, 1853–77), 5:721–23; Laurence Brockliss, "Richelieu, Education, and the State," in *Richelieu and His Age,* ed. Joseph Bergin and Laurence Brockliss (Oxford, 1992), 237–72; J. H. Elliott, *Richelieu and Olivares* (Cambridge, 1984), 82, 133–34; Marcel Bataillon, "L'académie de Richelieu, Indre-et-Loire," in *Pédagogues et juristes,* Congrès du Centre d'Etudes Supérieures de la Renaissance de Tours, 1960 (Paris, 1963), 255–70; A.-F. Théry, *Histoire de l'éducation en France depuis le cinquième siècle jusqu'à nos jours* (Paris, 1858), 2:105; *Déclaration du roy contenant l'establissement de l'académie ou collège royal en la ville de Richelieu, et privileges attribués à icelle, ensemble les statuts et règlements de ladite académie* (Paris, 1641); and Jules Caillet, *L'administration en France sous le ministère du Cardinal de Richelieu,* 2d ed. (Paris, 1861–63), 2:171–83.

With regard to French as the language of instruction, Richelieu argued that knowledge of Latin was irrelevant to a soldier: "Les difficultés qu'il faut surmonter et le long temps qui s'emploie pour apprendre les langues mortes avant que de pouvoir parvenir à la connaissance des sciences font que les jeunes gentilshommes se rebutent et se hâtent de passer à l'exercice des armes sans avoir été instruits suffisamment aux bonnes lettres" (Caillet, *L'administration en France sous Richelieu,* 2:176–77). He also insisted that the French language was capable of conveying the wisdom of the ancients as well as the moderns and worthy of study in its own right. These views echoed the platform of the Académie

Française, which Richelieu founded in 1635; see the foundation act of the Académie Française in *Recueil général des anciennes lois françaises,* ed François Isambert (Paris, 1829), 16:418–20.

51. Mazarin did not envision a reform curriculum. The foundation act of his Collège provides a thumbnail description of the course of study: "Plus il y aura audit Collège huit Classes et autant de Régents: scavoir, six d'Humanitez, et deux de Philiosophie; tous lesquels Régents seront Bacheliers en Théologie, et nommez par le Grand-Maistre" (Franklin, *Recherches historiques,* 152).

52. My interpretation of the academies differs from that of Laurence Brockliss in that he emphasizes the role of *académies d'équitation* in "emasculating" the nobility of the sword and distracting it from affairs of state: Brockliss, *French Higher Education,* 450. Like Roger Chartier in *L'education en France,* 183–84, I see the reform academies of Richelieu and Mazarin as a means of preparing young nobles for state service.

53. More precisely the library contained, at the time of Mazarin's death, 37,880 volumes, which was close to its pre-Fronde size: Louis Charles François Petit-Radel, *Recherches sur les bibliothèques anciennes et modernes* (Paris, 1819), 290. See the next note for further references on the library.

54. Mazarin may have reasonably expected that by reconstituting his library as a public institution, it would be safeguarded from future sackings. Perhaps the same concern led him to order an inventory of the library, whereas he did not want his other property inventoried. Ironically, it was the king who made claims on the collection in a crafty move engineered by Colbert. A royal edict of 1668 ordered the Bibliothèque Mazarine to surrender all of its manuscripts (numbering 2,156) and 3,677 of its most precious printed books to the Royal Library. In exchange, the Royal Library donated 2,341 books that it had in duplicate.

On Mazarin's collection of books and manuscripts, see two studies by Pierre Gasnault: "La bibliothèque de Mazarin à la Bibliothèque Mazarine," in *Histoire des Bibliothèques françaises,* ed. Claude Jolly (Paris, 1988–91), vol. 2, *Les bibliothèques sous l'Ancien*

Régime, 1530–1789 (1989), 135–145; "La bibliothèque de Mazarin et la Bibliothèque Mazarine au XVIIe et XVIIIe siècle," in *Les espaces du livre,* vol. 2, *Les bibliothèques,* Institut d'Etude du Livre, Deuxième Colloque (Paris, 1980), 38–56; and three books by Alfred Franklin: *Histoire de la Bibliothèque Mazarine et du Palais de l'Institut,* 2d rev. ed. (Paris, 1901), 210–13; "Collège Mazarin," *Les anciennes bibliothèques de Paris* (Paris, 1867–73), 3:37–100; *Histoire de la Bibliothèque Mazarine depuis sa fondation jusqu'à nos jours* (Paris, 1860); as well as an assessment by Leon de Laborde: *De l'organization des bibliothèques dans Paris, quatrième lettre: Le Palais Mazarin et les habitations de ville et de campagne au dix-septième siècle* (Paris, 1845), 5–50. On the fate of Mazarin's library during the Fronde, see two articles by Jean Kaulek: "Nouveaux documents pour servir à l'histoire de la bibliothèque du cardinal Mazarin, 1642–1652," *BSHP* 9 (1882):81–90; and "Documents relatifs à la vente de la bibliothèque du cardinal de Mazarin pendant la Fronde, janvier–février 1652," *BSHP* 8 (1880):131–45.

55. Mazarin transferred 45,000 *livres* in bonds issued by the Hôtel de Ville in Paris to the Collège. According to Dessert ("Pouvoir et finance," 178), Mazarin's annual income at the end of his life was between 1.7 and 2 million *livres*.

56. Cosnac, *Mazarin et Colbert,* 2:445–46.

57. "Qu'afin de parvenir à l'exécution de ce dessein, par une Fondation qui pust estre à la gloire de Dieu, et à l'avantage de l'Estat, il avoit fait de temps en temps un amas de deniers comptans, par des oeconomies et des épargnes des effets à luy appartenans. [The preceding sentence is not translated in the text.] Mais qu'ayant connu par expérience, qu'il estoit absolument necessaire d'avoir un fonds assûré de réserve, pour subvenir aux incertitudes des évenemens et aux occasions pressantes et inopinées, principalement durant une guerre très-fâcheuse, et contre de puissans ennemis; et son Eminence [Mazarin] sçachant que les Finances du Roy n'estoient point en estat de donner un si prompt secours, a conservé ses épargnes pour en secourir le Roy, s'il en estoit besoin, et pour soûtenir et défendre la grandeur du Royaume, en cas de necessité . . ." (Franklin, *Recherches historiques,* 142–43).

58. "Le Cardinal Duc supplie très-humblement Sa Majesté," reads the will, "que la présente Fondation soit en sa protection perpetuelle, et des Rois ses successeurs" (Franklin, *Recherches historiques,* 148).

59. The argument was put forward originally in Madeleine Laurain-Portemer, "Mazarin: Militant de l'art baroque au temps de Richelieu (1634–42)," (*BSHAF,* 1975:65–100), and was reprinted in her collected essays, *Etudes mazarines* (Paris, 1981).

This section does not address Mazarin's long-distance patronage in Italy. Although his modus operandi was similar to that in France, Mazarin was involved in more building projects, principally because of family ties in Rome. He had the facade of his baptismal church, Santissimi Vincenzo ed Anastasio, Rome (1646–50), rebuilt by Martino Longhi the Younger—Mazarin's most important architectural undertaking—and made modest changes to the palace he bought for his family, the Palazzo Mancini (originally the Palazzo Borghese). On Mazarin's building activities in Rome, see Antonio Pugliese and Salvatore Rigano, "Martino Longhi il giovane, architetto," in *Architettura barocca a Roma,* ed. M. Fagiolo dell'Arco (Rome, 1972), 7–192; and Armando Schiavo, *Palazzo Mancini* (Palermo, 1969). On his involvement with a project to build steps at the Trinità dei Monti, see Appendix B.

60. On the cultural politics of Cardinal Richelieu, see Anne Le Pas de Sécheval's excellent dissertation "La politique artistique de Louis XIII," Université de Paris (Sorbonne), 1992. She makes the point (1:128, 143) that Richelieu courted prestigious artists irrespective of their stylistic convictions; he was as eager to commission Pietro da Cortona as Sacchi and Guercino. I submit the same was true of Mazarin.

As for Mazarin's work on behalf of Cardinal Richelieu, Le Pas de Sécheval writes (1:114–16, 146–47, 176): "Sans minimiser la part prise par Mazarin dès les années 1630 dans ce que certains ont appelé 'l'offensive de l'art romain,' il faut reconnaître que dans les faits, il ne fut que l'héritier d'une politique systématisée par d'autres que lui."

61. An exception is Antoine Schnapper, who sharply differentiates collecting from patronage in his work on seventeenth-century French collectors, *Curieux du Grand Siècle: Collections et collectionneurs dans la France du XVIIe siècle, vol. 2, oeuvres d'art,* (Paris, 1994). Schnapper focuses solely on the cardinal's practices as a collector, and in this context, disputing Laurain-Portemer's perception of Mazarin as a "militant for Baroque art," he writes (2:213): "Je ne crois pas la notion très significative, d'autant que certains des peintres italiens modernes les plus appréciés du Cardinal, Sacchi ou Romanelli, sont parmi les moins 'baroques' du siècle. En revanche, il est sûr que Mazarin, proche en cela de la plupart des grands curieux français, restait fort attaché à la peinture italienne, qu'elle fût ancienne ou moderne."

62. On Mazarin's contribution to the French political system, see Treasure, *Mazarin: The Crisis of Absolutism in France;* Goubert, *Mazarin;* Madeleine Laurain-Portemer, "Monarchie et gouvernement: Mazarin et le modèle romain," in *La France et l'Italie,* 45–53; and Accademia Nazionale dei Lincei, *Il Cardinale Mazzarino in Francia,* Atti dei convegni Lincei 35 (Rome, 1977).

63. Laurain-Portemer, *Etudes mazarines,* pt. 2, 175–399. In these essays Laurain-Portemer tapped a previously unexplored source, Mazarin's correspondence with his Roman agent, Elpidio Benedetti (now in the Ministère des Affaires Etrangères, Paris), which provided fascinating information about Mazarin's efforts to recruit Italian artists. Reliance on this archival source, however, provides only a partial view of Mazarin's practices as a patron. Laurain-Portemer's other evidence for Mazarin's Baroque offensive rests on his predilection for Baroque furniture.

64. On the decoration of Mazarin's galleries and Romanelli's other work in France, see Laurain-Portemer, *Etudes mazarines,* 175–293, 383–91; and Didier Bodart, "Une description de 1657 des fresques de Giovanni Francesco Romanelli au Louvre," *BSHAF,* 1974, 43–50.

65. On Poussin's project for the Grande Galerie of the Louvre, see Joseph Forte, "Political Ideology and Artistic Theory in Poussin's Decoration of the Grande Galerie of the Louvre," Ph.D. diss., Columbia University, 1983; Doris Wild, "Nicolas Poussin et la décoration de la Grande Galerie du Louvre," *La Revue du Louvre* 16 (1966):77–84; and Anthony

Blunt, "Poussin Studies VI: Poussin's Decoration of the Long Gallery of the Louvre," *Burlington Magazine* 93 (1951): 369–76.

66. Letter from Romanelli to Cardinal Antonio Barberini, 6 July 1646, published in Laurain-Portemer, *Etudes mazarines* (267): "Proposi al signor Cardinale Mazzarino di dipingervi dentrò l'istorie romane ma mostrò haver più gusto delle metamorfose d'Ovidio, come più allegre e che siano per dare più nel genio des paese."

67. According to Schnapper (*Curieux du Grand Siècle,* chap. 6), Mazarin's purchases—tapestries, silver, crystal, and furniture inlaid with semiprecious stones—put him in a category of princely collectors. On his collection of artworks and furnishings, including inventories, see *Curieux du Grand Siècle,* 189–215; Bibliothèque Nationale, *Mazarin: Homme d'etat et collectionneur, 1602–1661,* exh. cat. (Paris, 1961); Arnauld Brejon de Lavergnée, "Note sur la collection de peintures du Cardinal Mazarin: Sa formation et son sort après 1661," in *La France et l'Italie,* 265–74; comte Gabriel-Jules de Cosnac, *Les richesses du Palais Mazarin* (Paris, 1884); C. de Boyer de Sainte-Suzanne, "Inventaire du cardinal Mazarin (1661)," in *Notes d'un curieux* (Monaco, 1878), 87–114; duc d'Aumale, ed., *Inventaire de tous les meubles du Cardinal Mazarin dressé en 1653 et publié d'après l'original conservé dans les Archives de Condé* (London, 1861); and BN MS Mélanges de Colbert 75, fols. 273v–365.

68. Dessert, "Pouvoir et finance," 171–72.

69. Bergin, *Cardinal Richelieu,* 253.

70. Dessert, "Pouvoir et finance," 165.

71. "J'ay esté contraint d'envoyer à Mayenne le sieur Leveau le jeune prendre le plan de la ville et du château, faire des dessins des bastimens, afin de dissiper les bruits qui ont couru que Vostre Eminence vouloit vendre ce duché, qui aliénoient tous les esprits, en sorte qu'il estoit non seulement impossible de faire réussir les augmentations prejetées, mais mesme nous courrions risque de voir diminuer toutes nos fermes" (letter from Colbert to Mazarin, 11 Dec. 1658, published in Cosnac, *Mazarin et Colbert,* 2:256 (see also 116–17, 212, and 249).

72. Colbert wrote Mazarin on 11 Oct. 1652, upon the death of the governor of Vincennes, Léon Bouthillier, the count of Chavigny: "Si M. de Chavigny est mort, Vostre Eminence doit penser, à mon sens, à prendre le chasteau de Vincennes pour elle, quand ce ne seroit que pour avoir un lieu à elle où pouvoir mettre quelque somme considérable, et, en ce cas, y establir quelqu'un de sa maison, des plus affidés, pour y commander. . . ." Colbert went on to discuss the need to select cities where Mazarin could deposit his money (Clément, *Lettres de Colbert,* 1:194).

On Vincennes in the seventeenth-century, see Edouard-Jacques Ciprut, "Documents inédits sur quelques château d'Ile-de-France," *Mémoires de la Société de l'Histoire de Paris et Ile-de-France* 16–17 (1965–66):175–81; Jean Cordey, "Colbert, Le Vau, et la construction du château de Vincennes au XVIIe siècle," *GBA* 9 (May 1933):273–93; Alain Erlande-Brandenburg and Bertrand Jestaz, *Le château de Vincennes* (Paris 1989); and Colonel de Fossa, *Le château historique de Vincennes* (Paris, 1907–9).

73. It should be noted that Louis XIV's interest in Vincennes was short-lived; his last visit was in 1667.

74. Erlande-Brandenburg and Jestaz, *Le château de Vincennes,* 99–100.

75. Mazarin's patronage of Sainte Anne-la-Royale is discussed in chapter 2. On Sainte Anne-la-Royale and the Theatines, see Susan Klaiber, "Guarino Guarini's Theatine Architecture," Ph. D. diss., Columbia University, 1993, which supersedes earlier studies of Guarini's project; Alan Boase, "Sant'Anna Reale," in *Guarino Guarini e l'internazionalità del Barocco,* (Turin, 1970), 2:345–58; Georges Cattaui, "Guarini et la France," in *Guarino Guarini,* 2:512–21; David Coffin, "Padre Guarino Guarini in Paris," *JSAH* 15 (1956):3–11; E. Picard, "Les Théatins de Sainte-Anne-la-Royale (1644–1790): Une acculturation manquée?," *Regnum Dei* 106 (1980):97–374; and Raymond Darricau, "Les Clercs Réguliers Théatins à Paris, Sainte-Anne-la-Royale (1644–1793)," *Regnum Dei* 10 (1954):165–204, 11 (1955):98–126, 13 (1957):257–77, 14 (1958):13–58, 15 (1959):19–68, 96–214.

76. The Palais Mazarin, on the rue Neuve-des-Petits-Champs, has a complicated building history. In 1643,

when Mazarin first rented the property, it comprised three adjacent *hôtels:* a large house on the corner of the rue Vivienne—known as the Hôtel Tubeuf— and two others, smaller and nearly uniform to the west, toward the rue Richelieu. Mazarin bought land behind the houses and asked Bernini to design additions (the first of Mazarin's many attempts, all unsuccessful, to commission Bernini). After Bernini declined, Mazarin turned to François Mansart; in 1645 Mansart designed along the garden a two-story wing that later housed Mazarin's lower and upper galleries, with a pavilion connecting to the Hôtel Tubeuf. Mansart also designed a new staircase in the rue Vivienne wing of the Hôtel Tubeuf.

A year later, in 1646, Pierre Le Muet and Maurizio Valperga, a Turinese engineer whom Mazarin favored throughout his life, built stables and another gallery to house Mazarin's library along the rue Richelieu. The palace was pillaged during the Fronde, and when the cardinal returned to power, he concentrated on interior renovations from 1653 until shortly before his death.

In 1659 Mazarin set Valperga to work on an ambitious expansion project. That the site was inspected by Gaspare Vigarani, an expert on theaters then at work on the Tuileries theater, suggests that a theater was under consideration. Colbert reported Vigarani's reaction to the site in a letter to Mazarin on 13 July 1659: "M. Vigarani a vu avec M. Valpergue le palais de Vostre Eminence, mais il n'a pas trouvé qu'il y eust assez d'espace pour faire les bastimens nécessaires pour l'exécution de ses dessins. . . . Pour ce qui est de son palais, M. Valpergue travaille au dessin de ce qui est à faire pour achever au moins le carré de la cour des écuries, mais comme il m'a fait voir que ce bastiment est attaché à celuy qui continue jusqu'à la rue Vivienne, je doute que nous puissions prendre aucune résolution sur ce sujet avant le retour de Vostre Eminence" (cited by Roger-Armand Weigert, "Le Palais Mazarin, architectes et décorateurs," *Art de France* 2 [1962]:169, no. 124).

Valperga scaled back the project and concentrated on completing a courtyard with additional stables. As a result of these piecemeal additions, the Palais Mazarin was a sprawling structure, palatial in size and decor perhaps, but not in building type or monumentality.

On the Palais Mazarin, see Claude Dulong, "Du nouveau sur le Palais Mazarin: L'achat de l'Hô-

tel Tubeuf par le cardinal," *Bibliothèque de l'Ecole des Chartes* 153 (1995):131–55; Madeleine Laurain-Portemer, "Le Palais Mazarin à Paris et l'offensive baroque, 1645–50, d'après Romanelli, P. de Cortone et Grimaldi," *GBA* 71 (1973):151–68, republished in *Etudes mazarines,* 237–78; comte de Cosnac, ed., *Les richesses du Palais Mazarin;* and several articles by Roger-Armand Weigert: "Le Palais Mazarin en 1657," *Humanisme actifs: Mélanges d'art et de littérature offerts à Julien Cain,* (Paris, 1968), 1:385–98; "Le Palais Mazarin, architectes et décorateurs," *Art de France* 2 (1962):146–69; "L'Hôtel de Chevry-Tubeuf et les débuts du Palais Mazarin," *BSHAF,* 1945, 1–33.

On Mansart's alterations, see Allan Braham and Peter Smith, *François Mansart* (London, 1973), 1:70–74, 223–26; and Jean-Pierre Babelon and Claude Mignot, eds., *François Mansart: Le génie de l'architecture* (Paris, 1998), 180–82.

77. Bergin, *Cardinal Richelieu,* 261. Richelieu asked the duc de Richelieu to build a new library; the project was never realized.

78. The key source on the pope's fusion of secular and religious power is Paolo Prodi, *The Papal Prince, One Body and Two Souls: The Papal Monarchy in Early Modern Europe,* trans. Susan Haskins (Cambridge, 1988). See also Carl Conrad Eckhardt, *The Papacy and World Affairs as Reflected in the Secularization of Politics* (Chicago, 1937).

A vast literature touches on the relationship between church and state in France. In addition to the comments of Philip Benedict (personal communication), I found the following sources helpful: Joseph Bergin, *The Making of the French Episcopate, 1589–1661* (New Haven and London, 1996); François Laplanche, *L'ecriture, le sacré et l'histoire: Erudits et politiques protestants devant la Bible en France au XVIIe siècle* (Amsterdam, 1986); Colette Beaune, *The Birth of an Ideology: Myths and Symbols of Nation in Later Medieval France,* trans. Susan Ross Huston, ed. Fredric Cheyette (Berkeley, 1991)—originally published as *Naissance de la nation France* (Paris, 1985); *Histoire de la France religieuse,* ed. Jacques Le Gott and René Rémond, vol. 2, *Du christianisme flamboyant à l'aube des Lumières (XIVe–XVIIIe siècle),* ed. François Lebrun (Paris, 1988); Aimé-Georges Martimort, *Le Gallicanisme* (Paris, 1973); and William Church, *Richelieu and Reason of State* (Princeton, 1972).

CHAPTER 2

1. This book draws on a rich bibliography, beginning with Alfred Franklin, *Recherches historiques sur le Collège des Quatre-Nations* (Paris, 1862), which tells the story of the foundation. Matters of design fall outside his scope, but Franklin, an archivist and historian of Paris, did an admirable job in culling useful information from the minutes of the building commission, Mazarin's will, and other early documents. My thanks to Orest Ranum for alerting me to an article by Claude Dulong, "Les origines du Collège des Quatre Nations," *Revue des sciences morales et politiques* (1996):247–56.

The focus of the next studies shifts to the nineteenth-century history of the Institut and the vicissitudes of the academies that Napoleon installed in Le Vau's buildings: Alfred Franklin et al., *L'Institut de France: Le Palais-l'Institut; L'Académie Française; L'Académie des inscriptions et belles-lettres* (Paris, 1907); Henry Lemonnier, *Le Collège Mazarin et le Palais de l'Institut (XVIIe–XIXe siècle)* (Paris, 1921); and Carl de Vinck and Alfred Vuaflart, *La Place de l'Institut, sa galerie marchande des Quatre Nations, et ses étalages d'estampes, 1660–1880* (Paris, 1928).

The restoration of the dome in 1962 and 1963 prompted a new wave of publications that, for the first time, addressed the architecture. André Gutton, the architect responsible for the building from 1943 through the restoration of the dome, presented a dossier on the dome in "La Restauration de la coupole de l'Institut," *Monuments historiques de la France* 9, no. 1 (1963):1–58. His memoirs touch on many other fascinating aspects of his career at the Institut, including his efforts to save the structure from demolition in the 1960s: Gutton, *De la nuit à l'aurore: Conversations sur l'architecture* (Saint-Léger-Vauban, 1986), 1:125–28, 241–47, 261–66; 2:352–55, 384–90, 485–89, 502. Louis Hautecoeur, a member of the Institut, put Le Vau's drawings in sequence and published many of them for the first time in an amply illustrated anniversary publication, *La chapelle du Collège des Quatre Nations, le tricentenaire 1662–1962, la coupole de l'Institut* (Paris, 1962). Since then several other commemorative volumes have been dedicated to the Institut de France. The most useful is the catalogue of an exhibition sponsored by the Délégation à l'Action Artistique de la Ville de Paris and the Société Historique du VIe Arrondissement, *L'Institut et la monnaie: Deux palais sur un quai* (Paris, 1990).

2. The instructions sent in December 1656 do not survive. In a letter to Mazarin dated 15 January 1657, Benedetti indicated that he had not yet approached Bernini about Mazarin's tomb: "Tra hieri et oggi che vennero le lettere dell'8 del passato non ho pututo vedere il s. cav. Bernino per pregarlo d'applicare ad un disegno di sepoltura.... Per d.a fabrica, ancora si haverebbe bisogno d'un poco di descrittione del sito e del numero di quei verrano destinati al collegio et al servitio della chiesa et biblioteca" (Affaires étrangères, Corr. pol., Rome 132, fol. 299; cited in Madeline Laurain-Portemer, *Etudes mazarines* [Paris, 1981], 391 n. 3).

3. "Non si può dare al s. cavalier Bernino alcune notitie del sito, che è ancora incerto, ma egli porrá fare il disegno con ogni libertà perché a me stará il sciierglierlo" (letter from Mazarin to Benedetti, 22 February 1657; Affaires étrangères, France 273, fol. 495v; cited in Laurain-Portemer, *Etudes mazarines,* 295 n. 5). Whether Mazarin refers here to the tomb alone or to the entire project is uncertain; either way, he had not chosen the site of the Collège.

4. "Mi dice che non sa mettere le mani a quello che desidera V. Em. se non ha le misure precise del luoco ove deve andare, ne si vuole apagare del libero campo che se gli lassa e del volersi che il luoco servi al suo pensiero, rispondendo che il principale non deve ceder all'accessario e che egli non ha tempo di dar colpo all'aria" (letter from Benedetti to Mazarin, 28 May 1657, Affaires étrangères, Corr. pol., Rome 132, fol. 409; cited in Laurain-Portemer, *Etudes mazarines,* 295 n. 5).

5. "Mando per questo ordinario a M. Colbert un cannelo di latta con dentro quattro disegni di pensieri per la sepoltura da farsi di quà a cento anni per V. Em.a. Sono del più pellegrino ingegno che oggi habbiamo e di meriti ad essere invediato anco da i Bernini" (letter from Benedetti to Mazarin, 19 November 1657, Affaires étrangères, Corr. pol., Rome 134, fol. 131; cited in Laurain-Portemer, *Etudes mazarines*, 392 n. 5).

6. Rainaldi mentioned the project in a letter to Mazarin dated 27 February 1660 (Affaires étrangères, Corr. pol., Rome 138, fol. 418): "Si compiacque il Signor Abbate Elpidio di farmi godere i favori segnalti della fortuna facendo comparire d'avanti gl'occhi di V. E.za alcuni miei Disegni per la construttione del sontuoso Tempio, con Palazzo et Biblioteca, che l'E. S.a pensava di far fabricare." Rainaldi mistakenly referred to a palace rather than a college. The letter, which otherwise concerns Rainaldi's project to enlarge the Palazzo Mancini, Mazarin's Roman residence, is published in full by Armando Schiavo, *Palazzo Mancini* (Palermo, 1969), 115–16.

7. "Pour le grand dessein de bastiment auquel V. E. m'a tesmoigné de vouloir faire travailler, je la suplie très humblement de me donner ses ordres si j'attendray response de M. E. Benedetti pour scavoir si l'architecte de Rome viendra pour voir les desseins qu'il a faitz, ou si j'en feray fere par quelque architecte de cette ville. Il me semble que l'on se peut servir pour cela que du sr. Le Vau ou du sr. Manssart ou du sr Le Muet. V.Em me fera scavoir s'il luy plaist lequel des trois elle desira que j'employe" (Letter from Colbert to Mazarin, 8 June 1657, BN MS Baluze 176, fol. 299; published in Ministère de la Culture, *Colbert, 1619–1683,* exh. cat. [Paris, 1983], 235).

8. "Il sera bon de soliciter le Benedetti à nous envoyer l'architteti [plural?], mais au mesme temps il faudroit faire travailler à Paris un des trois à un dessein, luy faisant entendre mon intention avec des gatteries pour Le Vau si vous employez un autre, mais en cela je me remet à vous" (marginal comment by Mazarin, 12 June 1657, BN MS Baluze 176, fol. 299; published in Ministère de la Culture, *Colbert,* 235).

9. Colbert left an ample right margin on his letters so that Mazarin could reply to each of his queries. Colbert's comment on 22 June 1657, "Je fais travailler le sr Le Vau au grand dessein de V. E," elicited a reply from Mazarin on June 25: "Bon, car aussi bien

il ne faut rien attendre de Rome, mais peut-être il serait bon de donner quelque gratification à celui que le Benedetti escrit avoir fait un beau dessein. Je m'en remet à vous" (BN MS Baluze 176, fol. 308; published in Adolphe Chéruel and Georges d'Avenel, *Lettres du Cardinal Mazarin pendant son ministère* [Paris, 1893], 7:529).

10. When Le Vau suggested the Porte de Nesle site on 31 December 1661, he stated that "on pourroit faire une place publique qui serviroit d'ornement à l'aspect du Louvre, qu'autrefois il avoit esté proposé d'y faire une grande place, de mesme facon que la place Royalle mais que depuis le dessein en a esté changé . . ." (AN MM 462, fol. 38v).

11. On 8 July 1657 Colbert wrote Mazarin: "J'envoye à Votre Eminence un projet que j'ay faict concernant son grand dessein. Je la supplie tres humblement de le voir et examiner à son loisir pour y changer et retrancher ce qu'elle estimera à propos estant tres important de bien poser et considerer un si grand dessein avant que le commencer." Mazarin's response on 15 July was written in the margin of Colbert's letter: "J'examineray ce project mais je voudrois seulement scavoir ce que couteroit la place qu'il faudroit achepter pour bastir, et dela je vous dis que je n'approuve pas tout ce qui concerne les casernes et lieux . . . d'iceux corps et des gardes cor. Quand pour mon credit, la chose seroit establie comme on la prepare, cela auroit peine à estre executer de mon vivant" (BN MS Baluze 176, fol. 324).

Colbert pressed Mazarin for a fuller evaluation of Le Vau's design a few days later, on 21 July 1657: "Pour le projet du grand dessein que j'ay envoyé, je scay bien qu'il y aura beaucoup de choses à changer et à corriger. Votre Eminence prendra, s'il luy plaist, la peine de le voir et le considerer à son loisir pour y employer quelque partie de ses grandes lumiere puisque c'est un dessein qui doibt porter son nom dans les siecles à venir" (BN MS Baluze 176, fol. 331).

The letters cited above are unpublished. The combination of Mazarin's irregular French spellings and his inscrutable handwriting makes it daunting to transcribe his autograph letters. I am grateful to Madame Le Pavec, curator in the Salle des Manuscrits, for help in deciphering this difficult passage. Mazarin's correspondence with Colbert contains no further comments on Le Vau's design.

12. "La pensée de faire une grande place carrée au delà de la rivière, disposée pour y loger les gendarmes, chevau-légers, mousquetaires et mesme partie du régiment des gardes, qui pourroit servir pour des grandes festes et divertissemens publics, au milieu de laquelle on pourroit élever quelque monument à la gloire du Roy" (Pierre Clément, ed., *Lettres, instructions, et mémoires de Colbert* |Paris, 1868|, 5:258).

13. The Louvre had originally been oriented to the river, which it was built to defend; only after the building was defortified and converted to a palace in the fourteenth century was the main entrance relocated in the east wing, facing the city center. François I confirmed long-standing practice when he closed the southern entrance altogether and built an enclosed garden between the palace and the river in the 1530s. The urban dimension of Le Vau's design of 1660 was noted by André Chastel and Jean-Marie Pérouse de Montclos, "L'aménagement de l'accès oriental du Louvre," *Monuments historiques de la France* 12, no. 3 (1966):180; and by Daniela del Pesco, *Il Louvre di Bernini nella Francia di Luigi XIV* (Naples, 1984), 16.

14. Etienne Dupérac and Filippo de Rossi reconstructed the Pons Triumphans as part of the ancient Via Triumphalis, the road emperors followed from the Vatican Circus (the Circus of Nero) to the Capitol. On the Via Triumphalis, see Ena Makin, "The Triumphal Route, with Particular Reference to the Flavian Triumph," *Journal of Roman Studies* 11 (1921):25–36; and E. Baldwin Smith, *Architectural Symbolism of Imperial Rome and the Middle Ages* (Princeton, 1956), 25–27. Smith discussed the importance of purification by water in the ceremonial entry of emperor-triumphator, an idea that may resonate in the background of Le Vau's royal bridge over the Seine. Le Vau owned books by Suetonius, Dio Cassius, and Josephus that described triumphal processions.

On Hadrian's bridge, the Pons Aelius, see Mary Boatwright, *Hadrian and the City of Rome* (Princeton, 1987), 161–81; Joël Le Gall, *Le Tibre, fleuve de Rome dans l'antiquité* (Paris, 1953), 214–15; and S. Rowland Pierce, "The Mausoleum of Hadrian and the Pons Aelius," *Journal of Roman Studies* 15, no. 1 (1925):75–103. Dupérac and Pirro Ligorio based their reconstructions of the Pons Aelius on antique bronze medals that show eight columns rising from the arches of the bridge, each supporting a statue, in addition to four smaller statues at the embankments. On Ligorio's reconstruction of the Pons Aelius, see Howard Burns, "Pirro Ligorio's Reconstruction of Ancient Rome: The *Antiquae Urbis Imago* of 1561," in *Pirro Ligorio: Artist and Antiquarian,* ed. Robert Gaston (Milan, 1988), 28–29.

Le Vau's Pont de la Paix emerges from the same traditions as Bernini's Ponte Sant' Angelo (1667–72), which had statues of colossal angels rising above the piers. On Bernini's design, see Mark Weil, *The History and Decoration of the Ponte S. Angelo* (University Park, Pa., 1974); and for related projects by other architects, see Werner Oechslin, *Bildingsgut und Antikenrezeption* (Zurich, 1972).

15. For other plans of Jesuit colleges, see Pierre Moisy, *Les églises des Jésuites de l'ancienne assistance de France* (Rome, 1958).

16. The phrase reads: "affin que la posterité puisse estre informée de la conduitte qu'on aura tenu pour parvenir à l'accomplissment de ce grand dessein . . ." (AN MM 462, fol. 56v, 29 July 1662).

17. Minutes of the meetings from 1661 to 1668 were compiled in a register titled "Collège Mazarin, Deliberations, 1661–1668" (AN MM 462). A duplicate register, AN MM 461, ends with the meeting on 27 February 1667. The register for 1669–1672 does not survive; however, there is one for 1673–1680: "Troisieme Registre contenant la suite des deliberations concernant l'execution de la fondation du college et academie appellez Mazarini" (Bibliothèque de l'Institut MS. 368).

18. The will states: "L'établissement dudit College, auquel la Bibliotheque est joint, et de l'Académie sera fait sous le bon plaisir du Roy en la Ville, Cité ou Université, ou aux Fauxbourgs de Paris, en mesme ou divers lieux, le tout selon que les Exécuteurs de la presente Fondation . . . le trouveront plus à propos" (Franklin, *Recherches historiques,* 150). I stress this point because most writers have followed the erroneous report of Germain Brice (in *Desciption nouvelle de ce qu'il y a de plus remarquable dans la ville de Paris*

[Paris, 1685]) that Mazarin had committed himself to the Porte de Nesle site before his death.

19. "Monsieur Colbert a dit que pour l'execution de ceste fondation, a laquelle il convient de travailler incessemment les deniers en estans comptans, il y a desja eu commission du conseil et commissaires nommez affin d'obliger les propriettaires des dernieres maisons et places scituées à la pointe du Pré aux clercs du costé de la Grenouillière de rapporter leurs tiltres affin d'en avoir leur remboursement suivant les estimations qui seront faites en cas que l'on ne puisse en composer à l'amiable, qu'on ne peult trouver de lieu plus commode pour establir le college, la bibliotèque et l'academye. Il y a trente cinq mille thoises ou environ de place, qui composent pres de quarante arpens, qu'on peut en prendre tout ce qui sera necessaire, tant pour cette fondation que pour l'establissement des Theatins et bastiment de leur Eglize en ce lieu . . ." (AN MM 462, fol. 21r–v, 21 Mar. 1661).

On the proposed site, now occupied by the Palais Bourbon, see Léo Mouton, "Le quai Malaquais," *Bulletin de la Société d'Histoire du VIe arrondissement de Paris* 16 (1913):253; and Adolphe Berty et al., *Topographie historique du Vieux Paris,* vol. 4, *Région du Faubourg Saint-Germain* (Paris, 1882), 5–6 and pl. 3.

20. In his will Mazarin also gave the Theatines title to the underlying property. My thanks to Giuseppe Dardanello for sharing information with me regarding Valperga's work for Mazarin. On Sainte Anne-la-Royale, see the works cited in chap. 1, note 75, above.

21. The citations in this paragraph were extracted from Father Angelo Bissaro's report, published by Raymond Darricau and Madeline Laurain, "La mort du Cardinal Mazarin," *Annuaire-Bulletin de la Société de l'Histoire de France,* 1958–59:100–102: "M. Colbert s'était mis en tête de rattacher notre couvent au collège que S. E. laissait à fonder au lieu d'y faire une église, il voulait que celle du collège fût la nôtre avec la seule permission aux prêtres qui gouvernaient et enseignaient dans le collège d'y dire la messe, prêtres qui sont de l'Université qui hait les réguliers. D. Camillo et moi nous opposâmes à ce dessein et nous en parlâmes à S. E. Eminence parce qu'il y au-

rait une pépinière de procès. S. E. fut immédiatement d'accord avec nous et réprouva le project de M. Colbert. Malgré cela, parlant du collège dans le testament il mit 'et si les Pères l'approuvent, l'Eglise du collège sera leur église,' etc. Le Cardinal dit: 'Non, non, ôtez cette clause, je veux que les Pères aient leur église à part.' 'Monseigneur,' dit Colbert, 'cela se fera avec leur approbation, si cela doit se faire.' 'Non,' dit S. E., 'ôtez la,' Colbert répliqua: 'Cela ne leur fait pas de tort puisque la décision dépend d'eux,' Alors elle se mit en colère: 'Les Pères ne le veulent pas, ne le veulent pas, ôtez la. Ils veulent leur église et moi je la veux aussi.' Ainsi il fallut supprimer la dite clause."

22. AN MM 462, fol. 25v, 11 Apr. 1661.

23. "L'affaire ayant esté jugée de tres grande importance pour faire le choix d'un lieu ou la fondation puisse estre establie, qu'à l'esgard du College il faut considerer surtouttes choses la commodité des escholiers externes que l'on doit y appeler pour y recevoir les instructions et celle des bacheliers, maistres es arts, et autres suppots de l'Université de Paris pour adsister aux actes et autres exercises, que c'est ce qui y donnera la plus forte consideration et qui le fera subsister" (AN MM 461, fol. 21v, 21 Mar. 1661).

24. The Theatines yielded the jobs in question—principal and assistant principal of the Italian nation—because they were prohibited from assuming fixed-income positions. We know that the priests occasionally made exceptions to this rule—for example, when Urban VIII asked them to administer the Collegio di Propaganda Fide in 1641—and they must have recused themselves in this instance, seeing little to gain from an association with Mazarin's Collège.

25. "Il n'y a rien qui puisse rendre le college illustre que la frequentation des echoliers externes et celle des officiers et suppots de l'université parce qu'autrement ce ne seroit qu'un college de soixante echoliers et qu'en ce cas on ne pourroit pas trouver de professeurs capables qui voulussent s'y appliquer" (AN MM 462, fol. 26v, 11 Apr. 1662).

26. For discussion of the rejected sites, see AN MM 462, fol. 22, 29 Mar. 1661. The second choice was the Jardin des Plantes, which at first the king was willing

to relocate to Vincennes or elsewhere, but when the Faculty of Medicine opposed the move, the crown vetoed the Jardin des Plantes site (AN MM 462, fol. 23v, 29 Mar. 1661, and fol. 24, 2 Apr. 1661). On the college, see Charles Jourdain, "Le Collège du cardinal Lemoine," *Mémoires de la Société de l'Histoire de Paris et d'Ile-de-France* 3 (1876): 42–82.

27. AN MM 462, fol. 23r–v, 29 Mar. 1661. The proposed consolidation had several precedents: the Collège de Presles had merged with the Collège de Dormans-Beauais in 1597; the Collège de France took over the Collèges de Tréguier and de Cambray in 1610; and Cardinal Richelieu merged three colleges—Calvi, Dix-Huit, and du Plessis—with the Sorbonne, to mention but a few instances. On this process of consolidation, see the Abbé Pierre Feret, *La Faculté de Théologie de Paris et ses docteurs les plus célèbres: Epoque moderne* (Paris, 1904), 3:7.

28. "Après la discution de toutes choses, il ne fut rien trouvé de plus à propos ny de plus beau ny plus commode que le derrière du Collège du Cardinal Le Moyne" (AN MM 462, fol. 37r, 24 Dec. 1661).

29. "Sur quoy ledit sieur Le Veau a dit qu'il avoit pensé à une autre place qui peut-estre seroit aussy advantageuse que celle du College du Cardinal Le Moyne, soit pour l'establissement du college, soit pour la decoration de la ville, et mesme pour rendre plus illustre la memoire du feu Monseigneur le cardinal Mazarini. C'est à scavoir de bastir le college proche la porte de Nesle vis-à-vis le Louvre auquel lieu on pourroit faire une place publique qui serviroit d'ornement à l'aspect du Louvre qu'autrefois il avoit esté proposé . . ." (AN MM 462, fol. 38r–v, 31 Dec. 1661).

30. "Le Roy . . . les a trouvé fort beaux et les desseins tres agreables pour faire la vue des appartemens et logemens de Sa Majesté, et pour l'execution de la fondation de Son Eminence" (AN MM 462, fol. 39v, 11 Mar. 1662).

31. The minutes carry several comments along these lines: "On a desja beaucoup d'obligation à M. Le Vau, que l'on doit à luy seul de ce que la fondation est establie en un lieu si avantageux . . ." (AN MM 462, fol. 67v).

32. "L'heureux effet des masses combinées du dôme et de ses pavillons, qui présentent une disposition pittoresque et théâtrale, assez commune en Italie, mais extrèmment rare à Paris où la plupart des monuments sont étouffés, et rarement disposés pour former un agréable point de vue" (Jacques Guillaume Legrand and Charles Paul Landon, *Description de Paris et de ses edifices* [Paris, 1806–9], 1:107).

33. The *prévôt des marchands* complained: "Il estoit à craindre que ceste advance de la demy lune, venant à etrecir le canal de la Riviere en cest endroit . . . ne porte prejudice à la navigation et au commerce, et que dans les grands desbordemens et lors que les glaces viennent à rompre en hyver a la riviere a charis que les batteaux n'en fussent pareillement endommages, et que le Louvre mesme n'en receut de l'incommodité . . ." (AN MM 462, fol. 54, 10 July 1662).

34. In patent letters dated 17 June 1662, the king had approved the quay which "sera un peu advancé dans la rivière en demie lune, dont le milieu respondra à celuy du Dosme de la face du Louvre, qui se construit à présent" (AN M174 nos. 57–58). For the expertise of the masons on 10 July 1662, see AN H3 2845, no. 49. Representatives of the king and the city reached the agreement on 24 July 1662, following which the crown issued an edict to proceed with the quay, "d'en retrancher seulement les cinq toises advancer en la rivière de Seyne au delà du premier picquet planté et qui avoit esté projetté de servir à faire un demi lune . . ." (AN MM 462, fols. 54v–55). These events, which unfolded between 8 and 24 July 1662, are described by Gomont (AN MM 462, fols. 53v–54) and in other minutes (AN H3 2845, no. 47 [in brown ink], 8–19 July 1662). Another plan (BN Est. Va443, film H187391) includes a pencil sketch of the flattened profile over the orginal projecting scheme.

35. AN MM 462, fols. 163v–164, 3 Jan. 1665.

36. N. N. Petit, "Considérations sur le dessein de la place et du quay proposez à faire vers la Tour du Nesle," Bibliothèque de l'Institut, Coll. Godefroy 190, fols. 49–54. A project for razing the *spina* of the Vatican borgo, drawn under Innocent X, is in Franz Ehrle, "Spada," *Atti della Pontifica Accademia Romana di Archeologia,* 1928.

37. Paul Fréart de Chantelou, *Diary of the Cavaliere Bernini's Visit to France,* trans. Margery Corbett, ed. Anthony Blunt, annotated by George Bauer (Princeton, 1985), 210.

38. Margaret Whinney, "Sir Christopher Wren's Visit to Paris," *GBA* 51 (Apr. 1958):235.

39. "Tout le public trouve à ce dire que les deux pavillons couppent la veue des maisons du quay. . . . M. Le Vau a toujours dit et soustient encore à présent que cela ne sera point difforme lors que les bastiments seront achevez. Et qu'au contraire, l'ornement sera plus beau, les pavillons estant advancées que s'ils estoient en droite ligne des maisons du quay, et principallement à la veue du Louvre" (AN MM 462, fol. 164r, 3 Jan. 1665). At this time Gomont acknowledged having given some consideration to aligning the pavilions with the Hôtel de Nevers (AN MM 462, fols. 163v–164, 3 Jan. 1665).

40. "Sans doute quelques considérations particulieres ont déterminés à avancer ce bâtiment si près la rivière, autrement il eût été plus à propos de supprimer ces pavillons et de reculer tout l'édifice, afin que la largeur d'un des plus beaux Quais de Paris n'en fût pas interrompue. Il est vrai que de l'autre côté de la rivière, l'ensemble de cet édifice considéré à part présente un aspect satisfaisant, et que ces pavillons, dont la saillie est si incommode pour la voye publique, servent à unir tout cet édifice par le revêtissement du parapet qui lui sert de soutien et d'empattement général. Ces différentes considérations semblent excuser l'Architecte d'en avoir usé ainsi; et même comme ce frontispice est en face du Louvre, on pourroit croire que Le Veau a voulu procurer à la demeure du plus grand Roi du Monde, le coup d'oeil d'un des beaux monumens qui se soyent élevés sous son Regne. Cette idée est bien digne de ce célebre Architecte, mais il n'en est pas moins vrai que dans un édifice de cette espèce, il faut toujours préférer la commodité publique. . . ." (Jacques-François Blondel, *Architecture françoise,* [Paris, 1752–56], vol. 2, bk 3, pp. 2–3).

41. I am grateful to Robert Berger for alerting me to this remark from Philip Skippon, "An Account of a Journey made thro' Part of the Low-Countries, Germany, Italy and France," in *A Collection of Voyages*

and Travels, ed. Awnsham Churchill, 3d ed. (London, 1746), 6:742.

42. For the debate about the academy, see AN MM 462, fol. 258r, 9 Nov. 1666; fols. 263v–264, 21 Feb. 1667; and fol. 294v, 20 May 1668. The possibility of separating the academy from the college had been considered at the outset, and various locations in faubourg Saint Germain and on the Right Bank were suggested (AN MM 462, fols. 28v–29, 11 Apr. 1661).

43. The minutes for 1673–1680 do not mention the academy at all. The king confirmed the fate of the academy in patent letters of March 1688 (Alfred Franklin, *Histoire de la Bibliothèque Mazarine et du Palais de l'Institut,* [Paris, 1860; 1901], rev. ed., 361, article 39).

44. For a description of the masonry work undertaken in the houses, see the *toisé* dated 31 Dec. 1663, AN H3 2845, no. 24 (in brown ink).

45. For Le Vau's reaction to the Sorbonne, which he visited on 18 Apr. 1664, see AN MM 462, fols. 106v–107.

46. AN MM 462, fol. 195, 27 Jan. 1665.

47. Gabriel Naudé, *Advis pour dresser une bibliothèque* (Paris, 1627; 2d rev. ed., 1644).

48. On the library in the Palais Mazarin and the Bibliothèque Mazarine, see two works by André Masson: "Mazarin et l'architecture des bibliothèques au XVIIe siècle," *GBA* 58 (1961): 355–66; and *Le décor des bibliothèques* (Paris, 1972), 270–72. The new vault is illustrated in an eighteenth-century sectional drawing, AN M176, no. 56. For further references about the holdings in Mazarin's library, see chapter 1, note 54.

    Interest in the history of reading and the book over the past decade has sparked new work on the architecture of early modern libraries—for instance, *Ikonographie der Bibliotheken,* ed. Carsten-Peter Warncke (Wiesbaden, 1992); in particular, see Warncke, "Bibliotheksideale: Denkmuster der architektonischen Gestaltung und abbildlichen Datstellung frühneuzeitlicher Büchereien," 159–97, and

Regina Becker, "Theorie und Praxis—zur Typologie in der Bibliotheksarchitektur des 17. und 18. Jahrhunderts," 235–69.

49. Visiting hours were Mondays and Thursdays, 8:00–10:30 a.m. and 2:00–4:00 p.m.

50. AN MM 462, fol. 240, 11 Jan. 1666. The Sorbonne objected to Le Vau's revised design because it required the public to enter the Collège. Le Vau replied that the first courtyard did not belong to the Collège (AN MM 462, fol. 293v–294, 20 May 1668), an answer that did not allay the Sorbonne's fear of students mingling with the general public en route to the chapel and library. Le Vau's staircase has been remodeled, but the entry sequence is otherwise unchanged today.

51. On Wren's library at Trinity College, see most recently, *The Making of the Wren Library, Trinity College, Cambridge,* ed. David McKitterick (Cambridge, 1995).

52. Le Vau set forth this proposal in a memo titled "Calcul general de la despense du Colleige des quatre Nations du xxvi juin 1662" (AN H3 2845, no. 29 [in red pencil]): "On pouroit faire un establissement d'academye pour y mettre quatre maistres differands quy auroient chucn une grande salle de plain pied avec leur entrees separex et leur logements au dessus. L'on seroit pour enseigner l'architecture avec touttes ses despandances pratiques comme la geometrie, mesures des superficies et des corps solides, montrer à dessiner et la couppe des pierres pour les appareilleurs. Un autre pour instruire des ingenieurs, leurs aprendre les fortifications, fors mouvantes, et touttes sortes de machines de guerres et aultres. Un aultre pour mettre l'academye de la peinture et sculpture quy est desja establie et fort mal logée en la gallerie du Louvre. L'autre pour touttes les matematiques, comme l'astrologie, la cosmographye, l'idrographye et les cartes, et sy l'on veult aussy pour la pratique phisique. Il ne faudroit a chacun qu'une petitte pension, leurs logements et quelque privileige. Ils enseigneroient à des heures choisyes aux escolliers du colleige et le reste du temps au publicq."

53. Charles Perrault described the project for a general academy comprising "personnes de quatre talens

differens, scavoir: belles-lettres, histoire, philosophie, mathématiques," in an undated memo to Colbert that Pierre Clément dated to 1666 (Clément, *Lettres de Colbert,* 5:512–13). Fontenelle described the project in greater detail in his *Histoire de l'Académie Royale des Sciences* (Paris, 1666); the relevant passage is cited also by Clément. See also David Lux, "Colbert's Plan for the *Grande Académie:* Royal Policy toward Science, 1663–67," *Seventeenth-Century French Studies* 12 (1990):177–88, which David Sturdy kindly brought to my attention. Colbert eventually created six separate academies: the Petite Académie, the Academie Française in Rome, and academies of science, music, dance, and architecture.

54. Le Vau's scheme was still under discussion in 1665 (AN MM 462, fol. 164) but is not mentioned thereafter.

55. On the workshops in the Grande Galerie, see Hilary Ballon, *The Paris of Henri IV: Architecture and Urbanism* (New York and Cambridge, Mass., 1991), 47–49.

56. Perhaps the most famous tenant was the painter Jean Jouvenet, who did not have a shop but rented an apartment where his paintings could be seen. After the shops were closed in 1804, they were used as administrative offices, as were the second-floor rooms. For detailed information about the tenants, see de Vinck and Vuaflart, *La Place de l'Institut,* 79; they attribute the absence of commercial activity in pre-revolutionary images of the Place Mazarine to a perception that business was at odds with the solemnity of the Collège and its relationship to the Louvre.

57. The memo concerns primarily the cost of the buildings. I have taken a few liberties in the translation to restore coherence to the excerpt. The original paragraph reads as follows: "La despence des bastiments quy font toutte la beauté de la place, la decoration publique, et la belle veue du Louvre, ayant la biblioteque d'un costé et les quatre academyes des arts de l'autre avec leur logements, cousteront au plus iiiic g lt [400,000 *livres*] et rapporteront au moins x g lt [10,000 *livres*] de rente. . . . Oultre la commodité que les artisans et marchands apporteront au colleige et la beauté qu'ils rendront à la place Mazarine quy sera tousjours rempli au moyen des privileigez de maistrises qu'on leur pourra donnez soubs le nom de Mazarini" (AN H3 2845, no. 29, fol. 3r).

58. James E. King, *Science and Rationalism in the Government of Louis XIV, 1661–1683* (Baltimore, 1949), 282.

59. See, for instance, Marcel Reymond, who described the Collège as "une très heureuse imitation de la façade de Sainte-Agnès;" in André Michel, ed., *Histoire de l'art,* vol. 6, *L'art en Europe au XVIIe siècle, 1re partie* (Paris, 1921), 44 n. 1.

60. Louis Hautecoeur, *Histoire de l'architecture classique en France,* vol. 2, *Le règne de Louis XIV* (Paris, 1948; reprint 1980), 260–63. The author identified both Roman churches and French châteaux as sources of the design but placed greater weight on the native context.

61. Robert Berger, "Antoine Le Pautre and the Motif of the Drum-without-Dome," *JSAH* 25 (1966):171

62. See Anthony Blunt, "Palladio e l'architettura francesa," *Bolle CISA* 2 (1960):14–18; Blunt, "Palladio in Francia," *Boll. CISA* 10 (1968):9–14; and Jean-Marie Pérouse de Montclos, "Palladio et la théorie classique dans l'architecture française du XVIIe siècle," *Boll. CISA* 12 (1970):97–105. Blunt also discounted the significance of Chambray's 1650 translation of the Four Books ("sembra aver exercitato alcun serio influsso").

63. James Ackerman noted the affiliation between this type of Palladian villa and Mazarin's Collège (see his *Palladio's Villas* [Locust Valley, 1967], 15–16). On the Villa Trissino and Villa Badoer, see also *Andrea Palladio, 1508–1580: The Portico and the Farmyard.* ed. Howard Burns (London, 1975), 237, 251–52; and Lionello Puppi, *The Villa Badoer at Fratta Polesine,* trans. Catherine Enggass, Corpus Palladianum 7 (University Park, Pa., 1975).

64. Laurence Brockliss, *French Higher Education in the Seventeenth and Eighteenth Centuries: A Cultural History* (Oxford, 1987), 58.

65. There were smaller false domes built of carpentry, for which see Jean-Marie Pérouse de Montclos, *Histoire de l'architecture française de la Renaissance à la Révolution* (Paris, 1989), 172. Only two churches in all of France are known to have had a temple front before 1650: the Sorbonne and the chapel of Villers-Cotterêts. Not long after the Collège was built, Charles Errard used a temple front at the Eglise d'Assomption (1670). Mansart's design for the facade of Val-de-Grâce (1645) included a projecting single-story portico, but it was part of a two-story facade of the Gesù type. Peter Smith remarked that "the concept of a single-storey portico applied to a two-storied classical façade is without precedent. This feature owes much to the complex château frontispieces which Mansart himself developed, and as such can be regarded as an exclusively French contribution to the classical church front" (Allan Braham and Peter Smith, *François Mansart* [London, 1973], 1:59).

66. The dome does not delineate a perfect circle, as Blondel noted, yet he misunderstood the rationale for the double-shaped dome: "Je dis presque sphérique, parce qu'il faut remarquer que son axe perpendiculaire est à son horizontal comme 15 est à 16 . . . L'inégalité de ces deux courbes intérieure et extérieure a été faite ainsi, pour pouvoir dans la plus grande épaisseur des murs placer les escaliers dont nous avons parlé" (Blondel, *Architecture françoise,* vol. 2, bk. 3, p. 4). He refered to the small spiral stairs that ascend to the lantern, but they surely do not account for the double shell.

67. According to Pérouse de Montclos, there were only two oval churches in France, and neither was oriented transversely: the Jesuit church in Besançon (date uncertain) and another in Carpentras (c. 1627) (see his *Histoire de l'architecture,* 181). Earlier longitudinal oval churches include Vignola's Sant'Anna dei Palafrenieri (begun 1565) in Rome and Ascanio Vitozzi's church of Vicoforte di Mondovi (1596) in Piedmont, an example of special relevance because it served as the mausoleum of the Savoy dynasty. The fundamental study of oval churches is Wolfgang Lotz, "Die ovalen Kirchenräume des Cinquecento," *Römisches Jahrbuch für Kunstgeschichte* 7 (1955): 9–99. See also Rudolf Wittkower, "Carlo Rainaldi and the Architecture of the High Baroque in Rome" (first published in 1937), in *Studies in the Italian Baroque* (London, 1975), 10–52; Milton Lewine, "Vignola's

Church of Sant'Anna de' Palafrenieri in Rome," *Art Bulletin* 47, no. 2 (1965):199–229; Nino Carboneri, *Ascanio Vitozzi: Un architetto tra manierismo e barocco* (Rome, 1966); and Howard Colvin, *Architecture and the Afterlife* (New Haven, 1991), 246–49.

68. The paving pattern is recorded also in an unsigned drawing by d'Orbay, "Plan du Collège Mazariny ce 15e mars 1684," Musée du Louvre, Département des Arts Graphiques, Inv. 30399.

69. Susan Klaiber rejects the possibility of a direct link between Le Vau's plan and that of Valperga, which was slightly earlier, and suggests that both architects were informed by the work of Carlo Rainaldi, Mazarin's architect in Rome. See Klaiber, "Guarino Guarini's Theatine Architecture," 8–16.

70. The side arms also reinforce the autonomy of the oval. In the first plan Le Vau repeated the oval shape in the small spaces flanking the side chapels, in part because they were also intended to house tombs. Then he made them simple rectangles with hemispherical domes so that the sequence of spaces encountered at the end of the main axis—domed altar flanked by groin-vaulted wings—is inverted in the side arms. The result is that the composition contains one unique oval, while the tripartite units wrapped around it refer only to one another.

71. During an inspection of the church in 1665, representatives of the Sorbonne complained that the sacristy was too far from the altars and the collegiate entrance too close to the high altar: "Apres avoir tout discuté et mesuré et faict diverses propositions, l'on est demeuré d'accord qu'il ne se pourroit mieux et attendu la scituation dees lieux, et que la sacristie n'estoit point trop esloigné . . . Neantmoings sur les difficultez que Messieurs les depputez de Sorbonne ont encore faites toutchant la sacristie et l'entrée de l'eglise, M. Colbert a dict à M. Le Vau de penser à ce qui pourroit faire la dessus" (AN MM 462, fol. 192, 27 Jan. 1665).

72. Even as Le Vau insisted on the public nature of the church, Gomont questioned the wisdom of that policy; in 1665 he informed the Sorbonne rectors that the church should be considered "une eglise du college" (AN MM 462, fols. 171v–172).

73. Anthony Blunt noted that the plan of the Sorbonne is based on the Roman church of San Carlo ai Catinari, which was begun in 1612 and under construction during Jacques Lemercier's sojourn in Rome (see his *Art and Architecture in France, 1500–1700,* 4th rev. ed. [New York, 1986], 198). The Roman church is notable for its fusion of centralized and longitudinal elements, and Lemercier saw that this spatial duality was a means of differentiating the collegiate and public roles of the Sorbonne. On the seventeenth-century reconstruction of the Sorbonne, see Claude Mignot, "La chapelle et maison de Sorbonne," in Chancellerie des Universités de Paris et Académie Française, *Richelieu et le monde de l'esprit* (Paris, 1985), 87–94; and Paolo Berdini, "The Sorbonne and Richelieu: Theological Controversies and Urban Renewal in XVIIth century Paris," *Arte Cristiana* 79 (1991):251–76.

74. Bernini visited the Sorbonne in 1665 and "held a long discussion on the right place for the monument to Cardinal Richelieu and the form it should take. The Cavaliere said he had made a sketch putting it beneath the cupola" (Chantelou, *Diary of Bernini's Visit,* 275). Like Le Vau at the Collège chapel, Bernini responded to the architectural cues of the dome. The prevailing view, however, was that Richelieu's tomb should be placed in the choir, in accordance with a long-standing tradition of treating the choir as a burial chapel.

On Richelieu's tomb, which was commissioned in 1675 and installed in the choir in 1695, see Mary Jackson Harvey, "French Baroque Tomb Sculpture: The Activation of the Effigy," Ph.D. diss., University of Chicago, 1987. The most famous French example of a tomb-filled choir was at the royal abbey of Saint Denis. On the choir as burial chapel, see especially Alain Erlande-Brandenburg, *Le roi est mort: Etude sur les funérailles, les sépultures et les tombeaux des rois de France jusqu'à la fin du XIIIe siècle* (Paris, 1975); Julian Gardner, *The Tomb and the Tiara: Burial Tomb Sculpture in Rome and Avignon in the Later Middle Ages* (Oxford, 1992), which addresses the special case of founder's tombs; and Christoph Frommel, " 'Cappella Julia': Die Grabkapelle Papst Julius II in Neu-St. Peter," *Zeitschrift für Kunstgeschichte* 40 (1977): 26–62, which argues that the intended location of the tomb of Julius II was not beneath the dome but in the choir.

75. Colbert naively thought that there would be no problem viewing the high altar if the tomb were elevated on columns (AN MM 462, fol. 291v, 20 May 1668). Gomont raised the issue of the tomb's location on several occasions (AN MM 462, fol. 263, 21 Feb. 1667; fol. 267v, 26 Feb. 1667; and fol. 291v, 20 May 1668). Perhaps the first sign of trouble came even earlier. According to a *toisé* plan of the foundations, a support was built for the tomb in the center of the church, but it would have been dismantled by the time of André Gutton's renovation in 1960, inasmuch as he found no such footings (see his article, "Restauration de la coupole de l'Institut de France," 33).

76. I refer to Albert Laprade's aggravating but occasionally informative book *François d'Orbay, architecte de Louis XIV* (Paris, 1960).

77. "L'eglise n'avoit este faite que pour le college, c'est à dire dans une espace assez resserré pour devoir estre conservée autant que l'on pourroit, que le mausolée estant placé sous le dome, il occuperoit tout le passage [et] offusqueroit le maître autel . . ." (Bibliothèque de l'Institut MS 368, fol. 9v, 2 Feb. 1673). Foucault recommended the space opposite the college entrance.

78. On the Académie's visit to the church on 15 July 1675 and the recommendations submitted in March 1676, see Bibliothèque de l'Institut MS 368, fols. 149–153 and 155v–178v; and Henry Lemonnier, ed., *Procès-verbaux de l'Académie Royale d'Architecture, 1671–1793*, vol. 1 (Paris, 1911), 103–4, 112. Lepautre suggested imitating the crossing of Saint Peter's by placing statues in the four piers: in one the cardinal looking up into the dome; opposite him an angel pointing heavenward; and in the other two pier niches, angels holding the cardinal's hat and coat of arms. Of his design he said tellingly, "[L]e tout conservera la regularité de son plan, la beauté de l'architecture et fera voir que ce n'est qu'un mausolée" (Bibliothèque de l'Institut MS 368, fols. 158v–159).

79. In 1676 Hardouin-Mansart complained that this location was too distant from the main entrance; he preferred the right side chapel, where he had designed Mazarin's effigy "eslevée en forme de priant et accompagné de ses attributs, ses vertus, ses armes et ses emplois." The executed scheme was faithful to this idea (see Bibliothèque de l'Institut MS 368, fol. 178r, 9 Mar. 1676; and Lemonnier, *Procès-verbaux*, 1:112).

80. Although Le Vau altered the shape of the entry vestibule in each plan, he never altered its size, which is disproportionately large in relation to the sanctuary. Since functional requirements are not relevant, two other factors might account for the large size of the narthex: (a) the plastic value of a projecting volume at the centerpoint of the composition and (b) the iconographic associations of a narthex with Saint Peter's and perhaps to antique temples.

81. In the second scheme Le Vau shrank the circumference of the oval slightly, diminished the overall height of the dome, and added considerable decoration.

82. In April 1664 Le Vau visited the Sorbonne and found it too dark, which might explain why the third design increases the number of windows in the drum from four to eight. But the Sorbonne visit does not explain the more profound changes in the third scheme. The Sorbonne visit is described as follows in the minutes: "Apres avoir considéré la beauté et la magnificence de l'architecture du portail [de la Sorbonne], ou estant led. sieur procureur a dict qu'il y avoit un deffaut qui estoit le peu de haussement qu'on avoit donné à lad. chapelle. Et M. Le Vau a remarqué que la gayeté des jours y manquoit aussy" (AN MM 462, fol. 107, 18 Apr. 1664).

83. For details on the pace of construction, see AN MM 462, fols. 90r–152.

84. On 21 Apr. 1665, the contractors complained that "les bastiments dud. college pour y mettre autant d'ouvriers qu'il s'en peut mettre, il est besoin que Monsieur Le Vau donne ses resolutions pour l'eglise dud. college et pour la hauteur des bastiments qui sont entre le pavillon des arts et l'eglise" (AN MM 462, fol. 204v). The details cited in the text were mentioned at the meeting two days later (AN MM 462, fol. 208v). On 7 May 1665, a member of the building commission, Meurset de La Tour, informed Colbert that "[Le Vau] n'a pas encore donné ses resolutions aux entrepreneurs qui ne s'en plaindre et

cependant je les vois par ce deffaut à la veille de retrancher le nombre de leurs ouvriers au lieu qu'ils
augmenteroient s'ils avoient les elevations fixees"
(BN MS Mélanges de Colbert 129, fols. 220–21).

85. On the size of the workforce in June 1665, see
AN MM 462, fol. 214.

86. "Il y avait encore quelque chose à faire à ses resolutions, et que la sepmaine prochaine il les [the draw-
ings] donneroit aux entrepreneurs" (AN MM 462,
fol. 223r, 30 July 1665).

87. "Le Vau a dit qu'il venoit du bastiment du college, et apres avoir visité quelques choses il avoit
donné ses ordres pour la disposition de ce qui restoit
à faire, notamment pour commencer l'elevation de
l'eglise au dessus du rez de chaussee; qu'il avoit
mesme fait lever le dessin des vazes qui doivent ornés
le dessus des corniches des pavillons des arts . . ."
(AN MM 462, fol. 226v, 12 Sept. 1665).

88. Guglielmo De Angelis d'Ossat, "Louis Le Vau,
architetto berniniano suo malgrado," in *Gian
Lorenzo Bernini, architetto e l'architettura europea del
Sei-Settecento,* ed. Gianfranco Spagnesi and Marcello
Fagiolo, (Rome, 1984), 2:511–24.

89. René Girard, *Deceit, Desire and the Novel: Self and
Other in Literary Structure* (Baltimore and London,
1965), 11. I am grateful to Rosalind Krauss for sug-
gesting Girard's book. A study by Harold Bloom—
The Anxiety of Influence: A Theory of Poetry (Oxford,
1973)—also points a way to conceptualize Le Vau's
struggle with the architecture of Bernini.

90. Le Vau's ideas for a courtyard west of the Cour
Carrée are first seen as a sketch in Musée du Louvre,
Département des Arts Graphiques, fol. 12, project 3,
and then developed more fully in AN O1 1678c, no.
495, an unfinished ground-floor plan, and AN F21
3567, no. 9 (fig. 80), also a ground-floor plan, both of
which illustrate Le Vau's fifth (postfoundation) project. On Le Vau's design of July 1665, see Chantelou,
Diary of Bernini's Visit, 90, 100, 103, 106; Mary Whiteley and Allan Braham, "Louis Le Vau's Projects for
the Louvre and the Colonnade," *GBA,* Dec. 1964,
350–52, 357, 360.

91. Chantelou recounted the story as follows (in
Diary of Bernini's Visit, 327): "The Nuncio asked
[Bernini] if he had not met this architect [Le Vau].
The Cavaliere replied that he had not, that there had
been a misunderstanding, for they had been staying
at the same inn, and Mancini had told him there
would be time for him to rest as Le Vau had not yet
dined, but, although he got up as he thought in
plenty of time to see him, Le Vau had already left; he
had regretted what must have seemed like rudeness
on his part."

92. The 1665 edict was confirmed in March 1688,
when the Collège finally opened. The 1688 patent
letters set forth the regulations governing the Collège
and were published in Franklin, *Histoire de la Bibliothèque Mazarine,* 357–62. Article 38 stipulates that
the Collège should enjoy "tous les droits qui appar-
tiennent aux Maisons de fondation royale."

93. Le Vau initially stressed the commemorative
aspect of the project; in January 1662 he described
his scheme as "fort avantageux et glorieux pour la
memoire de son Eminence" (AN MM 462, fol. 39,
18 Jan. 1662). Mazarin's escutcheon appears above
the main doorway, and his heraldry decorates the
dome.

94. The dedication of the church to Saint Louis—his
name and symbols appear on the entrance facade,
and his cipher decorates the drum—also underscores
the royal connection. A black marble tablet above the
doorway was inscribed D.O.M. SUB INVOCATIONE
SANCTI LUDOVICI. The wood door was decorated with
the symbols of Saint Louis: nails of the cross and the
crown of thorns. Both door and tablet were the work
of Etienne Le Hongre (Guillet de Saint-Georges,
"Etienne Le Hongre," in *Mémoires inédits sur la vie et
les ouvrages des membres de l'Académie Royale de Peinture et de Sculpture,* [Paris, 1854] 1:365–68.

The Collège was one aspect of a campaign to
associate Louis XIV with Saint Louis; on this effort,
see Lawrence McGinniss, "Royal Chapel Projects for
Louis XIV at St. Denis, the Louvre, and the Invalides, 1664–1683," Ph.D. diss., Columbia University, 1974, 15–16. He pointed to the refurbishment of
the Saint Louis reliquary at Saint Denis in 1657 and
to the new edition of Jean de Joinville's *Histoire de
S. Louis IX,* which Charles DuFresne du Cange

brought out in 1668. Under Louis XIV, royal chapels at Versailles and the Invalides were also dedicated to Saint Louis. In 1659 Le Vau designed a chapel in the Pavillon de l'Horloge that was dedicated to Saint Louis and Notre-Dame de la Paix.

This section does not address the dome frescoes because we have no information about Le Vau's intentions or about Charles de La Fosse's unexecuted design for the large dome. The estimated cost of frescoing the dome was 7,000–8,000 *livres;* in 1673 d'Orbay suggested leaving it unpainted to save money: "Quand a ce qui convient faire au dosme, il semble que les compartimens enrichis d'ornemens de dorures y seroient plus convenables et de moindre despence que la fresque et autres peintures a huile qui noircit et qui est de peu de durée" (AN H3 2845, "Memoire à M. Foucault pour le parachevement des ouvrages du College Mazarini et observations sur le memoire de Dorbay, delivré a Mr. Foucault," 12 Aug. 1673). After an initial discussion in 1673 of de La Fosse's design, the matter was dropped until 1676, when Le Brun approved the project and Colbert was consulted. Louis-Gabriel Blanchard, son of Jacques, was commissioned to paint the small dome and the three altarpieces, but those projects were unexecuted as well.

On the dome decorations, see Bibliothèque de l'Institut MS. 368, fol. 5, 16 Jan. 1673; fol. 192r, 15 Apr. 1676; and fol. 212, 15 June 1678. As for the altarpieces, they were installed at a later date and are of little interest. Martin Desjardins completed two decorative projects in the 1670s: eight reliefs of the Beatitudes in the spandrels of the crossing arches and twelve medallions of the Apostles in the dome. On his work at the Collège, see Saint-Georges, "Martin Van den Bogaert dit Desjardins," in *Mémoires inédits,* 1:393–95.

95. In fact, the changes in the second design express the sepulchral theme more clearly by transforming the figures into winged angels, who actively support the clock.

96. On medallion funerary portraits, see George Hanfmann, *The Season Sarcophagus in Dumbarton Oaks* (Cambridge, Mass., 1951; reprint, New York, 1971); and Johannes Bolten, *Die Imago Clipeata: Ein Beitrag zur Portrait- und Typengeschichte* (Paderborn, 1937).

97. Normally clocks appeared on church towers, and the pediment enclosed the founder's coat of arms. On pedimented church facades, clocks more often appear either below the pediment, as in the street facade of the Sorbonne, or above it, as in Mansart's design for the Minimes facade. The pediment clock was uncommon but not unprecedented: Inigo Jones placed a clock in the pediment of his church at Covent Garden. (Thanks to Tod Marder and Christy Anderson for information on this subject.)

The most likely explanation for the displacement of Mazarin's arms from the pediment was to deemphasize the cardinal, but it is tempting to speculate about another possibility: might the clock symbolize Louis XIV, who in his mythic guise as Apollo was Master of Time? On Louis in this personification, see Ernst Kantorowicz, "Oriens Augusti-Lever du Roi," *Dumbarton Oaks Papers* 17 (1963):173; and Brice Bauderon, *L'Apollon François ou . . . Louis le Grand, XIV de ce nom* (Mâcon, 1681), 331–38. Louis XIV is represented as the Master of Time in a Boulle clock at the Metropolitan Museum of Art, for which see James Parker, "A French Royal Clock," *Metropolitan Museum of Art Bulletin* 18 (1960):193.

It was Apollo's duty to lead the Hours, and his association with time is central to the program of Versailles; it pertains to the grotto of Thetis, as conceived by Charles Perrault, and to the clock that Hardouin-Mansart placed in the center of the Cour de Marbre in 1687 (on the clock in the Cour de Marbre, see Pierre Francastel, "Cloches et cadrans," *Revue de l'histoire de Versailles et de Seine-et-Dise* [1927]:113–20). If the clock at the Collège is symbolically charged, then the pediment conflates the triumph of Time with that of Louis XIV, and the displacement of Mazarin's arms from the customary niche in the pediment to a lower register constitutes a sign of deference to the king, symbolically present in the pediment. Le Vau also used a clock in the entry pavilion at Vaux, above the pediment. Obviously that clock refers not to Louis XIV but to the Apollonian theme in Le Brun's unexecuted design for the grand salon vault.

98. Le Vau originally intended to personify virtues, similar to those on the courtyard facade of the Sorbonne, where the figures represented Science, Truth, Prudence, Knowledge, and Grace, among other qualitites (Jean Bonnerot, *La Sorbonne* [Paris, 1927],

12). It is tempting to read the thirteen figures in Le Vau's second design as Christ and the Apostles, as at Saint Peter's; however, while the axial figure suggests a risen Christ, the flanking figures are clearly women. Judging from the absence of attributes in the first two facade projects, Le Vau had not determined their precise identities.

Whoever they were, it is fair to say that the program of the statuary changed from metaphysical abstractions to the historical church. The six pairs of figures were, from left to right, John and Luke, Matthew and Mark, Basil and Athanasius, John Chrysostom and Gregory of Nazianzus, Jerome and Augustine, Ambrose and Gregory: four fathers of the Latin church, four fathers of the Greek church, and the four Evangelists.

99. The pediment figures today hold additional attributes: a bell at the left, a scroll at the right. For a plausible interpretation of the iconography, see Blondel, *Architecture française,* vol. 2, bk. 3, p. 5. I am grateful to Roberto Rusconi for directing me to the writings of Anthony of Padua, who employed the metaphor of the hammer against heresy in *Malleus Hereticorum.* It should be noted that the hammer is not among the attributes Ripa assigned to Vigilance. If Ripa is taken as a strict guide, the figures with hammer and book might represent Necessity and Truth, respectively (Cesare Ripa, *Iconologie ou explication nouvelle de plusieurs images, emblems et autres figures...,* trans. Jean Baudouin [Paris, 1644], 125, 195–96).

100. For commentary on the device, see Charles Dreyss, ed., *Mémoires de Louis XIV pour l'instruction du Dauphin* (Paris, 1860), 2:569–70; Claude-François Menestrier, *La devise du roy justifiée* (Paris, 1679); and Académie Royale des Médailles et des Inscriptions, *Médailles sur les principaux événements du règne du Louis le Grand avec des explications historiques* (Paris, 1702), fol. 74, which states: "[A]insi que les rayons de cet Astre éclairent à la fois la Terre et plusieurs Globes célestes, de mesme le génie du Roy suffiroit à gouverner ensemble et la France et plusieurs Royaumes."

101. Perrault selected the passage from Ezekiel (31:17) at the base of the dome, *Sedebit sub umbra culo ejus in meio nationum.* He also composed the entablature inscription on the church facade. (See Bibliothèque de l'Institut MS. 368, fol. 5v, 16 Jan. 1673; fol. 14v, 14 Apr. 1673; and fol. 20, 8 Aug. 1673.) The facade sculpture was in place by 1673.

102. On Le Vau's foundations and the dating of his third and fourth projects, see Alain Erlande-Brandenburg, "Les fouilles du Louvre et les projets de Le Vau," *La vie urbaine* 4 (1964): 241–63. On Le Vau's drawings for the Louvre, see the second part of Erlande-Brandenburg's article in *La Vie Urbaine* 1 (1965):12–22; and Whiteley and Braham, "Louis Le Vau's Projects," 285–96 and 347–62. The Whiteley-Braham articles are essential for the sequencing of the drawings, but their chronology does not reflect Erlande-Brandenburg's findings (the articles were published simultaneously). The group of articles from 1964 and 1965 discuss several drawings unknown to Louis Hautecoeur (*Le Louvre et les Tuileries de Louis XIV* [Paris and Brussels, 1927]).

103. See Hilary Ballon, "Vaux-le-Vicomte: Le Vau's Ambition," in *Italian Villas and French Gardens in Context,* ed. Mirka Beneš and Dianne Harris (in press).

104. The masonry contract instructs the masons: "[d']observer aux encoignures des grandes bossages de la mesme saillie, haulteurs, et longueurs que ceux qui sont à present emploie aux murs du face des fosses du Louvre avec un gros cordon au dessus en saillie et couronnée au droict desdittes bossages en forme de doussine ainsy qu'aux fondations du Louvre..." (AN H3 2845, no. 50, 13 Aug. 1662, [in brown ink]).

The moat of the Louvre was filled in in 1668 to accommodate the Colonnade; thus the model for the Quai Mazarin disappeared from sight until the moat was excavated in 1964, by which time the Quai Mazarin had been altered. On the excavation of Le Vau's moat, see two articles by Erlande-Brandenburg: "Les fouilles du Louvre et les projets de Le Vau," and "Les fouilles du Louvre, Louis Le Vau," *Les dossiers de l'archéologie* 7 (1974): 85–93.

The inscription on the Quai Mazarin reads: "Ludovico Magno / Luparum absolvente / Ripam hanc ut ripae alterius / Dignitati responderet / Quadro saxo vestiri C. C. / Praef. & Aediles / Anno

MDCLXIX et MDCLXX." (The prefect and Echevins dedicate to Louis the Great this riverbank, having been freed from wolves, with the result that it might respond to the other riverbank and be worthy to be dressed in cut stone. 1669 and 1670.) It is said that François Blondel composed the inscription (Germain Brice, *Description nouvelle de la ville de Paris,* 9th ed. [Paris, 1752], 4:126).

105. According to the minutes, the foundations of the obelisks were completed by Feb. 1664: AN MM 462, fol. 90, 18 Feb. 1664. During the restoration of the church in 1960, André Gutton rediscovered the foundations (Gutton, "Restauration de la coupole," 33).

106. AN MM 462, fol. 277v, 25 Nov. 1667; fol. 291, 20 May 1668. The obelisk fountains were still slated for construction in 1673 (Bibliothèque de l'Institut MS. 368, fol. 26v, 3 Sept. 1673); thereafter they are no longer mentioned.

107. At the church of the Feuillants, Mansart had used obelisks similar to those in Le Vau's first elevation. On obelisk-finials, see McGinniss, "Royal Chapel Projects for Louis XIV," 71. Like Louis XIV, Augustus was associated with the sun; he dedicated a temple in his palace to Apollo and erected in Rome the largest sundial ever built, an obelisk that functioned as a gnomon. Le Vau may well have read about the gnomon obelisk in Pliny's *Natural History,* which was in his library. The gnomon obelisk exemplifies the same interconnections between solar symbolism, obelisks, and time that inform the iconography of Louis XIV and extend to the Place

Mazarine. On the gnomon obelisk, see Pliny, *Natural History,* bk. 36, chap. 15, sec.72; Erik Iversen, *Obelisks in Exile,* vol. 1 (Copenhagen, 1968), 142–49; Paul Zanker, *The Power of Images in the Age of Augustus* (Ann Arbor, 1988), 144.

108. Alfred Frazer, "The Iconography of the Emperor Maxentius' Buildings in Via Appia," *Art Bulletin* 48 (1966):386. On the circus as a site of the imperial cult, see John Humphrey, *Roman Circuses: Arenas for Chariot Racing* (Berkeley, 1986). Significantly, the relevant seventeenth-century text, Onofrio Panvinio's Latin treatise *De Ludis Circensibus* (Rome, 1642) was not in Le Vau's library, according to the posthumous inventory.

109. On the Piazza Navona, see Rudolf Preimesberger, "Obeliscus Pamphilius: Beiträge zur Vorgeschichte und Ikonographie des Vierströmbrunnens auf Piazza Navona," *Münchener Jahrbuch des bildenden Kunst* 25 (1974), 77–162.

110. On Bernini's conception of the Piazza San Pietro, see Hanno-Walter Kruft, "The Origin of the Oval in Bernini's Piazza S. Pietro," *Burlington Magazine* 121 (1979):796–801; Daniela Del Pesco, *Colonnato di San Pietro: 'Dei portici antichi e la loro diversità,' con un'ipotesi di cronologia* (Rome, 1988); and Peter Rietbergen, "A Vision Come True: Pope Alexander VII, Gianlorenzo Bernini and the Colonnades of St. Peter's," *Mededelingen van het Nederlands: Instituut te Rome* 44–45, n.s. 9–10 (1983):111–63. The relationship of church and palace also invites comparison with Bernini's work for the pope at Ariccia.

CHAPTER 3

1. The only earlier document with Le Vau's signature thus far uncovered dates from 24 June 1639 (AN Min. cent. XII 69). It is a contract to build the house of Melchior de Gillier on the Ile Saint-Louis.

2. Jonathan Goldberg, *Writing Matter: From the Hands of the English Renaissance* (Stanford, 1990), especially chap. 5, "Signatures, Letters, Secretaries: Individuals of the Hands." While the book as a whole is indebted to the writings of Jacques Derrida, this

chapter draws in particular on Derrida, "Signature Event Context," in *Margins of Philosophy,* trans. Alan Bass (Chicago, 1982). For the French context, see also François Furet and Jacques Ozouf, *Reading and Writing: Literacy in France from Calvin to Jules Ferry* (Cambridge, 1982); and on Descartes, Jean-Luc Nancy, "Dum Scribo," *Oxford Literary Review* 3 (1978):6–20.

Le Vau did not own any handwriting manuals; however, he did possess books by a leading author on the subject, Louis de Lesclache. The following French manuals on handwriting and spelling were available in Le Vau's lifetime: Jean de Beau Chesne, *Le trésor d'escriture* (Lyons, 1580); Chesne, *La clef de l'escriture* (London, n.d. [c. 1595]); Jean Puget de La Serre, *Le secrétaire à la mode ou méthode facile d'escrire selon le temps diverses lettres de compliment, amoureuses et morales . . .* (Paris, 1641); and Louis de Lesclache, *Traité de l'orthographe dans lequel on établit . . . les règles certaines d'écrire correctement . . .* (Paris, 1649)—the last reissued with a new title incorporating the phonetic spellings Lesclache recommended: *Les véritables règles de l'ortografe francèze, ou l'art d'aprandre an peu de tams à écrire côrectemant . . .* (Paris, 1668).

3. On François Le Vau, see Nicole Felkay, "François Le Vau 1623?–1676," in Ministère de la Culture, *Colbert, 1619–1683,* exh. cat. (Paris, 1983), 264–65.

4. For apprenticeship contracts with the master mason Louis Le Veau, see AN Min. cent. CV 401, 6 Dec. 1638; AN Min. cent. CV 402, 14 May 1639.

5. They formed a partnership to build nine houses on the Ile Saint-Louis (AN Min. cent. XXXVI 167, 13 Apr. 1641). Within a month of his marriage into the Le Vau family, Thoison and Le Vau joined forces on a building project on the Ile Saint-Louis, the first of many shared undertakings (AN Min. cent. XXXVI 169, fol. 49, 25 Jan. 1642).

6. The signatures discussed above pertain to the marriage contract (AN Min. cent. XXXVI, 168 fol. 530v, 23 Dec. 1641). Note that neither Louis Le Vau's sister Anne nor his mother, Estiennette Louette, could write: "Lad. future espouse et sa mère ont déclaré ne scavoir escrire ne signe."

7. The marriage took place on 2 May 1639; Jeanne Laisné brought a dowry of 150 *livres* in *rente* and 4,000 *livres* in cash. The marriage contract is the first document itemized in Le Vau's inventory after death (AN Min. cent. LXXXV 98 fol. 15r, 27 Nov. 1670).

8. What did Louis Le Vau look like? In writing this book, I thought the question was answered by a portrait at Versailles, which Albert Laprade identified as Le Vau in 1662 on the basis of the buildings depicted in the painting—Le Vau's designs to remodel the royal apartments at the Louvre, which were prepared soon after his elevation as *premier architecte.* (More specifically the painting illustrates the pavilion at the north end of the Petite Galerie, later named the Rotunda of Apollo, and the plan of the queen mother's summer apartment. See Laprade, "Portraits des premiers architectes de Versailles," *Revue des Arts,* Mar. 1955, 21–24.) However, the image was recently identified as a portrait of Pierre Rabon of Antoine de Ratabon, the Superintendant des Bâtiments, which means that we have no likeness of Louis Le Vau. On the reattribution, see Thierry Bajou, *La Peinture à Versailles. XVIIe siècle* (Paris, 1998), 76, which summarizes an unpublished thesis that I was unable to consult. See Christophe Hardouin, "La Collection de portraits de l'Académie royale de Peinture et de Sculpture: Peintures entrées sous le règne de Louis XIV (1648–1715)" (Mémoire de D.E.A., Université de Paris IV, 1994), 164–66.

9. The following details are drawn from Le Vau's inventory after death (AN Min. cent. LXXXV 198, 27 Nov.–30 Dec. 1670).

10. The inventory locates "le cabinet dud. deffunct ayant vue sur la cour et sur la rue" and details its contents (AN Min. cent. LXXXV 198, fols. 12v–33v 27 Nov. 1670).

11. "[Sept.] rangs de planches de bois de sappin faisant la longeur dud. cabinet, lesd. planches de petites bandes de serge verte bordé d'un petit molet de soye de pareille couleur [were these dust pelmets?], sur lesquelles planches sont les livres cy apres inventoriez" (AN Min. cent. LXXXV 198, fols. 12v–13r, 27 Nov. 1670). On the furniture used for storing books in private homes of the period, see Peter Thornton, *Seventeenth-Century Interior Decoration in England, France and Holland* (New Haven and London, 1978), 303–15; and Roger Chartier, "Urban Reading Practices, 1660–1780," *The Cultural Uses of Print in Early Modern France,* trans. Lydia Cochrane (Princeton, 1987), 200–202.

12. The literature on the history of reading has exploded in recent years. Pioneering work was done by Robert Darnton in, among other books, *The Great Cat Massacre and Other Episodes in French Cultural*

History (New York, 1984) and by Roger Chartier; see in particular his "Texts, Printings, Readings," in *The New Cultural History,* ed. Lynn Hunt (Berkeley, 1989), 154–75, and *The Cultural Uses of Print.* The field of English Renaissance studies has been a major site of studies on reading practices; these include Eugene Kintgen, *Reading in Tudor England* (Pittsburgh, 1996); Ann Moss, *Printed Commonplace-Books and the Structuring of Renaissance Thought* (Oxford, 1996); William Sherman, *John Dee: The Politics of Reading and Writing in the English Renaissance* (Amherst, 1995); Virginia Stern, *Gabriel Harvey: His Life, Marginalia and Library* (Oxford, 1979); and David McPherson, "Ben Jonson's Library and Marginalia: An Annotated Catalogue," *Studies in Philology* 71, no. 5 (Dec. 1974), 3–106. My thanks to Christy Anderson for many stimulating discussions on this subject, for supplying many helpful references, and for organizing with Alina Payne a seminar called "The Architect's Bookshelf," at the Center for Advanced Study in the Visual Arts, National Gallery of Art, Washington, D.C., on 19 Dec. 1997.

13. On Jones's library and reading practices, see two studies by Christy Anderson: "Inigo Jones's Library and the Language of Architectural Classicism in England, 1580–1640," Ph.D. Diss., Massachusetts Institute of Technology, 1993; and "Learning to Read Architecture in the English Renaissance," in *Albion's Classicism: The Visual Arts in Britain, 1550–1660,* ed. Lucy Gent (New Haven and London, 1995), 239–286. Jones's annotations of Palladio have been partially published in B. Allsopp, ed., *Inigo Jones on Palladio, Being the Notes by Inigo Jones in the Copy of* I Quattro libri dell'architettura *di Andrea Palladio, 1601, in the Library of Worcester College, Oxford* (Newcastle upon Tyne, 1970).

14. Lisa Jardine and Anthony Grafton, " 'Studied for Action': How Gabriel Harvey Read His Livy," *Past and Present* 129 (Nov. 1990):30–78. On Montaigne's library, see Adi Ophir, "A Place of Knowledge Re-Created: The Library of Michel de Montaigne," *Science in Context* 4, no. 1 (1991):163–89.

15. My reasoning about the timing of d'Orbay's trip relates to his drawings for the Spanish Steps, for which see Appendix B.

16. Albert Laprade believed Le Vau financed the trip because he paid d'Orbay 600 *livres* on 29 Dec. 1659, but there is no reason to suppose the money was for future travel as opposed to work completed in the past. Indeed, the latter explanation seems more likely given the context in which the payment is disclosed: an account of fees and pensions the crown owed Le Vau as of 1661 ("Etat des billets deubs au Sr Le Vau," 1655–60 [BN MS. Mélanges de Colbert 104, fols. 140–41). The document was published in part in Laprade, *François d'Orbay, architecte de Louis XIV* (Paris, 1960),112. There is no evidence that the crown reimbursed Le Vau for the payment to d'Orbay.

17. The minutes of the academy's meeting on 24 Oct. 1687 read: "M. d'Orbay a apporté une mémoire de plusieurs mesures d'attiques, qu'il a prises en différents endroits des plus considérables de Paris, et mesme à Rome à l'église de Saint Pierre" (Henry Lemonnier, ed., *Procès-verbaux de l'Académie Royale d'Architecture, 1671–1793,* vol. 2 [Paris, 1912], 151).

18. Père Louis Jacob, *Traicté des plus belles bibliothèques publiques et particuliers, qui ont esté et qui sont à présent dans le monde* (Paris, 1644). See also Albert de La Fizelière, *Rymaille sur les plus célèbres bibliotières de Paris en 1649 avec des notes et un essai sur les autres bibliothèques particulières du temps* (Paris, 1868). Of course, Cardinals Richelieu and Mazarin topped this class of bibliophiles. On Richelieu's library, see Jacqueline Artier, "La bibliothèque du cardinal de Richelieu," in *Histoire des bibliothèques françaises,* vol. 2, *Les bibliothèques sous l'Ancien Régime, 1530–1789,* ed. Claude Jolly (Paris, 1988), 126–33; Pierre Gasnault, "Note sur les livres de Richelieu," *Mélanges de la Bibliothèque de la Sorbonne* 8 (1988): 185–89; and Jean Flouret, "La bibliothèque de Richelieu," *Revue française d'histoire du livre* 24 (1979): 611–19. On Mazarin's library, see chapter 1, note 54; and on Colbert's library, see Denise Bloch, "La bibliothèque de Colbert," in *Histoires des bibliothèques française,* vol. 2, 156–79.

Consider some comparative English examples. Gabriel Harvey had about 100 books in the 1590s. The scholar Joseph Scaliger had 1,382 books at his death in 1608, John Lord Lumley had 2,800 volumes according to his catalogue of 1609, and John Dee had about 3,000 printed volumes. See Sears Jayne and Francis Johnson, eds., *The Lumley Library: The Cata-*

logue of 1609 (London, 1956), 12; David McPherson, "Ben Jonson's Library," 10; and Julian Roberts and Andrew Watson, *John Dee's Library Catalogue* (London, 1990).

19. On libraries of merchants, artisans, lawyers, and other non-nobles, see Henri-Jean Martin, *Livres, pouvoirs et société à Paris au XVIIe siècle (1598–1701)* (Geneva, 1969); Pierre Aquilon, "Petites et moyennes bibliothèques, 1530–1660," in *Histories des bibliothèques française,* 2:180–205; Aquilon, "Trois avocats angevins dans leur librairies," in *Le livre dans l'Europe de la Renaissance,* ed. Pierre Aquilon and Henri-Jean Martin (Tours, 1988), 502–49; and André Stegmann, "Comment constituer une bibliothèque en France au début du XVIIe siècle: Examen méthodologique," in *Livre dans l'Europe,* 467–501.

20. Henri-Jean Martin, *Livres, pouvoirs et société à Paris*; see, in particular, 1:492. For other broad surveys of book holdings, see Albert Labarre, *Le livre dans la vie amiénoise du seizième siècle: L'enseignement des inventaires après décès, 1503–1576* (Louvain, 1971); Henri-Jean Martin and M. Lecocq, *Livres et lecteurs à Grenoble: Les registres du libraire Nicolas (1645–1668)* (Geneva, 1977); and Chartier, "Publishing Strategies and What the People Read, 1530–1660," in *The Cultural Uses of Print,* 145–82. Lucy Gent assembled a list of books on art, perspective, and architecture in English libraries from 1580 to 1630 in her *Picture and Poetry, 1560–1620: Relations between Literature and the Visual Arts in the English Renaissance* (Leamington Spa, 1981).

Jan Bialostocki surveyed the libraries of artists in a useful article, "The *Doctus Artifex* and the Library of the Artist in the XVIth and XVIIth Centuries," in *The Message of Images: Studies in the History of Art* (Vienna, 1988) 150–65. Le Vau's library was large relative to the painters mentioned by Bialostocki; for example, Andrea Sacchi had 54 books and Velazquez 154. The subject is explored further in a forthcoming article by Claude Mignot "Bibliothèques d'architectes au XVIIe siècle," in *La bibliothèque artistique idéale,* ed. Sylvie Deswarte (in press).

Stegmann gives a cursory treatment of his subject in "Comment constituer une bibliothèque en France."

21. For a partial publication of Lemercier's inventory see Annalisa Avon, "La biblioteca, gli strumenti scientifici, le collezioni di antichità e opere d'arte di un architetto del XVII secolo, Jacques Le Mercier (1585–1654)," *Annali di Architettura, Rivista del Centro internazionale di studi di architettura Andrea Palladio* 8 (1996):179–96. Unfortunately, the transcription is flawed, the book list is abridged, and the document is not edited.

22. For Herrera's inventory in 1597, see Agustin Ruiz de Arcaute, *Juan de Herrera* (Madrid, 1936), 97 and 150–71. Joseph Connors gave the figure for Borromini's library in *Borromini and the Roman Oratory* (New York and Cambridge, Mass., 1980), 140 n. 44; but he now believes Borromini's holdings were far greater than the inventory suggests.

23. At the time of Mansart's death, 119 books were in his house, and 47 books he owned previously have been located (Allan Braham and Peter Smith, *François Mansart* [London, 1973], 1:175–77.

24. On Cortona's library, see Karl Noehles, *La chiesa dei SS. Luca e Martina nell'opera di Pietro da Cortona* (Rome, 1970), 365–67; and on Maruscelli, see Connors, *Borromini and the Roman Oratory,* 112. My thanks to Susan Klaiber for information on Castellamonte's library, for which see Franco Monetti and Arabella Cifani, "Un capitolo per Vittorio Amedeo Castellamonte (1613–1683), architetto torinese," in *Arte e artisti nel Piemonte del '600: nuove scoperte e Nuovi orientamenti,* ed. Franco Monetti (Cavallermaggiore, 1990), 71–84.

The library of gentleman-architect Roger Pratt (died 1685) has not been fully reconstructed; in *The Architecture of Sir Roger Pratt,* ed R. T. Gunther (Oxford, 1928), Appendix 2, "Sir Roger Pratt's Library," 302–4, sixty-nine titles are identified.

25. Jean-Pierre Babelon published de Brosse's inventory after death in "Documents inédits concernant Salomon de Brosse," *BSHAF,* 1962, 150; he suspected that the library was larger at an earlier point in time.

26. The 1602 inventory, which also mentions fourteen books of portraits, was published by David Thomson in Jacques-Androuet Du Cerceau, *Les plus excellents bastiments de France,* ed. David Thomson (Paris, 1988), 314.

27. AN Min. cent. II 140, fols. 10v–11v, 26 June 1632.

28. Published in AN Min. cent. XC 210, fols. 5v–6r,
31 Jan. 1647, is the following inventory:
   Dans une petite armoire estant aud. cabinet:
   Item ung grand de bastimens du Cerceau couvert
      de veau
   Item ung autre livre de petitz bastimens dud. du
      Cerceau
   Item ung livre de porticques et épitaphes de Rome
   Item ung aute livre de fortiffications, le trois et
      quatrième livres du Cerceau
   Item ung livre de petitz bastimens de Muet
   Item les ordres de colonnes de Vignolle
   Item la porticque de Francine . . . prisé le tout en-
      semble LXXV [75] l[ivres] t[ournois]
   Item une bible in follio ouverte de veau rouge 10 lt

29. AN Min. cent. XLV 260, 23 Sept. 1652.

30. "Dans le cabinet au second estage ayant veue sur
la cour. Soixante trois petits volumes de livres de different autheurs partie reliée en veau et l'autre en par-
chemin, en quarto, en octavo, en douze, prisée xii
[12] lt" (AN Min. cent. LXII 232, fols. 3v–4r, 18 Jan.
1685).

31. Howard Hibbard, *Carlo Maderno and Roman Architecture 1580–1630* (London, 1971), 98 and 103. For
Guillain's inventory after death, see AN Min. cent. V
75, 3 July 1630.

32. I am grateful to Christy Anderson for information on Jones's library for which no book list survives. She has located 46 he owned and identified 23
other titles in his collection; her estimate of 200 books
in total is based on extensive analysis of his writings

on architecture. For comparative information about
the libraries of other English architects and masons,
see Anderson, "Inigo Jones's Library," 182–83.

33. On Hardouin-Mansart's library, see Fontegrive,
"Une bibliothèque d'architecte au siècle de Louis
XIV," *Architecte des collectivités publiques* 2 (Mar.
1955):22–23. My thanks to Michael Rabens for this
reference.
   For the inventory of d'Orbay's library, dated
18 Sept. 1697, see Laprade, *François d'Orbay,* 348–50.
The inventory enumerates 943 volumes but specifies
only 163 titles. A typical item reads "un pacquet de
16 volumes in-16 dont la Coutume de Paris de
Tourneux," which explains the problem in sorting
out the number of books d'Orbay owned.

34. Chartier, "Urban Reading Practices," in *The Cultural Uses of Print,* 194–95.

35. On the orders in sixteenth-century French architecture, see Jean Guillaume, ed., *L'Emploi des ordres
dans l'architecture de la Renaissance* (Paris, 1992), and
Henri Zerner, *L'Art de la Renaissance en France: L'Invention du classicisme* (Paris, 1996)

36. For François Le Vau's inventory after death, see
AN Min. cent. XII 172, 8 July 1676. The fate of the
library after his death is unknown. The Le Vau dynasty of masons and architects ended with François's
death. Neither Louis nor his brother had sons, and
the daughters did not marry architects. François's
inventory was undertaken in the presence of his
widow, fourteen-year-old daughter, and a cousin, a
lawyer in Parlement; with no architect in the family
to use the library, it may well have been dispersed at
that time.

CHAPTER 4

1. Paul Fréart de Chantelou, *Diary of the Cavaliere
Bernini's Visit to France,* trans. Margery Corbett,
ed. Anthony Blunt, annotated by George Bauer
(Princeton, 1985), 210. I have altered the translation
slightly.

2. These items and others are specified in the bequest

(Alfred Franklin, *Recherches historiques sur le Collège
des Quartes-Nations* [Paris, 1862], 155–56).

3. The first budget broke the whole project down
into three lump sums totaling 2,058,800 *livres* (see
AN H3 2845, no. 14 [in red pencil], "Mémoire pour
commancer à l'exécution du Collège des Quatre Na-

tions," 8 June 1662). For Gomont's response, see AN MM 462, fols. 43–45v, 8 June 1662.

Soon thereafter, Le Vau submitted a revised and more detailed budget, which lowered the grand total to 1,956,000 *livres,* just under the ceiling; see AN H3 2845, no. 15 (in red pencil), "Calcul général de la despense du Colleige des Quatre Nations du 26 juin 1662." (For a variant copy of the second budget with more detailed information about programmatic issues, see AN H3 2845, no. 29 [in red pencil].) Owing to the summary nature of the first budget, it is impossible to pinpoint where the savings came from, but the modest cutback—about 103,000 *livres*—points to the overriding problem: Le Vau could barely stretch the bequest to cover construction costs alone. All other items he encompassed in an evasive omnibus provision: "Ces travaux se feront plus ou moins grands suivant le fond."

4. Le Vau estimated 70,000 *livres* in annual income from the following sources: 10,000 *livres* in rent from the shops, 15,000 *livres* in rent from the houses, 25,000 *livres* from municipal bonds (*rentes de l'Hôtel de Ville*), and 20,000 *livres* from a benefice from the abbey of Saint Michel-en-l'Herme. These figures derive from Le Vau's second budget, AN H3 2845, no. 15 (in red pencil). Le Vau later recommended building additional shops and houses on the rue Mazarine to raise an additional 2,500 *livres* per annum in rental income (AN MM 462, fol. 109v, 21 Apr. 1664).

Initially Le Vau hoped that the capital fund, if wisely invested, would return 150,000 *livres* in interest, but the commissioners put the money in low-risk, low-yield properties. For a discussion of investment strategies, see AN MM 462, fols. 42–43, 8 July 1662.

As it turned out, Le Vau's estimates were overly optimistic. From 1665 to 1673 the annual rental income from the rue Mazarine houses averaged slightly under 11,000 *livres,* below Le Vau's guaranteed minimum of 15,000 *livres* (note that sixteen houses were built, not seventeen as Le Vau originally planned). This average was calculated on the basis of information provided by the Collège treasurer in AN H3* 2822, fols. 12v–13: "Compte rendu par S. Simon Mariage des recettes et depenses des années 1674–1673." The same source indicates that the shops in the Collège arcade generated about 3,000 *livres,* half what Le Vau had projected.

The benefice from the abbey of Saint Michel-en-l'Herme was one of the most lucrative benefices in Mazarin's portfolio; it had paid 36,000 *livres* a year on average, which means Le Vau's estimate was conservative, but this income stream lasted only three years because the abbey was dissolved in 1664. On Mazarin's benefices, and Saint Michel-en-l'Herme in particular, see Joseph Bergin, "Cardinal Mazarin and His Benefices," *French History* 1, no. 1 (Mar. 1987): 3–26; Dom G. Charvin, "Colbert, intendant des Abbayes de Mazarin," *Revue Mabillon* 36 (1946): 15–47, 87–119; Jules Sottas, "Le gouvernement de Brouage et La Rochelle sous Mazarin (1653–1661)," *Revue de Saintonge et d'Aunis* 39 (1921):218; Gabriel-Jules, Comte de Cosnac, *Mazarin et Colbert* (Paris, 1892) 2:430, 436–39; L. Brochet, *Histoire de l'abbaye royale de Saint-Michel en l'Herme* (Fontenay-le-Comte, 1891); and Pierre Clément, *Lettres, instructions, et memoires de Colbert,* (Paris, 1861–70), 1:162–63 and 5:317.

On the cost of furnishings and decoration, which Le Vau estimated at 150,000–200,000 *livres,* see AN MM 462, fol. 79r, 11 Feb. 1663.

5. On Armand Charles de La Porte (1632–1713), duc de Mazarin, see Georges Livet, *Le duc Mazarin, gouverneur d'Alsace (1661–1713): Lettres et documents inédits* (Strasbourg and Paris, 1954); on Abbé [François Timoléon] de Choisy, see Champollion-Figeac, ed. *Mémoires pour servir à l'histoire de Louis XIV,* in *Nouvelle Collection des mémoires pour servir à l'histoire de France,* ed. Joseph Fr. Michaud and Jean Joseph François Poujoulat, 3d ser., vol. 6 (Paris, 1850), 572; Clément, *Lettres de Colbert,* 6:280–81; and Adolphe Chéruel, ed., *Journal d'Olivier Lefèvre d'Ormesson* (Collection de documents inédits sur l'histoire de France, 3d ser., vol. 9; Paris, 1860–61), vol. 2:274–75, 603.

6. AN MM 462, fol. 46r.

7. "Monsieur Colbert . . . avoit eu l'honneur d'entretenir fort longtemps le Roy sur la proposition du Luxembourg et que Sa Majesté luy avoit demandé toutes les circonstances de ce dessein et les moyens que l'on avoit projettés pour l'executer. . . . Sa Majesté avoit fait grande consideration sur ce que Luxembourg estoit une maison royale bastie par . . . sa grandmere, . . . mais surtout que l'ornement que le bastiment du college apportera au Louvre quant il sera basti sur la fosse de la porte de Nesle avoit fort touché Sa Majesté, qu'elle approuvoit beaucoup plus cette pensée, et mesme qu'elle feroit bien aise qu'elle fust executé le plus promptement qu'il sera possible" (AN MM 462, fol. 52v, 1 July 1662).

8. Expenses can be divided into four categories: land costs (acquisitions, indemnities, taxes); infrastructure costs to build the Quai Mazarin and underground sewer; construction of the college buildings; and construction of the rental houses on the rue Mazarine. The following chart compares estimated versus actual expenses.

Building Costs

	Estimated	Actual	Overrun	
Land	420,750	575,000	154,250	37%
Infrastructure	164,000	245,000	81,000	49%
College	1,100,000	1,212,700	112,700	10%
Rental Houses	300,000	310,000	10,000	3%
Total	1,984,750	2,342,700	357,950	18%

This data is derived from the following documents: for land, the first budget of 8 June 1662 (AN H3 2845); for infrastructure, the second budget of 26 June 1662 (AN H3 2845) and Bibliothèque de l'Institut, Godefroy 190, fol. 193, 30 July 1672—the sewer cost 75,000 livres and the quay, 170,000 livres; for construction of the college buildings, the second budget of 26 June 1662, cited above, and a record of payments compiled by the treasurer Mariage between 1662 and 1670, AN S6506 (a variant copy of Mariage's register, AN H3* 2824, covers the period from 1662 to 1683 and gives slightly higher figures; I have not used those figures because they include postconstruction costs, including those for furnishings and decorations, which Le Vau explicitly excluded); and for rental houses, Le Vau's second budget of 26 June 1662, cited above, and "Journal de la despence qui est faite par M. Mariage pour le College Mazariny," AN H3* 2824.

9. For the terms dictated by Colbert, see AN MM 462, fols. 49 and 59. Before the Collège was planned, the crown had initiated an urban-renewal project around the Porte de Nesle. In order to finance construction of a new gate and quay, the city of Paris was authorized by royal edict of 1659 to sell the ditch

of Nesle, whereupon the city auctioned off the land in October 1660. The developers who purchased the land had to build a sewer to replace the ditch (see the masonry contract, AN M176, no. 36, 31 Mar. 1661), while the city remained responsible for the gate and quay (masonry contract, AN H3 2845, no. 54, 29 Dec. 1660). For further details about the complicated history of the site before Mazarin's Collège, see Adolphe Berty et al., *Topographie historique du Vieux Paris* (Paris, 1866–87), 5:61–62, 593–97.

10. Le Vau had expected to indemnify only the fifteen houseowners whose properties he delineated on the site plan (see figs. 23 and 26). At a meeting hosted by Colbert on 11 Feb. 1663, the building committee acknowledged the problem of escalating costs relating to the site (AN MM 462, fol. 77). By this time, the Collège had already paid 260,000 *livres* in indemnities; the final cost was higher because this figure does not include what the Collège eventually paid the abbey of Saint Germain des Prés. See the record of payments compiled by the treasurer of the Collège in AN H3* 2824, fols. 2–3, under the headings "Acquisitions de maisons qui ont esté demollies" and "Acquisition des places."

The abbey of Saint Germain des Prés asserted claims to seigneurial dues on the underlying land. Colbert asked three eminent scholars—the historian Denis II Godefroy; the librarian of the Oratory, Charles Le Cointe; and Henri Sauval, historian of Paris—to research the abbey's claims in the Trésor des Chartes. Sauval found a document that, in his view, discredited the abbey's claims; nevertheless, the Conseil d'Etat eventually ordered the Collège to pay taxes *(lods et ventes)* and indemnities on houses beyond the moat.

In a revealing offshoot of this episode, relations between Colbert and Sauval ruptured over the fee Sauval was paid for his research. He considered Colbert's payment of 2,000 *livres* as inadequate and requested a lifelong pension of 3,000 *livres,* which Colbert refused to provide. See Le Roux de Lincy, "Henri Sauval," *Bulletin du bibliophile,* 1862, 1122, 1176–78; and Henri Cordier, *Annales de l'Hôtel de Nesle* (Paris, 1916), 109–14.

The case of Henri de Guénégaud, who bought the Hôtel de Nevers in 1646, was equally difficult to resolve. In 1650 de Guénégaud ceded rights to the Tour de Nesle, the city walls, and the Porte de Nesle

that were partially on the grounds of the hôtel. In exchange, the city gave de Guénégaud 400 square *toises*
in the fossé de Nesle; some of this land was encompassed in the building site. De Guénégaud de-
manded 250 *livres* per square *toise*. After protracted
negotiations the king eventually intervened and pres-
sured de Guénégaud to accept 120 *livres* per *toise* plus
a bond for 1,500 *livres*. See Cordier, *Annales de l'Hôtel
de Nesle,* 102, 138–42; on Mansart's renovations to
what was renamed the Hôtel de Guénégaud, see
Allan Braham and Peter Smith, *François Mansart*
(London, 1973), 1:74–76.

11. Le Vau appealed to Colbert in September 1664:
"Pour la beauté de l'aspect du Louvre, Le Roy feroit
achever le quay jusques ou pont des Thuilleries; on
pourroit comprendre dans la même despence celle du
Quai Mazarini." Two months later Le Vau reiterated
the request; the financial problems of the Collège
would be remedied if the king would only pay for
the sewer and the quay (AN MM 462, fols. 138v and
151v).

    Le Vau also bickered with Colbert over the
length of the quay. Colbert wanted Mazarin's Collège to pay for a quay that extended the full length of
the Louvre. These parameters were specified in the
royal edict of 1659 and in the masonry contract for
the quay which the city passed in 1660: "A commancer les murs de quai ou ils finissent devant l'hos-
tel de Nevers jusques au devant la rue de Seine et au
dela d'icelle le long du quay de Malaquais" (AN H3
2845, 29 Dec. 1660). Le Vau argued that the Collège
was at most accountable for the segment on which its
buildings fronted, not the flanking parts (AN MM
462, fol. 75), and Colbert conceded this point.

12. For the specifications and contract for this pre-
Collège project, see AN M176, no. 36, 31 Mar. 1661.
The masons were to be paid 156 *livres* per cubic *toise*.

13. "Les mauvais odeurs qui en exhalent dans les
chaleurs de l'esté peuvent causer une infection dan-
gereuse au logement dud. Palais" (AN H3 2845, no.
43).

14. A group of expert masons examined the lay of the
land and determined that a new sewer main, fed by
smaller conduits in the region, should run beneath
the garden and courtyard of the Collège, turn onto

the rue Guénégaud, then empty into the river
through an arched opening in the quay. For the minutes of the inspection and report of the experts, see
AN H3 2845, no. 44 (all in ink), 8 Nov. 1662. For further details on the sewer, see AN H3 2845, no. 42.

15. For instance, the cost of the Cardinal LeMoine
site was estimated at 450,000 *livres*: 86 *livres* per
square *toise* for 4,000 *toises* plus 100,000 *livres* in indemnities (AN MM 462, fol. 32).

16. "Il parlera au Roy de rembourser le Collège de la
depense du quay qui est le plus beau quay de la ville,
que Le Roy avoit fait faire estant viz à viz le Louvre
comme aussy les despences de l'esgout qui est un ouvrage public" (AN MM 462, fol. 291, 20 May 1668).
For prior exchanges between Gomont and Colbert
on this subject, see AN MM 462, fol. 151v, 17 Nov.
1664; fol. 276r, 18 Nov. 1667.

17. The masonry contract specifies several different
local limestones: *pierre dure de Cliquart* for the
ground-level course; *pierre de Saint Leu* and *de Trossy*
for the walls above; *pierre de liais de Paris* and *du
faubourg Saint Jacques* or *pierre dure de Vernon* for the
bases of the pilasters; the hardest *pierre dure de Trossy*
for the pilaster shafts and capitals; *pierre dure de Cliquart* for the flat arches; and solid blocks of *pierre
dure de Saint Cloud* for the bottom third of the
columns, the rest of *pierre de Trossy* (AN H3 2845,
13 Aug. 1662). On the Parisian limestones, see Louis
Savot, *L'architecture française des bastimens particuliers*
(Paris, 1624); Charles Pomerol and L. Feugueux,
*Bassin de Paris, Ile-de-France, guides géologiques ré-
gionaux* (Paris, 1968); and on the stone of the Louvre,
Robert Berger, *The Palace of the Sun: The Louvre of
Louis XIV* (University Park, Pa., 1993), 66.

18. Another problem was that Le Vau requested bids
in the form of a lump-sum price, rather than a schedule of piecework or unit rates, in order to lock in a
fixed price for the masonry. Masons complained
about the difficulty of calculating a block amount
given the uncertainties about the job—for instance,
what was the required depth of foundations at the
shoreline? The city's lead architect, Michel Noblet,
explained the problem: "This large enterprise with
a range of work required by the site, such that the
foundations are at different heights and depths,

makes it impossible to judge properly the total cost. . . . That is why I did not satisfy Monsieur Le Vau's terms" (AN H3 2845, no. 40, 26 July 1662). His bid consisted of unit prices, and the other masons followed suit. For complaints about the specifications, the bids, and the device, see AN H3 2845, no. 15, 13 Aug. 1662, which contains a narrative of the entire process.

Bernini wanted to pay workers at the Louvre by the day in order to retain maximum control over construction, but Colbert considered that method foolish; "there would be a great deal of swindling as no one felt any loyalty under those conditions, also there could be no planning as there was in the case of contracts being given for piece work" (Chantelou, *Diary of Bernini's Visit,* 155, 170). Colbert shared Le Vau's preference for a lump-sum payment.

19. The losing bids were apparently discarded. The terms of the winning bidders are stated in AN H3 2845, nos. 38–40, 26–27 July 1662. In *Demeures parisiennes sous Henri IV et Louis XIII* (Paris, 1965; rev. ed., 1991), Jean-Pierre Babelon adopts the spelling *Thoizon;* I have chosen to retain the standard spelling in period documents: Thoison. On Lambert, see Albert Laprade, *François d'Orbay, architecte de Louis XIV* (Paris, 1960), 131.

20. On 13 Aug. 1662 Lambert and Thoison signed a contract with Mazarin's executors to build the Collège and the quay. The two also signed a separate contract to build the rental houses on the rue Mazarine. The masonry contract for the Collège does not include the rental houses on the rue Mazarine, but other documents indicate the same masons took them on (see AN H3 2845, no. 50 [in brown ink], 13 Aug. 1662).

21. Chantelou, *Diary of Bernini's Visit,* 172.

22. These procedures are set forth in the masonry contract (see AN H3 2845, no. 50, fol. 26r). Uncertain how to handle Le Vau, who was obviously a commanding figure, Gomont questioned Colbert about the scope of Le Vau's powers. Beside each of Gomont's queries, Colbert penned an answer (see AN MM 462, fol. 63, 11 Sept. 1662). Should someone oversee Le Vau's requisitions to determine if the Collège had sufficient funds? Colbert replied: Le Vau

could spend only what was given to him. Was it Le Vau's job to oversee the contractors and the assistant controller? Le Vau supervised the contractors, but the assistant controller had to check up on Le Vau. Should Gomont make reports to the building committee about Le Vau's orders? Again Colbert answered yes.

23. On Meurset's complaints, see AN MM 462, fol. 88, 6 Oct. 1663; fol. 91, 18 Feb. 1664; and fol. 116, 9 June 1664; BN MS Mélanges de Colbert 119 bis, fols. 998–99, 19 Mar. 1664; and AN H3 2845, 31 Mar. 1665. Meurset was the second assistant controller; reports for his predecessor named Aubery, did not have the same stringent tone; see BN MS Mélanges de Colbert 112 bis, fols. 845–47, 20 Nov. 1662.

24. "Je cognois bien qu'on vous a desguisé ma conduite pour vous la rendre desagreable, et que l'exactitude et l'assiduité que j'ay apportées a m'acquiter de l'employ dont il vous a plu me charger en sont la seule cause" (BN MS Mélanges Colbert 119 bis, fol. 998, 19 Mar. 1664).

25. Gomont tried to calm Le Vau; "[he] begged Monsieur Le Vau to assist [Meurset] de La Tour in every reasonable way because the controller's work is necessary; surely Le Vau had already treated him well but he was asked to do even better, for the satisfaction of Monsieur Colbert . . . and the good of the building . . ." (AN MM 462, fol. 89, 6 Oct. 1663). Gomont felt he had either to fire Meurset or take his findings seriously, but he took no decisive action (AN MM 462, fols. 101v–102, 2 Mar. 1664).

26. "Il ne s'est jamais voulu mesler ny de delivrer, ny de faire deslivrer des ordonnances, ny de prendre cognoissance d'aucun payment, ny mesme de scavoir ce qui payé, parce que cela n'est pas de son profession, ny de la fonction qui luy est commise pour l'execution de la fondation, ny de son interest, ny de son esprit" (AN MM 462, fol. 266v, 26 Feb. 1667). Gomont made similar comments at other times as well (see for instance, AN MM 462, fol. 273, 17 June 1667).

27. "Toutes ces malfacons peuvent aisément faire connoistre l'intelligence des entrepreneurs avec cet architecte preposé pour en estre l'ordonnateur et le controlleur general, les aiant laissé construire tels qu'ils sont, et les aiant fait paier de la moitié plus qu'ils ne vallent quant mesme. . . . On peut aisement prejuger de ce qui s'est passé aux autres ouvrages de la maconnerie dud. College montant à des sommes tres considerables et la necessité qu'il y avoit de faire veriffier et examiner par une personne intelligente et desinteressé tous les toisés. . . . Joint la preuve qui a esté découverte apres le deces dud. Le Veau qu'il avoit pris interest en tous les ouvrages de maconnerie dud. College [crossed out: avec feu Thoison, son beaufrere], apres avoir entrepris seul le bastiment de plusiers maisons construictes pour faire des revenues aud. College [crossed out: aussi sous le nom dud. Thoison] ce qui a esté veu, sceu, et tolleré pendant le vivant dud. Le Veau [crossed out: tant par Mond. Seigneur Colbert que le Controlleur de la fondation dud. College] sous apparence d'un plus grand bien et de voir bastir plus diligement lesd. [crossed out: 16] maisons [crossed out: le tout a la persuasion dud. Le Veau] et faire bon au public à la persuasion dud. le Veau ce beau quay et pavillons avancez vis-à-vis du Louvre" (AN H3 2845, no. 55 [unsigned and undated but after Le Vau's death in 1670]).

28. This number was calculated by adding the difference in cost between the Quai Mazarin and the city's quay (86,000 *livres*) to the estimated value of demolition materials (8,000 *livres*).

29. Chantelou, *Diary of Bernini's Visit,* 157–58, 161, 204.

30. Upon signing the masonry contract with the Collège officials, Thoison and Lambert revised the terms of their partnership in the rue Mazarine houses. Three transactions took place. First, Lambert split his half-interest in the Collège and rental houses with the city's top-ranking mason, Michel Noblet, so that they each had a 25 percent share of the project. Second, Thoison sold his 50 percent stake to Etienne Blondet for 8,000 *livres.* Third, Blondet declared that he was acting on behalf of his employer, Louis Le Vau. In reality, Le Vau owed the money to his brother-in-law, who had merely loaned his name for the original transaction. For these transactions, see AN H3 2845, no. 19, 16–20 Aug. 1662; and AN H3 2845, no. 21 (written in ink), 13 Aug. 1662. Le Vau's part in the rental houses is also mentioned in an un-

dated account (AN H3 2845, no. 4): "Constructions des 16 maisons, 1662–1665, 310,000 livres. Le Vau a esté l'entrepreneur de ces 16 maisons sous le nom de C. Thoison, maçon, son beaufrère et à present décédé [Thoison died in 1666]." Le Vau's liability for the 8,000-*livres* payment is confirmed in the posthumous bankruptcy agreement negotiated by the trustees of his estate (AN S6506, 20 Sept. 1674, p. 19).

31. It is less likely that Chantelou was referring to the fact that Simon Lambert owned a house near the Porte de Nesle for which he received an indemnity of 10,000 *livres* from the Collège, the lowest of all indemnities it paid; for the figures, see AN S6506.

32. For Le Vau's salary and those of other architects, see Clément, *Lettres de Colbert,* 5:456.

33. For masonry contracts in which Le Vau hired his father, see AN Min. cent. XXXVI 167, 13 Apr. 1641; AN Min. cent. LXXXVI 167, fol. 376, 13 Apr. 1641 (same day, different notary—in this case, Le Vau's father-in-law); and AN Min. cent. CV 406, 1 May 1641.

For loans see, for example, AN Min. cent. XXXVI 169, 25 Jan. 1642; and AN Min. cent. XXXVI 167, 27 Mar. 1641. We know that Le Vau bypassed notaries in many (or most?) cases because some notarized documents refer to others passed "sous seing privé."

On Le Vau's role in the development of the Ile Saint-Louis, see Délégation à l'Action Artistique de la Ville de Paris, *L'Ile Saint-Louis,* ed. Béatrice de Andia and Nicolas Courtin (Paris, 1997), which has an extensive bibliography; and Maurice Dumolin, "La construction de l'Ile Saint-Louis," in *Etudes de topographie parisienne* (Paris, 1929–31), 3:1–288. Other sources focus on particular *hôtels* and design issues—for example, Dietrich Feldmann, "Das Hôtel de la Vrillière und die Raüme 'à l'italienne' bei Louis Le Vau," *Zeitschrift für Kunstgeschichte* 45, no. 4 (1982): 395–422; Feldmann, *Maison Lambert, Maison Hesselin und andere Bauten von Louis Le Vau auf der Ile Saint Louis in Paris* (Hamburg, 1976); and Constance Tooth, "The Early Private Houses of Louis Le Vau," *Burlington Magazine* 109, no. 774 (Sept. 1967): 510–18.

34. The rent did not consistently reach the targeted

level of 15,000 *livres* per year until the 1680s. For the figures, see AN H3* 2282 and AN H3* 2283.

35. On 10 February 1676, the Académie Royale d'Architecture "a délibéré sur le project de l'arrest que Monseigneur Colbert a accordé à l'Académie portant deffense à tous maîtres massons, entrepreneur et autres gens se meslans des bastimens, de prendre la qualité d'architecte du Roi, que Sa Majesté a réservée à ceux qui composent ladite Académie" (Henry Lemonnier, ed. *Procès-verbaux de l'Académie Royale d'Architecture, 1671–1793,* [Paris, 1911], 1:109).

36. See the loose sheet inserted in Bibliothèque de l'Institut MS. 368.

37. The pledge reads as follows: "Toutes les sommes montant à 100,000 livres tournois, et ce pour la delivrer et payer aux entrepreneurs des bastiments dud. College Mazariny, desquelz entrepreneurs led. Le Vau sera tenu et promet fournir des quittances aud. sr Mariage en sa demeure à Paris quand il l'en requierra. Sinon, et à faute de ce faire, sera aussy tenu et promet rendre et restituer icelle somme de 100,000 l au dr Mariage à sa volonté et premiere requeste . . ." (AN S6506, 14 Apr. 1666). This document lists the thirteen payments in question and was co-signed by Le Vau's wife. Another document in the same register and dated 31 July 1668 concerns an ineffectual appeal by Mariage to bring Le Vau into compliance.

38. AN S6506 (n.d.), "Memoire pour Mariage au sujet de 100,000 lt [livres tournois] avancé à Le Vau." The cited passages read as follows: "Il a suivi en cela la bonnefoy de celuy qu'on luy avoit nommé pour ordonnateur des paiements qu'on l'a chargé de faire sur ses ordonnances et certificats. Et il avoit cru manquer au devoir de sa commission . . . s'il n'avoit pas promptement fourni lesd.denier pour l'avancements desd. Ouvrages. . . . Et ainsy, il avoit toute apparance et il est encore à presumer que led. deffunct Le Vau avoit le mesme interest dans les autres ouvrages du College, et qu'il y a eu entr'eux des traités et des declarations secretes qui n'ont point encore paru, et qui pourront se decouvrir et faire voir que led. sr Mariage en paiant aud. Le Vau a payé au veritable entrepreneur et au principal interessé dans tous les ouvrages dud college."

39. According to Mariage, the split was documented in Blondet's registers, but the books were destroyed in 1666, when Thoison died and Lambert took over his share (Noblet remained involved in the rue Mazarine houses, although he is rarely mentioned in the records). "Et par la mesme transaction, il parroist qu'ils se sont fair rapporter les registres de recepte et despense pour les supprimer, et il est à presumer que par ces registres, la preuve estoit toute entiere que led. Le Vau estoit de part au gain de l'entreprise dud. College" (AN S6506, "Memoire pour Mariage au sujet de 100,000 lt [livres tournois] avancé à Le Vau").

Note that the partnership agreement entitled Le Vau to chose a successor should Lambert or Thoison die or wish to sell out. Le Vau's control of the partnership succession is open to two conflicting interpretations. Either the arrangement was intended to safeguard the quality of construction, for which Le Vau was responsible in his capacity as controller general, or it derived from his position as (senior) partner of the surviving contractor.

40. "Le Vau voulut faire servir l'argent du Collège à l'exécution de son entreprise; et pour cet effect dissimulant son dessein, il surprit du sieur Mariage la délivrance de plusieurs sommes qui formoient ensemble celle de 100,000 livres, sous prétext d'employer les deniers au payment des entrepreneurs et ouvriers" (AN M174, no. 68, 1689).

41. For the patent letters, see BN MS fr. 21789, fols. 342–47.

42. According to Le Vau's inventory after death (AN Min cent. LXXXV 198, fol. 22, 27 Nov. 1670, no. 25), Champion agreed to lend his name to Le Vau in a declaration dated 6 March 1665, but the summary description of the document does not indicate how Le Vau compensated Champion. Is it possible that Antoine Champion was related to the Champion family in England, like-minded metallurgists who dominated British brass and zinc smelting from the 1690s to the 1770s? On Nehemiah Champion and his sons John and William, see Joan Day, *Bristol Brass: A History of the Industry* (London, 1973), 62–74; and Joan Day, "Introduction" and "Copper, Zinc and Brass Production," in *The Industrial Revolution in Metals,* ed. Joan Day and R. F. Tylecoat (London, 1991), 19, 172, 180–84.

Champion was succeeded in November 1666 by Antoine Picquet. Because the edict had originally vested the privilege in Champion, the crown's approval was required for this change (BN MS fr. 21789, fols. 359–60, 10 Nov. 1666).

43. See, for instance, René Mémain, *Le marine de guerre sous Louis XIV: Le matériel Rochefort, arsenal modèle de Colbert* (Paris, 1937), 788, 833; there Le Vau is identified as a rich financier and is thought to be a person separate from the architect Louis Le Vau (the index has two separate entries). Even Jean Peter fails to make the connection in his well-researched book, the best source of information on Beaumont: *Maîtres de forges et maîtres fondeurs de la marine sous Louis XIV: Samuel Daliès de La Tour et les frères René et Pierre Landouillette de Logivière* (Paris, 1996). The first scholars to focus on Le Vau's work at Beaumont were Nicole Bourdel, "Nouveaux documents sur Louis Le Vau, premier architecte de Louis XIV (1612–1670)," *Paris et l'Ile-de-France, mémoires* 8 (1956):213–35; Guy Thuillier, "Les speculations malheureuses de l'architecte Louis Le Vau à Beaumont-la-Ferrière (1665–1670)," *Mémoires de la Société académique du Nivernais* 51 (1959):24–36 (which lacks citations).

44. On Colbert's industrial policies and initiatives, see Pierre Clément, *Histoire de Colbert et de son administration* (Paris, 1874); Germain Martin, *La grande industrie sous le règne de Louis XIV* (Paris, 1899); Prosper Boissonnade and Pierre Jacques Charliat, *Colbert et la Compagnie de Commerce du Nord (1661–1689)* (Paris, 1930); Prosper Boissonnade, *Colbert: Le triomphe de l'etatisme; La fondation de la suprématie industrielle de la France; La dictature du travail (1661–1683)* (Paris, 1932); Charles Woolsey Cole, *Colbert and a Century of French Mercantilism* (New York, 1939; reprint, Hamden, Conn., 1964); James King, *Science and Rationalism in the Government of Louis XIV, 1661–1683* (Baltimore, 1949); Geoffrey Treasure, *Seventeenth Century France,* 2d ed. (London, 1981), chap. 21; and the incisive, summary remarks of Emmanuel Le Roy Ladurie, *The Ancien Régime: A History of France, 1610–1774,* trans. Mark Greengrass (Oxford, 1996), 168. A key source remains Clément, *Lettres de Colbert,* especially vol. 2 on industry and commerce. See also Jacques Savary, *Le parfait négociant ou instruction générale pour ce qui*

regarde le commerce de toute sorte de marchandises, tant de France que des pays estrangers* (Paris, 1675), which is dedicated to Colbert but primarily concerns textiles.

45. The 60,000-*livre* subsidy to the tin foundry was modest by comparison with other grants—for instance, 200,000 *livres* to silk makers in Lyons and 1.7 million *livres* to cloth makers in Abbeville; for other comparative data, see Boissonnade, *Colbert: Le triomphe de l'etatisme,* 238–39.

46. Le Roy Ladurie, *The Ancien Régime,* 175.

47. Le Vau's trip to Germany is reported in the patent letters of 1665 (BN MS fr. 21789, fol. 343).

48. Another sign of contemporary interest in tinning comes from the Royal Society in London, which received two manuscripts on the subject—one by a Dr. Cotton in 1664, "An Account concerning the Tin-Mines in Devonshire," the other a report by an "Inquisitive Person" in 1671; the procedures they describe were probably very close to Le Vau's contemporary operation across the Channel. On the British efforts, see R. F. Tylecote, *History of Metallurgy* (London, 1976), chap. 8, "Post-medieval metallurgy"; Joan Day, "Introduction," and Bryan Earl, "Tin Preparation and Smelting," in *The Industrial Revolution in Metals;* and P. Brown, "Andrew Yarranton and the British Tinplate Industry," *Journal of the Historical Metallurgical Society* 22, no. 1 (1988):42–48.

49. See the discussion "Materials and Structure" written in collaboration with Rowland Mainstone in Robert Berger, *The Palace of the Sun: The Louvre of Louis XIV* (University Park, Pa., 1993), 65–74.

50. This account draws on numerous historical studies of metalworking, cast-iron cannon, and naval armaments in the seventeenth century: Centre Historique des Archives Nationales, *L'ame et la lumière: Armes et canons dans la Marine Royale fin de XVIIe–XVIII siècle,* exh. cat. (Paris, 1996); Carel de Beer, ed., *The Art of Gunfounding: The Casting of Bronze Cannon in the Late 18th Century* (Rotherfield, East Sussex, 1991); Archives Nationales, *Sur l'eau . . . Sous l'eau . . . :Imagination et technique dans la marine, 1680–1730* (Paris, 1986); Tylecote, *History of Metal-*

lurgy; John Francis Guilmartin, Jr., *Gunpowder and Galleys: Changing Technology and Mediterranean Warfare at Sea in the Sixteenth Century* (Cambridge, 1974); A. R. Hall, *Ballistics in the Seventeenth Century* (Cambridge, 1952); and Julien Felix Delaunay and Albert Charles Guittard, *Historique de l'artillerie de marine* (Paris, 1898).

The seventeenth-century treatises all postdate Le Vau and reflect the advances made under Colbert: Alain Manesson Mallet, *Travaux de Mars, ou la fortification nouvelle* (Paris, 1672); Casimir Simienowicz, *Ausführliche Beschreibung der groszen Feuerwercks* (Frankfurt, 1676); Louis de Gaya, *Traité des armes des machines de guerre* (Paris, 1678; reprint, Oxford, 1911); Pierre Surirey de Saint-Remy, *Mémoires d'artillerie,* (Paris, 1697).

Le Vau's installation at Beaumont was contemporary with John Winthrop's foundation of the Saugus Ironworks in colonial Massachusetts, for which see Robert Gordon, *American Iron, 1607–1900* (Baltimore, 1996); James Mulholland, *A History of Metals in Colonial America* (University, Ala., 1981); and E. N. Hartley, *Ironworks on the Saugus* (Norman, Okla., 1957).

51. Gun casting, although based on techniques of bell founding, presented special problems. First, a double furnace was required for a cast so large. Second, the founder had to reduce the molten metal to just the right degree of fluidity and fineness so that upon cooling, the metal had the proper density. Third, the mold required precise shaping to ensure that the metal cast had the proper thickness, a critical factor affecting ballistics. The gun mold had two parts: a clay mold for the outside of the gun was made on a wood frame or pattern, while an iron bar, covered in clay, was inserted in the barrel of the mold. This left a critical empty space between the two clay membranes, as illustrated in Saint-Remy's treatise on artillery, wherein the melt was poured. After cooling, the mold was broken to disengage the metal casting, whereupon the mouth was trimmed, the touch hole drilled, and the gun barrel reamed. For other products—tools, tableware, ingots, and tinplates—the metal went from the furnace into the forge, where it was reheated, refined, and hammered to remove charcoal and slag. After the forge, metal was ready for further shaping.

52. Those towns include Cosne, La Charité, Charbonnières, Arlot, and Landouillette à Cramin; see Louis Guéneau, *L'organisation du travail à Nevers aux XVIIe et XVIIIe siècles (1660–1790)* (Paris, 1919), 348. Charles Cole (*Colbert and a Century of French Mercantilism,* 2:324) confused Le Vau's foundry with others in the region.

53. For details of Le Vau's holdings in Beaumont, the key source is Gaston Gauthier, *Monographie de la commune de Beaumont-la-Ferrière* (Nevers, 1892), 12, 35, 118–19. According to Gauthier, Le Vau bought his first parcel of land in Beaumont from Henri de La Grange, marquis d'Arquian and captain of the guard for the king's brother, in 1660. However, Le Vau's inventory after death dates the sale to 4 Mar. 1665—that is, immediately after the foundation act of the foundry (AN Min. cent. LXXXV 198, fol. 23, no. 26). Gauthier described Le Vau's château as a *corps de logis* with round end towers and a service wing for stables and other farming functions, but we have no reason to believe his description matches its appearance in Le Vau's time. Le Vau's foundry was substantial, even comparable to the impressive foundry Colbert built at the arsenal at Rochefort (Mémain, *La marine de guerre,* 111–12, 989–95).

54. "L'on sait blanchir aussi bien qu'en Allemaigne. . . . Les fourneaux seront prests dans quinze jours pour blanchir plus de deux milles feuilles noires qui sont toutes disposées au blanchissage. Ainsy nous avons toutte la matière très-propre, et la forme des forges aussi bien disposée qu'on le peut souhetter. . . . Nous n'avons donc besoing que de bons martelleurs qui expédient l'ouvrage avec plus de promptitude que nos François. . . . J'ay disposé pour la manufacture de mousquets, canons et boullets, touttes choses pour y travailler quand il vous plaira l'ordonner. Je vous porteray quelque mousquet que je fais faire à des ouvriers que j'ay fait venir icy pour cognoistre la forme et la matière; et pour les canons, j'ay le meilleur fondeur du royaume avec lequel j'ay desjà faict marché soubz vostre bon plaisir, pour la façon, machine et mousle de chacun canon . . ." (G. B. Depping, ed., *Correspondance administrative sous le règne de Louis XIV,* [Paris, 1850–55], 3:743).

The shortage of skilled labor was a persistent problem, as Colbert had foreseen. In an early outline of his industrial program, he included a notation to hire workers in Nuremberg "at whatever price is needed to establish them in France" (Clément, *Lettres de Colbert*, vol. 2, pt. 1, cclx, "Discours sur les manufactures du Royaume"). Thanks to royal concessions, Le Vau could offer foreign employees an exemption from all taxes and a guarantee of French citizenship after eight years of work, but these measures were insufficient to induce Germans to settle in France. Colbert enlisted the help of the French ambassador to Germany, the abbé de Gravel, whose letters to Colbert from 1665 to 1668 chronicle his consistent lack of success in recruiting master founders. See Depping, ed., *Correspondance administrative sous Louis XIV*, 3:740–45.

Le Vau managed to hire some German journeymen but complained of their insolence and brutality. Although the French proved to be more disciplined workers, Le Vau still needed a seasoned master who would move permanently to Beaumont and cultivate a new generation of founders—someone like Jacob Momma, the German metalworker who had settled in Surrey, England, in 1649 and ran a brass foundry there for nearly thirty years. On the English experience, see Day, "Copper, Zinc, and Brass Production," in *The Industrial Revolution in Metals*, 137–38.

55. BN MS fr. 21789, fols. 361–62.

56. According to the terms of the royal edict, 30,000 *livres* were a gift; they show up as the royal subsidy. The other 30,000 *livres* were an interest-free loan to be repaid in six years; they have presumably been included in the outstanding debt of 320,000 *livres*. To qualify for the grant, the foundry had to meet certain production levels, which are spelled out in the royal edict (BN MS fr. 21789, fol. 342–47). The two payments are mentioned in the royal accounts: "A Antoine Champion, la somme de 30,000 lt pour achapt de terres et bastimens à Beaumont, la Ferrière et Grenan, en Nivernais, pour l'establissement de la manufacture de fer-blanc, de laquelle le Roy luy a fait don, pareille somme de 30,000 lt pour le prest que S. M. luy a fait pendant 6 années sans interest . . ." (Jules Guiffrey, ed., *Comptes des bâtiments du roi sous le règne de Louis XIV* [Paris, 1881], vol. 1, 60, 96). Le Vau used most of the money (47,000 *livres*) to buy property in Beaumont in Mar. 1665 (AN Min. cent. LXXXV 198, fol. 23, item 26).

57. "La première manière de société, à prendre la chose dès le commencement et rendre toute la dépense et les frais en commun, seroit à mon advis tres difficiles, ces sommes de bastiments, d'advances, et de faux frais seroient suspectes aux plus religeux, et comme l'ordre des payments n'a pas esté observé avec les formes, il seroit presque impossible de persuader ces grandes despences qui sont dans l'estat qu'on en fait plus foible que forte, c'est pourquoy il ne fault pas faire estat de cette maniere" (BN MS fr. 21789, fol. 367v).

Colbert's adviser remained enthusiastic about the foundry's prospects despite its problems: "Il y a sept forges prest à travailler, dont quatre sont garnies d'ouvriers françois et allemandz, et que la blanchisserie est aussy garnie. Il ne s'agit plus qu'à soustenir et continuer cette grande et utile entreprise ou, depuis près de trois ans, tous les obstacles, difficultez, frais, despences et industrie ont esté practiqués" (BN MS fr. 21789, fol. 367r).

58. Colbert originally sent his protégé, François Bertholet, commissioner general for gunpowder and saltpeter to Beaumont before dispatching Besch. The royal accounts record a payment on 22 June 1668, when Besch was installed: "[to Le Vau and Berthelot], entrepreneurs de la manufacture de canons de fer en Nivernois, 12,000 lt pour partie du desdommagement de la perte qu'ils ont faite de l'establissement de lad. manufacture, lequel ils ont remis par ordre du Roy entre les mains du sr. de Besch, gentilhomme suédois, auquel S. M. a accordé le privillège de fonte desd. canons à l'exclusion de tous autres . . ." (Guiffrey, *Comptes des bâtiments du roi*, 1:287).

An inspection report by Dalliez on 12 Apr. 1669 indicates that Besch set up a separate foundry in Beaumont: "M. de la Besche ayant bien réussy à une fabrique d'acier qu'il a establie à Beaumont, que je trouve, par l'espreuve que j'en ay faitte, aussy bon que celuy d'Allemagne, nous nous en servirons pour faire des coutelas, des haches d'armes, pertuizannes, hallebardes et picques . . ." (Depping, ed., *Correspondance administrative sous Louis XIV*, 3:727).

For Abraham Besch's reports about Beaumont, see BN MS Mélanges de Colbert 145, fol. 88, 8 Sept. 1667; and fol. 429, 29 Sept. 1667. On the Besch brothers in general, see Martin, *La grande industrie sous de Louis XIV*; Clément, *Lettres de Colbert*, 3:32, 55, 379;

and Boissonade, *Colbert: Le triomphe de l'etatisme,* 100.

59. As a director of the Compagnie du Levant, Dalliez secured numerous government contracts to supply the French navy with arms, building materials, food, and other supplies. (On Dalliez de La Tour, see Daniel Dessert, *Argent, pouvoir et société au Grand Siècle* [Paris, 1984], 567–69; and Peter, *Maîtres de forges,* 25–35, 45–46.) Dalliez's role as a peripatetic and trusted agent of Colbert, with responsibility for foundries and arms manufacturing across France clearly emerges in his correspondence with Colbert; see BN MS Mélanges de Colbert 140, Sept. 1666; and BN MS Mélanges de Colbert 140, Jan. 1668, which also has related letters to Besch.

60. "Je n'y songe plus que pour y servir M. Leveau, qui en a le privilege général pour tout le royaume," he assured Colbert in August 1665, "et pour contribuer de ma part au progrès d'une nouvelle fabrique advantageuse au royaume, et dont il est juste qu'il retire quelque utilité, comme en ayant la première pensée. Sans y avoir intérêt, je ne laisseray pas d'y apporter tous les soings possibles" (Depping, ed., *Correspondance administrative sous Louis XIV,* 3:718, 11 Aug. 1665; and 16 Aug. 1665, 720).

61. The contract was for one million *livres* of iron in different sizes, to be used in ships and sea vessels at Brest and Rochefort. Le Vau was represented in this transaction by Etienne Blondet (see AN Min. cent. XCV 20, 23 Mar. 1669).

A month later, Dalliez reported to Colbert that the tin foundry was "virtually abandoned," but the gun foundry, despite problems with the workers, was productive and casting cannons daily. Historians have failed to distinguish the two distinct missions of Le Vau's foundry, which has led to a misreading of Dalliez's report. It reads in full as follows: "Depuis la mort des maistres qui travailloient au fer-blanc, l'on peut dire que cette manufacture a esté comme quasy abandonnée; les garcons compagnons n'estant plus conduits ont vescu dans le désordre du plus grand libertinage du monde; ils travaillent quand il leur plaist, mais avec tant de nonchalance et de malice, qu'il semble que ce ne soit que par despit et pour user du charbon et du fer inutilement: sur le pied enfin où ils ont mis les choses, il n'y a pas de barril de fer-blanc qui ne revienne à plus de 300 livres tt, et pardessus tout cela il est mal faict. . . . Il est important de ne faire venir d'Allemaigne que de bons maistres; nous n'avons que trop de compaignons. . . . Mon desseing est de suivre un si bon commencement et accoustumer les François à bien travailler, qui sont bien plus disciplinables que les Allemans; et si toutte la perte qu'on a faitte jusques icy avoit esté employée à dresser des François, cette manufacture seroit establie, au lieu que c'est à recommencer. L'on coulle tous les jours deux canons, et s'il y avoit deux foreries icy comme nous en avons en Bourgogone, les choses iroient plus viste, mais enfin il y en a cent cinquante prestz à espreuver. Nous vous supplions de vouloir ordonner qu'un commissaire les vienne recevoir . . ." (Depping, ed., *Correspondance administrative sous Louis XIV,* 3:727–28, 16 Apr. 1669).

62. Payment was usually withheld until after the intendant general of the Navy, Colbert de Terron, inspected and certified the merchandise, but Dalliez was willing to pay Le Vau in advance, as long as Colbert approved. Le Vau beseeched Colbert: "[the loan] is of the greatest consequence; the operation and interest of my business rides on it" (BN MS Mélanges de Colbert 151 bis, fols. 625–26, 17 Apr. 1669).

63. A typical test entailed firing a gun with a large charge of powder followed by two smaller charges. The gun was then filled with water and a plunger pressed through the barrel to determine if any cracks had opened during firing. Colbert rebuked Besch for the poor results and was worried about similar flaws in other foundries Besch ran: "Although you tell me that the cannon of Sweden are no more beautiful or finer quality than those cast in the Nivernois, nonetheless, I have seen flaws, and I want you to apply yourself to the improvement of this foundry, to refine the metal, render it softer, and lighten the weight of each piece," he wrote on 25 Oct. 1669. He also promised to send lightweight cannon, weighing eight to twelve *livres,* as a model for the founders at Beaumont (Clément, *Lettres de Colbert,* vol. 3, pt. 1, p. 18; and, for other letters relating to the cannon trials, pp. 212–13, 379).

64. A stinging letter from Colbert dated 10 Oct. 1669 (AN Marines B2, 9, fol. 418r) preceded the one cited in the text: "Je ne vous ay pas écrit en intention de vous mortifier, mais seulement pour vous faire connoistre l'obligation où vous estes de faire réussir la manufacture de fer blanc. Je n'estois pas obligé de vous donner des associés; mais sur la prière que vous m'en avez faite, et pour vous assister, je vous en ay donné qui ont supporté toute la perte, en sorte que tous les changemens dont vous vous plaignez ne sont arrivés que pour vous donner des assistances trèsconsidérables, auxquelles je n'estois pas, dis-je, obligé. Je vous ay de plus donné un débit très-avantageux de vostre fer, en sorte qu'il se trouveroit que vous auriez l'argent que le Roy vous a donné pour acheter la terre de Beaumont, et pour faire vos établissements, que vous auriez reçu de grandes assistances de vos associés et un prix considérable de votre fer, et qu'après tout, Sa Majesté n'auroit pas de fer blanc. Vous voyez bien que cela ne se peut. C'est pourquoy il faut vous appliquer tout de bon à faire cet établissement en sorte qu'il réussisse selon les assurances que vous en avez données par le traité que vous en avez fait avec le Roi . . ." (Clément, *Lettres de Colbert,* vol. 2, pt. 1, pp. 493–94).

For other letters from Dalliez, Besch, and Le Vau to Colbert concerning Beaumont, see AN Marines B2, 9, 9, 10, 18, 26, Oct. 1669; and 1, 18 Nov. 1669. Colbert appointed François Le Vau an inspector of cannon and other manufactures in the Nivernois, which may also have been a favor to Le Vau.

65. "J'approuve le traitté que vous avez fait avec M. Le Vau pour [la manufacture] celle de fer blanc et il y a beaucoup d'apparence qu'ayant un notable interest pour la soustenir, il fera son possible pour la faire réussir" (AN Marines, B2, 9 fol. 470r, 1 Nov. 1669).

66. "Je suis bien ayse d'apprendre que la manufacture de fer-blanc aille mieux que par le passé, et quoyque ce soit bien peu de 4 martelleries [martelleurs]. Néanmoins il y a lieu d'espérer que, prenant un grand soin de conserver les ouvriers, ce nombre augmentera dans la suite, estant important que vous mettiez cet establissement en tel estat qu'il n'ayt pas si fréquemment besoin de vostre présence" (Clément, *Lettres de Colbert,* 3:190, 15 Nov. 1669). Colbert addressed the letter to Le Vau at Beaumont-les-Forges.

67. Colbert wrote Dalliez: "Le décès de M. Le Vau pouvant causer quelques altérations aux manufactures qu'il avait établies sous mes ordres en Niver-

nois, je vous écris ce mot pour vous dire qu'il est nécessaire que vous m'informiez de l'état où elles sont" (see Laprade, *François d'Orbay,* 83).

68. On Beaumont and the Compagnie du Nivernais in the 1670s, see Mémain, *La marine de guerre,* 832–47 (which does not, however, cover the early years under Le Vau), and Peter, *Maîtres de forges,* 45–46.

69. See letters from Colbert in which he tried to convert reluctant naval officers to his point of view: Clément, *Lettres de Colbert,* vol. 3, pt. 1, pp. 245, 397, 453.

70. The metal industries in general faltered without Colbert's support. Seignelay halted production at Beaumont and in the Nivernais in general in 1677. Nevertheless, a foundry continued to operate at Beaumont-la-Ferrière until the early eighteenth century.

Looking back from the 1690s, Charles Perrault judged Colbert's interest in mining as misguided. "Monsieur Colbert ordered a search for metals in several places in France, on the advice he had been given that there were minerals in abundance, of all types: because ministers never lack for people who give them advice in keeping with their own inclinations." Perhaps Perrault considered Le Vau one of those sweet talkers. "After spending 50,000 ecus [150,000 *livres*], it was found that the cost of mining far exceeded the product, and that it was much more expedient to purchase lead and tin from England, and copper from Sweden . . . instead of wanting to extract them in France" (Charles Perrault, *Memoirs of My Life,* ed. and trans., Jeanne Morgan Zarucchi [Columbia, Mo., 1989], 94–95).

For other assessments of Colbert's metallurgical activities, see Cole, *Colbert and a Century of French Mercantilism,* 2:328.

71. The creditors are listed in AN S6506, 20 Sept. 1670.

72. "Avant de procedder aud. present Inventaire, lesd. dames Guichard et Mignon ont déclaré que dans le temps de la maladie dud. sieur Le Vau leur pere luy ayant représenté qu'il leur debvoit plusieurs sommes de deniers et les depenses continuelles qu'il le convenoit faire et cependant qu'elles n'avoient point d'argent pour y subvenir, que mesme il ny en avoir point dans sa maison . . . ; il leurs dit en ces [mots?], 'Mes filles, prenez ma vaisselle d'argent et en disposer. Je voudrois qu'il y en eut davantage mais vous scavez bien que j'ay disposé de la plus grande partie il y a du temps' " (AN Min. cent. LXXXV 198 fol. 1, inventory after death, 27 Nov.–30 Dec. 1670).

73. Years later, when Jeanne Le Vau's husband, Henri Guichard, was charged with attempted murder of the composer Jean Baptiste Lully, a co-conspirator accused him of stealing Louis Le Vau's silver as well as his clothes (see Laprade, *François d'Orbay,* 94).

74. "[Le Vau} a esté notoirement connu pour homme très intelligent et plein d'artifice dans sa conduite . . ." (BN Factums Fonds Thoisy 408, fol. 278; cited by Laprade, *François d'Orbay,* 92).

75. The trustees included Nicolas Lambert, president of the Chambre des Comptes and brother of Jean-Baptiste Lambert for whom Le Vau designed the Hôtel Lambert, on the Ile Saint-Louis; Jacques de Chaumeau, a lawyer in the Parlement; Jean Richet, former controller general of Parisian municipal bonds; and Antoine Vitart, son-in-law of the mason Charles Thoison.

76. For the complaint against Dalliez de La Tour and Legoux, see BN MS nouv. acq. Fr. 2440, fols. 259–68.

77. A payment of 2,488 *livres* "au sieur Laisné, pour 101 contre-coeurs de fer qu'il a fourny au magazin du Roy" is recorded in Guiffrey, *Comptes des bâtiments du roi,* 1:548.

78. "Quoy que tout le monde scache qu'il s'en falloit plus de 100,000 escus [300,000 *livres*] que ce deffunt eust de quoy payer les debtes dont il estoit chargé lors qu'il entrepris les Manufactures et qu'il soit justifié par le Traité qu'il fit avec les deffendeurs un an et demy avant sa mort qu'elles luy avoient esté fort onereuses." As for proof of the abbé's complicity, the trustees referred to letters from Laisné to Le Vau's sons-in-law, Henri Guichard and Jacques Mignon; this tantalizing evidence is not included in the

record. The defendants, Dalliez and Legoux, replied that Mignon and Guichard were louts, "dont les noms et la mauvaise conduite ne sont que trop connues" (BN MS fr. nouv. acq. 2440, fols. 269–73, June 1677).

79. BN MS fr.nouv. acq. 2440, fols. 259–68, 19 June 1677.

80. For the schedule of payments to Le Vau's creditors, see AN S6505, 20 Sept. 1674.

81. These points are presented in AN M174, no. 68: "Factum pour M. les Grand Maistre et Procureur du College Mazarin contre M. le president Lambert et les sieurs Vitart et Gautier, se disans directeurs des creanciers de deffunt Louis Le Vau et Jeanne Laisné sa femme." The passage concerning the testimony of the notary reads: "Les sieurs Coquille et Le Fouyn, qui avoient été commis par les Executeurs pour l'examen de ce compte, ne voyant point de preuve que Le Vau eust été entrepreneur, ny associé à l'entreprise du college et des maisons."

82. The web of charges and lawsuits did not stop here. The Collège also pressed charges against the two contractors (or their heirs), Simon Lambert and Charles Thoison, for 60,000 *livres*—the amount of rent they guaranteed on the rue Mazarine houses. They claimed to have given the rent money to Mariage, and it was part of the 100,000 *livres* he had turned over to Le Vau. In an ironic twist dictated by these strange proceedings, the contractors denied that Le Vau was their copartner and to reduce their liability, turned against him (posthumously). Le Vau was liable for the rent money; the contractors were not. (See AN S6506.)

83. Documents concerning the proceedings against Mariage are in AN S6506.

84. AN S6506, 4 Oct. 1690.

85. Gauthier, *Monographie de la commune de Beaumont-la-Ferrière,* 44–49, 122–23, 230–31.

CONCLUSION

1. A roughly analogous phenomenon has been identified with regard to Colbert's literary patronage: "Colbert found himself the principal purveyor of patronage in 1661 without quite knowing what to support and what to ignore. His inclinations were businesslike, to the point of wanting to speed up the production of historical writing with little consideration for quality" (Orest Ranum, *Artisans of Glory: Writers and Historical Thought in Seventeenth Century France* [Chapel Hill, 1980], 164).

2. The passage begins: "As early as the end of the year 1662, when Monsieur Colbert had predicted or knew already that the King would make him Superintendent of Buildings, he began to prepare himself for carrying out this duty, which he considered much more important than it appeared to be in the hands of Monsieur de Ratabon" (Charles Perrault, *Memoirs of My Life,* ed. and trans., Jeanne Morgan Zarucchi [Columbia, Mo., 1989], 41).

3. "Il y a bien, Monsieur, d'autres moyens louables de répandre et de maintenir la gloire de Sa Majesté, desquels mesme les anciens nous ont laissé d'illustres exemples qui arrestent encore avec respect les yeux des peuples, comme sont les pyramides, les colonnes, les statues équestres, les colosses, les arcs triomphaux, les bustes de marbre et de bronze, les basses-tailles, tous monumens historiques . . ." (Pierre Clément, *Lettres, instructions, et mémoires de Colbert* [Paris, 1861–70], 5:589; also published in Josephe Jacquiot, *Médailles et jetons de Louis XIV* [Paris, 1968], lxxxviii–xc).

4. See Colbert's list of works projected in 1669 (Clément, *Lettres de Colbert,* 7:289–90).

5. Paul Fréart de Chantelou, *Diary of the Cavaliere Bernini's Visit to France,* trans. Margery Corbett, ed. Anthony Blunt, annotated by George Bauer (Princeton, 1985), 334.

6. On Bernini's hostility toward Colbert's questions, see Perrault, *Memoirs of My Life,* 65–66. An early sign of Le Vau's lingering influence on Colbert comes when the minister asked Bernini in 1664 to plan a royal square on the Left Bank to house gendarmes, evoking an element from Le Vau's first Collège design. Colbert asked Bernini to consider "la pensée de faire une grande place carrée au delà de la rivière, disposée pour y loger les gendarmes . . . qui pourroit servir pour des grandes festes et divertissements publics, au milieu de laquelle on pourroit élever quelque monument à la gloire du Roy" (Clément, *Lettres de Colbert,* 5:258).

7. For instance, Colbert asked Le Vau to enter his coach on 30 July 1665, while rumors of his new design for the Louvre were circulating at court. A few days later, on 6 Aug., Chantelou tracked down Colbert at the residence of the abbé Bruneau and found that the minister had gone there with Le Vau (see Chantelou, *Diary of Bernini's Visit,* 90, 104).

8. Colbert articulated this distinction in a letter of complaint to the king, dated 28 Sept. 1665, in which he hoped to redirect his interest from Versailles to Paris: "Cette maison [Versailles] regarde bien davantage le plaisir et le divertissement de Votre Majesté que sa gloire. . . . Pour concilier toutes choses, c'est-à-dire pour donner à la gloire de Votre Majesté ce qui doit lui appartenir, et à ses divertissemens de même elle pourroit faire terminer promptement tous les comptes de Versailles, fixer une somme pour y employer tous les ans, . . . et ensuite s'appliquer tout de bon à achever le Louvre, et si la paix dure encore longtemps, élever des monumens publics qui portent la gloire et la grandeur de votre majesté plus looin que ceux que les Romain ont autrefois élevés" (Clément, *Lettres de Colbert,* vol. 2, pt. 1, pp. ccx–ccxi).

Colbert blamed "two men" for piquing the king's interest in Versailles. Clément surmised that the men in question were André Le Nôtre and François Mansart; Hautecoeur suggested Le Vau and Le Nôtre, but it makes no sense to accuse Le Vau of neglecting the Louvre in 1665, when he was trying desperately to regain the commission from Bernini by designing ever more ambitious plans.

9. On the conflict between Bernini and Colbert over the location of the king's apartment, see Perrault, *Memoirs of My Life,* 66–68. Bernini was determined to relocate the apartment to the grander, more public, and wider east wing he designed, whereas Colbert insisted that the apartment remain in its historic position, in Lescot's Pavillon du Roi facing the river.

10. Chantelou, *Diary of Bernini's Visit,* 124.

11. Le Vau exemplifies an architectural strategy undervalued by historians but dominant at the French court in the sixteenth and seventeenth centuries whereby architects enlarged the royal châteaux over the centuries by historically sensitive additions. Michael Rabens explored this rich vein in "The Rebuilt Château in the Work of Jules Hardouin-Mansart," Ph.D. diss., Princeton University, 1992.

12. On the revised design of the south wing of the Louvre, see Robert Berger, *The Palace of the Sun: The Louvre of Louis XIV* (University Park, Pa., 1993), 41–44; Louis Hautecoeur, *Histoire du Louvre sous Louis XIV* (Paris, 1927), 171–73, 180; and Hautecoeur, "L'auteur de la Colonnade," *GBA,* 1924, 165–66.

13. In the debate between François Le Vau and an anonymous critic over the revised south facade, the critic favored retaining the dome and pavilion roofs on the south wing and argued that the Cour Carrée would look strange with domes and tall roofs on only the west and north wings. Le Vau's elevation evokes the same resistance to eliminating the dome and pavilion roofs. This fascinating document is transcribed in Berger, *The Palace of the Sun,* 129–130.

APPENDIX A

1. "[I quattro disegni di pensiere . . .]," Benedetti said, "sono del piu pellegrino ingego cheoggi habbiano e di meriti ad essere invediato anco da i Bernini" (Madeline Laurain-Portemer, *Etudes mazarines* [Paris, 1981], 392).

2. I am grateful to Giuseppe Dardanello, who discovered the drawings, brought them to my attention, and shared his research on the Valperga albums in the Biblioteca Nazionale of Turin. See his catalogue entries in Michela di Macco and Giovanni Romano, eds., *Diana trionfatrice: Arte di corte nel Piemonte del Seicento* (Turin, 1989); Ibid., "Cantieri di corte e imprese decorative a Torino," in *Figure del barocco in Piemonte,* ed. Giovanni Romano (Turin, 1988), 163–204, 237–52; and "Decorative and Architectural Drawings of the Valperga Albums in the Biblioteca Nazionale of Turin," in *CASVA Reports on Research* (Washington, D.C. 1990).

3. The inscription, which describes the materials and iconography, reads as follows: "La base di bianco e nero. Le armi di metallo dorato. La morte di metallo. Il libro di paragone. Le statue di marmo bianco rappresentano q[uest]te la Giust[izi]a, La Fame, e l'Immortalità sgrida la Morte che vogli registrare il nome

del Card[inale] nel lib[r]o di morte; avvertendola che se ben morto viverà immortale il nome di Sua Em[inenza] come gli mostra notato nel suo simbolo dell'eternità. L'urna di nero, o bianco e nero con i gigli, e modallone di metallo dorato. Le due angeli di marmo biano. Il ritratto simile et il festone di metallo dorato" (Biblioteca Nazionale di Torino, fl65, fol. 155).

4. Elpidio Benedetti, *Pompa funebre nell'esequie celebrate in Roma al cardinal Mazarini nella chiesa de SS. Vincenzo e Anastasio* (Rome, 1661); and *Il Mondo piangente, et il cielo festieggiante nel funerale apparato dell'essequi celebrate in Roma nella Chiesa di San Luigi de Francesi alla gloriosa memoria di Anna d'Austria* (Rome, 1666). On the catafalque for Mazarin, see Olga Berendsen, "The Italian Sixteenth and Seventeenth Century Catafalques," Ph. D. diss., New York University, 1962, 41–42.

5. Hempel, who first published the drawing, interpreted Benedetti's signature as a sign of approval rather than authorship. Wittkower agreed and posited François d'Orbay as the draftsman, a hypothesis that we can firmly reject. See Tod Marder, "Bernini and Benedetti at the Trinità dei Monti," *Art Bulletin* 62 (1980):286–89, an interpretation that has

not been convincingly refuted; Eberhard Hempel, "Die Spanische Treppe," in *Festschrift Heinrich Wölfflin* (Munich, 1924), 273–90; and Rudolf Wittkower, "Vicissitudes of a Dynastic Monument: Bernini's Equestrian Statue of Louis XIV (1961)," in *Studies in the Italian Baroque* (London, 1975), 285 n. 71. For complete bibliography on Mazarin's initiative in 1660, see Appendix B.

With regard to Benedetti's debt to Bernini, Wittkower pointed out explicit borrowings from Bernini in Benedetti's pamphlet about Louis XIV, *Le glorie della virtu nella persona di Luigi il magno re di Francia et di Navarra* (Lyons, 1682) (see Wittkower, "Vicissitudes of a Dynastic Monument," 97–98).

6. On Valperga's drawing, see Giuseppe Dardanello's catalogue entry in *Diana trionfatrice* 286–87.

7. For the Académie's discussion of the tomb in 1676, see Bibibliothèque de l'Institut MS. 368, fol. 178r, 9 Mar. 1676; and Henry Lemonnier, *Procès-verbaux de l'Académie Royale d'Architecture, 1671–1793* (Paris, 1911), 1:112.

8. For a new reading of the tomb, see Mary Jackson Harvey, "French Baroque Tomb Sculpture: The Activation of the Effigy," Ph.D. diss., University of Chicago, 1987, 1:183–85 and 2:473–75. The identification of Vigilance, who sits beside a crane, was made also by Harvey; writers had described her as Religion. The tomb was removed from the church in 1792 and reinstalled in 1963, at which time some changes were made in the surrounding niche (see André Gutton, "La restauration de la coupole de l'Institut," *Monuments historiques de la France,* 9, no. 1 | 1963|:48. On Mazarin's tomb, see also J. de Grouchy, "Le tombeau de Mazarin par Le Honge, Coysevox et Tuby," *Nouvelles archives de l'art français,* 3d ser. 8 (1982):69–77, for the contract dated 11 June 1689; R. Père Scheil, "Un document inédit relatif au mausolée de Mazarin," *Journal des savants,* June 1915:275–78; Georges Keller-Dorian, *Antoine Coysevox (1640–1720): Catalogue raisonné de son oeuvre* (Paris, 1920), 2:5-13; Pierre Pradel, "Le tombeau de Mazarin," *Art de France* 4 (1964):299–300; and François Souchal, *French Sculptors of the 17th and 18th Centuries: The Reign of Louis XIV* (Oxford, 1977–87), 1:202.

APPENDIX B

1. On Mazarin's unsuccessful attempt to build these steps, see Eberhard Hempel, "Die Spanische Treppe," in *Festschrift Heinrich Wölfflin* (Munich, 1924), 273–90; Pio Pecchiai, *La scalinata di Piazza di Spagna e Villa Medici* (Rome, 1941); Wolfgang Lotz, "Die Spanische Treppe: Architektur als Mittel der Diplomatie," *Römisches Jahrbuch für Kunstgeschichte* 12 (1969): 39–94; Cesare d'Onofrio, *Scalinate di Roma* (Rome, 1974); Tod Marder, "Bernini and Benedetti at the Trinità dei Monti," *Art Bulletin* 62 (1980):286–89; Madeleine Laurain-Portemer, "Mazarin, Benedetti et l'escalier de la Trinité des Monts" (1968) and "Nouvelles observations sur le projet de Benedetti pour l'escalier de la Trinité des Monts," in *Etudes mazarines* (Paris, 1981), 311–35 and 535–44; Tod Marder, "The Decision to Build the Spanish Steps: From Project to Monument," in *Projects and Monuments in the Period of the Roman Baroque,* ed. Hellmut Hager and Susan Munshower, Papers in Art

History from The Pennsylvania State University, no. 1 (University Park, Pa., 1984), 83–100. The four drawings by d'Orbay are in Paris: BN Est. Rés. B11, fol. 29; and Est. Vb132s, vol. 4, P66279–81.

2. "Questo è il disegno di Mr Orbais giovane francese mandato qui a studiare da Mr le Veau p[er] la scalinate della Trinità dei Monte. Se si havesse fatto in prospettiva si goderebbe meglio pur l'altro della Pianta ne fa da dichiarazione. Riesce troppa gran macchina, e di troppa spesa haverla a servire che p[er] un scala." (Letters from Benedetti to Mazarin, 2 and 9 Aug. 1660, Affaires étrangères, Corr. pol., Rome 139, fols. 353 and 369; cited by Albert Laprade, *François d'Orbay, architecte de Louis XIV,* [Paris, 1960], 112; and Lotz, "Die Spanische Treppe," 54–55.)

3. Letter from Benedetti to Mazarin, 16 Aug. 1660

and Mazarin's reply on 8 Oct. 1660 (see Lotz, "Die Spanische Treppe," 77) and Laprade, *François d'Orbay,* 111–12.

4. See Lotz, "Die Spanische Treppe," 54–55, 60–61, and 87, for catalogue entries on the four d'Orbay drawings.

5. "Non crederei che si dovesse incontrare difficoltà per l'espositione della statua del Re in publico poiché essende se può dire in casa di S. M.tà et in una iazza di suo sito, pare che sia l'istesso come che si esponesse in un cortile d'un palazzo d'un imbasciatore che non haverebbe eccetione alcuna" (see Lotz, "Die Spanische Treppe," 77).

6. Laprade, *François d'Orbay,* 113–14.

SELECTED BIBLIOGRAPHY

Accademia Nazionale dei Lincei. *Il Cardinale Mazzarino in Francia,* Atti dei convegni Lincei 35. Rome, 1977.

Anderson, Christy. "Learning to Read Architecture in the English Renaissance." In *Albion's Classicism: The Visual Arts in Britain, 1550–1660,* ed. Lucy Gent. New Haven and London, 1995.

Andia, Béatrice de, and Nicolas Courtin. *L'Ile Saint-Louis.* Délégation à Action Artistique de la Ville de Paris. Paris, 1997.

Aquilon, Pierre, and Henri-Jean Martin, eds. *Le livre dans l'Europe de la Renaissance.* Tours, 1988.

Aumale, duc d', ed. *Inventaire de tous les meubles du Cardinal Mazarin dressé en 1653 et publié d'après l'original conservé dans les Archives de Condé.* London, 1861.

Avon, Annalisa. "La biblioteca, gli strumenti scientifici, le collezioni di antichità e opere d'arte di un architetto del XVII secolo, Jacques Le Mercier (1585–1654)." *Annali di Architettura, Rivista del Centro internationale di studi di architectura Andrea Palladio,* 8 (1996):179–96.

Babelon, Jean-Pierre. "Le Château de Sucy-en-Brie, oeuvre de F. Le Vau." *BSHP,* 1974–75:83–102.

———. "La Cour Carrée du Louvre, les tentatives des siècles pour maîtriser un espace urbain mal défini." *Bulletin monumental* 142 (1984):41–81.

Babelon, Jean-Pierre, and Claude Mignot, *François Mansart: Le génie de l'architecture.* Paris, 1998.

Ballon, Hilary. "Constructions of the Bourbon State: Classical Architecture in Seventeenth-Century France." In *Cultural Differentiation and Cultural Identity in the Visual Arts,* ed. Susan Barnes and Walter Melion. Washington, D.C., 1989.

———. *The Paris of Henri IV: Architecture and Urbanism.* New York and Cambridge, Mass., 1991.

———. "Vaux-le-Vicomte: Le Vau's Ambition." In *Italian Villas and French Gardens in Context,* ed. Mirka Beněs and Dianne Harris. In press.

Benedetti, Elpidio. *Raccolta di diverse memorie per scrivere la vita del Cardinale Giulio Mazarini Romano.* Lyons, n.d. (c. 1653).

———. *Il Mondo piagente, et il cielo festigeggiante nel funerale apparto dell'essequie celebrate in Roma nella chiesa di San Luigi de francesi.* Rome, 1666.

———. *Pompa fundere nell esquie celebrate in Roma al Cardinal Mazarini, nella chiesa de SS. Vincenzo e Anastasio.* Rome, 1661.

Berger, Robert. "Antoine Le Pautre and the Motif of the Drum-without-Dome." *JSAH* 25 (1966):165–80.

———. "The Chronology of the Enveloppe of Versailles," *Architettura* 10 (1980):105–33.

———. "Louis Le Vau's Château du Raincy." *Architettura* 6 (1976):36–46.

———. "Louis Le Vau's Château du Raincy: An Addendum." *Architettura* 14 (1984):171.

———. *The Palace of the Sun: The Louvre of Louis XIV.* University Park, Pa., 1993.

———. *A Royal Passion: Louis XIV as Patron of Architecture.* Cambridge, 1994.

———. *Versailles: The Château of Louis XIV.* University Park, Pa., 1985.

Bergin, Joseph. "Cardinal Mazarin and His Benefices," *French History,* 1, no. 1 (Mar. 1987):3–26.

———. *Cardinal Richelieu: Power and the Pursuit of Wealth.* New Haven and London, 1985.

———. *The Making of the French Episcopate, 1589–1661.* New Haven and London, 1996.

Berty, Adolphe, H. Legrand, and L.-M. Tisserand. *Topographie historique du Vieux Paris.* 6 vols. Paris, 1866–87.

Bialostocki, Jan. "The *Doctus Artifex* and the Library of the Artist in the XVIth and XVIIth Centuries." In *The Message of Images: Studies in the History of Art.* Vienna, 1988

Bibliothèque Nationale. *Mazarin: Homme d'état et collectionneur, 1602–1661.* Exh. cat. Paris, 1961.

Blondel, Jacques-François. *Architecture françoise, ou Recueil des plans, élévations, coupes er profils des églises, maisons royales, palais, hôtels, et édifices. . . .* 4 vols. Paris, 1752–56.

Blunt, Anthony. *Art and Architecture in France, 1500 to 1700,* 4th rev. ed. New York, 1986.

Boissonnade, Prosper. *Colbert: Le triomphe de l'étatisme; La fondation de la suprématie industrielle de la France; La dictature du travail (1661–1683).* Paris, 1932.

Bonney, Richard. "The Secret Expenses of Richelieu and Mazarin, 1624–1661." *English Historical Review* 91 (1976):825–36.

Bordier, Cyril. *Louis Le Vau architecte.* Paris, 1998.

Borsi, Franco. *La chiesa di S. Andrea al Quirinale.* Rome, 1967.

Bourdel, Nicole. "Nouveaux documents sur Louis Le Vau, premier architecte de Louis XIV (1612–1670)." *Paris et l'Ile-de-France, Mémoires* 8 (1956):213–35.

Boyer de Sainte-Suzanne, C. de. "Inventaire du cardinal Mazarin (1661)." In *Notes d'un curieux.* Monaco, 1878.

Braham, Allan. "Bernini's Design for the Bourbon Chapel." *Burlington Magazine* 102 (1960):443–47.

Braham, Allan, and Peter Smith. *François Mansart.* 2 vols. London, 1973.

British Museum, Department of Printed Books. *Short-title Catalogue of Books printed in France and of French Books Printed in Other Countries from 1470 to 1600, Now in the British Library.* London, 1976.

Brockliss, Laurence. *French Higher Education in the Seventeenth and Eighteenth Centuries: A Cultural History.* Oxford, 1987.

———. "Richelieu, Education, and the State." In *Richelieu and His Age,* ed. Joseph Bergin and Laurence Brockliss, 237–72. Oxford, 1992.

Chantelou, Paul Fréart de. *Diary of the Cavaliere Bernini's Visit to France.* Trans. Margery Corbett, ed. Anthony Blunt, annotated by George Bauer. Princeton, 1985.

Chartier, Roger. *The Cultural Uses of Print in Early Modern France.* Trans. Lydia Cochrane. Princeton, 1987.

———, ed. *The Culture of the Print: Power and the Uses of Print in Early Modern Europe.* Cambridge, 1989.

Charvin, Dom G. "Colbert intendant des abbayes de Mazarin." *Revue Mabillon* 36 (1946): 15–47, 87–119.

Chastel, André, and Jean-Marie Pérouse de Montclos. "L'aménagement de l'accès oriental du Louvre." *Monuments historiques de la France* 12, no. 3 (1966):176–249.

Chéruel, Adolphe. *Histoire de France pendant la minorité de Louis XIV,* 4 vols. Paris. 1879–80.

Chéruel, Adolphe, and Georges d'Avenel, eds. *Lettres du Cardinal Mazarin pendant son ministère.* 9 vols. Paris, 1883–96.

———. *Histoire de France sous le ministère de Mazarin.* Paris, 1882.

Christ, Yvan. "L'Institut remis à neuf." *Connaissance des arts* 131 (1963):86–95.

Cioranescu, Alexandre. *Bibliographie de la littérature française du dix-septième siècle.* 3 vols. Paris, 1965–66.

Clément, Pierre. *Histoire de Colbert et de son administration.* 2 vols. Paris, 1874.

———, ed. *Lettres, instructions, et mémoires de Colbert.* 7 vols. Paris, 1861–70.

Cole, Charles Woolsey. *Colbert and a Century of French Mercantilism.* 2 vols. New York, 1939; reprint, Hamden, Conn., 1964.

Compère, Marie-Madeleine. *Du collège au lycée (1500–1850): Généalogie de l'enseignement secondaire français.* Paris, 1985.

Coope, Rosalys. *Salomon de Brosse and the Development of the Classical Style in French Architecture from 1565 to 1630.* University Park, Pa., 1972.

Cordey, Jean. "Colbert, Le Vau et la construction du château de Vincennes au XVIIe siècle." *GBA* 9 (May 1933):273–93.

———. "Le grand salon ovale de Vaux-le-Vicomte et sa décoration." *Revue de l'art ancien et moderne* 46 (1924):233–48.

———. *Vaux-le-Vicomte.* Paris, 1924.

Cosnac, Gabriel-Jules, Comte de. *Mazarin et Colbert.* 2 vols. Paris, 1892.

———. *Les richesses du Palais Mazarin.* Paris, 1884.

Darnton, Robert. *The Great Cat Massacre and Other Episodes in French Cultural History.* New York, 1984.

Darricau, Raymond, and Madeleine Laurain. "La mort du Cardinal Mazarin." *Annuaire-Bulletin de la Société de l'Histoire de France,* 1958–59:55–120.

Daufresne, Jean-Claude. *Louvre et Tuileries: Architectures de papier.* Liège, 1987.

De Angelis d'Ossat, Guglielmo. "Louis Le Vau, architetto berniniano suo malgrado." In *Gian Lorenzo Bernini, architetto e l'architettura europea del Sei–Settecento,* ed. Gianfranco Spagnesi and Marcello Fagiolo. 2 vols. Rome, 1984.

Del Pesco, Daniela. *Il Louvre di Bernini nella Francia di Luigi XIV.* Naples, 1984.

Depping, Georges-Bernard, ed. *Correspondance administrative sous le règne de Louis XIV.* 4 vols. Paris, 1850–55.

Desgraves, Louis. *Répertoire bibliographique des livres imprimés en France au XVIIe siècle.* Baden-Baden, 1978–.

Dessert, Daniel. *Argent, pouvoir et société au Grand Siècle.* Paris, 1984.

———. *Fouquet.* Paris, 1987.

———. "Pouvoir et finance au XVIIe siècle: La fortune du Cardinal Mazarin." *Revue d'histoire moderne et contemporaine* 23 (1976):161–81.

Dethan, Georges. *Mazarin: Un homme de paix à l'âge baroque, 1602–1661.* Paris, 1981.

———. *The Young Mazarin.* Trans. Stanley Baron. London, 1977.

Duchêne, Roger, and Pierre Ronzeaud, eds. *La Fronde en questions.* Aix-en-Provence, 1989.

Dulong, Claude. "Les comptes bleus du cardinal Mazarin." *Revue d'histoire moderne et contemporaine* 36 (1989):537–58.

———. *La fortune de Mazarin.* Paris, 1990.

———. "Mazarin et ses banquiers." In Accademia Nazionale dei Lincei, *Il cardinale Mazzarino in Francia.* Atti dei convegni Lincei (Rome, 1977):17–40.

———. "Le processus d'enrichissement du cardinal Mazarin d'après l'inventaire de l'abbé Mondin." *Bibliothèque de l'Ecole des Chartes* 148 (1990):355–425.

———. "Les signes cryptiques dans la correspondance d'Anne d'Autriche avec Mazarin, contribution à l'emblématique du XVIIe siècle." *Bibliothèque de l'Ecole des Chartes* 140 (1982), 61–83.

Dumolin, Maurice. *Etudes de topographie parisienne.* 3 vols. Paris, 1929–31.

———. "Notes sur quelques architectes du XVIIe siècle." *BSHAF,* 1930:11–22.

———. "Quelques nouveaux documents sur le Louvre de Le Mercier et de Le Vau." *GBA,* 1928, 123–48.

Erlande-Brandenburg, Alain. "Les fouilles du Louvre et les projets de Le Vau." *La vie urbaine* 1964 (no. 4), 241–63; 1965, (no. 1) 12–22.

———. "Les fouilles du Louvre, Louis Le Vau." *Les dossiers de l'archéologie* 7 (1974):85–93.

Erlande-Brandenburg, Alain, and Bertrand Jestaz. *Le château de Vincennes.* Paris, 1989.

Feldmann, Dietrich. "Das Hôtel de la Vrillière und die Raüme 'à l'italienne' bei Louis Le Vau." *Zeitschrift für Kunstgeschichte* 45, no. 4 (1982):395–422.

———. "Le Vau et l'architecture parisienne au 17e siècle," *Cahiers du Centre de Recherches et d'Etudes sur Paris et l'Ile-de-France* 1 (1983):191–96.

———. *Maison Lambert, Maison Hesselin und andere Bauten von Louis Le Vau auf der Ile Saint Louis in Paris.* Hamburg, 1976.

Fossa, Colonel de. *Le Château historique de Vincennes.* 2 vols. Paris, 1907–9.

Fossier, François. *Les dessins du fonds Robert de Cotte de la Bibliothèque Nationale de France: Architecture et décor.* Paris, 1997.

Fowler, Laurence Hall, and Elizabeth Baer. *The Fowler Architectural Collection of The Johns Hopkins University Press.* Baltimore, 1961.

Franklin, Alfred. *Les anciennes bibliothèques de Paris.* 3 vols. Paris, 1867–73.

———. *Histoire de la Bibliothèque Mazarine et du Palais de l'Institut.* Paris, 1860; rev. ed., 1901.

———. *Recherches historiques sur le Collège des Quatre-Nations.* Paris, 1862.

Franklin, Alfred, Gaston Boissier, and Georges Peirot. *L'Institut de France: Le Palais-l'Institut; L'Académie Française; L'Académie des Inscriptions et Belles-Lettres.* Paris, 1907.

Fumaroli, Marc. *Le poète et le roi: Jean de La Fontaine en son siècle.* Paris, 1997.

Gille, Geneviève, and Maurice Berry. *L'Institut et la monnaie: Deux palais sur un quai.* Délégation à l'Action Artistique de la Ville de Paris; Société Historique du VIe Arrondissement. Paris, 1990.

Girard, René. *Deceit, Desire, and the Novel: Self and Other in Literary Structure.* Trans. Yvonne Freccero. Baltimore and London, 1965.

Goldberg, Jonathan. *Writing Matter: From the Hands of the English Renaissance.* Stanford, 1990.

Goldsmith, V. F. *A Short Title Catalogue of French Books, 1601–1700, in the Library of the British Museum.* Folkestone and London, 1973.

Goubert, Pierre. *Mazarin.* Paris, 1990.

Gould, Cecil. *Bernini in France: An Episode in Seventeenth-Century History.* Princeton, 1982.

Guiffrey, Jules, ed. *Comptes des bâtiments du roi sous le règne de Louis XIV.* Vol. 1, *Colbert 1664–1680.* Paris, 1881.

Gutton, André. *De la nuit à l'Aurore: Conversations sur l'architecture.* 2 vols. [St. Léger-Vauban], 1986.

———. "La restauration de la coupole de l'Institut." *Monuments historiques de la France* 9, no. 1 (1963):1–58.

Hautecoeur, Louis. *La chapelle du Collège des Quatre Nations, le tricentenaire 1662–1962, la coupole de l'Institut.* Paris, 1962.

———. *Histoire de l'architecture classique en France.* Vol. 2, *Le règne de Louis XIV.* Paris, 1948; reprint, 1980.

———. *Le Louvre et les Tuileries de Louis XIV.* Paris and Brussels, 1927.

———. "L'origine du dôme des Invalides." *L'Architecture* 37 (1924):353–60.

Institut de France, Académie des Beaux-Arts. *Exposition Louis Le Vau, 1612–1670.* Exh. cat. Paris, 1970.

Jacob, Père Louis. *Traicté des plus belles bibliothèques publiques et particuliers qui ont esté et qui sont à present dans le monde.* Paris, 1644.

Jardine, Lisa, and Anthony Grafton. " 'Studied for Action': How Gabriel Harvey Read His Livy." *Past and Present* 129 (Nov. 1990):30–78.

Jestaz, Bertrand. *L'Hôtel et l'Eglise des Invalides.* Paris, 1990.

Jolly, Claude, ed. *Histoire des bibliothèques françaises,* 3 vols. [Paris], 1988–91

Jourdain, Charles. *Histoire de l'Université de Paris au XVIIe et au XVIIIe siècle.* 2 vols. Paris, 1888.

Kimball, Fiske. "The Genesis of the Château-Neuf at Versailles, 1668–1671. I: The Initial Projects of Le Vau." *GBA.* 35 (May 1949):353–72.

King, James E. *Science and Rationalism in the Government of Louis XIV, 1661–1683.* Baltimore, 1949.

Klaiber, Susan. "Guarino Guarini's Theatine Architecture." Ph.D. diss., Columbia University, 1993.

Laprade, Albert. *François d'Orbay, architecte de Louis XIV.* Paris, 1960.

Laurain-Portemer, Madeleine. *Etudes mazarines.* Paris, 1981.

———. "Monarchie et gouvernement: Mazarin et le modèle romain." In *La France et l'Italie au temps de Mazarin,* ed. Jean Serroy. Grenoble, 1986.

———. "La politique artistique de Mazarin." In Accademia Nazionale dei Lincei, *Il cardinale Mazzarino in Francia,* Atti dei convegni lincei 35 (Rome, 1977):41–74.

Lavin, Irving. "Bernini's Image of the Sun King." In *Past-Present: Essays on Historicism in Art from Donatello to Picasso.* Berkeley, 1993.

Lemonnier, Henry. *Le Collège Mazarin et le Palais de l'Institut (XVIIe–XIXe siècle).* Paris, 1921.

Lloyd, Howell A. *The State and Education: University Reform in Early-Modern France.* Hull, 1987.

Marder, T. A. *Bernini and the Art of Architecture.* New York, 1998.

Martin, Germain. *La grande industrie sous le règne de Louis XIV.* Paris, 1899.

Martin, Henri-Jean. *Livres, pouvoirs et société à Paris au XVIIe siècle (1598–1701).* 2 vols. Geneva, 1969.

Martin, Henri-Jean, and Roger Chartier, eds. *Histoire de l'édition française.* 4 vols. Paris, 1983–86.

Marvick, Elizabeth. "Psychobiography and the Early Modern French Court: Notes on Method with Some Examples." *French Historical Studies* 19, no. 4 (1996):943–66.

Masson, André. "Mazarin et l'architecture des bibliothèques au XVIIe siècle." *GBA* 58 (Dec. 1961):355–66.

McGinness, Lawrence. "Royal Chapel Projects for Louis XIV at Saint Denis, the Louvre, and the Invalides, 1664–1683." Ph.D. diss., Columbia University, 1974.

Mémain, René. *La marine de guerre sous Louis XIV: Le matériel; Rochefort, arsenal modèle de Colbert.* Paris, 1937.

Merrick, Jeffrey. "The Cardinal and the Queen: Sexual and Political Disorders in the Mazarinades," *French Historical Studies* 18, no. 3(1994):667–99.

Mignot, Claude. *Le Val-de-Grâce: L'ermitage d'une reine.* Paris, 1994.

Ministère de la Culture. *Colbert, 1619–1683.* Exh. cat. Paris, 1983.

Mirot, Léon. "Le Bernin en France: Les travaux du Louvre et les statues de Louis XIV." *Mémoires de la Société de l'Histoire de Paris* 31 (1904):161–288.

Mortimer, Ruth. *Harvard College Library Department of Printing and Graphic Arts Catalogue of Books and Manuscripts.* Part 1, *French 16th Century Books.* 2 vols. Cambridge, Mass., 1964

Möseneder, Karl. *Zeremoniell und monumentale Poesie: Die 'entrée solennelle' Ludwigs XIV, 1660 in Paris.* Berlin, 1983.

Moss, Ann. *Printed Commonplace-Books and the Structuring of Renaissance Thought.* Oxford, 1996.

Motley, Mark. *Becoming a French Aristocrat: The Education of the Court Nobility, 1580–1715.* Princeton, 1990.

Mousnier, Roland, ed. *Un nouveau Colbert.* Paris, 1985.

———. *Richelieu et la culture.* Paris, 1987.

Murat, Inès. *Colbert.* Trans. Robert Francis Cook and Jeannie Van Asselt. Charlottesville, 1984.

Naudé, Gabriel. *Advis pour dresser une bibliothèque.* Paris, 1627; 2d rev. ed., 1644.

Nora, Pierre, ed. *Les lieux de mémoire.* Vol. 2, *La Nation.* Paris, 1986.

Pérouse de Montclos, Jean-Marie. *L'architecture à la française XVIe, XVIIe, XVIIIe siècles.* Paris, 1982.

———. *Histoire de l'Architecture française de la Renaissance à la Révolution.* Paris, 1989.

———. *Vaux-le-Vicomte.* Paris, 1997.

Perrault, Charles. *Memoirs of My Life.* Ed. and trans. Jeanne Morgan Zarucchi. Columbia, Mo., 1989.

Petzet, Michael. "Der Obelisk des Sonnenkönigs: Ein Projekt Claude Perraults von 1666." *Zeitschrift für Kunstgeschichte* 47 (1987):439–64.

Pfnor, Rodolphe, and Anatole France. *Le Château de Vaux-le-Vicomte.* Paris, 1888.

Picon, Antoine. *Claude Perrault, 1613–1688, ou la curiosité d'un classique.* Paris, 1988.

Ranum, Orest. *The Fronde: A French Revolution, 1648–1652.* New York, 1993.

———. *Paris in the Age of Absolutism: An Essay.* New York, 1968.

Renting, A. D., and J. T. C. Renting-Kuijpers, eds. (with introduction and notes). *The Seventeenth-Century Orange-Nassau Library.* Utrecht, 1993.

Saint-Fare Garnot, Nicolas. *Le décor des Tuileries sous le règne de Louis XIV.* Paris, 1988.

Saint-Fare Garnot, Nicolas, and Emmanuel Jacquin. *Le Château des Tuileries.* Paris, 1988.

Salet, Francis. "Le Vau et le Bernin au Louvre." *Bulletin monumental* 123 (1965):144–48.

Schnapper, Antoine. *Curieux du Grand Siècle: Collections et collectionneurs dans la France du XVIIe siècle.* Vol. 2, *Oeuvres d'art.* Paris, 1994.

———. *Le géant, la licorne, et la tulipe: Collections et collectionneurs dans la France du XVIIe siècle.* Vol. 1, *Histoire et histoire naturelle.* Paris, 1988.

Serroy, Jean, ed. *La France et l'Italie au temps de Mazarin.* Grenoble, 1986.

Sherman, William H. *John Dee: The Politics of Reading and Writing in the English Renaissance.* Amherst, 1995.

Smyth-Pinney, Julia. "The Geometries of S. Andrea al Quirinale," *JSAH* 48 (1989):53–65.

Thornton, Dora. *The Scholar in His Study: Ownership and Experience in Renaissance Italy.* New Haven, 1997.

Thuillier, Guy. "Les speculations malheureuses de l'architecte Louis Le Vau à Beaumont-la-Ferrière (1665–1670)." *Mémoires de la Société Académique du Nivernais* 51 (1959):24–36.

Tooth, Constance. "The Early Private Houses of Louis Le Vau," *Burlington Magazine* 109 no. 774 (Sept. 1967):510–18.

Treasure, Geoffrey. *Mazarin: The Crisis of Absolutism in France.* London and New York, 1995.

Vaudoyer, A. L. T. *Plan, coupe, et élévation du Palais de l'Institut impérial de France suivant sa nouvelle restauration.* Paris, 1811.

Vinck, Carl de, and Alfred Vuaflart. *La Place de l'Institut, sa galerie marchande des Quatre Nations, et ses étalages d'estampes, 1660–1880.* Paris, 1928.

Walton, Guy. " 'L'Enveloppe' de Versailles: Réflexions nouvelles et dessins inédits." *BSHAF,* 1977:127–44.

Waquet, Françoise. *Le modèle français et l'Italie savante: Conscience de soi et perception de l'autre dans la République des Lettres (1660–1750).* Rome, 1989.

Whiteley, Mary, and Allan Braham. "Louis Le Vau's Projects for the Louvre and the Colonnade." *GBA,* Nov. 1964, 285–96; and Dec. 1964, 347–62.

Wiebenson, Dora, and Claire Baines. *The Mark J. Millard Architectural Collection.* Vol. 1, *French Books Sixteenth through Nineteenth Centuries.* Washington, D.C. and New York, 1993.

GENERAL INDEX

The Collège des Quatre Nations is cited within other index headings as Mazarin's Collège. An index of Le Vau's library inventory follows the general index.

INDEX OF LE VAU'S LIBRARY INVENTORY

This index lists authors of works inventoried in Le Vau's library, as determined in Appendix D. Numbers provided are inventory numbers. Uncertain attributions are indicated by (?), and works by undetermined authors are listed under their inventory descriptions at the end of the index, in order of appearance.

PHOTOGRAPHY CREDITS